Working with Grief and Traumatic Loss

Working with Grief and Traumatic Loss

Theory, Practice, Personal Reflection, and Self-Care

Elisabeth Counselman Carpenter
and Alex Redcay, Editors

cognella® | ACADEMIC PUBLISHING

Bassim Hamadeh, CEO and Publisher
Amy Smith, Project Editor
Abbey Hastings, Associate Production Editor
Emely Villavicencio, Senior Graphic Designer
Stephanie Kohl, Licensing Associate
Jennifer Redding, Interior Designer
Natalie Piccotti, Senior Marketing Manager
Kassie Graves, Vice President of Editorial
Jamie Giganti, Director of Academic Publishing

9781516577965

cognella® | ACADEMIC PUBLISHING

www.cognella.com 800-200-3908

In memory of my mother, Terry Dankel Counselman
(July 4, 1937–December 17, 2018)

For my children.
— Beth Counselman Carpenter

Brief Contents

Detailed Contents

Preface

Genesis of this Book

Both of my parents died when I was in my 30s. Beth lost her father when she was young and her mother a few months ago during the writing of this text. So, we were both orphaned young. As social workers training in various clinical models, none of which we felt thoroughly explored loss, we decided to collaborate on developing a textbook that would provide meaningful examples of a variety of personal loss and grief stories while considering a range of cultural and religious perspectives. We define loss broadly and do not limit it to the death of a loved one, which is how it is framed in many other grief and loss textbooks. We made this decision because we hope to strengthen the clinical lens through which grief is viewed and help the next generation of clinicians understand the global context of loss.

Overview of the Book

Any textbook for clinicians must begin with historic and current theories that guide clinical practice. Solid clinical practice and evidenced-based treatment is guided by good theories, so that is where our book starts. Chapter 1 reviews the main theories of grief, loss, bereavement, and mourning that have frame modern clinical behavioral health practice. This chapter begins with historic theorists like Sigmund Freud's *Mourning and Melancholia* and Elisabeth Kübler-Ross's *The Stages of Grief.* It addresses important factors such as attachment theory, anticipatory grief, and cultural relativity. Finally, the chapter reviews significant modern theorists (a) Neimeyer: Meaning reconstruction, (b) Stroebe and Schut: Dual-process model, (c) Rando: six Rs of mourning, (d) Worden: Tasks for the bereaved, and (e) Klass: Continuing bonds.

Neimeyer emphasized meaning reconstruction as one of the processes of grief in that understanding our response to the loss is significant. Grief interrupts our life story, and processing the grief changes our narrative. Stroebe and Schut, in the dual-process model, discuss how to cope with grief, in particular the loss of a partner or spouse. Stressors are global and can co-occur and our mourning is not a phase or stage; it is an ongoing process. Rando describes grief in three stages: avoidance, confrontation and accommodation. Rando's six Rs of mourning instruct us to pay attention to the 6 Rs: recognize the loss, react to the separation, recollect or re-experience the deceased person and the relationship, relinquish old attachments, readjust to the new world without the person in it, and reinvest.

The next theorist is Worden, who describes four tasks for the bereaved such as to accept the loss, to process the grief, to adjust to the world without the loved one, and to find connection with the deceased while starting a new journey. The final major modern grief theorist is Klass with continuing bonds. Klass argues that those in mourning do not need to "let go" of the past or move on to process the grief. The person can have a continuing bond with the deceased, which is an ongoing inner relationship that assists in the grieving process.

Chapter 2 reviews some of the major evidenced-based interventions defined by the Substance Abuse and Mental Health Services Agency (SAMHSA) and some promising new approaches. *Evidenced-based interventions* utilize research to examine whether a particular approach is useful to reduce mental health symptoms of grief, loss, and trauma such as depression, anxiety, nightmares, guilt, anger, post-traumatic stress disorder (PTSD), emotional regulation, coping skills, and social adjustment. These selected approaches are the ones that have demonstrated the most improvement in symptoms and are supported by the existing research literature. However, we did not review every approach that exists. The second part of this chapter reviews new and promising approaches such as expressive arts therapy, group therapy, and animal-assisted therapy including equine therapy.

Chapter 3 moves us from the intellectual theories and academic research to the intimate personal stories of loss from licensed clinicians, counselors, psychologists, marriage and family therapists, and social workers. Our goal was to broadly represent the range of personal loss that you may be exposed to in your clinical work but also to hear these stories from the full clinical community. Our goal was to share our lessons as mature clinicians for (a) the benefit of students just entering the field or (b) for the experienced professional who needs more information on the topic. Our passion is that the reader views clients not as subjects or as the "other", but as equal participants in grief. This chapter is about people who happen to be clinicians, in their own voice, telling us about their most vulnerable moments. Take care as you read this chapter as we may become quickly overwhelmed, exhausted, and saddened by the losses. However, we believe that clinicians must hold the space for clients to grieve as they need, and clinicians must be prepared. Exposure to loss is part of the preparation. One may not be able to read this chapter in its entirely at one time so it is recommended that faculty thoughtfully consider the best method for how students might consume this chapter over the course of a semester. There are a few notable regrets that we have for this chapter because there are certain topics that clinicians need to understand more deeply. We unsuccessfully sought a personal story on genocide, war, or seeking asylum. However, in the Religion and Culture chapter, there is a story that discusses how the Mayan people understand grief and loss in relation to the Guatemalan genocide and 36-year civil war. This story is written by a person who understands the culture but did not personally experience the civil war. We also unsuccessfully sought a personal story from a loved one of someone who had an opioid overdose. Opioid overdoses are a crisis that parallels HIV of the 80s and 90s. And finally, we were unable to secure a chapter reflecting on working with those who have survived a mass shooting, a challenge and fear that faces every behavioral health clinician in some way today. These examples of loss are very important for clinicians to understand. We hope to add these chapters in future editions of the book.

Chapter 4 describes a wide range of religions and cultures. Our goal for this chapter to broaden the clinical understanding of worldwide grief, loss, and death traditions. We offer comprehensive descriptions of all the major religions from Hinduism to Islam, except for Christianity. We intended to include a chapter on Christianity but our attempts to receive a suitable chapter failed. We wanted a balance between academic and the personal, the accurate description versus proselytizing, but we were unable to find this balance despite our personal attempts to recruit authors for over a year. Perhaps this is also because as editors, we are the most familiar with Christianity but there are hundreds of Christian denominations, so we did not want a chapter that painted a picture of Christianity as one religion. We encouraged all our other authors to write about their specific understanding. They were not expected to describe all of, say Judaism, just the part that they knew well and any notable variations. We hope to educate others about religion and culture within the context of loss, we did not want to create any misunderstandings or stereotypes about a group of people. We also included a chapter on people who are religiously unaffiliated as this is a rapidly growing population. The second part of chapter 4 discusses cultures from around the world and stories range from Africa, Asia, Central America, North America, and the Caribbean. We also included a part on the unique considerations of the LGBT community and provided introductory information on hospice. Again, we are aware that we were not able to include all cultures and spiritual traditions, but we hope this broad overview will deepen the reader's experience with religions and cultures that may be unfamiliar.

Chapter 5 is dedicated to self-care. Our original idea for this chapter changed after Beth's mother was hospitalized and died within weeks of this book's submission. Beth was not sure that she was willing or able to write this chapter, but I encouraged her to do so anyway. Our goal for this book was to help clinical students and active clinicians to become better practitioners, and part of doing that is to learn how to take care of themselves. In addition, I insisted on an *authentic self-care* chapter. If one more person suggests that I meditate, I am liable to throw my meditation pillows at them. It is not that I disagree with meditation—meditation is extremely effective, useful and is an evidenced-based intervention. My complaint is that we have a one-dimensional understanding of how to take care of ourselves. Suggestions, advice, or bossiness usually come from people who think they are "okay" and it comes across as pedantic, condescending, and superior. The reality is that sometimes we are a mess; sometimes we have shame, are depressed, drink too much, or eat too many cheeseburgers, but we hide it like any good therapist. We pretend that everything is okay. How do we practice self-care when we are on the verge of being a mess? Chapter 5 describes Beth's real life, expression of grief, and how she managed—reality television, if you will, hopefully with more taste and a clinical viewpoint.

This chapter is not just about self-care but it is also an example of how, as clinicians, we must examine ourselves again and again to see what issues or baggage we bring to the therapist office. Our "stuff" will always interfere in our clinical practice to some degree. The question is, "How much insight do you have into your baggage? How much reflection have you done on these issues today?" If you are confident in that all issues are resolved, then I might be the most concerned about you. Our goal is not for you to be confident in your ability to resolve such countertransference issues; our goal is for you to have steady, constant awareness of the issues that live in you and your office like the ocean waves. Waves can be calm and quiet or dangerous and life threatening. This chapter serves as that example of how to pay attention to the waves successfully and to have a toolbox of skills that will help you manage them.

Chapter 6 provides 10 examples of classroom exercises to help students learn how to be better clinicians. Faculty are encouraged to use or modify these exercises as they determine appropriate. We find that experiential exercises are very useful and enjoyable for students. Several of the exercises include reflection questions, instructions, and case studies. We encourage all faculty to read each exercise thoroughly prior to implementing it as they are designed to provoke strong and personal experiences for students.

The final chapter is an annotated bibliography created by our guest authors. These are books and articles suggested to either deepen your experience with the material or to share with your clients as they navigate the journey of grief. This is by no means a complete list of all the wonderful books and articles that cover these topics, but they were selected to highlight the narratives and experiences woven throughout the text.

—Alex Redcay, PhD, LCSW

Acknowledgments

The authors would like to thank Kassie Graves for believing in our project, as well as Amy Smith and the rest of the Cognella team. We would also like to thank all the contributing authors for their hard work and vulnerability in sharing their stories.

The deepest of thanks and love to my wife, Mayte Redcay, for her unwavering support and patience as I worked on this project and all other projects. Without her, I would be lost. Thank you to my incredible co-editor and friend, Beth, for all of her agendas, fierce determination, inspirational strength of character, marathon work calls, and pep talks over the last 2 years. Thank you to all of my interdisciplinary colleagues at Millersville University, particularly the chair of the School of Social Work, Karen Rice, Dean George Drake, and Provost Vilas Prabhu.

—Alex Redcay

First and foremost, I would like to thank my co-editor Alex for being such a wonderful collaborator on this project. I am so glad we sat next to each other that day at CSWE; thank you for planting the seed that grew into this book, your tireless work through all of our texts, emails and calls, and for your friendship! I am grateful to Jonathan Singer and Laurel Iverson Hitchcock for their wise words and professional mentorship in the early days, particularly the encouragement to believe we could do it. Thank you to my colleagues at Southern Connecticut State University, especially Chair Todd Rofuth and Dean Sandy Bulmer for their support. To my family, especially Colin & Brady, thank you for your patience with me through all the rounds of writing and editing. And finally, to my many clients who allowed me to companion them on their journey through loss and healing, I am so thankful to have been on this path with you.

—Beth Counselman Carpenter

PART I

Foundations in Grief Counseling

CHAPTER ONE
Grief Theories

Introduction

In this chapter, we discuss the main theories of grief, loss, bereavement, and mourning that have framed 20th-century counseling theories and practice. The first working model of grief came from Sigmund Freud, who in 1919 wrote *Mourning and Melancholia*. He posited that there were two phases to grief: the first in which the survivor maintains and wishes to nurture strong ties to the person who has died, tests the loss as part of an unwillingness to accept it, and then eventually realizes that maintaining these ties is impossible. Freud describes the next step in the process as *decathexis*, the withdrawing of libidinous energy from the loss object, and then a subsequent re-investment in other relationships and other objects. While a number of other psychoanalytic theories developed following Freud's work, this working model of mourning remained primary, followed by Elisabeth Kübler-Ross's critical work, *The Stages of Grief*, which became the primary theory framing clinical practice with the bereaved. Stage theory framed most classic texts and models of grief theories, with each theorist typically clarifying his or her own nuanced definitions of grief, mourning, and bereavement. Current models have moved away from stage theories and their linear understanding of bereavement and loss.

Reflective Questions to Frame the Chapter

1. How would you rate your level of comfort in reaching out to a bereaved person? Are you confident in the strategies you employ to you express your support? What has framed your confidence and experience in expressing your support?
2. When a friend or colleague you know has lost someone, what are the types of statements you've been socialized to say as a response? What gestures or overtures do you make to this person?
3. How are these words similar or different to something you may say to a client?
4. How do these words and actions relate to the different models and theories listed?
5. As you read this chapter, think about which theories/models resonate with you the most or the least. How do you think that relates to your culture of origin and positionality of identity?

THANATOLOGY: The scientific study of death and related practices. Includes the experience of terminally ill people and their families. Includes physical, psychological, and social processes.

We encourage the readers to approach each theory by examining their own cultural identity and relationship to loss, trauma, grief, and death. As you unpack your positionality, consider each theory with the lens of cultural relativity—particularly in terms of race, gender, and sexual identity along with educational and socioeconomic status. What roles do historical and structural oppression play in how these theories might be applied to clients and understanding their losses?

As many of the more recent grief models comment on their departure from Elisabeth Kübler-Ross's model, we will open the chapter with a review of her ground-breaking theory.

Stages of Grief Theory

Key Theorist: Elisabeth Kübler-Ross
From: Zurich, Switzerland
When: 1969

"Death has always been a fearful thing to men.
We have a hard time conceiving of our own death"

- Kübler-Ross

Kübler-Ross's seminal work in 1969 *On Death and Dying* is a collection of case studies that recount the experiences of dying patients in hospitals and outlines the five stages of grief that dying patients move through as they grapple with their own mortality. These stages involve acknowledging that they are dying and subsequent coping and preparation for their impending death. Kübler-Ross is credited with providing a platform for and amplifying the dying person's voice (Kuczewski, 2004). This stage model, in which a patient completes certain tasks before moving onto the next stage, became the foremost Western model of understanding grief and loss for the majority of the 20th century. The theory then expanded not only to include the experience of the dying but was also accepted as the resolution process for those who have survived their loved one's deaths. Eventually, this work also became the foundation for the field of palliative care.

When interacting with terminally ill patients, Kübler-Ross (1971) asked questions such as, "What is it like? How does it feel? What fears, needs, fantasies do you have? What kind of things are we doing that are helpful? What kind of things do we do that are detrimental?" to get a better understanding of patients' needs, feelings, and experiences.

THE FIVE STAGES OF GRIEF

DENIAL: A reaction to discovering one's own mortality. "No, not me!"
ANGER: Death is acknowledged as a reality and unavoidable. The patient becomes angry about this and displaces the feelings onto his or her immediate environment. "Why me?"
BARGAINING: The dying person looks for ways to escape death by promising certain things, being a "good person," and showing guilt. At the end of this stage, the person's condition has usually worsened and he or she realizes bargaining is futile. "Yes, me, but ..."
DEPRESSION: With this realization, the patient experiences despair and loss. "Yes, me ..."
ACCEPTANCE: Characterized by silence, the individual begins to prepare for his or her death. A lack of emotions is present.

In her interviews, Kübler-Ross found that hospitals' organizational and normative structures made dying more unpleasant for the patients she was talking to. Dying patients often felt lonely, isolated, and dehumanized in the hospital due to the limitations placed on visiting loved ones and being in an uncomfortable and unfamiliar environment. Kübler-Ross asserted that patients need to be more psychologically adjusted when they are dying outside their home in a hospital than when they are dying in an environment they have grown accustomed to (i.e., their homes) and in her later work argued that hospitals diminish the spiritual meaning death might have for the dying individual, noting that other cultures have a significantly different perspective: viewing death as an essential part of life.

While it is agreed on that understanding the psychology of a terminally ill patient can help build empathy and establish relationships, there have been a number of criticisms of Kübler-Ross's assertions on death and grief. Kuczewski (2004) notes that because stages suggest development and completion before moving to a bigger and more challenging stage, establishing stages of death suggests that earlier stages are not as important and are just stepping stones to later stages. Additionally, he notes that none of the patients who were interviewed for Kübler-Ross's *On Death and Dying* described passing through the five stages of death as a result of talking to Kübler-Ross. Kuczewski (2004) argues that it is acceptable to listen to patients discuss their thoughts and feelings, but it is not acceptable for the professional to insist that a person is not coping with death successfully or that he or she knows what the patient is experiencing because he or she can see the underlying psychological reality. This attitude of expertise can lead professionals to ignore what patients are telling them and highlights the power differential between professional and patient (Kuczewski, 2004).

Other criticisms include the lack of collaboration with peers by Kübler-Ross herself, who passed away in 2004. Not identified as an academic, she was known to have isolated herself from her colleagues due to her self-promotion and unwillingness to work in the medical field. In addition, her reputation suffered when she began working and collaborating with spiritualists who had unsubstantiated views on the afterlife of which Kübler-Ross was easily persuaded (Murray-Parkes, 2013). Published in 1971, Kübler-Ross's *Death: The Final Stage of Growth*'s focused on placing death in a context that is meaningful and significant. However, this text has been criticized for not answering the question, "If death is the final stage of growth, then this growth moves toward what?" (Sullivan, 1974) While Sullivan (1974) credits Kübler-Ross for confronting death and offering a solution that many people, religious or otherwise, will accept and understand, her answers are characterized as incomplete and weak and ultimately her book is more useful for healthcare practitioners and individuals studying religion than teachers and professionals looking for an in-depth scholarly analysis.

Strengths

- Kübler-Ross's theory was paramount in getting practitioners to think about how patients cope with death.
- Kübler-Ross made the voices of terminally patients heard through her work, especially her book *On Death and Dying* (1969).
- The theory helps develop empathy and understanding for family and friends who are mourning.
- The theory can be used by people of all ages.

Challenges/limitations

- No real evidence exists that any stages actually occur when coping with death.
- No evidence exists that people coping with their impending death move through all five stages.

- Patients may rush themselves, or may be pressured by family members, to move through the stages on some imaginary schedule.
- The theory does not consider the patient's environmental factors and how they may influence the coping process. Someone in a toxic environment may feel worse than those who have healthy relationships and support.
- Society can interpret and misuse this theory and its stages.

Reflection Questions

1. Kübler-Ross's model is now 50 years old. How does it resonate with you as a 21st-century mental health practitioner?
2. Do you think that Kübler-Ross needed to have an academic background to develop a grief theory that became such a seminal foundation to the thanatology field? Why or why not?
3. How have you seen clients or people in your personal life move through the stages of grief?
4. Do you believe, culturally or spiritually, that people ever accept their own mortality? Why or why not?

Attachment Theory, Anticipatory Grief, and Grief Work

Key Theorists: John Bowlby and Erich Lindemann

Where: England and Germany

When: Late 1940s, 1960s–1980s

John Bowlby (19873, 1980) posited that humans, similar to other animals, are programmed biologically to seek, form, and maintain attachment relationships, particularly with one significant caregiver, and to resist and avoid being separated from those attachments (Bowlby, 1973, Bowlby, 1980, Shear, M.K., McLaughlin, K., Ghesquiere, A., Gruber, MJ, Samson, N, Kessler, 2011). Attachment relationships help regulate psychological and biological functions such as learning and performing, along with building relationships with others, cognitive functioning, self-esteem, coping and problem-solving skills, and emotion regulation (Bowlby, 1980,; Shear, 2011). These relationships are developed in childhood through the strength of the child's primary care relationship and the ability of the caregiver to assist the child in making sense of the child's and others' emotions The child's fundamental needs are the freedom to explore while also feeling safe. A secure attachment develops when the primary caregiver can provide the child with this security and safety (Bowlby, 1980).

Attachment behavior was defined by Bowlby (1980) as any form of behavior that "results in a person attaining or retaining proximity to some other differentiated and preferred individual" (p. 39) and that this relationship serves as the basis for relationships throughout the developmental life span. Mary Ainsworth would later test this theory with her now famous and heavily replicated "Strange Situation" experiment. *Attachment theory*, heavily based on studies of how humans and animals form attachments with specific individuals (e.g., caregivers) early in life through their need for security and safety, provides a way to make sense of the strong emotional reactions (e.g., intense anxiety, emotional protest) that occur when bonds between humans are threatened or broken (Worden, 2009). Bowlby's theory relates directly to a child's connection to and separation from the child's mother For example, when a child is separated from his or her primary caregiver, the child responds by protesting and trying to reunite with him or her. However, the child's separation anxiety will gradually be replaced by despair, and the child will eventually stop searching and become despondent, creating a particular model of attachment, characterized as secure, insecure, avoidant, and disorganized.

Later, Bowlby (1973), along with Colin Murray Parker, deepened his attachment work to include stages of loss and mourning.

BOWLBY AND PARKES'S (1970) FOUR STAGES OF MOURNING INCLUDE THE FOLLOWING:

1. Numbness
2. Yearning and searching
3. Disorganization and despair
4. Reorganization of life without the deceased

Numbness is characterized by a surreal feeling that the loss is unreal, and yearning and searching is characterized by the emptiness left by the loss. This stage is particularly noteworthy because Bowlby and Parkes (1970) felt if this phase remained unworked the survivor would continue to try and fill the void left by the absence of the loved one. Disorganization and despair are characterized by hopelessness and questioning while re-organization, sometimes referred to as recovery, begins to reestablish a new life, new routines, and rituals, and while the loss does not disappear and continues to have influence, it is integrated into experience.

Bowlby (1973) noted that the four phases can occur in any order and are not linear in nature. In fact, individuals may move back and forth between any two stages for any given time and individuals' attachment styles (secure or insecure) become triggered during a state of loss, injury, or illness. Death is conceptualized as a loss of an attachment and, subsequently, the way a mourner grieves and handles his or her loss depends on his or her attachment style. For example, those who have secure attachment styles are able to maintain clear memories of others (Bowlby, 1972, Bowlby, 1973), while those with less secure attachment styles are dismissive, anxious, and preoccupied. This leads the mourner to suppress his or her need for others, struggle to cope with and maintain coherent memories in the absence of the other, and/or be unable create an organized narrative of the other in the other's absence (Bowlby 1973). This may lead to a person never entirely working through any one of the three first stages.

ANTICIPATORY GRIEF: Grief that occurs prior to a loss (i.e., the impending loss between the diagnosis of a terminal illness and the death itself).

Coined by psychiatrist Erich Lindemann in 1944 and heavily influenced Bowlby's work, *anticipatory grief* occurs prior to a loss and refers to the time of the impending loss between the diagnosis of a terminal illness and actual death (Bouchal, Rallison, Moules, & Sinclair, 2015; Evans, 1994; Lindemann, 1979). Lindemann, who observed the grief responses of people nearing bereavement (the experience of attachment-relationship loss), described grief as a reaction to separation or loss and anticipatory grief as a *reaction to impending death* rather than death itself (Bouchal et al., 2015; Shear, 2011).

Lindemann's Theory of Grief Work

After interviewing family members of individuals and survivors who died in the Coconut Grove nightclub fire in 1942, Lindemann (1979) developed six characteristics of normal or acute grief. These include the following:

1. Somatic or bodily distress of some type
2. Preoccupation with the image of the deceased
3. Guilt relating to the deceased or circumstances of the death
4. Hostile reactions
5. The inability to function as one had before the loss
6. The development of traits of the deceased in his or her own behavior

He was one of the first theorists to focus on the somatic experience of grief—looking at the physicality of loss, motivation, and appetite. In addition, Lindemann described a path of recovery that took 6 to 8 weeks and involved the task of becoming emancipated from bondage to the lost loved one (Bouchal et al., 2015, Lindemann, 1979). In order to process one's grief, one must engage in the "act" of doing grief work. However, there are limitations to Lindemann's studies, which include a lack of clarity about the relative frequency of the group of symptoms; no notation on how many interviews he conducted with the patients; and no mention as to how much time had passed between the interviews and the date of the death (Worden, 2009). In addition, the current literature suggests that recovery needs to be measured in years rather than weeks. However, his contributions to understanding overall grief highlight the importance of the somatic response to loss, that grieving is a type of "work" and that the grief process moves through a sequence and has a beginning and end (Bouchal et al., 2015).

Anticipatory Grief

While conventional grief can carry on for an unlimited amount of time after death, anticipatory grief, by definition, comes to an end at the time of death (Evans, 1994). Both griefs are reactions to loss. However, complete loss or death has not occurred in the case of anticipatory grief. Individuals witness many ongoing losses during terminal illness, including the loss of their loved one's mobility, their independence, and a general loss of control and certainty. Anticipatory grief is a reaction to losses that have occurred in the past, those that are occurring in the present, and those that will happen in the future (Evans, 1994).

Research that has been conducted to gauge the positive effects of anticipatory grief has been mixed (Evans, 1994). The long-established view of anticipatory grief and the emphasis on loss because of the death event does not take in account the other losses that occur as a result of a terminal illness (Evans, 1994). In addition, the literature does not confirm that helping members of the dying patient's family care for their loved one helps them recover post-death (Evans, 1994). Additionally, studies have shown that anticipatory grief is not always conscious or visible (Bouchal et al., 2015).

Reflection Questions

1. Have you ever experienced anticipatory grief? Was it related to the death of a person, the end of a developmental life cycle chapter, or loss of identity? Discuss the different ways in which anticipatory grief may be experienced.
2. How is grief somatically experienced in your family of origin? In your culture of origin? How might somatic bereavement be treated?
3. How do you define the work of grieving? Do you believe grief work can ever be completed?
4. How do you think the experience of working with survivors of a fatal fire influenced the development of Lindemann's theory? What can we compare Coconut Grove to in terms of mass losses today?

Recent research has suggested that grief is not a staged, temporal process, but an enduring process that changes over time (Bouchal et al., 2015). Grief is different for every individual, and it is shaped by the circumstances and consequences of the loss, the mourning individual's personality traits, and the individual's relationship to the deceased (Shear, 2011). In addition, psychodynamic views of grief suggest that grief is multi-dimensional and depends on the nature and meaning of the loss, how the mourner processes the loss, how the loss is socially constructed, and how the loss may transform the bereaved individual in a positive way. While grief may leave the bereaved individuals with regret, despair, and longing, it may also allow them to continue a relationship with the deceased and grow from the experience (Berzoff, 2003).

Strengths

- Bowlby and Parkes (1970) highlighted the concept that grief is present, but after working through the stages, is not always at the forefront of the bereaved's mind.
- Bowlby and Parkes's (1970) theory acknowledges that the phases of mourning do not always occur in the same order.
- Lindemann highlighted the experience of those waiting to lose someone to a terminal illness and attempted to capture their experience.

Challenges/limitations

- Attachment theory initially does not consider the father or couples outside a hetero-centric framework or kinship care such as friends, aunts, uncles, teachers, grandparents.
- Research that has been conducted to measure the positive effects of anticipatory grief has been mixed.
- The literature does not confirm that assisting members of a dying patient's family helps in the family's post-death recovery.

Meaning Reconstruction

Key Theorist: Robert A. Neimeyer
From: Memphis, Tennessee
When: 2000

In his book, *Meaning Reconstruction and the Experience of Loss,* Neimeyer (2001) opens the book by framing his two most significant losses: the suicide of his father at age 12, and his mother in her later years battling health problems and near the end of life. Under the umbrella of the construct of the Meaning Reconstruction model are Stroebe and Schut's (1999) *dual process model* and Calhoun and Tedeschi's *post-traumatic growth*, which is discussed in chapter 2.

Meaning reconstruction is defined as "response to a loss [that] is the central process in grieving" (Neimeyer, 2001, p. 4). Originally developed in reaction to a Western model of viewing grief as pathology, Neimeyer wanted to explore how grief interrupts an individual's narrative. There is a heavy focus on discourse and rhetoric as meanings are viewed as personal and socially constructed. This modality was developed with the clinician in mind, and the work that takes place between client and therapist as the therapist helps the client making meaning out of the loss.

IMPORTANT CONCEPTS OF MEANING RECONSTRUCTION

There are shared constructs of stage theories (e.g. Kübler-Ross) and models of loss and bereavement:

- Doubt that there is a clear series of stages that leads from psychological dysfunction to re-calibration and adaptation
- A movement that the grieving process requires an emotional connection from the lost loved one toward a continued symbolic connection to the deceased
- New models that focus less on the emotional impact of loss and focus more on cognitive processes
- Less of a focus on a universal model of grief and more focus on a greater understanding of cultural needs in grieving
- More focus on how the loss impacts an individual sense of identity
- Understanding that post-traumatic growth can enhance one's life after loss
- More inclusiveness of families and social systems in the constructs of loss

Neimeyer believes that key losses in our life interrupt a narrative in which we have taken our identity as related to this person for granted. After the loss, the bereaved person needs to redefine his or her identity and how he or she engages with others. Meaning reconstruction is grounded in the narrative that occurs as the client is telling the story to the therapist. Rather than focusing on the lens through which the therapist sees the client and his or her loss, or the therapist's interpretation of the loss, the language that the client uses to describe the loss and tell his or her story is considered the focal point of the clinical work. The client comes to therapy because he or she wants to make meaning of the loss and understand how his or her life has changed, and he or she asks the therapist to help him or her tell, and then re-tell, his or her story. Regardless of the type of loss, whether it's normative or traumatic, the therapist helps the client re-write the story with the loss integrated in such a way that the past and future are connected. Neimeyer refers to the process of bereavement therapy as one that needs to be approached with reverence and respect. The therapist is a sculptor of the client's words. The therapist also helps validate the client's new identity as he or she figures out who he or she is without this person in his or her life. This process includes preserving features of the self-narrative that include the person who has died as well as trying on or experimenting with new identities.

The work in session must go deeper than discussing coping skills for managing emotions related to the loss. Neimeyer, describing this as a highly experiential type of therapy, clearly states that this is not enough to honor the subtleties of loss, nor is it enough to give advice or reassurance to the client. Instead, the client is to guide the session with his or her narrative, and the therapist is to listen to tension or unfinished narrative while letting the implicit meaning of the client's story guide the session.

Strengths

- Neimeyer believes that any theory of grieving cannot stand alone without looking through the biopsychosocial lens of broader experience.
- Neimeyer also believed that the narrative of our losses can only be viewed through how loss is experienced in our identified community and culture.
- The concept of reworking one's identity after the loss resonates closely with Calhoun and Tedeschi's post-traumatic growth theory discussed in chapter 2.

Reflection Questions

1. Think about a loss of your own. How did you identify yourself before the loss and how did you identify yourself afterward? Who or what helped shape the changes in your story?
2. What does it mean to you to be a "sculptor" in a therapy session?
3. How much do you rely on advice giving or concrete skills in a therapy session? What might it look like for you to not reassure a grieving client?

Dual Process Model

Key Theorists: Margaret Stroebe and Hank Schut
From: The Netherlands
When: Mid-1990s

Stroebe and Schut's (1999) seminal work on the dual-process model was first published in the journal *Death Studies* in 1999. Described by the theorists as a "taxonomy" that was initially developed to understand how someone copes with the death of a primary partner, at the time it was developed, it had not yet been tested on other types of loss.

GRIEF WORK HYPOTHESIS: Grief work is an active and ongoing effort to come to terms with loss, and one must confront the experience of bereavement to come to terms with the loss and to avoid future health problems.

IMPORTANT CONCEPTS

- Two types of stressors: loss oriented and restoration oriented
- Need for respite from grieving is critical to adaptive coping
- Coping process embedded in everyday life
- *Oscillation*: movement between the two types of stressors

The dual-process model grew from the question, "What comprises effective coping with bereavement?" Stroebe and Schut (1999, 2001) challenged what they identify as the grief work hypothesis, arguing that it was simply inadequate to represent the experience of coping and bereavement. Other aspects of current grief work that they challenged included the following:

- That suppressing grief is pathological in nature and that one must be aware of the reality of their loss in order to process it
- Lack of clarity in the definition of grief work
- Poor quality of operationalizing grief work in empirical studies
- Absence of sound evidence for the grief work hypothesis
- Lack of application across cultures

The roots of the dual process model are based in Lazarus & Folkman's (1984) cognitive stress theory and Horowitz's (1986) work in terms of stress response syndromes. Stroebe and Schut (1999) approach bereavement as a *global stressor* but feel that neither theory adequately addresses that different stressors can co-occur after loss, nor do they thoroughly address how these different stressors are coped with. They believe that while most grief theories share the common belief that a major task in bereavement is learning to live without the loved one, but that they do not address the other stressors that occur, nor to do they address general coping with loss and how coping processes may ebb and flow over time.

Coping occurs in responses to two categories of stressors, and occurs throughout everyday life, but is not a constant experience. The first category, loss oriented, follows the traditions grief work

FIGURE 1.1. The dual process model

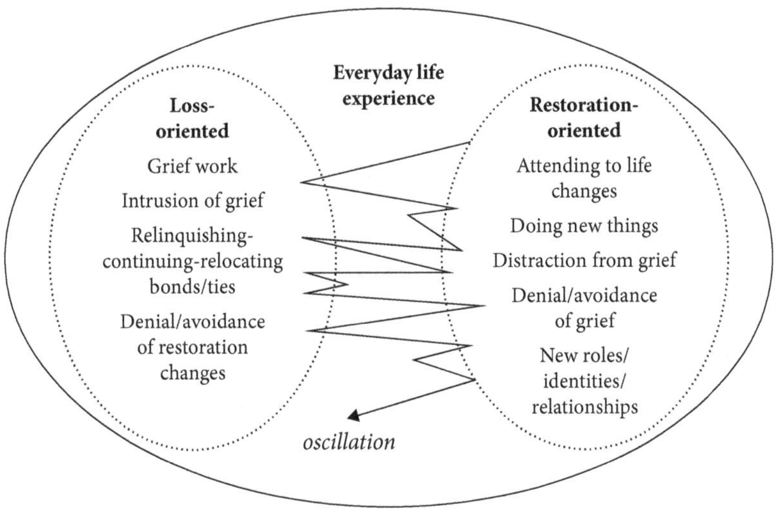

Source: Stroebe and Schut, (1999)

hypothesis. In *loss-oriented coping*, the person feels emotions typically associated with bereavement, longing, yearning, sadness, happiness that the deceased person is no longer suffering, and they engage in mourning behaviors such as looking at old pictures or memorabilia. *Restoration-orientation* refers more toward secondary adjustments related to the loss, such as the what and how as opposed to any end result of grieving. The concept does not relate to actually experiencing restoration as a final step or stage in grieving, but addresses the emotional and logistical "other" challenges related to the loss.

> **KEY POINT:** Dual process is a model where feelings and behaviors flexibly occur over time. It is not a phase or stage model.

Some of these challenges can include tackling the tasks in the home that had been managed by the lost loved one, the gaining of a new identity post-loss, and managing any financial challenges or other life changes (e.g., changing one's work schedule to care of children as a single parent). A variety of negative and positive feelings may occur with mastering or "failing" at these tasks. While this model is similar to Worden's (2009) task-centered model of bereavement, there are three significant differences:

- One needs to take time and respite from the grieving process.
- One needs to reorganize one's subjective environment.
- One needs to develop new roles, identities, and relationships that do not include the deceased.

Another important difference to the dual process coping model is reflecting on the cognitive processes that give attention to managing these different aspects of the loss. The term Stroebe and Schut (1999, 2001 give to process of attending is known as *oscillation*. This process occurs when the bereaved moves between avoiding or being distracted from the grief due to the needs of the other stressors, and then is confronted with the loss. Taking a break from the emotional and physical stress of grief, Stroebe and Schut argue, can have great physical and behavioral health implications over time.

Strengths

- Highlights the uniqueness of everyone's grieving and coping style
- Has a fluidity to the model that highlights the dance between grief and the need to manage everyday tasks
- Discusses the long-term physical and mental health consequences of loss

Challenges/limitations

- Cumbersome nature of the definitions within and description of the model can make it difficult to convert to practice
- Only looks at bereavement within the gender binary and culturally ascribed binary sex roles

Reflection Questions

1. What are some initial tasks your clients need to address in their first 3 months of grieving?
2. How has their role in the family changed?
3. How has their public identity changed?
4. What tasks will your client need to undertake in the first year of bereavement?
5. What activities can your client do to "take a break" from the grieving process?
6. Writing exercise: If you have lost someone significant in your life, take a few moments to write about how you saw your identity evolve and change, the tasks you had to shoulder after the loss, and how you might have taken a break from the grieving process.

Six Rs of Mourning

Key Theorist: Therese Rando
From: Warwick, Rhode Island
When: 1988

Like many other grief theorists, and even the editors of this textbook, Rando's interest in the theories of grief and loss came from her own personal losses. Rando (1984, 1988) experienced the very sudden death of her father while she was in high school and the unexpected death of her mother less than a year later.

Unlike Kübler-Ross, Rando conceptualizes grief has having three stages: *avoidance*, *confrontation*, and *accommodation*. These stages are understood to be fluid and flexible rather than ordered and rigid and allow for the unique and personal experience that each grieving person experiences. The three phases also allow for movement and regression between each phase. Although Rando does not identify this as a stage model, modern critics often challenge this, stating that it is presented as needing to complete a phase, and the R tasks within a phase, before moving to the next one (1988, 1993).

RANDO'S DEFINITIONS

GRIEF: The process of experiencing social, psychological, and physical reactions to an individual's perception of loss

MOURNING: This includes both the conscious and unconscious processes that allow you to release your psychological ties that connect you to deceased person, help you adapt to the loss of the person, and help you live in this new world without the person present

BEREAVEMENT: The state of having suffered a loss

KEY CONCEPTS

- Losses can be physical, symbolic, or competency based. Physical losses are more likely to be recognized, while symbolic losses relate to social interaction and may not be recognized by others.
- Competency-based losses may be positive/related to change and may not be grieved even though a loss has occurred.
- Grief requires active work to be resolved.
- Significant losses bring up unresolved emotional conflict and issues.
- Active grief work requires acknowledgement and recognition that the loved one has died and makes both internal and external changes to reconcile this reality.

The *avoidance* phase is characterized by strong negative emotions, typically denial, disbelief, and shock. Typically occurring immediately after the death, this phase encompasses receiving the news of the death. Some individuals may respond with numbness as part of their shock, while others are overwhelmed and disorganized by the reality of the news. The *confrontation* phase is when the reality that the loved one has died begins to set in. Rando argues that this is the time when grief is most acute and the survivor experiences the most intense emotional reactions to the loss. This phase is also characterized by fluctuations in mood and varied emotional reactions and conflict as emotions, and needs may be at war with one another. The *accommodation* phase signifies an ebbing of the grief, as the acuteness of emotions begin to fade and new attachments are made. While the process of mourning is still taking place, the survivor is learning to live with the loss. This phase often occurs and ebbs and flows along with the confrontation phase and may be accompanied by guilt at starting a new life without the loved one present.

The six Rs of mourning take place during each of the three phases.

There is only one R that occurs in the *avoidance* phase and that is to **recognize** the loss. The tasks of this phase involve acknowledging that the person has died and trying to understand the death. Three Rs occur in the confrontation phase. The first, **reacting** to the separation, typically means feeling the pain of the loss, identifying the feelings accompanying the loss, and expressing reactions. It also involves understanding, identifying, and reacting to the secondary losses that occur. These secondary losses are typically related to identities as well as the existential, like losing faith in a spiritual tradition or in a higher power or losing the identity of a whole family or the role of spouse or child. **Recollecting and re-experiencing** allow the survivor to remember experiences and feelings related to his or her deceased loved one and the relationship shared between then. These memories should include the good and the bad and allow for the integration of the entire relationship through and past the loss. In **relinquishing** old attachments, the survivor lets go of the assumptive world prior to the loss, along with attachments to the lost loved one. **Readjusting** occurs in the accommodation phase and involves remember the "old" world as well as the old relationship with the person who died and developing a new relationship with them. This R also involves developing new identities in the world, both internally and externally recognized, and new ways of negotiating oneself in the world. **Reinvesting** means taking one's energy and investing it in the new world, the new identity and the new experiences with the old world. Like the other theorists in the chapter, Rando emphasizes the idea that grief cannot be rushed (1986, 1988).

Recognize the loss.
React to the separation.
Recollect and **re-experience** the deceased person and the relationship.
Relinquish old attachments.
Readjust to the new world without the person in it.
Reinvest.

One of the limitations to Rando's writing is that the books are written with a hetero-centric and gender binary lens, where she often discusses the typical male and female reactions to loss. Other critics challenge the idea of reinvesting and believe that it should actually be referred to as investing. Another limitation is that most people view this as a linear model moving from one step to the other, as opposed to a more inclusive cyclical model.

Rando's writings are dated in terms of their cultural relativity (1988). In addition to the gender binary division (there is an entire chapter dedicated to male and female differences in mourning in her book *How to Go on Living When Someone You Love Dies),* she does not typically discuss the role of culture in loss and grief. However, much of Rando's work does focus on the need for rituals throughout the bereavement process as a way of giving structure and meaning to the feelings that come with the grieving process. She gives concrete examples of rituals and defines different various funeral practices that can facilitate meaning and healing, as well as the importance of funeral rites, although she does not identify the cultural and spiritual traditions to which these rites are historically tied.

Reflection Questions

1. In reflecting on your culture of origin, are there gender-based differences expected in grief and bereavement, and if so, what are they?
2. Do you see Rando's model as a stage model or a phase model? Why?
3. List the physical aspects of grief you've seen in your clients or experienced personally. How do you create a treatment plan that addresses both the physical and emotional aspects of grief?
4. Rando states that her model of grief and mourning is applicable to all kinds of loss, not just death. Do you agree with this statement? Why or why not?

Worden: Tasks for the Bereaved

Key Theorist: J. William Worden, PhD
From: Massachusetts and California
When: 1982

In *Grief Counseling and Grief Therapy: A Handbook for the Mental Health Practitioner* (4th ed.), psychologist J. William Worden (2009) establishes four tasks to help clinicians and scholars understand how individuals grapple with and work their way through grief. Worden challenges the concept of stages, stating that people do not pass through stages in any particular sequence and there is a tendency to take the stages too literally. Worden notes that the phases approach implies that there is something that the mourner must pass through and complete. As an alternative, he suggests the task-oriented approach because it reflects Freud's concept of grief work. In addition, the tasks approach implies that the mourner can act and do something to understand grief and to adapt to the loss he or she has experienced.

KEY CONCEPT: THE TASKS

How individuals grapple with and work their way through grief:

- Accept reality of loss.
- Process grief and pain.
- Adjust to the world without the deceased loved one.
- Find a connection with the deceased while embarking on a new journey.
  Grieving individuals work on the four tasks in no specific order, can revisit tasks over time, and work on tasks simultaneously.

In his handbook, Worden (2009) describes **mourning** as the process that occurs after a loss and **grief** as the personal experience of the loss.

Accepting the reality of the loss, the first task, indicates that the individual might intellectually accept that a loved one has died but not be able to emotionally accept it. In other words, the mourning individual may be aware of the loss long before his or her or emotions allow him or her to accept the loss as real. Examples of this include the survivor still experiencing a sense of disbelief, calling out for the deceased person, misidentifying someone in the environment as the deceased, getting rid of or keeping the deceased's belongings, or denying the meaning of his or her loss by making it seem less significant. Timing of the reality of the loss is fluid. It may begin to set in immediately after the death, when an individual must call the funeral home, attend the memorial service, or pick up the loved one's ashes. Additionally, it can occur weeks, months, or years later when an occasion arises that the deceased would have been part of such as a holiday, birthday, or anniversary.

Processing the pains of grief is the second task and is felt in a myriad of ways. Worden notes that grief is experienced emotionally, physically, cognitively, and spiritually, and that individuals experience different levels of intensity and pain when grieving. However, it is impossible for individuals to not feel any pain after losing someone to whom they were deeply attached. Thus, it is important to acknowledge and work through the pain of grief or else, the pain may manifest itself through physical symptoms, to the point of somatic conversion, or unhealthy behavior. Individuals may hinder this task by cutting off their feeling and emotions and denying any pain. This can look like a survivor only thinking pleasant thoughts of the deceased so he or she does not confront the discomfort of unpleasant memories; idealization or complete avoidance of any reminders of the deceased; or using alcohol or drugs to numb the grief. A newly bereaved individual often does not know how to grapple with the intense emotions that follow a loss like death and may receive invalidating messages from loved ones who tell them to "get over it," "move on," or be strong. Worden suggests that grief support groups are an appropriate counter-balance to these messages as they encourage and facilitate an expression of grief naturally.

THREE AREAS OF POST-DEATH ADJUSTMENT:

1. External
2. Internal
3. Spiritual

The third task is adjustment to a world without the deceased. Worden notes three areas of adjustment that need to be acknowledged after the death of a loved one. External adjustments relate to how death can affect a bereaved individual's everyday functioning and may include coming to terms with living alone, raising children and/or managing finances alone, taking on the deceased's previous responsibilities, and learning new skills. Making sense of the loss and finding benefit in the loss are two dimensions of making meaning after loss.

Internal adjustments refer to how death or loss affects an individual's sense of self, including self-esteem, self-definition, and self-efficacy. These adjustments are made as the individual adapts to his or her new identity without the deceased in his or her life. The bereaved individual must relearn the world after the loss of a loved one and focus on its impact by addressing questions like, "Who am I now?" and "How am I different from loving him or her?"

The final adjustment, spiritual, is how an individual's beliefs, values, and assumptions about the world are challenged by the death of a loved one. This adjustment occurs as individuals grapple with questions about their belief systems and the purpose and meaning of their lives. Common feelings after the death of a loved one include feeling lost and directionless and characterized by a sense of seeking to make sense of the loss so that the survivor feels that he or she has regained some sense of control.

When individuals work against themselves by feeling helpless, by not developing appropriate coping skills, or by avoiding reality through withdrawal from the world, they hinder this third task. However, most individuals decide that they must fill the roles to which they are unaccustomed, develop skills they never had, and move forward with a new sense of themselves and the world.

The fourth and most difficult task is finding an enduring connection with the deceased as the individual embarks on a new life. Some bereaved individuals do not lose their attachment to the deceased and instead develop ways to continue those bonds, which is very similar to the grief model described by Klass. A challenge that can delay completion of this task is when the bereaved cannot let go of the past attachment, which prevents him or her from forming new attachments. Mourning was identified as ending when the survivor no longer needed to focus on or highlight the lost loved one throughout everyday life. Thus, the task of the counselor is to help the bereaved end his or her relationship with the deceased and to help him or her find an appropriate place for the dead in his or her emotional lives, a place where he or she can live effectively in the world (Worden, 2009). Gradually, the bereaved survivor can maintain a balance between remembering the deceased person and living a meaningful and full life.

Strengths

- Worden's model is flexible; tasks can be done in order, can be skipped, or can be worked on simultaneously.
- Individuals do not feel pressured to "achieve" one task before another.
- The model explains grief as natural and normal and that the process is gradual.
- It encourages the griever to be engaged in his or her grieving process.

Challenges/limitations

- The model assumes there is a "goal" or "destination" to grief, with a suggested sense of completion.
- The term "tasks" sounds like a chore or something that must be done.
- According to Worden, these tasks must be accomplished during the process of mourning. However, these tasks might happen after the mourning phase and suggests a firm timeline.

Reflection Questions

1. Think of a client with whom you work; how might he or she experience external, internal, and spiritual adjustment? What might that look like when assessing a client's level of functioning during bereavement?
2. For someone who is engaging in numbing behavior following a loss, what might that look like?
3. What are some concrete and abstract ways in which a grieving person might maintain his or her connection to his or her lost loved one?

Continuing Bonds

Key Theorists: Dennis Klass, Phyllis Silverman, and Steven Nickman

Where: St. Louis, Missouri

When: 1996

Continuing bonds theory first appeared in the literature in the mid-1990s as a direct challenge to current models. Klass, Silverman, and Nickman (1996) state that modern grief work is rooted in a misinterpretation of Freud in which those who are mourning must let go of the past and their lost loved one and move on for healing and that we need to consider an alternative model. Continuing bonds has been defined as "the presence of an ongoing inner relationships with the deceased person by the bereaved individual" (Stroebe & Schut, 2001 p. 477). Whereas Freud believed that energy toward the loved one had to be severed in order to pursue new relationships and bonds, Klass and colleagues believe that these bonds help the grieving process and that this natural attachment not only helps the survivor heal but will continue through the developmental life stages regardless of the amount of time that passes.

KEY CONSTRUCTS

- The survivor not only maintains a bond with the deceased, but this bond then changes to become multidimensional.
- There are physical aspects to this continued bond, including a sense of presence, hallucinations in any of the five senses, and belief that the deceased still has an active impact on the survivor.
- Continuing bonds are more than mental constructs but are experienced on many different levels.

Klass and colleagues' work demonstrates that continuing to hold a bond with a lost loved one does not indicate pathology but is a rather common and adaptive experience. Rather than death punctuating the end of relationship, it is a period in which the relationship is restructured and re-defined. Rather than being based in the physical world, post-death the relationship is characterized by a symbolic interaction. However, early on post-loss, the bereaved may actively seek physical connection such as wanting to smell his or her loved one, leaving personal items exactly as they were, or even thinking he or she sees the deceased in a crowd or in his or her peripheral view.

These bonds, over time, may be defined by actions and emotions related to the deceased and include but are not limited to rituals around the deceased's life and interests, concrete actions such as holding on to possessions of the deceased, looking at pictures, recounting stories and more abstract experiences such as internalizing the value system and beliefs of the deceased, and using the deceased as a role model. Other examples include grievers' communication rituals with the deceased such as talking to them in their head or out loud, praying to the deceased, and writing letters to the deceased; dreams and nightmares about the deceased can also be considered continuing bonds. Concrete examples of this theory involve the rituals of burial, choosing a headstone or memorial plaque, and anniversary observances involving visiting the spot where the deceased was buried or had their ashes scattered. This theory focuses on what Klass (1996) refers to as the nature of social and communal continuing bonds that are collectively held to the deceased. The rituals around staying connected to the deceased tend to evolve as a person moves through different stages of the developmental life cycle. A continuing bond is seen as a dynamic connection or relationship to the deceased that is different simply because the deceased is no longer alive.

KEY CONSTRUCT

Grief is intersubjective:

1. Grieving is a relationship between the living and the dead.
2. Grief is biologically social.
3. Those who can make sense of their grief have improved outcomes over those who cannot.

Klass, Nickman, and Silverman (1996) caution against the idea that the presence of continuing bonds leads to healthy adjustment following loss. The authors do not feel that bonds are either present or absent, nor do they believe that continuing bonds mitigates the impact of a loss. Rather, behaviors related to staying connected to the dead are normalized. This continuing relationship often reflect the same nature of the relationship when the deceased was alive (positive, negative or neutral) and the continuing bonds based on a complex interaction between relationships, conscious and unconscious aspects, as well as roles previously held by those in the dynamic. If the relationship in life was characterized by tension or negativity, then it is likely that this will be replicated following the death as well. Bonds are not only influenced heavily by culture, but by faith systems.

Strengths

- Highlights cultural relativity as a construct of continuing bonds. In his research, Klass (1996) particularly focused on Japanese Buddhist culture and honoring the dead, along with Confucian mourning rites and Muslim traditions, to name a few.
- De-pathologizes the grief experience through the lifespan.
- Highlights how bereaved children connect with their lost loved one.

Challenges/limitations

- There are mixed results related to continuing bonds and improved coping, although Klass (1996, 2015) believes that this may be a cultural artifact stemming from a Western lens.
- It is often misinterpreted that continuing bonds to the deceased automatically equal a healthy adjustment to the loss.

Reflection Questions

1. What rituals can you identify in your culture that relate to honoring the dead?
2. What connection do you see between continuing bonds theory and the increase in technology and social media?
3. How does the intersection of major life events/developmental life cycle changes intersect with continuing bonds theory?

References

American Psychiatric Association. (2013). *Diagnostic and Statistical Manual of Mental Disorders (5th ed., text rev.)*. Washington, DC: Author.

Bouchal, S., Rallison, L. Moules, N., Sinclair, S. (2015). Holding on and letting go: families' experiences of anticipatory mourning in terminal cancer. *OMEGA—Journal of Death and Dying, 72*, 42–68. Bowlby, J. (1973). *Attachment and loss: Separation, anxiety and anger*, Vol. 2. London, UK: Hogarth Press.

Bowlby, J. (1980). *Attachment and loss: Sadness and depression*, Vol. 2. London, UK: Hogarth Press.

Bowlby J. & Parkes C.M. (1970) Separation and loss within the family. In Anthony E. J. (Ed.) *The Child in His Family, pp.197–216*. New York: Wiley.

Evans, A. J. (1994). Anticipatory grief: a theoretical challenge. *Palliative Medicine, 8*(2), 159–165. https://doi.org/10.1177/026921639400800211.

Horowitz, M. J. (1986). Stress response syndromes. USA: Jason Aronson

Klass, D. (1996). Ancestor worship in Japan: Dependence and the resolution of grief. *Omega: Journal of Death and Dying, 33*(4), 279–302.

Klass, D. (2015). Continuing bonds, society, and human experience: Family dead, hostile dead, political dead. *OMEGA: Journal of Death and Dying, 70*(1), 99–117.

Klass, D., Silverman, P., & Nickman, S. (1996). *Continuing bonds: New understandings of grief.* Washington, DC: Taylor & Francis.

Kübler-Ross, E. (1969), *On Death and Dying.* New York, NY: Touchstone Press.

Kuczewski, M. G. (2004). Re-reading on death and dying: What Elisabeth Kübler-Ross can teach clinical bioethics. *American Journal of Bioethics, 4*(4), W18–W23.

Lazarus, Richard S. & Folkman, Susan. (1984). *Stress, appraisal, and coping.* New York : Springer Publishing.

Lindemann, E. (1944). Symptomology and management of acute grief. *American Journal of Psychiatry, 101*(3), 41–149.

Lindemann, E. (1979). *Beyond grief: Studies in crisis intervention.* Lanham, MD: Jason Aronson.

Neimeyer, R. (2001). *Meaning construction and the experience of Loss.* Washington, DC: American Psychological Association.

Rando, T. (1986). *Loss and anticipatory grief.* Lexington, MA: Lexington Books.

Rando, T. (1988). *How to go on living when someone you love dies.* Lexington, MA: Lexington Books.

Shear, M. K., McLaughlin, K., Ghesquiere, A., Gruber, M. J., Samson, N, Kessler, R. (2011). Complicated grief associated with hurricane Katrina. *Depression and Anxiety, 8*, 648–657.

Stroebe, M. and Schut, H. (2001). Meaning making in the dual process model of coping with bereavement. In: R. Neimeyer, ed., *Meaning reconstruction and the experience of loss*, 1st ed. Washington DC: American Psychological Association, pp.55–73.

Stroebe, M. & Schut, H. (1999). The dual process model of coping with bereavement: rationale and description. Death Studies, 23 (3), 197–224.

Worden, J. W. (2009). *Grief counseling and grief therapy. A handbook for the mental health practitioner* (4th ed.). New York, NY: Springer.

Credit

Fig. 1.1: Margaret Stroebe and Henk Schut, A Dual Process Model of Coping with Bereavement, from "The Dual Process Model of Coping with Bereavement: Rationale and Description," *Death Studies*, vol. 23, no. 3, pp. 213.

CHAPTER TWO
Evidenced-Based and Promising Interventions for Grief and Loss

As we discussed in chapter 1, there are numerous theories of grief, loss, and bereavement. As clinicians, how do we choose the right theory to guide our practice? How is grief measured and how can we understand outcomes for effective practice?

THE ROLE OF SAMSHA

WHO: The federal agency known as the Substance Abuse and Mental Health Services Agency (SAMHSA), under the Department of Health and Human Services of the United States Government
MISSION: Reduce the impact of mental illness and substance abuse on America's communities

---

In counseling, we refer to this as "evidence-based" practice. SAMHSA's protocol ensures that the interventions are assessed and reviewed independently. The interventions discussed in first section of this chapter have been identified as SAMHSA-endorsed practice to treat grief, loss, and trauma. Review SAMHSA's Evidenced Based Practices Resource Center for more information. The second section of this chapter covers treatment and that are promising practices. Each summary describes the description of implementation of the intervention, the primary theorist, current research including outcome variable and measurement, and information on training.

Grief and Trauma Intervention (GTI) for Children

Description of Intervention

Grief and trauma intervention (GTI) for children is a specific treatment for **children ages 7–12** who have been diagnosed with post-traumatic stress disorder (PTSD). GTI is designed is to improve a child's PTSD, traumatic grief, and depression symptoms (Salloum & Overstreet, 2012). GTI has been implemented in the United States in states such as Louisiana, California, Florida, and Texas and internationally in Ethiopia, Lebanon, and Turkey. Originally developed by Dr. Alison Salloum (SAMHSA, 2018) it is theoretically grounded both in cognitive-behavioral and narrative techniques.

CIRCUMSTANCES INCLUDE THE FOLLOWING:

- Surviving community violence
- Witnessing the death of a loved one
- Surviving a natural disaster

IMPLEMENTATION

- Individual or group format
- Ten sessions in total
- One session conducted with child's caregivers for strengths assessment
- Sessions are held in schools and community-based environments
- Grounded in CBT, narrative therapy, and expressive arts therapy

GTI is developmentally specific in that it considers the developmental stage of the child and incorporates developmentally appropriate activities like art, drama, play, and storytelling designed to help children express their thoughts and feelings about their experiences (SAMHSA, 2018; Salloum et al., 2009). Other considerations include the following:

- The child's gender
- Time since the death of the loved one
- Identified culture
- The type of relationship the child had with the deceased
- The type of violence to which the child was exposed

The intervention utilizes an ecological perspective and because many children who witness and experience violence live in oppressed neighborhoods, the intervention takes into account the child's environment and natural supports by sharing his or her story with an identified "support person" (Salloum, 2008, 2015). GTI also uses culturally relevant approaches by incorporating intervention strategies based on the child and his or her family's cultural and spiritual beliefs about death and loss. Issues confronted in GTI are common among both grieving and lived trauma experience such as dreams and nightmares, questioning, and anger and guilt. Activities includes drawing, talking, and writing, the development of positive coping strategies, (Salloum, 2015; SAMHSA, 2018).

CONNECTION MOMENT

- Focuses on how the child can make meaning of the loss. Remember Neimeyer's meaning reconstruction from chapter 1?

Primary Theorist

GTI was developed in 1997 by Dr. Alison Salloum of the University of South Florida. An expert in organizational psychology, she developed the program from her work in the Children's Bureau of New Orleans, which works with urban children, primarily African American with low socioeconomic status, who had been witness to multiple types of violence and often had a murdered family member.

Dr. Sollum's work is guided by the blend of research-informed practice and practice-informed research as she began to gather data and solidify the framework.

Research and Measurement

Salloum and Overstreet (2008, 2012) conducted significant research in two different studies using grief and trauma intervention with children from urban New Orleans who had experienced Hurricane Katrina (2005). The outcome variables for both studies included post-traumatic stress symptoms, depression symptoms, and internalizing and externalizing behaviors.

Theorists	Year	Research Focus	Measurement Tool	Outcome
Salloum & Overstreet	2008	Individual or group GTI	UCLA-PTSD Index; MFQ-C;	Decrease of PTSD and depression symptoms in child subjects who survived Hurricane Katrina
Salloum & Overstreet	2012	Cognitive-behavioral skill-based methods and trauma narrative processing	UCLA-PTSD Index; MFQ-C; CBCL	Decrease of PTSD and depression symptoms in child subjects who survived Hurricane Katrina; decrease in internalizing behaviors; decrease in externalizing behaviors

The instruments used to assess GTI effectiveness by measuring symptoms of post-traumatic stress disorder, depression, stress, and internalizing (e.g., depression, anxiety) and externalizing behaviors (e.g., hyperactivity, aggressiveness) were the following:

- UCLA PTSD Reaction Index for DSM-IV (UCLA PTSD RI, 22-item, Likert Scale 0–4). A self-report questionnaire to screen for exposure to traumatic events and assess PTSD symptoms in school-age children and adolescents.
- Mood and Feelings Questionnaire: Child Version (MFQ-C, 33-item). A series of descriptive phrases regarding how the subject has been feeling or acting recently, most of the time, sometimes, or not at all in the past 2-week period.
- Child Behavior Checklist (CBCL, 20 competence-item, 120 problem item). A standardized measure completed by the parent/caretaker who spends the most time with the child. It includes open-ended items covering physical problems, concerns, and strengths and is used to measure symptoms of both internalizing and externalizing behaviors. Parents rate how true each item is now, or was within the past 6 months, using a same three-point scale.

Training

The program manual, *Grief and Trauma in Children* (Salloum, 2015), is available on the program's website http://www.childrens-bureau.com/gti.html. The manual includes the following:

- The layout of the session's content and the flow of the sessions
- Guidance for session implementation, including missed sessions
- Training specifically indicated for master's level clinicians
- Session handouts and worksheets with case vignettes in addition to standardized assessment tools and recommended evaluation techniques
- Two days of on-site training, recommended for first-time practitioners. Trainers offer consultation via phone, e-mail, and the Internet. In addition, fidelity tools and standardized assessment instruments that measure child outcomes are provided to support quality assurance (Children's Bureau of New Orleans, 2014).

References and Additional Readings

Achenbach, T. M., & Rescorla, L. A. (2001). *Manual for the ASEBA school-age forms and profiles.* Burlington, VT: University of Vermont, Research Center for Children, Youth, & Families.

Angold, A. & Costello, E. J. (1987). Mood and feelings questionnaire. Developmental epidemiology program. *Duke University.* Retrieved from http://devepi.mc.duke.edu/mfq.html

Children's Bureau of New Orleans. (2014). *Grief and traumatic inventory.* Retrieved from www.childrens-bureau.com/gti

Pynoos, R. S., Rodriguez, N., Steinberg, A., Stuber, M., & Frederick, C. (1998). *The UCLA posttraumatic stress reaction index for DSM-IV.* Los Angeles, CA: UCLA Trauma Psychiatric Program.

Salloum, A. (2008). Group therapy for children after homicide and violence: A pilot study. *Research on Social Work Practice, 18*(3), 198–211.

Salloum, A. (2015) *Grief and trauma in children: An evidence-based treatment manual.* New York, NY: Routledge.

Salloum, A. Garside, L.W., Irwin C. L., Anderson, A. D. & Francois, A. H. (2009). Grief and trauma group therapy for children after hurricane Katrina. *Social Work With Groups, 32*(1–2), 64–79.

Salloum, A., & Overstreet, S. (2008). Evaluation of individual and group grief and trauma interventions for children post disaster. *Journal of Clinical Child and Adolescent Psychology, 37*(3), 495–507.

Salloum, A., & Overstreet, S. (2012). Grief and trauma intervention for children after disaster: Exploring coping skills versus trauma narration. *Behaviour Research and Therapy, 50*(3), 169–179.

Substance Abuse and Mental Health Services Agency (SAMHSA). (n.d). National registry of evidence-based programs and practices (NREPP). *Grief and Trauma Intervention (GTI) for Children.* Retrieved from https://nrepp.samhsa.gov/Legacy/ViewIntervention.aspx?id=259

Credit

Cognitive-Behavioral Intervention for Trauma in Schools (CBITS)/Bounce Back

Alex Redcay, PhD, LCSW, Lisa Jaycox, PhD, RAND Corporation, Washington D.C. & Audra Langley, PhD, Division of Child and Adolescent Psychiatry at the UCLA Semel Institute for Neuroscience and Human Behavior, Los Angeles, California

Description of Intervention

Bounce Back (Langley Gonzalez, Sugar, Solis, & Jaycox, 2015) is a cognitive-behavioral, skills-based intervention to treat the symptoms of trauma in school children and is an adaptation of the school-based program, Cognitive-Behavioral Intervention for Trauma in Schools (CBITS) (Jaycox, 2003). The aim of the program is to improve the well-being of traumatized students and can be used both as an individual or group modality.

BASED ON COGNITIVE-BEHAVIORAL INTERVENTION FOR TRAUMA IN SCHOOLS (CBITS)

- Focuses on psychoeducation
- Relaxation training
- Cognitive coping
- *In vivo* mastery of trauma reminders and generalized anxiety
- Processing traumatic memories
- Social problem solving

The population for which CBITS is designed to support is middle–high school students who have witnessed community and/or school violence, experienced physical abuse or intimate partner violence, have survived natural and/or man-made disasters, and have survived accidents and/or injuries (CBITS, 2018; NCTSN, 2012).

There are also one to three individual sessions in which participants complete a trauma narrative in order to process their traumatic memories and grief, two parent education sessions, and one teacher education session. CBITS is designed to be culturally and organizationally appropriate for the school setting. Students screened or referred for trauma exposure and elevated PTSD are selected to receive the intervention (NCTSN, 2012; SAMHSA, n.d.). The goals of the program are to reduce symptoms of post-traumatic stress disorder (PTSD), depression, and behavioral problems and to improve functioning, grades and attendance, peer and parent support, and coping skills (CBITS, 2018; NCTSN, 2012).

IMPLEMENTATION OF CBITS

Group format:

- Ten sessions, 1 hour in length
- Group size: 6–8 students
- Skills based: Feelings identification, relaxation, reducing avoidance, increasing positive activity, combating negative thoughts, social problem solving, conflict resolution, and processing traumatic memories and grief

Bounce Back has some **core differences** from CBITS in terms of how it addresses grief. The primary differences are the following:

- The focus of individual sessions that offer children the opportunity to share their trauma narratives with a parent/caregiver
- No teacher education sessions; parent education focuses on how parents can support the children with at-home practicing

The clinician helps each child develop a "My Story" trauma narrative. Near the end of the program, the clinician meets with the parent and child to share the child's story. The Bounce Back program is appropriate for children and families of diverse ethnic and social backgrounds (SAMHSA, n.d.).

BOUNCE BACK IMPLEMENTATION

- Ten weeks, 1 hour a week
- Group size: 4–7 students
- Skills based: Session content includes coping skills, feelings identification, relaxation exercises, positive activities, social support, and problem solving

Primary Theorists

CBITS was developed by a team of clinician-researchers from the RAND Corporation, the University of California at Los Angeles (UCLA), and the Los Angeles Unified School District (LAUSD) and includes Alejandra Acuna, LCSW; Pia Escuardo, LCSW; Lisa Jaycox, PhD; Sheryl Kataoka, MD, MHS; Joshua Kaufman, LCSW; Audra Langley, PhD; Bradley Stein, MD, PhD; Ailleth Tom, MSW; and Marlene Wong, PhD (RAND, n.d.).

Kataoka and colleagues (2011) and Langley and colleagues (2015) conducted two studies to determine the effectiveness of CBITS and its later adaptation, Bounce Back, at treating the symptoms of trauma in school children who had been exposed to violence and reported moderate or high levels of post-traumatic stress symptoms. The outcome variables for the Bounce Back study included trauma- and stress-related disorders and symptoms, anxiety disorders and symptoms, social competence, non-specific mental health disorders and symptoms, self-concept, depression and depressive symptoms, and self-regulation. The outcome variable for the CBITS study was educational achievement.

Research and Measurements

Theorists	Year	Research Focus	Measurement Tool	Outcome
Kataoka et al.	2011	Cognitive Behavioral Intervention for Trauma in Schools (CBITS)	Pediatric Symptom Checklist (PSC); school records	Short-term effectiveness at reducing child's emotional and behavioral problems; educational achievement improvement was mixed
Langley et al.	2015	Bounce Back (adaptation of CBITS)	Pediatric Symptom Checklist (PSC); UCLA-PTSD Index; Screen for Child Anxiety Related Emotional Disorders (SCARED-C); Social Adjustment Scale: Self-Report for Youth (SAS-SR-Y); Strengths and Differences Questionnaire (SDQ); Coping Self-Efficacy Scale; Child Depression Inventory (CDI); emotion regulation checklist	Short-term effectiveness at reducing child's emotional and behavioral problems; significant improvement at 3-month post-test in trauma and stress-related symptoms, anxiety disorders and symptoms, non-specific mental health disorders and symptoms, self-concept, depression and depressive symptoms, self-regulation, and social competence.

The instruments used to assess CBITS/Bounce Back program effectiveness by measuring academic achievement, self-concept, social competence, self-regulation, and symptoms of trauma- and stress-related disorders, anxiety disorders, non-specific mental health disorders, and depression were as follows:

- Pediatric Symptom Checklist (PSC). A 35-item parent-report questionnaire designed to identify children with difficulties in psychosocial functioning.
- UCLA PTSD Reaction Index for DSM-IV (UCLA PTSD RI, 22-item, Likert scale 0–4). A self-report questionnaire to screen for exposure to traumatic events and assess PTSD symptoms in school-age children and adolescents.
- Screen for Child Anxiety Related Emotional Disorders: Child Version (SCARED-C, 41-item, three-point Likert-type scale). A screen for signs of anxiety disorders in children.
- Social Adjustment Scale: Self-Report for Youth (SAS-SR-Y). A self-report that measures the level of both behavioral and emotional social adjustment across six major areas (work, leisure, extended family, primary relationship, parental unit, and family unit).

- Strengths and Differences Questionnaire (SDQ, 25-item). A brief emotional and behavioral screening questionnaire that includes emotional symptoms, conduct problems, hyperactivity/inattention, peer relationships problems, and prosocial behaviors.
- Coping Self-Efficacy Scale (CSE). Provides a measure of a person's perceived ability to cope effectively with life challenges, as well as a way to assess changes in CSE over time in intervention research.
- Child Depression Inventory (CDI). A brief self-report test that helps assess cognitive, affective, and behavioral signs of depression in children and adolescents 7 to 17 years old.
- Emotion Regulation Checklist (ERC, 24-item, four-point Likert-type scale). Measures children's emotional regulation (ages 6–12).

Training

- Options for training include in-person or virtual formats.
- CBITS website also offers implementation assistance, virtual training, and support for clinicians (www.cbitsprogram.org, www.bouncebackprogram.org) over the course of 10 weeks.
- Providers traditionally are identified as school-based mental health professionals with a master's degree in counseling, psychology, or social work (SAMHSA, n.d.; NCTSN, 2012).

References and Additional Readings

Cognitive-Behavioral Intervention for Trauma in Schools (CBITS). (2018, July 28). *CBITS At-a-Glance*. Retrieved from https://cbitsprogram.org/

Gonzalez, A., Monzon, N., Solis, D., Jaycox, L., & Langley, A. K. (2016). Trauma exposure in elementary school children: Description of screening procedures, level of exposure, and posttraumatic stress symptoms. *School Mental Health, 8*(1), 77–88.

Jaycox, L. (2003). *Cognitive-Behavioral Intervention for Trauma in Schools*. Santa Monica, CA: RAND Corporation.

Jaycox, L. H., Cohen, J. A., Mannarino, A. P., Langley, A. K., Walker, D. W, Gegenheimer, K., ... & Schonlau, M. (2010). Children's mental health care following Hurricane Katrina: A field trial of trauma-focused psychotherapies. *Journal of Traumatic Stress, 23*(2), 223–231.

Jaycox, L. H., Stein, B. D. & Wong, M. (2014). School intervention related to school and community violence. *Child and Adolescent Clinics of North America, 23*(2), 281–293.

Jaycox, L. H., Kataoka, S. H., Stein, B. D., Langley, A. K. & Wong, M. (2012). Cognitive-behavioral intervention for trauma in schools. *Journal of Applied School Psychology, 28*(3), 239–255.

Kataoka, S., Stein, B. D., Jaycox, L. H., Wong, M., Escudero, P., Tu, W., Zaragoza, C. & Fink, A. (2003). A school-based mental health program for traumatized Latino immigrant children. *Journal of the American Academy of Child and Adolescent Psychiatry, 42*(3), 311–318.

Kataoka, S., Jaycox, L., Wong, M., Nadeem, E., Langley, A., Tang, L., & Stein, B. (2011). Effects on school outcomes in low-income minority youth: preliminary findings from a community partnered study of a school trauma intervention. *Ethnicity & Disease, 21*(3), S1-71-7.

Langley, A. K., Gonzalez, A., Sugar, C. A., Solis, D., & Jaycox, L. (2015). Bounce Back: Effectiveness of an elementary school based intervention for multicultural children exposed to traumatic events. *Journal of Clinical Psychology, 83*(5), 853–865.

National Child Traumatic Stress Network (NCTSN). (2012). *Cognitive Behavioral Intervention for Trauma in Schools (CBITS) fact sheet.* Retrieved from https://www.nctsn.org/interventions/cognitive-behavioral-intervention-trauma-schools

RAND. (n.d.). *Cognitive Behavioral Intervention for Trauma in Schools (CBITS).* Retrieved from https://www.rand.org/health-care/projects/cbits.html

Stein, B. D., Jaycox, L. H., Kataoka, S. H., Wong, M., Tu, W., Elliott, M. N. & Fink, A. (2003). A mental health intervention for schoolchildren exposed to violence: A randomized controlled trial. *Journal of the American Medical Association, 290*(5), 603–611.

Substance Abuse and Mental Health Services Agency (SAMHSA). (n.d.). National Registry of Evidence-based Programs and Practices (NREPP). *Cognitive-Behavioral Intervention for Trauma in Schools (CBITS)/Bounce Back.* Retrieved from https://nrepp.samhsa.gov/ProgramProfile.aspx?id=205

Credit

Traumatic Grief Cognitive-Behavioral Therapy (TG-GBT)

Description of Intervention

TG-CBT is based on the foundation of *trauma-focused cognitive-behavioral therapy* (TG-CBT). Core components, which have a heavy focus on gradual exposure, are known as PPRACTICE: **p**sychoeducation (about trauma, loss and grief), **p**arenting, **r**elaxation skills, **a**ffect modulation (in response to trauma cues), **c**ognitive coping, **t**rauma narration and processing, **i**n-vivo mastery (to overcome trauma fears), **c**onjoint parent-child session, and **e**nhancing safety (Cohen, Mannarino, & Deblinger, 2006; Cohen, Mannarino, & Deblinger, 2010). TG-CBT has been adapted specifically for grieving through five additional components:

- Acknowledging the death and addressing the scope of loss including providing grief psychoeducation
- Addressing ambivalent feelings about the loss
- Preserving positive memories of the person who has died
- Developing new or ongoing positive relationships
- Treatment closure, which involves planning for the future

TG-CBT SNAPSHOT

- Evidence-based treatment model for children and teens with a concurrent parent treatment component
- Twelve- to 16-week treatment for children and caregivers

TG-CBT for grief is utilized for children experiencing what Cohen and colleagues (2006) define as traumatic grief, in which children and adolescents develop symptoms of post-traumatic stress disorder following the traumatic death of a loved one. However, traumatic grief does not necessarily predict the onset of complicated grief.

CONNECTION MOMENT

- While this may sound like Shear's model of complicated grief, the primary difference is that in addition to ineffective or prolonged grieving, there is additional distress reactions to the loss.

Primary Theorists

TG-CBT was developed, adapted, and tested by Judith Cohen, Anthony Mannarino, and Esther Deblinger. Dr. Cohen is a professor of psychiatry at the Drexel College of Medicine as well as the medical director of the Center for Traumatic Stress in Children and Adolescents at Allegheny General Hospital. Dr. Deblinger is a clinical psychologist and professor of psychiatry and cofounder and codirector of the Child Abuse Research and Education Services (CARES) Institute at the Rowan University School of Osteopathic Medicine in New Jersey. Dr. Mannarino is the director of the Center for Traumatic Stress in Children and Adolescents and a professor of psychiatry at Drexel University. Together, they have published the seminal works on TG-CBT including *Treating Trauma and Traumatic Grief in Children and Adolescents* (2006) and *Trauma-Focused CBT for Children and Adolescents Treatment Applications* (2012).

Research

Theorist	Year	Research Focus	Measurement Tool	Outcome
Cohen, Mannarino and Knudsen	2004	PTSD		Lower levels of PTSD in child subjects
Cohen, Mannarino, and Staron	2006	Grief, depression, anxiety, PTSD		Lowered levels of grief, depression, anxiety, and post-traumatic stress
O'Donnell et al.	2014	PTSD, grief, depression	Grief Screening Scale UCLA PTSD-RI Strengths and Difficulties Questionnaire Short Mood and Feelings Questionnaire	Reduced post-traumatic stress and depression of children in Tanzania

Much of the research on general TG-CBT focuses on various traumas that impact children through the early developmental lifespan. There are 21 randomized and controlled trials that have taken place in the United States, Europe and Africa. Currently, TG-CBT has the most significant empirical support of all treatment models that are trauma focused for children and their families (Cohen & Mannarino, 2011). Recently, the focus of TG-CBT has been adapted specifically for certain populations, including bereaved military families. In addition to the randomized studies, research also focuses on the case-study approach, demonstrating the trajectory of the treatment process and application of the specific skills.

Assessment and Outcome Variables

As TG-CBT for grief is typically used to treat PTSD, scales that measure symptoms of PTSD are most frequently employed. These scales include the UCLA Post-Traumatic Stress Disorder, Reaction Index (UCLA PTSD-RI), (Steinberg, Brymer, Decker, & Pynoos, 2004) as well as grief-oriented instruments such as the Grief Screening Scale, which is assessed by child report for a total grief score (GSS) (Layne, Pynoos, Savjak, & Steinberg, 1998).

Training

- Free Web-based training through TF=CBT Web, accessible through https://tfcbt2.musc.edu/resources

- There is an eight-step certification process:
    - Must hold a degree in a mental health discipline and professional licensure in one's home state.
    - Complete the online course.
    - Complete 2 days of live TG-CBT training.
    - Receive supervision in TG-CBT.
    - Use TG-CBT instruments and complete written case studies.
    - Pass a TG-CBT knowledge-based exam (Trauma-Focused CBT National Certification program).

References and Additional Readings

Allen, B., Oseni, A., & Allen, K. (2012). The evidence-based treatment of posttraumatic stress disorder and traumatic grief in an adolescent: A case study. *Psychological Trauma: Theory, Research, Practice, and Policy, 4*(6), 631–639. doi:10.1037/a0024930

Brown, E. J., Amaya-Jackson, L., Cohen, J., A., Handel, S., De Bocanegra, H. T., Zatta, E., … & Mannarino, A. P. (2008). Childhood traumatic grief: A multi-site empirical examination of the construct and its correlates. *Death Studies, 32*(10), 899–923. doi:10.1080/07481180802440209

Cohen, J., & Mannarino, A. (2011). Trauma focused CBT for traumatic grief in military children. *Journal of Contemporary Psychotherapy, 41*(4), 219–227.

Cohen, J., Mannarino, A. P., & Deblinger, E. (2006). *Treating trauma and traumatic grief in children and adolescents.* New York, NY: Guilford.

Cohen, J. A., Mannarino, A. P., & Deblinger, E. (2010). Trauma-focused cognitive behavioral therapy for traumatized children. In J. R. Weisz & A. E. Kazdin (Eds.), *Evidence-based psychotherapies for children and adolescents* (pp. 295–311). New York, NY: Guilford.

Cohen, J. A., Mannarino, A. P., & Knudsen, K. (2004). Treating childhood traumatic grief: A pilot study. *Journal of the American Academy of Child & Adolescent Psychiatry, 43*(10), 1225–1233. doi:10.1097/01.chi.0000135620.15522.38

Cohen, J. A., Mannarino, A. P., & Staron, V. R. (2006). A pilot study of modified cognitive-behavioral therapy for childhood traumatic grief (CBT-CTG). *Journal of the American Academy of Child & Adolescent Psychiatry, 45*(12), 1465–1473. doi:10.1097/01.chi.0000237705.43260.2c

Layne, C. M., Pynoos, R. S., Savjak, N., & Steinberg, A. (1998). *Grief Screening Scale* Los Angeles, CA: University of California, Los Angeles.

Layne, C. M., Saltzman, W. R., Poppleton, L., Burlingame, G. M., Pasalic, A., Durakovic, E., … & Pynoos, R. S. (2008). Effectiveness of school-based group psychotherapy program for war-exposed adolescents: A randomized controlled trial. *Journal of the American Academy of Adolescent Psychiatry, 47*(9), 1048–1062.

Melhem, N. M., Moritz, G., Walker, M., Shear, M. K., & Brent, D. (2007). Phenomenology and correlates of complicated grief in children and adolescents. *Journal of the American Academy of Child & Adolescent Psychiatry, 46*(4), 493–499.

O'Donnell, K., Dorsey, S, Wenfeng, G., Ostermann, J., Whetten, R. Cohen, J., … & Whetten, K. (2014). Treating maladaptive grief and posttraumatic stress symptoms in orphaned children in Tanzania: Group-based trauma-focused cognitive–behavioral therapy. *Journal of Traumatic Stress, 27*(6), 664–671.

Steinberg, A. M., Brymer, M. J., Decker, K. B., & Pynoos, R. S. (2004). The University of California at Los Angeles Posttraumatic Stress Disorder Reaction Index. *Current Psychiatry Reports, 6*, 96–100. doi:10.1007/s11920-004-0048-2

Short-Term Interpretive Group Therapy for Complicated Grief

Description of Intervention

First implemented in 1986, short-term interpretive therapy for complicated grief is a group therapy treatment for adults that consists of weekly 90-minutes sessions over a 12-week period. Symptoms for complicated grief include shock, denial, sadness, irritability, insomnia, preoccupation with loss, physically and mentally searching for a lost person, and experiencing intrusive images and memories of a lost person. This treatment has been implemented in almost 100 therapy groups in outpatient psychiatric clinics in Edmonton, Alberta, and Vancouver, British Columbia in Canada (Kealy et al., 2017; Piper, McCallum, & Azim, 1992).

SYMPTOM SNAPSHOT

- Shock
- Denial
- Sadness
- Irritability
- Insomnia
- Preoccupation with loss
- Physical and mental searching for the lost person
- Experiencing intrusive images/memories of the lost person

Complicated grief can be intense and enduring if not treated. The treatment for grief is important, especially when factors like depression, anxiety, family dysfunction, or health-compromising behaviors like drinking or substance use are involved. Therapists performing short-term interpretative group therapies ask two questions to determine if treatment is appropriate for individuals with complicated grief:

- During the last week, did pictures about your loss pop into your mind?
- During the past week, did you try not to think about your loss?
- Short-term interpretive group therapy is designed to reduce complicated grief symptoms and improve patients' social functioning, confidence, and life satisfaction. The goal of the therapy is to reduce psychiatric symptoms by applying probing and confrontation techniques. Consistent with psychodynamic orientation, probing and confrontation techniques are used to enhance patients' insight. For example, clinicians keep pressure on their patients to talk and open up so patients can explore uncomfortable feelings and emotions. Clinicians provide patients with possible interpretations of their internal conflict, make links between their relationships with others, and focus attention on the present. The treatment is based on the psychodynamic assumption that patients can overcome obstacles to their mourning process by understanding and resolving the unconscious conflicts that underlie their complicated grief. Once patients overcome these conflicts, the mourning process will naturally resume and continue until its resolution (Kealy et al., 2017; Piper, McCallum, & Azim, 1992).

Participants were patients who entered a walk-in clinic and reported interpersonal problems or psychiatric symptoms without identifying grief as the cause of their symptoms. They were assessed for complicated grief and were randomly assigned to short-term interpretive group therapy or to a wait list control group. Both groups were assessed at the beginning and end of the 12-week course. Participants were all Canadian and mostly female (72%), but no race or ethnicity demographics were reported. The outcome variables included interpersonal functioning, psychiatric symptoms, self-esteem, life satisfaction, and personalized target objectives (Piper, McCallum, & Azim, 1992; SAMHSA, 2018).

Primary Theorist

The primary theorist for the intervention is Dr. William Piper, the director of the psychotherapy program in the Department of Psychiatry, and a professor at the University of British Columbia, in Vancouver, Canada. He has published six books, including two that focus specifically on grief: *Adaptation to Loss Through Short-Term Psychotherapy* and *Short-Term Group Therapies for Complicated Grief*. He has also served as editor of the *International Journal of Group Psychotherapy* and as president of the Society for Psychotherapy Research.

Research and Measurements

Theorist	Year	Research Focus	Measurement Tool	Outcome
Piper, McCallum, and Azim	1992	Short-term interpretive group therapy effectiveness with interpersonal functioning and community adjustment	Interpersonal functioning Social Adjustment Scale (SAS-SR)	Improvement in interpersonal functioning and community adjustment in the following areas: work, social and leisure activities, and relationships with family, sexual partners, parents, and family unit
Piper, McCallum, and Azim	1992	Short-term interpretive group therapy on psychiatric symptoms	Global Severity Index (GSI); Beck Depression Scale (BDI); Impact of Events Scale (IES)	Significant improvement in symptoms of somatization, obsessive compulsion, interpersonal sensitivity, depression, anxiety, hostility, phobic anxiety, paranoid ideation, and psychoticism. The current distress of intrusion significantly improved.
Piper, McCallum, and Azim	1992	Short-term interpretive group therapy on self-esteem	Rosenberg Self-Esteem (RSE) scale	Significant improvement to self-esteem, self-worth, and self-acceptance.

Theorist	Year	Research Focus	Measurement Tool	Outcome
Piper, McCallum, and Azim	1992	Short-term interpretive group therapy on life satisfaction	1 item, seven-point Likert scale question	Significant improvement patient satisfaction with their life
Piper, McCallum, and Azim	1992	Short-term interpretive group therapy on patient's psychotherapy outcomes based on treatment goals assessment	Target Complaints Scale (TCS)	Significant improvement to patient's assessment of treatment goal severity

The instruments used to assess the effectiveness of short-term interpretive group therapy for complicated grief by measuring interpersonal functioning, psychiatric symptoms, self-esteem, life satisfaction, and personalized target objectives were the following:

- Interpersonal functioning, (30-item, seven-point Likert scale). Self-report rating current level of functioning and ideal level.
- Social Adjustment Scale (SAS-SR, 42-item, five-point scale). A self-report to assess the following interpersonal functioning areas for the previous 2 weeks: work, social and leisure activities, and relationships with family, sexual partners, parents, and family unit.
- Global Severity Index (GSI, five-point Likert scale). Questionnaire asking how much participants had been bothered during the past week by symptoms of somatization, obsessive compulsion, interpersonal sensitivity, depression, anxiety, hostility, phobic anxiety, paranoid ideation, and psychoticism.
- Beck Depression Inventory (BDI, 21-item, four-point Likert scale). Measures characteristic attitudes and symptoms of depression.
- Impact of Events Scale (IES, 15-item). Measures current distress by identifying intrusion and avoidance events.
- Rosenberg Self-Esteem scale (RSE, 10-item, four-point Likert scale). Measures self-esteem, self-worth, and self-acceptance.
- Target Complaints Scale (TCS). Measures psychotherapy outcomes based on the patient's treatment goals.
- One life satisfaction question (1-item, seven-point Likert scale). Asks, "All things considered, how satisfied or dissatisfied are you with your life as a whole these days?"

Training

Training for psychologists, psychiatrists, nurses, social workers, and occupational therapists interested in short-term interpretive group therapy for complicated grief implementation is available through the developer and at occasional professional meetings.

References and Additional Readings

Kealy, D., Sierra-Hernandez, C. A., Piper, W. E., Joyce, A. S., Weideman, R., & Ogrodniczuk, J. S. (2017). Short-term group therapy for complicated grief: The relationship between patients' in-session reflection and outcome. *Psychiatry, 80*(2), 125–138.

Piper, W. E., McCallum, M., & Azim, H. F. A. (1992). *Adaptation to loss through short-term group psychotherapy.* New York, NY: Guilford.

Piper, W. E., Ogrodniczuk, J. S, Joyce, A.S., & Weideman, R. (2007). Group composition and group therapy for complicated grief. *Journal of Consulting and Clinical Psychology, 75*(1), 116–125.

Piper, W. E., Ogrodniczuk, J. S, Joyce, A. S., & Weideman, R. (2009). Follow-up outcome in short-term group therapy for complicated grief. *Group Dynamics: Theory, Research, and Practice, 13*(1), 46–58.

Complicated Grief Treatment

Description of Intervention

Complicated grief is typically conducted as an individual intervention, specifically designed for those who experience persistent and intense grief. Complicated grief is framed by maladaptive thoughts, which are usually counterfactual and in which the loved one's death is second-guessed, and dysfunctional behavioral, which relates to escaping from reality and/or avoiding any reminders of the loss. Typically, rumination regarding the death and the lost loved one characterize the survivor's thoughts accompanied by intense feelings. Complicated grief prevents the person from moving forward and integrating the loss. *Typically, interpersonal functioning of the survivor is disrupted, which leads to disrupted social relationships, a sense of hopelessness about the future and a belief that one's life has been ruined by the experience of the loss.* Often these symptoms can present as depression, but there is a significant difference between depression and grief.

Bereavement is experienced by all and is shaped by a variety of individual factors, which includes the type of relationship between the person and his or her lost loved one, the circumstances of the loss, prior emotional experiences and other loss, and the person's temperament.

Acute grief, which occurs immediately after the death, is an intense and painful reaction that slowly ameliorates over time as we integrate it into our present life. **Complicated grief** is different in that grief disrupts this integration process. The *goal* of CGT as an intervention is to release the blockage and allow the natural healing process to occur.

Treatment lasts 16 weekly sessions in total, with four sessions for each of the four phases, which include (a) getting started, (b) a core revisiting sequence, (c) midcourse review, and (d) a closing sequence. The role of the therapist is one as companion-guide who helps the client recognize the blocks to integration of the loss, and the focus of the tasks takes place primarily between therapy sessions. A significant portion of the session is planning activities for the client to do during the week, with motivational support to accomplish these activities.

Sessions one through three, *getting started,* focus on developing the therapeutic alliance, the juxtaposition of the loss in the client's life, psychoeducation about complicated grief and CGT, developing weekly plans and monitoring grief, goal setting, and sitting down the client and one other significant person in his or her life. Sessions four through nine, the *core revisiting sequence,* have an end goal of developing a new normal and allowing the client to do imagined and situational revisiting work. The focus of this sequence is to address avoidant behavior surrounding the loss, to resolve the more difficult aspects of the loss, and to set longer-term goals. The *closing sequence* covers sessions 11–16 and highlights the termination process of the grief work and the client evaluates the treatment and the clinician. A highlight of this stage is the imaginal sequence, which is a 15–20-minute imagined conversation between the client and his or her lost loved one, during which the client can say everything he or she wants to say. After the imagined conversation, the client processes his or her feelings and reactions with the clinician. The final session revisits and summarizes the goals of CGT and the treatment experience overall.

Primary Theorist

M. Katherine Shear began researching the phenomenon of CGT in 1995 and is the Marion E. Kenworth professor of psychiatry in social work at the Columbia University College of Physicians and Surgeons. She is the director of the Bereavement and Grief Program and director of the Complicated Grief Research and Training Program at Columbia University School of Social Work. She is also director of the Complicated Grief Treatment Program at the New York State Psychiatric Institute. Dr. Shear also currently serves on the advisory council for the National Institute of Health's National Center for Complementary and Alternative Medicine (NCCAM). She has helped develop the current evaluation instruments and the short-term treatment modality specifically designed to address CGT.

Research

Research regarding complicated grief treatment began at the University of Pittsburgh in the 1990s. Early studies indicated that CGT was nearly two times as effective as interpersonal psychotherapy (2008); CGT in older adults has shown similar results regarding efficacy when used with older adults (Shear, Wang & Skritskaya, Duan, Mauro & Ghesquiere, 2014), and in 2016, Shear and Bloom's study found that when comparing CGT to antidepressant medication symptoms of depression improved when compared to a placebo.

Assessment

The Center for Complicated Grief publishes a number of validated instruments that assess for symptoms of CG. These instruments span different symptomology areas such as those that focus on social support:

- Grief Support Inventory (GSI, two-item)
- LOSS SUM. Explores the experience of multiple losses for the respondent
- Typical Beliefs Questionnaire (TBQ). Focuses on beliefs related to the loss
- Grief-Related Avoidance Questionnaire (GRAQ). Asks the respondent about what he or she is avoiding.
- Difficult Times Questionnaire. Highlights difficult dates on the calendar.
- Brief Grief Questionnaire (BGQ). Short self-report screen tool.
- Structured clinical interview for complicated grief (SCI-CG). More extensive semi-structured clinical interview.

Training

Training is provided virtually and through in-person trainings through the Center of Complicated Grief at Columbia University. There is also a 16-session treatment manual that helps clinician guide their clients through what seems to be endless grief and instead to integrate the loss into their life.

References and Additional Readings

Shear, M. K. (2012). Getting straight about grief. *Depression and Anxiety, 29*(6), 461–464.

Shear, M. K. (2015). Clinical practice. Complicated grief. *New England Journal of Medicine, 372*(2), 153–160.

Shear, M. K., & Bloom, (2016). Complicated grief treatment: An evidence-based approach to grief therapy. *Journal of Rational-Emotive and Cognitive-Behavioral Therapy, 35*(1), 6–15.

Shear, K., Frank, E., Houck, P. R., & Reynolds, C. F, III. (2005). Treatment of complicated grief: A randomized controlled trial. *Journal of the American Medical Association (JAMA), 293*(21), 2601–2608.

Shear, M. K., Wang, Y., Skritskaya, N., Duan, N., Mauro, C., & Ghesquiere, A. (2014). Treatment of complicated grief in elderly persons: A randomized clinical trial. *JAMA Psychiatry, 71*(11), 1287–1295.

Additional Evidence-Based Practices and Promising Approaches

Groupwork for Uncomplicated Grief

Description of Intervention

This type of group focuses exclusively on uncomplicated grief, which is defined as a bereavement response that does not impair physical, social, or occupational functioning but does result in acute distress within the first 6–12 months of the loss (McKinnon et al., 2016, Shear et al., 2011; Stroebe, Hansson, Schut, & Stroebe, 2008). Although a brief Internet search will reveal literally hundreds of residential and virtual support groups for those who are grieving, academic literature regarding mutual aid and/or support groups that focus on uncomplicated bereavement is more difficult to find. Rice (2011) reports that attendance in grief groups has been increasing, in part due to the accessibility through the Internet. In general, support groups have tremendous support regarding their efficacy, despite the dearth of visible research for grief group participants.

The website myGriefAngels.org claims over 100,000 people use their grief resources annually. This organization has also developed the Grief Support Network application, which includes a grief group chat feature for smart phones and other mobile devices.

- GriefShare.org lists thousands of grief recovery support groups that meet in over 12 countries.
- Grief.com lists 16 different types of grief recovery support groups on their resource page and state that bereavement groups are important to the healing process, particularly if they are loss specific, because of the importance of the experience of being with others through healing.

The core of a support group experience is *the participants being seen and heard by other group members, installation of hope* that things can and will get better (from those who are further along in the grief process), and *universality* that they are not alone in their feelings and experiences (Yalom, 2005). Participants who choose to attend bereavement support groups report that they attend grief groups to be with others who have shared experience with loss and who understand the impact the loss has had and the overall need for emotional support (Finley & Payne, 2010; Picton, Cooper, Close & Tobin, 2001; Umphrey & Caccitore, 2011). A common goal of a bereavement group is for participants to explore their reactions to grief and share authentic emotions without becoming dysregulated, and, should dysregulation occur, the facilitator and other group members can provide support (Parkes, 2001, , Paine et al., 2017). Benefits of support groups are as follows:

- They are often offered free or at low costs.
- They are usually voluntary.
- They are usually offered in a time-limited fashion, to which it may be easier to commit.

Typically, a bereavement support group is facilitated or co-facilitated by mental health professionals at a counseling center, or a center specifically related to grief and loss. Most uncomplicated bereavement groups follow a narrative process in which group members tell the story of their loss, describe how it has impacted their life, and discuss how they may or may not be coping currently. Often, particularly in long-term groups, the phenomenon of grief mentoring in which attuned group members support one another through anniversaries and next developmental steps without their loved one present is key to facilitating the healing process (Prior, 2015).

Recently, a closed-ended 12 session form of bereavement counseling referred to as meaning-based group counseling (MBGC) for bereavement has shown promising efficacy. MBGC is based on Yalom And Leszcz's (2005) model of *brief group psychotherapy* and Stroebe and Schut's (1999) *dual process model of grief (DPM).* This type of group therapy is a 12-session, highly structured and manualized program, which involves both a pre-screening protocol and specific facilitator training (Mackinnon et al., 2016.

Primary Theorists

Bereavement groups are typically based on the same eleven theoretical principles for all group as described by Yalom and Leszcz (2005). However, there are three particular aspects of these principles that are relevant for groupwork:

- Interpersonal learning and attachment
- Social support
- Meaning making of the loss (Rice, 2014)

These occur through three particular developmental stages: (a) engagement and affiliation, (b) control and power, and (c) intimacy and genuine cohesion (Yalom & Leszcz, 2005). The first stage involves seeking answers or advice regarding the loss and fantasies about the group facilitator, the second stage involves uncertainties and ambiguities regarding other group members and how they may trigger unresolved feelings toward the loss, and the third phase, of group maturity, involves how group members can be vulnerable about how the loss has impacted their lives and work toward growth and resilience (Paine et al., 2017).

Group therapy for uncomplicated bereavement can also be based in the attachment work of John Bowlby (1980), in which group participants can work out the attachment rupture that has happened because of the death.

Research

Historically, research on the efficacy of bereavement groups has struggled with design issues include the poorly controlled studies, a lack of randomization and small sample sizes, which have made it difficult to draw accurate conclusions from the data, can obscure any significant findings from the study and make it hard to generalize overall y outcomes (Linde, Treml, Steinig, Nagle, Kersting, 2007; Maryuma & Atencio, 2008).

- Currier, Neimeyer, and Berman (2008) state that a number of meta-analyses have highlighted the minimal effectiveness of psychotherapeutic interventions for uncomplicated grief.
- Linde and colleagues (2017) found in their meta-analysis of treatment for bereaved individuals who lost someone to suicide that four studies showed moderate-to-strong study design, with three of the four demonstrating randomization and overall findings being mixed.
- Farberow (1992) found that uncomplicated grief in group members was significantly reduced after attending a bereavement support group, but the study design showed limited validity and difficulty in replication.
- Constantino and Bricker (1996) found in their original study that despair, rumination, and depersonalization were reduced after attending group when they later replicated the study (Constantino et al., 2001) with a larger sample size; these symptoms were reduced in both the intervention and comparison groups.
- Maryuma and Atencio (2008) found that bereavement groups are more effective for those who participate voluntarily and have an overall improvement in grief post-group experience. Other findings from this study indicate that gender plays a role, including improving depressive symptoms for women and worsening ebullience and high energy for men.
- Wittouck, Van Autreve, Portzky, and van Heeringen (2014) explored the effect of CBT used in an an uncomplicated bereavement group but found that it had had no intervention effect.

Specifically, MBGC demonstrated improvement in four particular areas for attendees, including that being with others in group who have experienced a loss had benefits, that group as an experiential forum promoted learning, that written exercises were particularly helpful, and that participating in the group helped participants developed a sense of meaning making of the loss (Mackinnon et al., 2015).

Research and Measurement

Often behavioral symptoms are measured as the outcome variables regarding grief groups. Typically, depressive symptoms, loneliness, difficulty attaching to others, stress, and anxiety are examined prior to and after attendance of the group (Prior, 2015). Some examples of measurements used to assess the efficacy of group work in an uncomplicated bereavement format were the following:

- Grief Cognitions Questionnaire (GCQ) (Boelen, Van den Bout, Van den Hout., 2003)
- Revised Grief Experiences Inventory (RGEI) (Lev, Munro & McCorkle, 1993).
- Texas Revised Inventory of Grief (TRIG), which is a 21-item questionnaire that measures an individual's experience of grief with scales of past behavior and present feelings (Faschingbauer, Zisook, & DeVaul, 1987).
- Unresolved Grief Index (UGI). This instrument looks at three items that identify unresolved grief (Zisook & DeVaul, 1983)

There continues to be a call for additional measures that look at grief and mood symptoms separately to differentiate between depression and other mood symptoms as opposed to mood symptoms related to bereavement, with particular attention paid to gender differences (Maruyama & Atencio, 2008).

Implementation and Training

Bereavement groups for those who are experiencing uncomplicated bereavement typically are facilitated by those who have also received some groupwork training and/or have experience a loss themselves.

Other bereavement group facilitators may come from faith-based or pastoral counseling backgrounds. Programs that provide certifications in bereavement facilitation that include groupwork training include the following:

- Association for Death Education and Counseling
- Center for Loss and Transition
- American Grief Academy
- Marian University, Madonna University, Hood College, Grand Valley State University, Arizona State University's School of Social Work, University of Maryland, and the University of Wisconsin-Madison

Other private practitioners and foundations often offer single-day, weekend trainings, and/or special supervision hours related to grief and bereavement work. International programs include King's College in Canada.

References and Additional Readings

Boelen, P., Van den Bout, J., Ven den Hout, M. (2003). The role of cognitive variables in psychological functioning after the death of a first degree relative. *Behaviour Research and Therapy, 41*, 1123–1136.

Bowlby, J. (1980). *Loss: Sadness and depression*. New York, NY: Basic Books.

Constantino R., & Bricker P. (1996). Nursing postvention for spousal survivors of suicide. *Issues Mental Health Nursing, 17*(2), 131–152.

Constantino R., Sekula L., & Rubinstein E. (2001). Group intervention for widowed survivors of suicide. *Suicide Life Threatening Behavior, 31*(4), 428–441.

Currier, J., Holland, J., & Neimeyer, R. (2008). The effectiveness of bereavement interventions with children: A meta-analytic review of controlled outcome research. *Journal of Clinical Child and Adolescent Psychology, 36*(2), 253–259. doi:10.1080/15374410701279669

Farberow, N. (1992). The Los Angeles survivors-after-suicide program: An evaluation. *Crisis Journal of Crisis Intervention Suicide Prevention, 13*(1), 23–34.

Faschingbauer, T. (1981). *The Texas Inventory of Grief – Revised*. Houston, TX: Honeycomb Publishing.

Finley, R., & Payne, M. (2010). A retrospective records audit of bereaved carers' groups. *Groupwork: An Interdisciplinary Journal for Working with Groups, 20*(2), 65–84.

Grief.com. (n.d.). Retrieved from http://www.grief.com/

GriefShare.org. (n.d.). Retrieved from https://www.griefshare.org/

Lev, E., Munro, B., McCorkle, R. (1993). A shortened version of an instrument measuring bereavement. *International Journal of Nursing Studies, 30*, 213–226.

Linde, K., Treml, J., Steinig, J., Nagl, M., & Kersting, A. (2017). Grief interventions for people bereaved by suicide: A systematic review. *PLoS ONE, 2*, e0179496.

MacKinnon, C., Smith, N., Henry, M., Milman, E., Berish, M., Farrace, A., … & Cohen, S. (2016). A pilot study of meaning based group counseling for bereavement. *OMEGA: Journal of Death and Dying, 72*(3), 210–233.

Maryuma, N. C., & Atencio, C. V. (2008). Evaluating a bereavement support group. *Palliative and Supportive Care, 6*(1), 43–49.

My Grief Angels. (n.d.). Retrieved from www.mygriefangels.org

Paine, D., Moon, S., Langford, R., Patel, S., Hollingsworth, A., Sandage, S., Bronstein, M., & Salimi, B. (2017). Group therapy for loss: Attachment, intersubjectivity, and healing, *International Journal of Group Psychotherapy, 67*(4), 565–589, doi:10.1080/00207284.2016.1278172

Picton, C., Cooper, B. K., Close, D., & Tobin, J. (2001). Bereavement support groups: Timing of participation and reasons for joining. *Omega: Journal of Death and Dying, 43*(3), 247–258.

Prior, A. (2015). A Guide to Setting up a College Bereavement Group: Using Monologue, Soliloquy, and Dialogue. *Journal of College Student Psychotherapy, 29*, 111–119.

Rice, A. (2015). Common therapeutic factors in bereavement groups. *Death Studies, 39*(1–5), 165–172.

Shear, K. K., Simon, N., Wall, M., Zisook, S., Neimeyer, R., Duan, N., Reynolds, C…Kesyaviah, A. (2012). Complicated grief and related bereavement issues for DSM-V. *Depression and Anxiety, 28*, 103–117.

Stroebe, M., Hansson, R., Schut, H. & Stroeve, W. (Eds.) (2008). Handbook of bereavement research and practice: advances in theory and intervention. Washington, DC: American Psychological Association.

Stroebe, M. & Schut, H. (1999). The dual process model of coping with bereavement: rationale and description. Death Studies, 23, 197–224.

Umphrey, L. R., & Cacciatore, J. (2011). Coping with the ultimate deprivation: Narrative themes in a parental bereavement support group. *OMEGA: Journal of Death and Dying, 63*(2), 141–160. doi:10.2190=OM.63.2

Wittouck, C., Van Autreve, S., Portzky, G., & van Heeringen, K. (2014). A CBT-based psychoeducational intervention for suicide survivors: a cluster randomized controlled study. *Crisis, 35(3)*, 193–201. doi:10.1027/0227-5910/a000252

Yalom, I. D., & Leszcz, M. (2005). *The theory and practice of group psychotherapy.* New York, NY: Basic Books.

Zisook, S., & DeVaul, R.A. (1983). Grief, unresolved grief, and depression. *Psychosomatics, 24*(3), 247–256.

Expressive Arts as a Developing Grief Modality

Description of Intervention

Expressive arts therapy combines the creative arts, the creative process, rituals around art, and the imagination with therapeutic purpose and healing intention. This type of work uses different creative expressive arts (CAT) techniques to facilitate therapeutic healing, personal growth, community building, and/or political action. Other terms for expressive arts therapy include *intermodal therapy* and *integrative arts therapy* (Donahue, 2011; McNiff, 2009). Historically, there has been significant debate of the exact definitive parameters of what constitutes expressive arts therapy, but it may include music, dance, art, poetry, drama, and photography therapies, as well as other forms of creative expressions (Donahue, 2011; Kalmanowitz & Potash, 2010; Malchiodi, 2005; Thompson & Berger, 2011). Play therapy is sometimes included under the expressive arts umbrella but for the purposes of this text will be considered a separate modality. Expressive arts may be used both as its own standalone treatment modality and as a tool for diagnosis (Malchiodi, 1998).

FUN FACT

Although SAMSHA does not yet recognize art therapy as an evidence-based grief and bereavement practice, but more than 80% of certified ATs report working with grieving clients.

Some examples of how expressive arts is used in grief work is through the intentional creation of scrapbooks or photo albums of the lost loved one as part of the loss narrative (Shear, Frank Houck, & Reynolds, 2005), mandala work and thematic collage, as well as cultural practice of visual memorials during mourning rites and burial practices in other cultures. Expressive arts therapy for grief allows the client to move between mediums and to choose the one that most resonates with his or her experience as different senses are engaged through kinesthetic experience (Thompson & Berger, 2011). Other attributes of expressive arts in bereavement work is attributed to the transformative process of engaging the imagination and making art, which then brings forth the words to make sense of the death, creating meaning and facilitating healing.

Primary Theorists

The start of expressive arts as a therapeutic modality is sometimes attributed to Carl Jung (McNiff, 2009; Niemeyer, 20011), although there is no one identified theorist in the use of expressive arts to treat bereavement and grief. Widely recognized contributors to the field of expressive arts therapy include Shaun McNiff, who published *The Arts and Psychotherapy* in 1981, which is considered a seminal contribution to the field, and four subsequent books focusing on research and practice, and Cathy Malchiodi, who has written 16 books on expressive therapies theory and practice. Typically, expressive arts treatment recognizes two types of bereavement: the dual process model of bereavement (Stroebe & Schut, 2001) and the meaning reconstruction model for understanding (Neimeyer, 2001). The dual-process model of bereavement is built on traditional theories of attachment and loss and focuses on orientation to the loss and subsequent restoration. The focus of therapy in the dual-process model is on both the negative and positive aspects of grief (Stroebe & Schut, 2001; Wood, 2015).

The meaning reconstruction model is grounded more in narrative and post-traumatic growth frameworks. This model posits that people are able to create meaning after loss and that the death of the loved one is a challenge that allows them to create a new narrative both about the death and what it means to their life (Neimeyer, 2001).

Research and Measurement

Expressive arts therapy research has not typically focused on grief and bereavement.

Outcome studies with significance typically focus on the following:

- Adults with severe mental illness (Crawford et al., 2014; de Morais, Roecker, Salvagioni, & Eler, 2014; Montag et al., 2014; Richardson, Jones, Evans, Stevens, & Rowe, 2007)
- Academic settings (Jang & Choi, 2012; Roghanchi, Mohamad, Mey, Momeni, & Golmohamadian, 2013;)
- PTSD (Chapman, Morabito, Ladakakos, Schreier, & Knudson, 2001; Lyshak-Stelzer, Singer, St. John, & Chemtob, 2007).

There is promising research in limited control group studies regarding expressive arts treatment and grief, particularly how visual arts can help with the adaptation to loss and bereavement through continued meaning making and facilitating continuing bonds. However, the majority of studies remain non-experimental (, Schut, De Keijser, Van den Bout, & Stroebe, 1996). Early studies have demonstrated positive effect on visual arts in treating bereavement and grief (Kalmanowitz & Potash, 2010).

Outcome variables remain significant areas of growth for this modality. Lister, Pushkar, and Connolly (2008) call for improved operational definitions, clearer experimental research designs, and the development of empirically validated assessments, and Wisekettle and Gramling (2018) call for increased use of measurements of growth-oriented measures such as the PTGI scale, which looks at post-traumatic growth and other scales focused on self-efficacy and benefit finding. Many studies still rely on client-reported scales and therapist-observed changes.

CURRENT RESEARCH QUESTIONS

What is the exact relationship between expressive arts treatment and the grief experience? How does visual arts treatment mitigate the pain of the loss?

Typically, single-subject case design has been used for most art therapy research studies. There has been a strong call from the American Art Therapy Association to implement outcome-oriented research, to have a neuroscience focus, and to develop instruments with assessment validity and reliability. Some examples of instruments that have been used specifically for grief and loss in AAT are the following:

- The Coping Resources Inventory and Grief Scale (Morton, 1994)
- Levels of symptoms on the General Health Questionnaire (Schut, De Keijser, Van den Bout, & Stroebe, 1996).
- The Chapman Art Therapy Treatment Intervention (CATTI), which was implemented as an urban trauma center as an art therapy research project to reduce symptoms of acute stress and PTSD in children (McNamaee, 2006).

- Art Therapy Trauma Protocol (ATTP) designed to address the 'non-verbal core' of encoded traumatic memories
- The Bilateral Art Protocol, which was designed to address general issues presented in psychotherapy using both dominant and nondominant hands while challenging negative cognitions and beliefs (McNamaee, 2006). However, none of these protocols have been adapted exclusively for grief.

Implementation and Training

Training programs specifically to become an art therapist typically involve a masters' degree from an art therapy program accredited through the Commission on Accreditation of Allied Health Education Programs (CAAHEP) and managed by the Accreditation Council for Art Therapy Education. As of the writing of this book, there are not undergraduate or doctoral programs in art therapy (American Art Therapy Association, 2007). There is a board-certification process through the Art Therapy Certification Board. However, there is no specific training for art therapy for grief and bereavement, although regional chapters and individual counselors may offer trainings on this particular sub-topic.

For expressive arts therapists, there are a number of different avenues available, including the following:

- International Expressive Arts Therapy Association, which offers two different levels of registered acknowledgement:
  - Registered Expressive Arts Consultant/Education (REACE)
  - Registered Expressive Arts Therapist (REAT), which requires meeting specific criteria in education, training, supervision and a blind review by others licensed in the field
- American Music Therapy Association (AMTA)
- National Drama Therapy Association (NADT)
- American Dance Therapy Association (ADTA)
- National Poetry Therapy Association (NAPT)

Case Study: Singing an Imaginal Dialogue

Yasmine A. Iliya, PhD, MT-BC, LCAT, FT, New York University, New York City, New York

FIGURE 2.1. Yasmine A. Iliya

Yasmine A. Iliya, PhD, MT-BC, LCAT, FT is a music psychotherapist from Long Island, New York, who teaches in the graduate programs at Molloy College, New York University, and St. Mary-of-the-Woods College. She received her doctorate in expressive arts therapies from Lesley University and her master's degree in music therapy from NYU. Yasmine spent 7 years working in inpatient and outpatient psychiatric units at Interfaith Medical Center in Brooklyn. Her research and writing focus on music therapy, especially singing, with bereaved adults. Her work on using the voice with men living with mental illness and homelessness was published in *Music Therapy Perspectives*. She is also a performing singer. Yasmine can be reached at yai202@nyu.edu.

Singing an Imaginal Dialogue

In response to my own grief experience of losing my father, I developed and researched an intervention of singing an imaginal dialogue. Using singing instead of talking, it is influenced by Austin's (2008) method of vocal psychotherapy. Musically, it consists of the client and therapist singing together while the therapist plays a continuous, repetitive, and predictable two-chord harmonic structure on the piano with vocal components of the intervention including repetition, singing in unison with the client, and doubling (Austin, 2008). *Doubling* is a psycho-dramatic technique where the therapist sings in the first person on behalf of the client, using intuition and countertransference to express what the client might wish but is presently unable to express (Moreno, 1946). The client and clinician both actively sing words, phrases, and melodies, sometimes together, other times in repetition of one another. The clinician aims to match the client's emotional quality, volume, timbre, and pitch of voice.

Vocal warm-up exercises such as sighing and humming can help clients feel more comfortable with hearing and using their voices (Austin, 2008). Resourcing the client to his or her strengths and sources of safety (i.e., people/places/things that create a sense of safety) is equally important. Breathing exercises can also be utilized to help the clients feel grounded as well as connected to their bodies and the vocalization process. The therapist can then play various chords on the piano, asking which ones the client prefers. Once two chords are chosen, a repetitive vamp can be established, where the chords are played consistently and slowly, back and forth.

Throughout the imaginal dialogue, clients are asked to focus on creating a sense of connection with the deceased person and to sing directly to him or her, imagining that he or she could hear (Iliya, 2014; Iliya, 2015a; Iliya, 2015b; Iliya, 2015c; Iliya & Harris, 2015). While they sing, clients can face an empty chair that is representative of the deceased. Clients are then invited to switch chairs and respond to themselves from the role of the deceased person. The method is completely improvisational; music, words, and phrases are not planned or pre-composed, and clients are encouraged to completely improvise. The intervention typically ends organically when clients stop singing. After singing, it is important to verbally process the experience with the client in an attempt to make sense of uncovered emotional reactions and insights.

The circumstances of the loss can influence the imaginal dialogues (Iliya, 2014). For example, if the relationship with the deceased was complicated, clients may find it helpful to exchange apologies and/or seek some closure. If the loss was sudden, clients may find it helpful to say goodbye to the deceased. If the loss was traumatic, clients may find it helpful to ask questions of the deceased, especially regarding the final moments of life. It can also be beneficial to express feelings of anger, guilt, sadness, and shame, especially regarding unresolved issues, survival guilt, and moving on from the loss.

Case Illustration

Lindsay was a 52-year-old African American woman with a history of bipolar disorder, alcohol abuse, crack/cocaine abuse, and marijuana abuse. She began individual grief-focused music therapy with me 6 years after the death of her friend and employer, Jill, due to cancer. Lindsay was a survivor of cancer herself and suffered from complicated grief surrounding Jill's death. She had not been invited to the funeral and had never felt a sense of closure from the loss. Lindsay was simultaneously enrolled in a mental illness and chemical abuse (MICA) day treatment outpatient program at the same location where our sessions took place.

Lindsay was tentative about opening up in music therapy. Articulate and anxious, she would often try to derail sessions by bringing up less emotional content. Lindsay may have told long, unrelated stories as a way of avoiding her feelings of grief and loss. Indeed, when she spoke about Jill at the start of music therapy treatment, she would be overcome with sadness, guilt, and tears. Singing an imaginal dialogue facilitated an expression and subsequent lessening of feelings of guilt. Lindsay sang of her feelings for her deceased friend while also asking for forgiveness that she was not a "better" friend to her.

In our second session, Lindsay sang to Jill:

I'm sorry, I'm sorry [THERAPIST DOUBLES: will you forgive me?]
I really loved you
I will always miss you
And I hope that, wherever you are, you will forgive me. [THERAPIST DOUBLES: Please forgive me, Jill]
Please forgive me
Will you forgive me?
I want you to forgive me.
I need you to forgive me.
I did not mean to hurt you.
I did not mean to leave you
I did not mean it.

At the end of the singing, Lindsay was sobbing. If Jill had heard her, Lindsay felt Jill would have said: "It's okay, Lindsay, it's okay." Lindsay cried, sobbing more and more. To end the session, I invited her to take a deep breath and feel the connection with Jill, here and now.

In the last session, Lindsay demonstrated that singing an imaginal dialogue had helped her find an enduring connection with Jill while moving forward with her life. Lindsay sang directly to her deceased friend in imaginal dialogue to say goodbye and establish and strengthen a sense of connection with her:

It's strange that I feel a little happy
To get to say goodbye
I feel like I'm letting go of something
That I don't need
And, I'm hoping that there's gonna be more space
For me to move on to something new

And I'm happy that I got to know you (pointing at therapist)
And also to say goodbye
To say goodbye to Jill, and goodbye to [name of former employment],
And see you later, Yasmine [laughing]
And I'm grateful that I had this chance to work with you, and to work through the grief that I was feeling ...

Over the 10-week treatment, Lindsay went from sobbing and avoiding the grief to saying goodbye, feeling grateful for closure, and laughing. In terms of her complicated grief scores, in a pre-test of the ICG-R, her score was 92. After 10 weeks of music therapy sessions, her ICG-R post-test score was 64.

References and Additional Readings

American Art Therapy Association. (2007). *American Art Therapy Association Newsletter,* Vol. I. Alexandria, VA: Author.

Austin, D. (2008). *The theory and practice of vocal psychotherapy.* Philadelphia, PA: Jessica Kingsley.

Chapman, L. M., Morabito, D., Ladakakos, C., Schreier, H., & Knudson, M. M. (2001). The effectiveness of art therapy interventions in reducing posttraumatic stress disorder (PTSD) symptoms in pediatric trauma patients. *Art Therapy: Journal of the American Art Therapy Association, 18*(2), 100–104.

Crawford, M., Killaspy, H., Kalaitzaki, E., Barrett, B., Byford, S., Patterson, S., ... & Waller, D. (2010). The MATISSE study: A randomized trial of group art therapy for people with schizophrenia. *BMC Psychiatry, 10*(65), 1–9.

de Morais, A., Roecker, S., Salvagioni, D., & Eler, G. (2014). Significance of clay art therapy for psychiatric patients admitted in a day hospital. *Investigación y Educación en Enfermería, 32*(1), 128–138.

Donahue, K. (2011). Expressive arts therapy. *Encyclopedia of Creativity* (2nd ed.). Cambridge, MA: Elsevier Academic Press.

Iliya, Y. A. (2014). *Singing an imaginal dialogue: A study of a bereavement-specific music therapy intervention.* (Doctoral dissertation, Lesley University). Retrieved from http://ir.flo.org/lesley/institutionalPublicationPublicView.action?institutionalItemId=2175

Iliya, Y. A. (2015a). Music therapy as grief therapy for adults with mental illness and complicated grief: A pilot study. *Death Studies. 39*(3), 173–184.

Iliya, Y. A. (2015b). Singing an imaginal dialogue. In R. Neimeyer (Ed.), *Techniques of grief therapy: Assessment and intervention (series in death, dying, and bereavement)* (pp. 236–238). New York, NY: Routledge.

Iliya, Y. A. (2015c). Singing for connection after loss. In S. L. Brooke & D. A. Miraglia (Eds.), *Using the creative therapies to cope with grief and loss* (pp. 197–209). Springfield, IL: Charles C. Thomas.

Iliya, Y. A., & Harris, B. T. (2015). Singing an imaginal dialogue: A qualitative examination of a bereavement intervention. *Nordic Journal of Music Therapy,* 1–25. DOI: 10.1080/08098131.2015.1044259

Jang, H., & Choi, S. (2012). Increasing ego-resilience using clay with low SES (socioeconomic status) adolescents in group art therapy. *The Arts in Psychotherapy, 39*(4), 245–250.

Kalmanowitz, D. & Potash, J. (2010). Ethical considerations in the global reaching and promotion of art therapy to non-art therapists. The Arts in Psychotherapy, 37 20–26.

Lister, S., Pushkar D., & Connolly, K. (2008). Current bereavement theory: Implications for art therapy practice. *Art Therapy, 35*(4), 245–250.

Lyshak-Stelzer, F., Singer, P., St. John, P., & Chemtob, C. M. (2007). Art therapy for adolescents with posttraumatic stress disorder symptoms: A pilot study. *Art Therapy: Journal of the American Art Therapy Association, 24*(4), 163–169.

Malchiodi, C. (2005). *Expressive therapies.* New York, NY: Guilford.

Malchiodi, C. A. (1998). *Understanding children's drawings.* New York, NY: Guilford.

McNamee, C. (2006). Experiences with bilateral art: aAretrospective study. *Art Therapy: Journal of the American Art Therapy Association, 23*(1), 7–13.

McNiff, S. (2009). *Integrating the arts in therapy.* Chicago, Illinois: Charles C. Thomas, Limited.

Montag, C., Haase, L., Seidel, D., Bayerl, M., Gallinat, J., Herrmann, U., & Dannecker, K. (2014). A pilot RTC of psychodynamic group art therapy for patients in acute psychotic episodes: Feasibility, impact on symptoms and mentalizing capacity. *PLoS ONE, 9*(11), 1–11.

Moreno, J. L. (1946). *Psychodrama, vol. 1.* Beacon, NY: Beacon House.

Neimeyer, R. (2001). Introduction: meaning reconstruction and loss. In R. Neimeyer (Ed.)'s *Meaning Construction and the Experience of Loss (pp. 1–13).* Washington, D. C: American Psychological Association.

Orton, M. (1994). A case study of an adolescent mother grieving the death of her child due to sudden infant death syndrome. *American Journal of Art Therapy, 33*(2), 37–44.

Richardson, P., Jones, K., Evans, C., Stevens, P., & Rowe, A. (2007). Exploratory RCT of art therapy as an adjunctive treatment in schizophrenia. *Journal of Mental Health, 16*(4), 483–491.

Roghanchi, M., Mohamad, A. R., Mey, S. C., Momeni, K. M., & Golmohamadian M. (2013). The effect of integrating rational emotive behavior therapy and art therapy on self-esteem and resilience. *The Arts in Psychotherapy, 40*(2), 179–184.

Rosal, M. L. (1993). Comparative group art therapy research to evaluate changes in locus of control in behavior disordered children. *The Arts in Psychotherapy, 20*(3), 231–241.

Schut, H. A. W., De Keijser, J., Van den Bout, J., & Stroebe, M. S. (1996). Cross-modality grief therapy: Description and assessment of a new program. *Journal of Clinical Psychology, 52*(3), 357–365.

Shear K., Frank E., Houck P., & Reynolds C. (2005). Treatment of complicated grief: A randomized controlled trial. *Journal of the American Medical Association, 293*(21), 2601–2608.

Stroebe, M. & Schut, H. (2001). Models of coping with bereavement: a review. In M.S. Stroebe, R.O. Hansson, W. Stroebe, & H. Schut (Eds.), Handbook of bereavement research: consequences, coping and care (pp. 375–403). Washington, DC: American Psychological Association.

Talwar, S. (2007). Accessing traumatic memory through art making: An art therapy trauma protocol (ATTP). *The Arts in Psychotherapy, 34*(1), 22–35.

Thomson, B., & Berger, J. (2011). Grief and expressive art therapy. In R. Neimeyer (Ed). *Grief and Bereavement in Contemporary Society: Bridging Research and Practice* (pp. 303–315). New York, NY:Taylor and Francis.

Weiskittle, R., & Gramling, E. (2018). The therapeutic effectiveness of using visual art modalities with the bereaved: A systematic review. *Psychology Research and Behavior Management, 11*, 9–24.

Animal-Assisted Therapy

Description of Intervention

Animal-assisted therapy (AAT), originally developed in the 1970s, is gaining traction as both an adjunctive and standalone treatment modality for a number of behavioral health concerns, including grief and loss. Since the early days of humans, the importance of the animal-human bond and its role in spirituality and healing has been documented (Walsh, 2009). Pet ownership has been found to have significant physical and behavioral health benefits including for adults living with schizophrenia (Searles, 1960), facilitating pro-psychosocial development in children (Melson, 2003) and improved physical health of the elderly (Friedmann & Tsai, 2006).

> **ANIMAL-ASSISTED THERAPY:** The use of an animal in the goal-directed delivery of psychotherapy-oriented services by trained and certified professionals in order to promote improved well-being in the physical, social, emotional, and/or cognitive functioning of an individual or group (Pet Partners, n.d.).

AAT is developed with a clear treatment plan, documented throughout the treatment process and formally pre and post treatment (Fine, 2010; Parks, 2016). Specific to the treatment of grief and bereavement, AAT is typically used as an adjunctive therapy to traditional talk therapy and other therapeutic modalities as a way enhancing the client's coping in the ability to calm and to create new behavioral responses (Wood, Fields, Rose & McClure 2015). Dogs, cats, and horses are most typically used as the animals in AAT, although other animals can serve in a therapeutic capacity.

CLINICAL NOTE

There is a subgroup of practitioners who engage in animal-assisted counseling (AAC), which is practiced exclusively by mental health practitioners and endorsed by the American Counseling Association (Hartwig & Smelser, 2018).

One particular organization, Hope Animal Assisted Crisis Response, deploys teams of dogs and their handlers to respond to mass crises and loss, including on one of the first 20th-century mass shootings in 1998, 9/11, the Pulse massacre in Orlando, and the Emanuel AME Church shooting in Charleston, South Carolina. Known as "hope dogs," dogs and their handlers have received specialty training in AAT and crisis response to provide support to survivors, family members of those who have died, and first responders. Hope AACR handlers and animals often provide grief and crisis services in conjunction with the Red Cross or CERT teams.

Primary Theorist

There is no one primary identified theorist regarding animal-assisted therapy. However, Walsh (2009) and Fine (2010) are two of the most frequently cited sources and are considered two of the most visible theorists and authors on the use of AAT. Levinson and Mallon (1977) are credited with developing and publishing the first guide to AA entitled "Pet-Oriented Child Psychotherapy." Theoretically, AAT is used with intention by the clinician who has received specific training in AAT, as has the animal. The clinician must not only be attuned to the client in the room, but the needs of the therapy animal, including looking for signs of burnout, distress, and/or health concerns (Stewart, Chang, & Rice, 2013).

CLINICAL NOTE

AAT is chosen by the clinician to enhance the therapeutic relationship and experience, and the clinician (known as the handler) has a very strong and highly developed relationship with the therapy animal (Parks, 2016).

Historically, AAT does have roots in the counseling theories of Gestalt, which moves a client toward a self-identified goal through experiential exercises; existential therapy, which teaches techniques that allow clients to make choices that move them toward a more authentic self (Yelvington, 2013); and attachment theory (Zilcha-Manoa, Mikulincera & Shaverb, 2011). The National Association of Social Workers formally recognizes AAT and has made the public statement that change can occur through the relationship/bond between animals and humans. Hartwig and Smelser (2018) have found that nearly 92% of 300 practitioners surveyed identified AAT as a legitimately based counseling modality. The research and theory behind AAT tends to target the behavioral and emotional symptoms that come from experiencing grief and bereavement, including increased stress, depressive symptoms, difficulty with attachment, and emotional regulation, as opposed to grief and loss directly.

Research and Measurement

Animal-assisted therapy has been found to have significant outcomes in the following areas:

- Emotional regulation (Bachi, 2013; Geist, 2011; Walsh 2009)
- Reducing anxiety and decreasing loneliness (Knisely, Barker, & Barker, 2012)
- For children experiencing stress (Fawcett & Gullone, 2001)
- Helping individuals who are developing social skills (Lanning, Baier, Ivey-Hatz, Kreneck & Tubbs, 2014)
- Building a therapeutic alliance for breast cancer survivors involved in counseling (White et al., 2015)
- Improved compliance with treatment for adults struggling with SUDs

Aoki and colleagues (2012) conducted one of the first neurobiologically based studies on the impact of AAT through the use of near-infrared spectroscopy (NIRS) as an observational tool for patients diagnosed with mood disorders participating in AAT. The spectroscopy results indicated that the prefrontal cortex has increased activity during the AAT session, which signified the presence of biological and physiological changes. Depressive disorders often signify lower prefrontal cortex activity, so this study may provide promising results related to both mood disorders and perhaps even complicated bereavement.

AAT is frequently used in PTSD treatment for veterans, including the following:

- Warrior Canine Connection
- Canines for Combat Vets

Typically, AAT focuses on addressing symptoms of depression and the ability to re-attach to others at home.

Specific to grief and loss, McCardle, McCune, Griffin, Esposito, and Freund (2013) and Pichot (2012) specifically found efficacy with AAT and bereavement counseling, and Yelvington (2013) found that equine-assisted psychotherapy (EAP) can help bereaved parents process their loss, engage in meaning making of their child's life, and connect with other grieving parents, and has overall integrative properties in healing from profound loss. However, there continues to be a dearth of rigorous and well-designed research studies for AAT, particularly related to grief and bereavement.

Typically, the effects of animal-assisted therapy are assessed in interventions studies in which behavioral health factors and/or treatment goals are assessed prior to the intervention's introduction; subjects are assigned to control groups and then re-assessed following a standard course of AAT. There are not yet specific quantitative measures designed to assess the efficacy of AAT and there is a continued call for AAT to engage in stronger research design and larger sample size studies (Fine, 2010; Parks, 2016; Renzi, 2005; Walsh, 2009). Historically, the *case study model* is most frequently used, which challenges the ability to generalize the findings (Yelvington, 2013). *Phenomenological studies* have recently attempted to answer the call for more substantial research into the relationships between AAT and bereavement, including Yelvington (2013) whose doctoral qualitative study looked at the impact of equine-assisted psychotherapy (EAP) in treating parental bereavement following the loss of a child.

Implementation and Training

Since 1990, Pet Partners (n.d.) (formerly the Delta Society) has been the largest North American nonprofit institution that provides training and volunteer partnering in AAT.

- Pet Partners provides in-person and virtual trainings in AAT, animal-assisted education, and other animal-assisted interventions. There are nine core and intermediate competencies provided for AAT practitioners:

    1. Knowledge regarding therapy animals
    2. Animal behavior and care and training techniques
    3. Ability to train animals
    4. Ability to work effectively with a team
    5. Ability to understand multicultural implications of human-animal bonding
    6. Basic infection control
    7. Understanding of animal-related trauma and burnout
    8. Attending to animal wellness
    9. Attitudes about animal welfare, advocacy, and professional comportment

Typically, licensure is held through the practitioner's mental health licensing board in his or her state of practice while post-graduate training and coursework is provided by an AAT-specific organization.

Academic institutions that offer training programs that are considered continuing education are the following:

- University of Denver (Colorado)
- Oakland University (Michigan)
- Camden County College of New Jersey
- Harcum College (Pennsylvania)
- Other national pet-oriented programs, such as the ASPCA, often offer regional training workshops

For-profit training institutions:

- Animal Behavior Institute
- International Association of Animal Assisted Play Therapy (www.iiapt.org) offers both a level I and level II certification program and supervisory training program. There is a call for a full licensure and training track to be developed for AAT (Hartwig & Smelser, 2018)
- Internationally accredited programs by the International Association for Animal-Assisted Therapies are available in Germany, Israel, Italy, and Austria and the European Society of Animal-Assisted Therapies accredits additional programs in Switzerland and Luxembourg.

References and Additional Readings

Aoki, J., Iwahashi, K., Ishigooka, J., Fukamauchi, F., Numajiri, M., Ohtani, N., & Ohta, M. (2012). Evaluation of cerebral activity in the prefrontal cortex in mood [affective] disorders during animal-assisted therapy (AAT) by near-infrared spectroscopy (NIRS): A pilot study. *International Journal of Psychiatry in Clinical Practice, 16*(3), 205–213. doi:10.3109/13651501.2011.644565

Bachi, K. (2013). Application of attachment theory to equine-facilitated psychotherapy. *Journal of Contemporary Psychotherapy, 43*(3), 187–196.

Chandler, C. K. (2012). *Animal assisted therapy in counseling.* New York, NY: Routledge.

Fawcett N., & Gullone E. (2001). Cute and cuddly and a whole lot more? A call for empirical investigation into the therapeutic benefits of human-animal interaction for children. *Behavioral Change, 18*(2), 124–33.

Fine, A. H. (2010). *Handbook on animal-assisted therapy theoretical foundations and guidelines for practice* (3rd ed.). San Diego, CA: Academic Press.

Friedmann, E., & Tsai, C. C. (2006). The human-animal bond: Health and wellness. In A. Fine (Ed.) *Animal-assisted therapy: theoretical foundations and practice guidelines* (2nd ed.) (pp. 95–117). San Diego, CA: Academic Press.

Geist, T. S. (2011). Conceptual framework for animal-assisted therapy. *Child & Adolescent Social Work Journal, 28*(3), 243–256.

Hartwig, E., & Smelser Q. (2018). Practitioner perspective on animal-assisted counseling. *Journal of Mental Health Counseling, 40*(1), 43–57.

Knisely, J. S., Barker, S. B., & Barker, R. T. (2012). Research on benefits of canine assisted therapy for adults in non-military settings. *United States Army Medical Department Journal*, 30–37.

Lanning, B. A., Baier, M. M., Ivey-Hatz, J., Krenek, N., & Tubbs, J. D. (2014). Effects of equine assisted activities on autism spectrum disorder. *Journal of Autism and Developmental Disorders, 44*(8), 1897–1907. doi:10.1007/s10803-014-2062-5

Levinson, B. M., & Mallon, G. P. (1997). *Pet-oriented child psychotherapy (rev. ed.).* Springfield, IL: Charles C. Thomas

McCardle, P., McCune, S., Griffin, J. A., Esposito, L. & Freund, L. S. (2013). *Animals in our lives: Human-animal interaction in family, community, & treatment settings.* Baltimore, MD: Brooks.

Melson, G. F. (2003). Child development and the human-companion animal bond. *Animal Behavioral Scientist, 47*(1), 31–39.

Pet Partners. (n.d.). *Animal-assisted therapy.* Retrieved from http://www.petpartners.org/

Pichot, T. (2012). *Animal-assisted brief therapy: A solution-focused approach* (2nd ed.). New York, NY: Routledge.

Parks, Y. (2016). *Review of the literature regarding animal-assisted therapy as a beneficial health service psychological intervention* (Doctoral dissertation). Retrieved from from ProQuest Dissertations & Theses Global. (1815800936).

Renzi, K. A. (2005). *An evaluation of the benefits of animal assisted therapy* (Order No. 3177436). Available from ProQuest Central; ProQuest Dissertations & Theses Global. (305373745).

Searles, H. F. (1960). *The nonhuman environment in normal development and in schizophrenia.* New York, NY: International Universities Press.

Stewart, L. (2014). *Competencies in animal assisted therapy in counseling: A qualitative investigation of the knowledge, skills and attitudes required of competent animal assisted therapy practitioners* (Doctoral dissertation). Retrieved from https://scholarworks.gsu.edu/cps_diss/100

Stewart, L. A., Chang, C. Y., & Rice, R. (2013). Emergent theory and model of practice in animal-assisted therapy in counseling. *Journal of Creativity in Mental Health, 8*(4), 329–348. doi:10.1080/15401383.2013.844657

Walsh, F. (2009). Human-animal bonds I: The relational significance of companion animals. *Family Process, 48*(4), 462–447.

Wesley, M. C., Minatrea, N. B., & Watson, J. C. (2009). Animal-assisted therapy in the treatment of substance dependence. *Anthrozoös, 22*(2), 137–148. doi:10.2752/175303709X434167

White, J., Quinn, M., Garland, S., Dirkse, D., Wiebe, P., Hermann, M., & Carslson, L. E. (2015). Animal-assisted therapy and counseling support for women with breast cancer: An exploration of women's perceptions. *Integrative Cancer Therapies, 14*(5), 460–467.

White, S. A. L. (2018). *Harnessing the healing powers of animals: Treatment through animal-assisted therapy* (Doctoral dissertation). Retrieved from ProQuest Dissertations & Theses Global. (2036843719).

Wood, W., Fields, B., Rose, M., McClure, M. (2017). Animal-Assisted Therapies and Dementia: A Systematic Mapping Review Using the Lived Environment Life Quality (LELQ) Model.*American Journal of Occupational Therapy, 71*, 1–7

Worden, J. W. (2009). *Grief counseling and grief therapy: A handbook for the mental health practitioner* (4th ed.) (pp. 222–230). New York, NY: Springer.

Yelvington, D. (2013). *Bereaved parents' perceptions about their participation in an equine assisted grief-group experience* (Doctoral dissertation). Available from ProQuest Central; ProQuest Dissertations & Theses Global. (1491162909).

Zilcha-Mano, S., Mikulincer, M. & Shaver, P. (2011). Pet in the therapy room: an attachment perspective on Animal-Assisted therapy. *Attachment and Human Development, 13*, 541–561.

Equine-Assisted Therapy

Meghan Morrissey, MSW, NYU School of Medicine, Department of Child and Adolescent Psychiatry, New York, NY

Meghan Morrissey, LCSW is a PATH-certified therapeutic riding instructor and a licensed clinical social worker. Meghan achieved her BS in psychology from Fordham University and MSW from New York University, where she continues to hold a clinical instructor position and is actively engaged in research of therapies utilizing equine interactions. Meghan is a creator of the Reining in Anxiety protocol, an equine-facilitated group therapy with cognitive-behavioral components for youth with anxiety. She also completed her post-master's certificate in equine-assisted mental health at Denver University. Meghan has facilitated various models of equine-assisted activities and therapies in Argentina, Bolivia, New York City, and now at Miracles Therapeutic Riding Center in Lafayette, Colorado. When not with horses, Meghan works as a co-responder crisis clinician for Longmont Public Safety, responding to 911 calls for mental health and substance abuse crises in the community with police officers.

Description of Intervention

Equine-assisted therapy can take many different forms. Facilitated by mental health professionals staying within their scope of practice, equines can be integrated into different therapeutic approaches. Equine-assisted therapy can be done in individual or group format; with families or couples; indoors or outdoors; mounted or unmounted; with youths or adults. Given the flexibility and diversity of equine interactions, the treatment can be a challenge to evaluate and study.

Equine-assisted therapy has many moving parts, some of which cannot be controlled. Similar to groupwork, where facilitation is key and therapeutic learning may arise from organic interactions between group members, interactions between equines, clients, and the environment provide ample grist for the therapeutic mill. Highlighting any communication (verbal or nonverbal), reflecting incongruences, or supporting change talk are opportunistic benefits of the novel interactions found in sessions. In fact, animal-assisted therapies can also be done without an actual animal present; for example, herd observation of horses (in person or via video) can be reflective of object relations in a client's life. Furthermore, depending on the presentation of grief, the therapist can target individual symptoms such as mood, sleep disturbance, or somatic issues (especially given the physical exercise element of some equine interactions). Mood can be targeted via simple emotion identification aside horse communication cues; sleep issues can be addressed through psychoeducation of sleep hygiene comparing sleep habits of horses; and somatic issues can be ameliorated through mindfulness activities practiced on/around a horse and with engaging senses. The horse can mitigate the physical touch that ethics of traditional therapies disallow, as Beetz (2017) cites evidence that shows physical touch of dogs produces oxytocin in humans, which can assist in coping and processing.

Primary Theorist

There is no main theorist for the development of equine-assisted psychotherapy, as it is a structure that can be utilized in conjunction with varying therapeutic perspectives. Lentini and Knox (2015) cite Trotter (2012) as suggesting there are four main theories: brief therapy, Gestalt therapy, reality therapy, and Adlerian therapy, but current trends indicates therapists are often using their individual perspectives and clinical judgment about client presentation to guide the therapeutic approach. As with anything flexible, therapeutic intention is paramount. The milieu of the arena inherently takes clients out of their familiar environment, which can sometimes provide a needed safe space to process grief. It can be difficult to put into words one's experience of grief, so providing a nonverbal sentient being with different sensory experiences can put clients at ease.

Interactions between humans experiencing grief can sometimes be frustrating due to the discomfort of the human bystander witness of bereavement phenomena where grief is avoided or not discussed. Conversely, a horse provides a genuine interaction that does not invalidate feelings, inject perceived spirituality, or attempted to distract with its own past experience of grief. Additionally, equine-assisted therapy does not always feel like therapy or address feelings directly, so it can often be a great option for clients who do not buy into traditional treatment methodologies. Furthermore, pet loss is often identified as disenfranchised grief and a self-selecting population of clients who feel connection with animals could benefit from animal-assisted treatments (Hoy-Gerlach & Wehman, 2017).

Case Study

Sarah is a 14-year-old female who lives in a small town with her mother, father, 16-year-old brother, and two dogs. Sarah does not have experience with mental health treatment but has a stable family who is supportive and engaged. Sarah and her brother perform well in school and extracurricular activities. Last year, Sarah's maternal grandmother, Anne, received a diagnosis of cancer, which was treated intensively and invasively. However, after significant intervention, Anne's cancer persisted and she decided to not to pursue additional treatment; this was met with sadness and understanding by family members, who had witnessed her suffering. Anne's 68th birthday celebration was at her deathbed; she died within days.

Sarah came to her first individual equine-assisted therapy session with a loose guideline that she could discuss her grief if she wanted. Session included mounted work, as requested by the client. During session, Sarah, who had limited understanding of how to steer a horse, voiced a theme of lack of control throughout the session. The therapist reflected this loss of control and validated Sarah's frustration, to which Sarah responded by drawing on recent experiences in which well-intentioned friends offered unsolicited advice about her grief; the therapist prompted Sarah for her thoughts and emotions associated with that experience and noted Sarah's response of isolating from friends because friends cannot "relate." Through psychoeducation and connection (or lack of connection) with the horse, the theme of loss of control and external and unwanted impetuses (which can exacerbate bereavement pain), Sarah developed some insight, which was later shared with her parents about her personal and individualized bereavement experience. Especially given Anne's prolonged battle with cancer, which Sarah witnessed and created a sense of ambiguity that anyone would find unsettling, loss of control is an abundant theme through which to process grief.

Research and Measurement

Rigorous research is difficult to fund and find when it comes to equine-assisted activities and therapies. Many peer-reviewed articles are case studies or philosophical discussions of grief and the metaphor and lore associated with equines in various cultures (Symington, 2012). Since grief and PTSD symptomology may overlap with populations (such as veterans), looking to trauma research with human and equine interactions can be somewhat extrapolated to some symptoms of bereavement. Naste and colleagues (2017) found equine-assisted therapy to show promising positive results in decreasing PTSD symptoms, while Mueller and McCullough (2017) found no statistical significance in decrease of symptoms between traditional office treatment and the equine-facilitated psychotherapy studied; if equine-assisted therapies do not outperform traditional treatments, the added financial cost of treatment with a horse, which is already a barrier, is emphasized. In regard to standardized measures, any of the scales utilized and recognized as measuring grief and bereavement symptomology could be applied. Additionally, there are some scales that aim to measure human-animal bond, such as the Human Animal Interaction Scale (Fournier, Berry, Letson, & Chanen, 2016).

Implementation and Training

The nomenclature of the field of equine-assisted therapies is inconsistent and full of ever-changing acronyms, like any developing field. This makes research difficult, especially meta-analyses that use different words, so the International Association of Human-Animal Interaction Organizations (IAHAO, 2018) established a task force to solidify definitions within the field of animal-assisted interventions. Words used depend on the person providing the session, the sessions' goals, and the type of client served. "Assisted" versus "facilitated" are commonly interchanged. Most states have a definition for "psychotherapy" versus "therapy" that is protected for qualified mental health professionals only; EAP is equine-assisted psychotherapy. "Activities" are usually done by a teacher or non-mental health professional. "Activities" can include vaulting, carriage driving, or other "learning" that includes a client-equine interaction; EAL is equine-assisted learning, which is commonly used when goals include occupational or educational objectives, such as team building. "Therapeutic riding" is provided by a non-mental health professional with horsemanship as the main session goal. "Hippotherapy" in the United States must be provided by a physical therapist, occupational therapist, or speech pathologist. It is important to make these distinctions and understand that someone calling themselves an equine therapist could have various educational backgrounds; there are many practitioners of coaching, for example.

There are also many independent certifications that are proprietary, but not necessarily recognized by others in the field nor regulatory agencies or insurance. There are also more educational institutions adding animal-assisted therapies to their curriculum. It is important for a new social worker to take into consideration the syllabus of any training or certification and the educational experience of the instructor (in equines and in mental health) and assure that it fits with his or her individual therapeutic paradigm and his or her professional ethics and scope of practice as defined by his or her credentialing agent. Thus far, the American Counseling Association (Stewart, Chang, Parker, & Grubbs, 2016) has created animal-assisted therapy in counseling competencies that can be a guide for new practitioners hoping to include this promising treatment into their work.

CLINICAL NOTE

Sarah Schlote (2018), MA, RP, CCC, SEP created a list of equine-assisted practice trainings and certifications that practitioners may find useful.

References and Additional Readings

Beetz, A. M. (2017). Theories and possible processes of action in animal assisted interventions. *Applied Developmental Science, 21*(2), 139–149. doi:10.1080/10888691.2016.1262263

Fournier, A. K., Berry, T. D., Letson, E., & Chanen, R. (2016). Human-animal interaction in a prison setting: Impact on criminal behavior, treatment progress, and social skills. *Behavior and Social Issues, 16*(1), 89–105. doi:10.1037/t64133-000

Hartwig, E. K., & Smelser, Q. K. (2018). Practitioner perspectives on animal-assisted counseling. *Journal of Mental Health Counseling, 40*(1), 43–57. doi:10.17744/mehc.40.1.04

Hoy-Gerlach, J., & Wehman, S. (2017). *Human-animal interactions: A social work guide*. Washington, DC: NASW Press.

International Association of Human-Animal Interaction Organizations. (2018). *The IAHAIO definitions for animal-assisted intervention and guidelines for wellness of animals involved In AAI*. Retrieved from http://iahaio.org/wp/wp-content/uploads/2019/01/iahaio_wp_updated-2018-19-final.pdf

Lentini, J. A., & Knox, M. S. (2015). Equine-facilitated psychotherapy with children and adolescents: An update and literature review. *Journal of Creativity in Mental Health, 10*(3), 278–305.

Mueller, M., & McCullough, L. (2017). Effects of equine-facilitated psychotherapy on post-traumatic stress symptoms in Youth. *Journal of Child & Family Studies, 26*(4), 1164–1172. doi:10.1007/s10826-016-0648-6

Naste, T. M., Price, M., Karol, J., Martin, L., Murphy, K., Miguel, J., & Spinazzola, J. (2017). Equine facilitated therapy for complex trauma (EFT-CT). *Journal of Child & Adolescent Trauma, 11*(3), 289–303. doi:10.1007/s40653-017-0187-3

Schlote, S. (2018). *The list*. Retrieved from https://equusoma.com/trainings/the-list/

Stewart, L. A., Chang, C. Y., Parker, L. K., & Grubbs, N. (2016). *Animal-assisted therapy in counseling competencies*. Alexandria, VA: American Counseling Association.

Symington, A. (2012). Grief and horses: Putting the pieces together. *Journal of Creativity in Mental Health*, 7(2), 165–174. doi:10.1080/15401383.2012.685017

Trotter, K. (Ed.). (2012). *Harnessing the power of equine-assisted counseling: Adding animal assisted therapy to your practice*. New York, NY: Routledge.

Credit

PART II

Contextualizing Loss and Influencing Factors

CHAPTER THREE
The Nature of Loss

Personal Stories

The Insider-Outsider Perspective in Life and Grief: Moving Across the Divide

Erica Goldblatt Hyatt, DSW, MSW, MBE, Rutgers, The State University of New Jersey, Brunswick, New Jersey

FIGURE 3.1. Dr. Erica Goldblatt Hyatt

Dr. Erica Goldblatt Hyatt is an administrator, clinician, and author with over a decade's worth of experience in the field of death, dying, and bereavement. She received her doctorate of social work, master of social work, and master of bioethics degrees from the University of Pennsylvania and a bachelor of arts from McGill University. A notable figure in thanatology, Dr. Goldblatt Hyatt is the author of the only self-help book available for bereaved teen siblings, entitled *Grieving for the Sibling You Lost* (2015). She is a special editor for aging for the journal *Reflections: Narratives of Professional Helping*, and a peer reviewer for several peer-reviewed publications. Her commercial blogs can be found on websites including The Mighty, *Huffington Post*, Elephant Journal, and Scary Mommy. A nationally recognized speaker, Dr. Goldblatt Hyatt is also a passionate advocate for women's reproductive rights and has been featured in media campaigns by Planned Parenthood of Pennsylvania as well as repeatedly welcomed at press conferences alongside Pennsylvania Governor Tom Wolf. Her clinical practice focuses on working with women who have terminated desired pregnancies due to fetal anomaly, as well as individuals coping with a fear of death. She is also passionate about working with adolescents. Dr. Goldblatt Hyatt is currently serving as the assistant director of the doctorate of social work at Rutgers, the state university of New Jersey.

Introduction

I have often wondered if anyone ever feels like an "insider" as an adult in his or her adopted home community. Growing up as a liberal daughter of a socially active labor lawyer, I never questioned that my reality, one in which I accompanied my father as he advocated on the picket lines for same-sex healthcare benefits, equal access rights for disabled workers, and fair wages for physicians, was the *only* reality that existed. Certainly, it is not unusual for children to erroneously assume that every child grows up in a home just like theirs: If I am raised by loving parents, aren't all children? If social justice is a priority in my household, isn't it, then, in others?

As we journey beyond the bubbles of our individual childhoods and gain perspective into a greater world, our perspectives become more nuanced and colored by the multiple settings we encounter. Observation and experience can deceptively convince us that we are foreigners in new environments populated by endemic, insider populations. Transitioning into new professions, extended family relationships, and physical locations, we may perceive ourselves as outsiders to our new worlds, concluding that those in place before us, the insiders, have never questioned or experienced conflict with this status.

When I moved into a unique, conservative Christian community as an adult, I mistakenly assumed that my new community was full of homogenous insiders. However, my experience of ending a wanted pregnancy caused me to better understand that insider and outsider status truly only exist within the eye of the beholder.

Context and Setting

I live in the world center of a very unique Christian religion. My initial interest in the theology of this particular church arose from personal and professional experiences exploring death and dying.

In childhood, I acquired an early awareness that all humans must die, and I spent many anxious nights trying to grasp the implications of this stark and unchangeable truth. My head was full of questions about death: How does it happen? Does it hurt? and What happens to us after? Yet, everywhere I looked for answers, more questions abounded. In those days before the Internet existed, I had no quick access to Google to explore narratives of near-death experiences or a Wikipedia description of any particular religious philosophy about the afterlife. I was isolated, confused, and worried that my anxiety about death was abnormal. I felt compelled to be close to death to understand it, yet did not know how or where to begin. Perhaps that was *my* first true outsider experience: the painful, sickening realization of our imminent deaths, and bewilderment because nobody really talked about it. Everyone else appeared to live their lives unaware of their unwavering terminal trajectory. I could barely ever speak about it: nausea, hopelessness, fear, and confusion, swirled within my mind and body, but nobody else seemed bothered by the same concerns.

I chose social work as a path that married my lifelong interest in death with my inherent love of helping others. It provided me with a pedagogy to explore and understand many themes that arose across childhood and adolescence: human development, pedagogy of oppression and liberation, power and privilege, death and dying.

My first job opportunities were within oncology units. There, at the intersection of intractable pain and suffering, I experienced beautiful resilience in my patients. I abided with the encounter of wordless, unintelligible transition, as formerly animated bodies breathed their last and were transformed into lifeless containers. I pondered over the intangible yet *still-there* feeling of a presence in the room in the moments after. Working at the end of life was a spiritual experience.

While I was completing my doctoral degree, I met my husband, who was raised in a small church. As we got to know each other, I moved beyond descriptions of the work I did in end of life and began to self-disclose regarding the bigger questions I had about what happens when we die. As a result, he began to educate me about the theology of his upbringing. It included detailed descriptions of what happens in the afterlife, where children were raised by angel mothers and people lived in communities organized by their love for each other. I wanted to learn more, and, after discovering there was a small liberal arts college in the town originally created by the church community, I applied for a position. Shortly after we were married, I was appointed as a professor and we moved.

I threw myself into embracing life in our new home, but community members met me with trepidation. Most women my age did not work full time; those who did focused their vocation on educating children according to church prescription at the local elementary or high school. Those who did not work in the schools were more liberal in religious orientation and commuted, so I encountered them infrequently at community gatherings. Most of my peers had several children, because they married in their late teens.

I was warmly received at work, but the wider community regarded me with suspicion. Community members asked many questions about my Jewish heritage and why I chose my particular career path. They seemed concerned that I might not take their faith seriously or wanted to take advantage of it for the purposes of academic research. Kurzban and Leary (2001) offer some evolutionary insight into the phenomenon of social exclusion; they suggest that stigmatization and identification of "others" may protect groups against unpredictability, losses, exploitation, uncooperative social interactions, and even unfamiliar pathogens. My new community was long labeled by outsiders as a cult, full of fundamentalist, in-breeding members. I did not agree with this perspective and desperately wanted to be accepted, but was not open to thoughtful explanations that might help me understand *why* the community seemed so defensive. Rather, my feelings centered on my perceived label as an outsider: as a Jew, an outsider to the church; as a Canadian, an outsider to the country; as a professor, an outsider to the feminine vocation of homemaking. I noticed my feelings about this outsider status first as a tight knot in my stomach, and then, almost, as an invisible physical wall that sprouted between church insiders and me. I felt as though I was always trying to climb that wall, to justify my existence in the community, to connect. It was rare that I felt I was able to successfully scale it to the other side and be truly heard and seen.

Conceiving a child offered me a way in. When I became excitedly pregnant with our first child, a new world blossomed: Ministers' wives offered me birthing advice and threw me baby showers. I was gifted with a book of wisdom completed by many community wives who wanted to share. I announced the news very early, eager to join a cadre where pregnancy was interpreted as one important way of serving God. It was clear that conceiving a child with a husband born and raised in the church allowed me true insider privilege, as the doctrine of the church indicated that child-bearing was also an example of spousal commitment and unity in marriage that extended to a unity with God. The community clucked over my growing belly, invited us to dinner, and invited me to speak widely about my area of research and clinical practice on grief and loss. They seemed to care about me—all of me—and trust that I had something of value to offer beyond my future child. With each passing month of pregnancy,

I felt more connected to my new home. I loved teaching at the college and connecting with my community on weekends. After church services, I savored time in the choir hall munching on cookies and drinking tea furnished by volunteers as I made small talk with our neighbors. Life was sweet.

The Experience of Loss

I returned to Toronto at nearly 20 weeks pregnant to visit my family. My aunt, the director of an obstetric clinic at one of the city's largest hospitals, offered me an early anatomy ultrasound where my husband and I eagerly awaited to learn the baby's sex. I had experienced scans previously in the pregnancy, but this was the first time the internal structure of our future child would be seen more clearly. As the screen flashed on, I marveled at the fish-bone cascade of the baby's spinal column, the blurred and wand-like fingers floating in an inky black sea of fluid, leaving milliseconds-long bursts of sparkling gray mist behind. We waited for over an hour for the doctor to read the results of the scan.

Before I could ask, "Is it a boy or a girl?" the doctor told us that he had some unsettling news. The ultrasound screen leaped to life once more, revealing the profile of our baby's face and long, elegant neck. The physician spoke.

"We believe that your baby has an extremely rare anomaly. The name of it is congenital high airway obstruction syndrome, or CHAOS, for short. See here?" he pointed to an area of the scan that, in my untrained view, looked no different than others. "No viable airway. No trachea. It did not form early in the pregnancy. Instead, it is sealed off at the top. There is nowhere for amniotic fluid in the body to exit. Can you see, here, the lungs and heart?" *Flip to another image.* "The heart is crushed by the lungs. The lungs, as you can clearly see," *which I couldn't. I couldn't clearly see,* "are stretched beyond appropriate size. They are placing pressure on the diaphragm, here." *Where?* "And it is becoming inverted. We would like you to meet with our genetic counselor and arrange from some follow-up tests to tell you more about the CHAOS," *CHAOS—how appropriate,* "as babies diagnosed this early, with this level of disorder, usually die in the womb, or are born in a state of brain death. There is the option of termination." *Termination? As in, to end? An abortion?* "I know you live in Pennsylvania, where the rules might be different. Here, you have the option of aborting until 24 weeks."

"Is it a boy or a girl?" I asked meekly, as if the answer might create some hope or change the outcome.

"Congratulations, it's a boy." *Congratulations. Your son is dying inside of you.*

CHAOS is an extremely rare presentation housed within a very rare disorder itself, tracheal atresia, that affects less than one in every 50,000 births (Javia, Harris, & Fuller, 2016). In our case, the structural malformation was linked to a chromosomal anomaly, Trisomy 16, the most common cause of first-trimester miscarriages (Benn, 1998). Our son survived into the second trimester, but the anomaly snaked its way through the cellular structure of his internal organs, and CHAOS was the first symptom. We hurried home to Pennsylvania, where, after extensive testing and consultation, we were informed that the son we named Darby Joss would likely not survive to term: He was nearly in heart failure. If he did, his fate was consigned to the cold, sterile environment of the neonatal intensive care unit, where, without consciousness, he would survive in body only. He would never know our tender touch, the depth of our love, the wetness of the tears we would shed. His body would suffer; his existence would be bleak.

We pursued several thought experiments around abortion or continuing the pregnancy; we knew that if we continued to term, the baby was likely to die anyway, but we wouldn't be making the decision for the baby's end of life. Yet how could I continue to grow visibly pregnant and cope with questions or excitement about my baby-to-be when the dark secret was that our child would never grow up? At what point in fetal development would our unborn child begin to feel the imaginably painful effects of heart failure in the womb, and what mother would sanction this if she could stop it? Yet, how could I live with myself if we decided to end the pregnancy, making no room for divine intervention or miracle? Every hypothetical path we walked led to more shades of gray; more nuance and what-if questions cluttered my brain. I later learned that our decision-making process was not uncommon. In fact, my now-colleague, Judith McCoyd (2008) has documented similarities along the path of women burdened with deciding the outcome of a pregnancy following the heartbreaking diagnosis of fetal anomaly. Like McCoyd's (2008) subjects, I considered the social context of our experience; the lack of societal support and community resources in the face of raising a critically ill child weighed heavily. Could I continue to carry and possibly birth a child into brain death in my community, where support was already tenuous? Further and consistent with McCoyd's (2008) research, I struggled with the impact of carrying the pregnancy to term on future siblings: How would they live alongside a critically ill brother, if he even survived? In the unlikely event that he lived into adulthood, would they be responsible for him when we died? And, how would we pay for the enormous cost of healthcare to preserve Darby in an unconscious state? He would require round-the-clock care. Would I have to quit my job? Did we have the emotional resources to endure this, and would our marriage last under all of the strain? Psychologically, could I?

Ultimately, we decided to end the pregnancy. On August 3, 2012, I went from pregnant to grieving in a matter of hours. Cramping and bleeding from the procedure that removed my unborn son from my womb and released my pregnancy into the eternal realm of my memory, I returned home. My breasts swelled with milk that would never feed our son. I buried myself under the covers of my bed and slept for days, waking only to cry or vomit, praying for the abyss of sleep. I was accompanied by the gentle sighs of my large dog, as he readjusted into the warmth and curve of my deflating, empty belly. My husband rubbed my back in the morning, sat by my side holding my hand after work, crawled into bed and held me at night. He told me to take my time.

In the aftermath, I hid the abortion from our community. When I began to share our story, I only referred to Darby's death as "a loss." I felt so broken and ashamed, always pro-choice for others but never anything but pro-life for myself in ideation, never predicting a scenario like ours. Isolated in my grief, I ventured into the murky world of community discussions on social media around the abortion debate. Perhaps I did this to reconcile my own sense of brokenness about our decision, or to explore whether there might be sensitivity and understanding aimed at my unique scenario. I know that I hoped to find some surprising support. The first posts that popped up when I typed "abortion" into the search box, per the website algorithm, involved my own online "friends": members of my community. To my knowledge, they had never experienced my form of loss, but they had much to say about abortion. "People who have abortions are murderers and should be tried as such," one minister's wife opined. "It's the killing of babies: sweet, innocent lives from the Lord." I scrolled to similar responses. While I found some outside groups that welcomed me with sympathy and understanding, the majority of my local community had decided on the issue. Now, I was an outsider and a murderer. How could I continue to live there?

The Aftermath of Disclosure

Ironically, the path to staying put was found in slowly, tentatively, telling the truth. I struggled with feeling suffocated by the secret of our abortion and realized that I could no longer hold back as long as I continued to live in my community, as well as be privy to the chatter on social media. Our closest friends and family already knew our story, and my mother-in-law had initially encouraged me to only tell our community that the baby had died and spare the details. Though she did not disapprove of my choice, she knew that more conservative community members would, and she wanted to protect me from harsh judgment. In the early days of grief, I agreed with her. But the more I sought to clarify who was "for" and who was "against" abortion in our community, the more I realized very few people talking about it had ever heard a story like ours before.

I could no longer abide with reading one-dimensional characterizations about women like me or any woman making the difficult choice of abortion. My fire for social advocacy began to build. I began to disclose the first and truest parenting decision that my husband and I ever had to make: to release Darby from life so that he would not suffer. I began to reveal the narrative of our much-loved, much-wanted son.

The response was predictable: Women who had once delivered meals accompanied by Bible verses lovingly written in cursive retreated. I was unfriended, online and in real life. This only fueled my desire to narrate, to give voice to Darby's story. To our story, and the story of women and families like ours. I wrote poems. I connected and worked with Planned Parenthood and spoke alongside our pro-choice governor at press conferences. I began to author articles and chapters on loss. With every passing moment of narrating my truth and engaging in social advocacy, I began to grow and find comfort. I cared less about my outsider status. I wanted my voice to be heard.

As time passed, my clinical practice focusing on grief expanded and I began to counsel women privately from beyond my community who had also been affected by fetal anomaly. I struggled in these cases with self-disclosure and published about that too, asking "*Who* needed to know about my abortion in order to heal?" In writing, I found solace and wrestled with my desire to have more children, to venture into the anxiety and abyss of a subsequent pregnancy after our devastating loss. I wrote and I wrote and I wrote, sometimes privately, often publicly, for journals and blogs and websites.

And, unpredictably, within the community, I began to collect misfit outsiders like myself.

The private messages began to arrive a few years, via Facebook and text message, after our loss. People found me through my posts and advocacy work, or through friends of friends who knew my story. Nobody ever called; it was almost as if the requests were too shameful or shocking to speak about aloud.

"Can you help me? I know you know a thing or two about loss and trauma. I need a therapist to talk to about something I can't write about. Can we talk on the phone?": a minister within the church community, frantic and fearful about a sense of disillusionment with the church organization, with nowhere to turn, on the bridge of loss of faith.

"You may know about my family. My wife ended her life last year. We did not really see it coming until it was too late. We had tried to get her counseling with the minister, and we sent her for holistic healing. She left behind our daughter, who is struggling with self-harm and suicide. Can you talk to her? I am sure you'll understand that you'll need to keep this quiet, as our family minister doesn't support secular psychotherapy": a father, well-connected in our community, reaching out after discovering rows of fresh cuts on his daughter's arms and legs.

"I'm looking for someone to help and was sent your way. I go to the high school and I'm having sexual feelings about girls in my class. We are taught that having lust toward the same sex is against the Lord's will. I'm scared and I don't know what to do": a teenager, experiencing the frightening but normal changes of adolescence, afraid to disclose her sexual orientation to her parents.

"I'm thinking of leaving my husband. Can we talk about this?": The minister's wife who stated that women who have abortions should be tried as murderers.

I could not refuse any of them. Of course, I was familiar with Doka's (2002) concept of disenfranchised grief; he theorized that individuals who have experienced certain losses may encounter the bias from others that their grief is not valid or sanctioned. According to Doka (2002), disenfranchised grief is accompanied by "fear and shame, those experiencing the loss believe that they are incapable or unworthy of support" (p. 161). While I battled these feelings in the aftermath of our abortion, I was unaware that fighting my sense of disenfranchisement with self-disclosure and advocacy would also create a deep sense of compassion. Every request for help from an insider caused me to abandon my prior assumptions about who appeared to "fit" in our community. Maybe all of us, in less dramatic ways, exist as insiders *and* outsiders on a spectrum. Maybe our self-perception varies across our realities and experiences. Maybe we should never assume what category another person belongs to.

My experience as a clinician became rich, and I began to appreciate my clients' struggles with self-identity. Working with teens, I relied on literature on theories of identity development to support and encourage my teen patients to begin to explore their confusing feelings. I delved into research on organizational trauma in conservative churches and found that I could apply it to the sense of identity loss that my minister client experienced. And, amazingly, I found my heart opening to the very members of the community who had cast me out: those mislabeled insiders, who, as I learned through clinical sessions, thought that their own upbringings applied to everybody else, that it was normal to love the sinner and hate the sin, to believe that they were exempt from life's hardships because they believed in a loving and merciful God who protected his faithful. Insiders who encountered life experiences that challenged their sense of safety and beliefs. Insiders who became outsiders like me.

Today I work across modalities supporting clients from all backgrounds. I often apply techniques from cognitive behavioral therapy to challenge the automatic thoughts my religious clients have about what the world, or life, or God, owe them. My clients struggle with understanding and reconstructing their identities in the context of loss across the lifespan. I work from a humanistic and existential foundation to support them. I have even met my fair share of outsiders who, as children, thought that they were the only people with a fear of death.

Ultimately, the disenfranchised grief resulting from my abortion experience and my refusal to be silent about it enriched my professional perspective as a clinician who creates safe spaces for the expression of many different forms of grief and loss. It has also provided me with a humbling education about too quickly labeling others experiencing a different perspective. The grief of my abortion and my growth as a result is one of the many gifts that Darby gave me. While today not every community member speaks to me about Darby, many do. People know his name and I am often approached, in-person and online, to talk about him or, not unfrequently, I am thanked for "the good [I] created from a terrible situation." I am not sure how many community members agree with the decision we made, but I believe that my husband and I have established a level of acceptance. We have made unexpected friendships with women and families who I never thought would accept me; some of them refer to my son as "sweet Darby" or "your angel boy," which means more than they ever could know. I've been told that I muddied the waters and introduced an important but difficult public narrative, though I also now know that there are many stories filled with shades of gray amongst the secret "outsiders" I see in therapy. All of this exists as part of Darby's legacy, and for that I am incredibly grateful.

Questions for Reflection

1. Do you ever feel like an outsider in your clinical work? How do you connect with people from different backgrounds than your own?
2. Is it important for social workers to categorize people as insiders or outsiders to better treat them? Why or why not?
3. Do you feel you are open to hearing different viewpoints on controversial or polarizing issues like abortion?
4. What are some forms of disenfranchised grief that you have encountered in your life? Do they emerge in your clinical work?

References

Benn, P. (1998). Trisomy 16 and trisomy 16 mosaicism: A review. *American Journal of Medical Genetics, 79*(2), 121–133.

Doka, K. J. (Ed.). (2002). *Disenfranchised grief: New directions, challenges, and strategies for practitioners.* Champaign, IL: Research Press.

Javia, L., Harris, M. A., & Fuller, S. (2016). Rings, slings, and other tracheal disorders in the neonate. *Seminars in Fetal & Neonatal Medicine, 21*(4), 277–284.

Kurzban, R., & Leary, M. R. (2001). Evolutionary origins of stigmatization: The functions of social exclusion. *Psychological Bulletin, 127*(2), 187–208.

McCoyd, J. L. M. (2008). "I'm not a saint": Burden assessment as an unrecognized factor in prenatal decision making. *Qualitative Health Research, 18*(11), 1489–1500.

Losing Linden

Allison J. Spinneweber, MSW, LCSW, East End Therapists, LLC Pittsburgh, Pennsylvania

FIGURE 3.2. Allison Spinneweber

Allison Spinneweber, LCSW, is an EMDRIA-certified EMDR therapist with over 17 years of experience in community mental health and private practice. She received her BS in family and child sciences from Florida State University and her master's of social work from the University of Pittsburgh with a specialization in mental health. Allison currently provides individual outpatient clinical services in her Pittsburgh-based private practice where her focus is perinatal mental health, women's issues, trauma, anxiety, and depression. Allison balances her professional life while juggling being a wife and a mom to three kids ranging in ages from 2.5-10. The experience of being "in the weeds" of motherhood, and also grieving both a miscarriage and a stillbirth, prompted Allison to further specialize around these issues in her practice. Allison can be reached at www.eastendtherapists.com or AllisonSpinneweberLCSW@gmail.com or 412-467-6042.

Introduction

I was a 34-year-old mother of two healthy girls, working full time as a supervisor at a community mental health agency, while also spending two evenings a week building my private practice. My husband was in graduate school and we had decided that if we were going to have a third child, this would be the best time as I was just hitting "advanced maternal age." The previous summer we had had a surprise pregnancy followed by an early miscarriage. However, this time around, we tried and got pregnant quickly and easily. As the weeks went on and we hit week 13, we breathed a sigh of relief as, statistically, the risk of something going wrong dropped dramatically.

At our 20-week ultrasound we were excited to find out the gender (it was a girl!). However, the baby appeared smaller than expected. We were sent for genetic testing and set up another scan for a few weeks later. In between scans, we received the results of the genetic testing; everything came back normal and we felt a sense of relief. At 24 weeks, I showed up to the next ultrasound scan and did not think twice about going by myself. However, as I lay there, the tech got a strange look on her face, and after several moments told me that there was not a heartbeat.

Since the baby was so small, I had the option to go through labor or to have a procedure called a dilation and evacuation. I could not imagine going through hours of labor knowing that the baby was dead. I am at peace with the decision now, but there have been times over the past few years when I wished I would have opted for labor and getting to hold our little baby. At the time, though, I did not feel strong enough to make that choice.

The hospital sent home a memory box with us. I was asked if I wanted a memorial service. I said maybe later, but this was more my way of saying no without making a hard/strong decision. We named our baby girl Linden. Linden had been at the top of our list for names around this time, but we hadn't researched the meaning. I just liked how Linden sounded. We would have had three girls with L names: Lydia, Lorelei, and Linden. After we lost her, I realized that Linden is also the name of a tree. This provided the opportunity for beautiful symbolism and a way to keep her in our lives. My mother bought me a beautiful white metal decorative tree that sits on a table in our living room. I also bought a gorgeous painted picture of a tree and a sunset. This picture hangs on our wall with our other family pictures. The first few years we got our family pictures taken, we included Linden's tree picture with them.

The next days, weeks, and months were excruciating. Two weeks after the loss, while at work I did a school visit and noticed a teacher who was pregnant. My eyes welled up with tears, but I quickly swallowed them and redirected my thoughts, allowing me to remain professional. Two hours later I returned to the office for a meeting. We had personal "check-ins" at the beginning of each meeting that included how we were feeling at that moment. Another coworker was pregnant at the table, and the group spent a few minutes joking about how she should get used to not having sleep. They then looked at me and asked me to check in. As I began to open my mouth, big sobs started to come out and I had to leave the room. My immediate peers and supervisors were very supportive to me that day, even though it was uncomfortable.

Upper management was more difficult. They were very nice and supportive to my face, but my tears in that meeting were used against me in the future when applying for other positions within the company. I was seen as emotionally unstable even though my crying that one particular day was one of the few times strong emotions were ever shown. It should be noted that this represented the general culture of our office. In my department, we were all supportive of each other. However, upper management was not trustworthy and talked behind almost every worker's back. This toxic management style greatly contributed to the difficulty of the summer and fall after Linden's death.

My husband Jason grieved right along with me, but it looked different. I am a verbal processer and needed to talk through my grief. My husband is an internal processer and was often quiet about our loss. Jason was very supportive of me, while steadily working to keep the house going, taking care of our daughters, working his full-time job, and completing his graduate course work. A few times per week I would cry and would talk through my feelings. My husband would listen and hug me but wouldn't say much himself. Two weeks into the loss I asked him how he was feeling and what he had been thinking about. Jason responded with a few sentences that allowed me insight into his grieving process and helped me to connect with what he was feeling. All along Jason had been feeling sadness and anger but hadn't expressed these feelings verbally. I expected him to feel this way, but it was helpful for me to hear him say these things out loud. It was a reminder that we all grieve and process in different ways.

For the most part, I was able to function well. I was able to show up to my day job and enjoyed my private practice clients in the evenings. I was able to separate what was going on personally and professionally and work was a nice distraction from my grief. My individual clients at the time were not struggling with grief or loss. It was easy for me to be focused and attentive during sessions—and

I appreciated that break from my own thoughts. The week after the loss I did cancel my sessions and needed to tell my clients what happened as they had all known I was pregnant. My clients all expressed sympathy when I shared the news. A few of them checked back in with me during our first session back. I was able to kindly give a short, generic yet appropriate answer, and then redirected the attention back to them. Six months after the loss I was able to resign from my full-time job to focus exclusively on my private practice.

However, the weekends were when the grief came out, and I had several weekends where I would just lay on the couch and cry. As time went on, I began to cry less, and the time in between actively grieving got longer. There were several months where the crying stopped altogether and I began to have a routine again. Six months after the loss, it really caught me by surprise when an interaction with another pregnant woman triggered me, and I went home and cried for several hours. This was completely frustrating as I had thought everything was getting easier, and it felt like a setback. Thankfully, this was the last major trigger for me—but I continued to struggle with a low level of sadness and jealousy around others having healthy babies. I unfollowed friends on Facebook who were pregnant or had new babies—which allowed me to look at their pages when I was prepared, instead of being hit with a triggering image or post.

I'm hesitant to write this next struggle for fear of judgement and being misunderstood. However, one of the most shocking thoughts that came through my mind in the first few months after my loss was a wish that the other women with healthy pregnancies would lose their babies too. It wasn't fair. Why did they get to keep their babies, and mine was dead? To be very clear, I did not *actually* want anyone else's baby to die. I would never wish this pain on anyone, and I am so thankful for the healthy children that they currently have. I just wanted some company in my misery—and I was angry in my loss. Thankfully I was aware enough to edit who I verbalized my anger to. I was able to confide my feelings in my therapist, my husband, and a close friend. I am a verbal processor, and the most effective way for me to work through anger is to talk to someone who is patient, non-judgmental, and validating. In the midst of this pain I was blessed with a really great support system.

As the months went on, I had one or two pregnant clients. These were clients who came to me to work through other life issues, but then ended up becoming pregnant during the time we worked together. Even though treatment was focused around other realms of their life, it was normal to process through general life stressors as a part of treatment. These women would bring up aches or pains, or feeling tired, or feeling stressed about getting the baby room together. These were the times I had to really watch out for counter-transference. I had to work really hard to keep my jealousy in check when they would complain about pregnancy but were still healthy—and still pregnant. I would notice my heart beating a little faster, and my foot would start to tap. I would also have internal thoughts along the lines of, "You don't know how lucky you have it." As soon as I noticed what was happening, I would work to calm myself. All of these things, the thoughts, the physical reaction, could happen in 15–30 seconds. If I allowed them to progress it would greatly interfere with my ability to be present and supportive and could also damage the therapeutic relationship. Through taking subtle deep breaths and reminding myself that it is my job to support them, I was able to keep my emotions in check. If anxiety around the pregnancy was pressing, I would allow the client to process. However, if these were passive complaints, I would empathize, and then follow up with a relevant question about another area of their life, redirecting away from the pregnancy topic. I did not shy away from the pregnancy topic. Yet, I did not encourage continued conversation around the topic if it did not appear to be important for the client that day. I continued to support them as a therapist and kept my experience of loss to myself (*I had been working in the mental health field for 13 years and was able to read people and clinical needs fairly easily. However, if I was newer to the field, or if I continued to struggle with this, I would have contacted my clinical supervisor to process and problem solve how to best handle my struggles around this.*). I did make sure to process my emotions around this with other trusted therapists in peer supervision. Being able to verbally process in a trusted space was very helpful in getting my emotions and thoughts out of my head.

Through the loss, I had a lot of support from friends and family. I had one friend who always remembered to check in with me on tough anniversaries. A few said the wrong thing, or nothing at all—and this hurt. I also realized that sometimes people aren't necessarily saying something wrong, but more that I am angry and hurt and their inability to say exactly the right thing makes them an easy target for my feelings.

Through my vulnerability and sharing my struggle with friends around me, I realized that I am not alone in my loss. There are many women and couples out there who are grieving losing babies and/or who are also struggling with infertility. This place feels very lonely as we are inundated by social media posts of ultrasounds, belly pics, and newborn announcements. The world appears to move on without us, and we are a part of a special club of which no one ever wants to be a member.

As I began to heal, I also felt a strong desire to help others who were experiencing similar grief. Through word of mouth and targeted advertising, I began to get clients who were working through the grief of stillbirth or miscarriage. Had these clients come to me when I was in deep grief, it would have been very difficult to separate my grief from theirs, and counter-transference would have been a struggle. However, since a lot of my healing took place before this point, it was fairly easy for me to attend to their needs as a therapist without emotional entanglement from my end.

If clients access my advertising profile online, they are aware that I have children but have also experienced loss. During the first session I will briefly mention that I have also experienced loss, while also reminding clients that everyone's loss and experience with loss is different. These women will often express relief that I understand what they are going through. Limited self-disclosure on my part often helps these women to not feel as alone. The majority of time in session revolves around clients and what they need. Every so often I chose to share parts of my story or a decision I made during the grieving process.

When I choose to share bits of my story, this choice has to meet the following criteria:

1. *Sharing this information is only for the benefit of the client.* An example of this is sharing a decision I made for keeping mementos of Linden around the house. This is typically shared with choices others have made, providing a variety of options and examples that can be helpful for clients to make their own decisions. While this is sharing a part of my life and my story, it is a very small amount with the purpose of helping the client.
2. *Sharing is not for the purpose of my own healing or processing.* I need to have my own therapist and/or friends to process my own loss. The only time I share more of my story is when I have an established, trusting relationship with a client, and he or she asks for my story. At this point I will share a 2–5-minute synopsis of my loss story, highlighting the grief process and how things have changed over time.

One of my biggest emotional transference/countertransference struggles was related to clients and parents of clients who would ask if I was pregnant. My body type is one that the stomach is the first place I gain weight, and my abs do not easily bounce back after pregnancy. I work hard to eat well and exercise, and was actively working on losing the baby weight from the baby I no longer had. I would be having a day where I felt good about myself, only to be asked when I was due. I tried multiple styles of clothing, but this did not prevent inappropriate questions or assumptions from being verbalized. Whenever I was asked this, it really threw me off. I would say, "No, I'm not," with most likely a small smile and a mortified face. The accidental offender would always apologize, and most of the time would be embarrassed. I tried to move past this a quickly as possible. However, in session, it would take a good 5 minutes to fully move past what had happened. My thoughts would be scattered and internally I would feel angry, embarrassed, and frustrated that people continued to ask. It was a very difficult transition to make from being personally offended and hurt to being able to support this client in a therapeutic manner. If the parent in the waiting room asked the offending question, I moved through this quicker as the child/client was not responsible for what his or her mother said. If it was an adult client in the room with me, I continued to take subtle deep breaths while continually redirecting my thoughts back to the client. Doing this helped me to become reabsorbed in what the client was sharing for the remainder of the session. After the client left, I allowed myself a minute to process my emotions before preparing for the next client. Within the next 24–48 hours I would also process these incidents with a coworker as it would really throw my self-confidence for a while.

Around 1.5 years after our loss we decided to take the risk and try again for another baby. We debated over trying again, but I finally came to the realization that if we tried again and lost, that the pain would be excruciating but temporary. If we were successful, the reward far outweighed the risk. While pregnancy for me was not life-threatening, it was a difficult pregnancy that required layers of medical management. At 37 weeks the pain and uncertainty were worth it as I delivered a beautiful baby boy who is now an adorable, active 2-year-old.

A common theme that appears with clients in my practice is how to manage the fear and anxiety during subsequent pregnancies. My friend once mentioned something to the effect of "Once you experience pregnancy loss, you lose the gift of naivety in subsequent pregnancies." Before loss, a positive pregnancy test means that you will have a baby. After loss, a positive test means that there is only a chance you will having a living, healthy baby. Many will say, "I'm not getting excited yet." The belief is that if you aren't excited, then the grief will be easier when you lose again. The reality is that grief is excruciating whether you expect a loss or not. During my last pregnancy I did have a lot of fear. However, I also made it a point to enjoy the time I had with the baby I was carrying—whether it was only for a few weeks, or he was born healthy at full term. I would talk to him and appreciate the life I got to live with him right there with me.

I learned through this experience that control is an illusion. There are so many things that can daily threaten our safety and health. However, we just don't think about them. We expect if we do everything right, that everything will turn out okay. This loss taught me that I am not immune to awful things happening. I was terrified to let my husband and daughters leave the house. I quickly made a plan where we would all just stay home indefinitely. We would order groceries in, not leave the house, and stay safe. As I continued to think through my plan, I realized that if someone really wanted to break in, they could find a way. Or, wait a minute, we could all die of carbon monoxide poisoning! There was absolutely no way that I could figure out how to keep my family 100% safe. And if we all stayed home 100% of the time, we would be missing out on meaningful life experiences and the ability to provide for ourselves. This realization of lack of control provided some relief. I was able to let go of trying to control our safety (while still reasonably wearing seatbelts and watching before crossing the street). I realized that worrying about what may or may not happen only ruined my experience in the moment.

In closing, the following quote was very helpful during my grieving process:

> Grief is like a long valley, a winding valley where any bend may reveal a totally new landscape. … Sometimes the surprise is the opposite one you are presented with, exactly the same sort of country you thought you had left behind miles ago. That is when you wonder whether the valley isn't a circular trench. But it isn't. There are partial recurrences, but the sequence doesn't repeat. (Lewis, 1961, p. 60)

This quote beautifully encapsulates my experience with grief. It felt like it would go on forever. However, as time went on, I began to heal. The time I spent crying slowly waned in intensity and length. The time in between feeling the hard feelings got longer. I was able to more consistently experience joy. I still have occasional days when I feel the grief. I will always miss Linden and feel a sense of loss as I see who would have been her peers grow and develop. She would have been attending kindergarten soon, and I wonder what her personality would have been like.

I am also content with our life as it is. I have been able to help others through their loss and have an understanding of grief that allows me to hold space while others experience theirs. I delight in our 2-year-old. He could never replace Linden, but he certainly brings a lot of joy to our lives. Grief is ridiculously hard. But as you honor it and sit in it, the grief will lessen, and, with time, will allow you to experience joy again.

Reflection Questions

1. Related to grief or not, we all have triggers/things we are sensitive about. What are some of your triggers and how might transference/counter-transference occur around these triggers in the therapist/client relationship?
2. Are you an internal or verbal processer? What positive coping strategies do you have in place for handling stressors?
3. What are the risks of self-disclosure? When can it be appropriate/helpful?
4. What are some ways in our professional life that we assume we have control, when really it is an illusion? How might this illusion play out in our relationship with clients, and/or how we view our work as clinicians?

Experiential Suggestion

I have mentioned deep breathing as a way for me to manage difficult emotions. I used to think that breathing as a coping mechanism is pretty worthless—I mean, it could help, but more as a placeholder—something to do while the passage of time allowed you to calm down. However, I eventually learned the physiological reason behind deep breathing being a helpful coping mechanism, and it encouraged me to use this much more myself, as well encourage my clients to do the same.

In many of Dr. John Gottman's talks and papers, he shares that in a social situation, if our heart rate is 100 beats per minute or higher, that it is extremely difficult for us to process information. If we are angry, our heart rate increases. If we are anxious, our heart rate increases. This makes it very difficult for us to listen, respond, or process information. Dr. Gottman discusses this more in a relationship context here: https://www.gottman.com/blog/manage-conflict-part-4/

However, there is nerve in our body called the vagus nerve. It controls many things, one of which is how quickly our heart is beating. When we take deep belly breaths, this stimulates the vagus nerve, helping our heart rate to slow. Which in turn calms us down and helps us to process information. This is the reason I use deep breathing so often in my sessions. It actually works, and there's an explanation into why/how. How cool is that? How might you strengthen your use of deep breathing in session with a client? In your own personal life?

References

Gottman, J. (2015, June 4). Manage conflict: Part 4. *The Gottman Institute*. Retrieved from https://www.gottman.com/blog/manage-conflict-part-4/

Little Ones to Him Belong: Re-experiencing Traumatic Loss as a Clinician

Kathleen Leilani Ja Sook Bergquist, LCSW, JD, PhD,
University of Nevada, Las Vegas

Dr. Bergquist is an associate professor in the School of Social Work at the University of Nevada, Las Vegas. She earned her master's in social work at Norfolk State University, her PhD in counselor education at the College of William and Mary, and her JD at UNLV's Boyd School of Law. Dr. Bergquist has always actively worked in the field throughout her academic career, practicing both as an LCSW/PhD and an attorney. She can be reached at kathleen.bergquist@unlv.edu.

Introduction

Mental health clinicians are often drawn to their respective fields due to personal or tangential experiences in their private lives. The death of a child, regardless of the circumstances, age of the child, or time since the death is a traumatic loss. Even if one does not choose to work specifically with grieving families, it is often unavoidable in clinical practice. My story contextualizes the grieving process as the mother of a child who died of sudden infant death syndrome (SIDS) and navigating the intersections of others' grief.

Despite having almost 20 years of clinical experience, I continue to feel the need to brace myself when I encounter parents who have suffered the loss of a child. Many people, myself included, believe that I should be uniquely well equipped to connect with grieving families and walk with them through their healing, yet much of my own grief has been unexamined. A couple of early experiences shook my confidence in being able to provide professional support, which led me to believe that all I had to offer was as not as a professional, but only as another grieving mother regardless of my many years of training and a career spent helping others. Fortunately, recent evidence-based research has examined the connections between attachment and bereavement and provided a framework to scaffold and contextualize my experience (Maccallum & Bryant, 2018; Schenck, Eberle, & Rings, 2016).

> *Your absence is inconspicuous, nobody can tell what I lack.*
>
> \- Sylvia Plath (2008, p. 152)

Losing a child to SIDS is something that no one is prepared for. My son, Alex, was 6 months old and presumably a healthy happy baby when he simply did not wake up on December 20, 1986. I recall the feeling of depersonalization and detachment immediately following his death. I struggled with my faith and the illogical senselessness of it all. A hospital chaplain who I can only assume was inexperienced tried to comfort me by telling me that "Alex is in a better place," which devastated me because the best place for my baby was to be with me. So many simple yet complex tasks, like picking an outfit for him to be buried in, designing a headstone for his grave, looking for a death announcement in Hallmark (they don't exist), and worst of all, finding the words to explain to his 4-year-old twin brothers that Alex was not coming home seemed impossible. My faith gave me some resolve if not peace. Alex's headstone marked my releasing him from my care with the quotation "Little ones to Him belong."

FIGURE 3.3. Alex Whitman

At the time, I only went to one support group as a grieving parent. I needed to know that I wasn't alone, that I wasn't crazy when I sometimes heard him cry, and that I couldn't have prevented his death.

My coping response was to keep busy. Shortly after Alex's death I started working and returned to school. I learned everything I could about SIDS and how to manage sibling bereavement, met with a SIDS researcher, and learned about the different ways that mothers and fathers grieve. I became a SIDS educator and affiliated with a local advocacy and support group. All of this busy work allowed me to function on the periphery of my grief. That is, until my safe zone was threatened in very different ways by two grieving moms I met through peer support.

The first was a young mother I'll call "Sarah," who had two sons, the youngest who died of SIDS. She had struggled prior to his death with unstable partners, limited education, and financial vulnerability. I did not know what role I could play in her healing and found myself vacillating between providing peer support and recognizing the significant psycho-emotional impact on her ability to function. She was overwhelmed and out of control. I am not sure how she saw my role in her life, but she was not a client. We had met informally as bereaved parents, and I served as a mentor of sorts since I was an "experienced" SIDS parent. Sarah then asked me after a support meeting if I would lend her money, which I knew she was not able to repay. My years of ethics training about dual relationships and boundaries as a professional set alarm bells off and I became immobilized. I was unsure of how to respond, so I gave myself some space to consider. I examined the nature of our relationship and whether lending her money would be helpful. I was concerned that if I lent her money, I could be setting precedent for future requests. I concluded that because Sarah and I did not have a formal client/social worker relationship I could make a decision based on my own personal rather than professional values. I lent her the money but made it clear that I did not want to be paid back and that I was only able to offer assistance that one time, removing the possibility for future uncomfortable situations. I felt I made a well-thought-through decision. However, in my honest moments I can admit that I felt resentment.

The other mother, "Mary," was a first-time mom. We met in the support group that I had organized. Her grief response was to fundraise for SIDS research; she organized events and a GoFundMe account, and reached out to local media. Both moms were drawn to images of angels and memorializing their children through tattoos, Web pages, releasing balloons, and other such commemorations. The more they made their grief public, the more I distanced myself from them. Sarah and Mary led me to some uncomfortable and confusing insights about myself. I felt inadequate where I believed I should have been competent. I both wanted to be able to provide support to them and felt overwhelmed by what felt like their bottomless grief. I over-empathized with their pain and struggled with understanding their emotional immobility. I felt like the ill-guided aspiring clinician who wanted to help others move forward because I thought I had, although I knew better. I was aware that I engaged in distracting behaviors that allowed me to defer my grief. Rather than reflect on my reaction at that time, I focused my attention elsewhere. Although Sarah and Mary were not my clients, I was viewed as having a certain level of expertise both as a mentor and group facilitator, and because of my education and training. I wrongly believed that if I assumed a facilitative or mentoring role I could somehow deflect attention from my own grief because I felt productive. However, this actually served to impede my own recovery; in truth I was the one who was immobilized.

Stress-coping theory identifies two predominant strategies for coping; emotion focused and problem focused (Lazarus, 1993). *Emotion-focused coping* involves affective responses and expression of feelings, while *problem-focused coping* is more likely to involve affect-avoiding task-oriented action. I relied heavily on information seeking as a problem-focused coping strategy immediately following Alex's death. I consumed everything and anything I could about SIDs, especially research that might help me understand how a seemly healthy baby could die without explanation. The one support group meeting that I attended was part of my information-gathering process. The group affirmed for me that my grief responses (such as sensory experiences of Alex after his death) were normative, so I did not feel the need to return. Although, with the death of a child there is really no problem to be solved. Huh, Kim, Lee, and Chae (2018) hypothesized a model whereby one's coping strategy is a moderating strategy in the relationship between attachment and trauma-related emotions. They found in their study of bereaved parents who lost children in a 2014 ferry accident that the problem-solving coping associated with avoidant attachment was correlated with complicated or complex grief, while emotion-focused coping associated with anxious attachment was correlated with shame and guilt. According to Bowlby (1980), avoidant and anxious attachment systems are prevalent in insecurely attached individuals. Avoidantly attached persons may have discomfort relying on others and value self-reliance, while anxiously attached persons may be preoccupied with the responsiveness and availability of others. Huh, Kim, Lee, and Chae (2018) explained that anxiously attached parents *hyperactively coped,* seeking reassurance and support externally, while avoidant parents *deactively coped*, internalizing or otherwise directing their grief.

> *Everything that irritates us about others can lead us to an understanding of ourselves .*
>
> - Carl Jung (1963, p. 351)

The problem-solving, task-oriented, information seeking that I engaged in after Alex's death is congruent with an avoidant attachment response. My early life was spent in a Korean orphanage and I experienced the deprivation that many infants do in institutions. I am aware that my ability to securely attach has been a lifelong journey, contributing to my greater comfort in personal and professional relationships and roles where I have a sense of autonomy. However, despite my tendency to cope through *avoidant problem solving,* I have not struggled with the associated experience of complex bereavement. Attachment theory describes avoidant-attached persons as having a negative view of others as a form of self-defense, while having a positive self-view. I do not negatively evaluate others as a general rule and know that I could not be effective in my clinical work if that were the case. However, the mothers whose grief was publicly displayed and whose need seemed without boundaries triggered in me the impulse to avoid. I did not understand my response at the time, but it was visceral. Hayes, Yeh, and Eisenberg (2007) summarize previous research that found that when therapists' unresolved grief is triggered by clients' bereavement, they may respond with reactive rather than reflective thinking, have distorted perceptions of clients, and seek to avoid.

Through education and training mental health professionals are inundated with guidance about self-care and awareness of transference and countertransference. I was fully aware at an intellectual level but did not readily understand the countertransference reaction I had with Sarah and Mary. They needed to connect to others to share the burden of their sorrow, ensure that their sons' names were spoken and their memories sustained, while I needed to keep my memories of Alex private and safe and find ways to proactively understand SIDS so that I could help others by disseminating information. In the end, Sarah, Mary, and I all needed to memorialize our babies; we just chose different ways.

Many believe, clinicians and clients alike, that we can better understand and help our clients if we have walked in their shoes. Jackson (2001) describes the wounded healer as someone who through growth and lessons learned from his or her own struggles and can later constructively assist others. However, my experience has reinforced for me that shared circumstances do not necessarily mean shared responses or meaning making. It has also reminded me that we must do our own healing before we can help others. I took on the role of support group facilitator and/or professional prematurely, without realizing that I was not yet ready, to the detriment of Sarah, Mary, and myself. Healing could not be measured in months, years, or even decades but rather in my ability to create and maintain healthy boundaries and to be fully present for my clients. Today I carefully keep my roles of SIDS parent and mental health professional separate. As a SIDS parent I can serve as an educator and draw from my own experience as well as teach about prevention and grief; however, I do not take on participants who approach me after a workshop or training as clients. If I work with a grieving parent as a clinician, I do not self-disclose. I'm not sure that is necessary for everyone, but it is important for me to not confuse the two roles. It's taken me years to be able to examine my grief, gain insight from the countertransference, let go of the guilt for not being able to be the "expert," and strive to understand and be mindful of the ways that my life experiences intersect those I seek to help.

Reflection Questions

1. Is there an event in your life, or in the life of someone you know, that has drawn you to want to help others? If so, do you believe you are better equipped to help because of your own experiences?
2. If a client's faith, worldview, and experiences inform his or her grief response differently than you might anticipate, how should you respond?
3. Grief is a deeply personal experience, yet there are common emotional and behavioral responses, three which are illustrated by Sarah, Mary, and myself. Do you know your own grieving style? When will you know you are healed enough to support others in their grief?

References

Bowlby, J. (1980). *Attachment and loss*. New York: Basic Books.

Hayes, J. A., Yeh, Y. J., & Eisenberg, A. (2007). Good grief and not-so-good grief: Countertransference in bereavement therapy. *Journal of Clinical Psychology, 63*(4), 345–355. doi:10.1002/jclp.20353

Huh, H. J., Kim, K. H., Lee, H. K., & Chae, J. H. (2018). Attachment styles, grief responses, and the moderating role of coping strategies in parents bereaved by the Sewol ferry accident. *European Journal of Psychotraumatoloy, 8*(6). doi:10.1080/20008198.2018.1424446

Jackson, S. W. (2001). Presidential address: The wounded healer. *Bulletin of the History of Medicine, 75*, 1–36.

Jung, C. & Jaffe, A. (1963). *Memories, Dreams, Reflections.* New York: Pantheon Books

Lazarus, R. S. (1993). Coping theory and research: Past, present, and future. *Psychosomatic Medicine, 55*(3), 234–247.

Maccallum, F., & Bryant, R. A. (2018). Prolonged grief and attachment security: A latent class analysis. *Psychiatry Research, 268*, 297–302. doi:10.1016/j.psychres.2018.07.038

Meier, A. M., Carr, D. R., Currier, J. M., & Neimeyer, R. A. (2013). Attachment anxiety and avoidance in coping with bereavement: Two studies. *Journal of Social & Clinical Psychology, 32*(3), 315–334. doi:10.1521/jscp.2013.32.3.315

Plath, S. (2008). *The Collected Poems.* New York: Harper Collins

Schenck, L. K., Eberle, K. M., & Rings, J. A. (2016). Insecure attachment styles and complicated grief severity. *Omega: Journal of Death & Dying, 73*(3), 231–249. doi:10.1177/0030222815576124

A Therapist as a Suicide Survivor Working With Client Suicide

Elizabeth Murdoch, LCSW, Family and Children's Agency, Norwalk, Connecticut

FIGURE 3.4. Elizabeth Murdoch

Elizabeth Murdoch, LCSW is a clinical social worker in Norwalk, Connecticut. She is the director of Behavioral Health at Family and Children's Agency in Norwalk, a large community social service agency. She oversees the Outpatient Mental Health clinic, a substance abuse program for women, and an intensive in-home program for seriously emotionally disturbed children and their families. She has a private psychotherapy practice and is an adjunct lecturer in the graduate MSW program at the Silver School of Social Work at New York University, her MSW alma mater. She has taught Advanced Clinical Practice, Clinical Work With Children, and Clinical Work With Substance Abusing clients and their families. Her clinical interests are attachment, family systems, and the effect of trauma on risk for substance abuse, problematic interpersonal relationships, and mental health. She has a post-graduate certificate in advanced clinical supervision from Smith College. She particularly enjoys supervising interns and new graduates. Her first career was in finance, and she has been practicing social work for 15 years. Elizabeth's 20-year-old son died by suicide, as did other family members, and when working with clients who are suicidal, the challenges of being a clinician with a lived experience of being a suicide survivor have been considerable. The stigma of suicide is weighty, and Elizabeth hopes that the open discussion of the considerations in this work could be of assistance to other practitioners. Elizabeth can be found on LinkedIn: https://www.linkedin.com/in/elizabeth-murdoch-2924b18/

Framing the Loss

I am director of behavioral health services at a community social service agency where I provide clinical supervision to a number of therapists. I have a private practice and am an adjunct lecturer on clinical social work in the Master's of Social Work program at a major local university. My personal experience with suicide is, unfortunately extensive. My father killed himself when I was 14, and my mother when I was 31, the day I returned from my honeymoon. Almost unbelievably, my artistic, athletic, bright wonderful son, R., died by hanging on his 20th birthday in 2004, after several years battling addiction. My son died 2 months after I received my MSW from New York University, where I attended graduation in Washington Square Park wearing the light blue high-top Converse sneakers he had given me. He was living in another state, having just left a halfway house where he was living after yet another stint in rehab. We were due to all meet up for a family vacation in South Carolina the week after his birthday. I know he wanted to discuss if he could come home. It was reported to us he had friends over the night before he died and was talking to them about where in his apartment he was going to set up his art supplies. They then went out to a club, he did a lot of cocaine, came home, and killed himself, saying in a note that he was sorry, but "just couldn't do it anymore."

His death was completely shattering. It was literally unbelievable. After my father died, I thought I was safe from any other suicides, because obviously my mother, despite having some mental health problems, knew the impact of suicide and would never kill herself, an incorrect assumption. Although my son did not know about my parents' suicides, I was quite sure that suicide was done with me. I had contemplated the possibility that R. could die from drug use, but it had not crossed my mind that he would commit suicide. How were I, my husband, and R.,'s younger brother going to go on?

In the first days after R.'s death, our house was filled with kids, friends of both boys, and their parents. In the evenings our front door had a sign saying, "Come on in." We had a constant stream of shell-shocked, unbelieving kids. One of my casual friends told me, "The kids really need you." True, perhaps, but it seemed an impossible task. Nevertheless, there I was, 2 days after my son's death, with seven or eight devastated young people in my living room, talking with them about my son, their friend. Many brought food, presents, wine, more food, books about grief, and poems about grief.

What was most helpful in the early days was people coming to the house and sitting with me, encouraging me to tell them about my son. I remember two women who visited, who I would characterize only as friendly acquaintances; each came and just sat on the couch with me. One, inexplicably, brought a loaf of Wonder Bread. My closest friends came from afar, and a couple of close local friends were always quietly available. My husband and I did not know how to help each other. I remember R.'s brother, who was 18, saying to me "Don't let this ruin your life." After a couple of weeks of feeling numb and disconnected, the tears came.

At the time of R.'s death, I was 2 months into my first post-MSW job at a crisis shelter for children and adolescents. I took 3 months off from work, but do not remember what I did. My husband went back to work a week after the funeral. I know that I cried for hours every day for 6 months. I thought that I probably should go to therapy but did not see the point when all I could do was cry. I was flattened by thoughts of failure, guilt, deep depression, fear about whether my other son would be okay, if my marriage would survive, and mostly, if it was my fault. I began to wonder who I could talk to who was a survivor of suicide, because I recognized that this grief was different from bereavement following other kinds of deaths.

I called a local agency where I had volunteered in the aftermath of 9/11, knowing that they had grief and bereavement services. I began attending a suicide survivors' group, where I sat and cried every other week for months. Despite the floods of tears, it was helpful to know that the other people there had some empathy for the extreme and desperate feelings connected with suicide. I was the only parent of a child who killed himself in the group, but the feelings of survivors of other family member's deaths were similar. There was no one there who had experienced three suicides in the immediate family. The group was helpful in normalizing the extent of the grief, and I attended for about 10 months, until a man whose son had also hung himself, joined. The father had discovered him hanging in the basement. I found his stories too difficult to hear, and they were causing me intrusive visual images of hangings that I had not actually seen. I asked the group leader if I could see her individually instead, and she agreed. It was a good decision, because by this time, I was able to begin to explore in helpful and meaningful ways what my son's death meant to me and was able to express, in the safety of her therapy

FIGURE 3.5 In memory of my son.

room, the difficult rational and irrational feelings that plagued me.

I had returned to work and found it helpful to be occupied and focused on helping other young people. My supervisors had wanted me to take longer than the 3 months, but I begged them to return, as the prospect of not having much to do was frightening. Industrial grief, I have subsequently heard it called, is when one throws themselves into work, or other ways to stay busy. What was most helpful in grieving was having people, family, friends (those who did not flee), a good therapist who I knew could tolerate my story and provide a safe place, and wonderful colleagues who were therapists, so they were not scared of me. We lost friends; I saw people hiding from me in the grocery store more than once. Suicide is just too much for many people. Stigma of suicide remains, but more often perhaps, it is just too difficult for people to imagine, and they do not want to envision what it would be like for them. These losses, of friends, a community, made an impossible situation that much harder.

I would not wouldn't do much differently, but EMDR (eye movement desensitization reprocessing) might have been helpful for some visual imagery that was troubling. Suicide of a child can produce any number of irrational thoughts, such as "I could have saved him," "It was my fault," and "I'm a failure as a mother," and my therapist incorporated CBT-informed techniques into challenging some of them. Some of those thoughts remain, and probably always will. I have learned to not ignore my sadness and lingering grief, but I am able to gently move it to the background, much of the time.

Some may disagree that this is possible, but for me, there was an element of choice in deciding to not only weather this tragedy, but maybe even feel better as time went on. There was an event that contributed to this decision. For the first several years I visited R.'s grave in a local cemetery fairly often. On many occasions I saw a woman there at a gravesite, and I had an idea that she must have lost a child. One day when she was not there, I looked at the grave where she stood day after day, and indeed, she had lost her son who was 22 when he died. The next time I saw her there, I went over to her, told her that my son had died a year before, and tearfully asked her, "Does it ever get better?" She stonily replied "No, it does not." I thanked her, and returned to my car, and thought "Well, fuck that. That will NOT be me. I WILL find a way to have it be better." That day I decided that my son's death, while knowing there would be pain every day of my life, was not going to, as my younger son said, "ruin my life." For me, part of eventually feeling better, if not great, was deciding to find joy where joy can be had, to appreciate the sound of the ocean, the softness of my cats' fur, my dear friends, and my small remaining family. Deciding to feel better, and believing that feeling better was not a betrayal of my son, helped.

Many therapists would agree that their greatest fear is that a former or current client dies by suicideeither while in treatment with them or even after treatment has ended. . We work with depression, anxiety, psychosis, life transitions, and myriad other client challenges, and do our best to collaborate with our clients to help them live their lives in the most satisfying way possible. Helping to keep a client alive, or working with a family in the aftermath of a suicide, is among the most challenging, and emotionally fraught situation for a therapist. Clinical academic curricula include how to conduct a suicide assessment, create safety plans, and discuss responsibilities in terms of referring to higher levels of care, but these interventions can seem disconnected from witnessing clients' pain and despair.

When working with extremely depressed and/or suicidal clients, the obvious goal is to preserve life and help them return to a more hopeful way of thinking and functioning while considering their right to self-determination. All health care providers have the same goal: curing, healing, restoring good health, caring. Mental health providers, including psychiatrists, clinical social workers, psychologists, and professional counselors, can find themselves in the position of working to prevent a client from killing him- or herself. The question of responsibility is a complex one, and it is this that plagues mental health providers, as well as feelings of failure, grief, loss, and powerlessness, among others, when there is a completed client suicide. Survivors of suicide, whether family, friends, therapists, are left with the multifaceted task of wrestling with excruciating questions like "Why?" "How could or should this have been prevented?" and "Whose fault was it?" while typically experiencing grief that is unlike any other.

Therapists can be charged tasked with providing therapy to a suicidal client and perhaps his or her family, and/or working with family members or friends after a completed suicide. They must be prepared to tolerate highly emotional content in both circumstances, but particularly if working with survivors of someone who has taken his or her life.

Suicidal clients, in my direct and supervisory practice, have fallen into two categories: those who are extremely depressed, whether situational or not, and see no relief in sight, and those who are in troubling situations where the client sees no solution other than to die. Despite the conventional wisdom that all people who are suicidal are depressed, and while that is frequently the case, some may feel they are in a rock-and-a-hard-place circumstance where no solution can be seen to problems that may, in fact, be solvable. It was what I have come to think of as the "suicidal tunnel"; there is only one way forward.

Individual interventions with suicidal clients can include dialectical behavioral therapy to provide skills to increase distress tolerance, and particularly cognitive-behavioral therapy to identify and replace irrational thinking. Examples of common irrational thoughts a suicidal client may have include "Everyone would be better off without me," "I don't matter," or "I'm a burden." Feeling heard and validated, essentially supportive psychotherapy, has been reported to be helpful, as well as psychodynamic therapy to explore the origins of feelings that can include anger, poor self-worth, despair, and hopelessness. Work with a suicidal client ideally should include family members, who, if they know their loved one is suicidal, may be in denial, frightened, angry, sad, anxious, or depressed. A therapist may be with a suicidal client an hour or two a week, but a client's friends and family in the best-case scenario can be critical in providing support.

Considerations of level of care are important when working with a suicidal client. Safety is paramount, and sometimes an in-patient setting is necessary for an acutely suicidal client. However, treatment must be chosen carefully and ideally with the client, because if a therapist is fearful for emotional or liability reasons and jettisons a client to a different treatment, the impact on the client of a perceived abandonment at a critical time can be considerable. Family members, friends, and others impacted by a suicide are typically referred to as survivors of suicide. As with other unexpected deaths from unnatural causes, it can be anticipated that loved ones will be overwhelmed and traumatized. Questions arise immediately, including "How did it happen? Who found the body? Did he or she suffer? Was it violent? How could they leave me?" and the often unanswerable, "Why?"

It is possible that friends and family left behind are at increased risk for depression, complicated grief, and suicidal ideation themselves. Struggling to understand, shame, guilt, feelings of abandonment, and looking for something or someone to blame are all common responses. It is widely believed that the loss of a child is the most difficult of all losses, and if the child died by suicide the parents' and close family members' grief responses can be expected to be greatly intensified. There can be an inability to find meaning in the loss, which can result in myriad agonizing emotions.

The intensity of therapeutic work with a suicidal client, or with survivors of suicide can be expected to be challenging for any provider, due to the life and death nature of the work. After a completed suicide, the exposure to intense grief can be difficult to tolerate. Competent therapists utilize supervision and other supports to recognize vicarious traumatization and transference and countertransference reactions that arise in their provision of therapy to their clients. A therapist's lived experience of any issue a client presents with may affect the therapeutic relationship and the work done within.

All of our life experiences color our interaction with clients, and in the psychoanalytic sense, produce countertransference responses. A therapist who is a suicide survivor can be expected to face unique challenges in working with suicidal clients, or with those who have experienced a loss due to suicide. In my work as a clinical supervisor in an agency, I have had supervisees who were working with suicidal clients a number of times. In the agency work, the suicidal clients have not, until recently, been my own, and I have found that the distance that exists between me and the supervisee's clients has been a sufficient buffer to prevent any problematic reactions on my part. In the last few years, I have had three cases of my own involving suicide or suicidality. Two of the clients were suicidal, and one family experienced a completed suicide of their 20-year-old son. In all three of these cases, there are considerations of treatment modalities, self-disclosure, and countertransference.

Case 1: Sam

The first suicidal client I saw directly for therapy, 2 years ago, was a 20-year-old young man, Sam, who was the same age as my son when he died, and similar in appearance. He was a student at a local university, hated it, and had recently been dumped by his girlfriend. He had near-genius IQ, was not challenged by his physics curriculum, had no interest in partying or drinking, and for reasons that were not entirely clear, felt that he had no options in his life. I had been told by the referral source that he was depressed, but was not aware that he actually was profoundly suicidal at the time we met. A few months prior, he had been hospitalized for a week for suicidality with a plan, which was followed by a stint in intensive outpatient treatment. He detested both, and said he would never go back to either one. He was astute enough to know what to say and what not to say to stay out of the hospital. He came to his intake with his parents who were tearful and terrified. In that session, he asked his mother to make sure he had no access to money so he could not buy a gun.

Despite his physical appearance, he was not, and the situation was not, anything like my son's. I was surprised that it did not appear that I was experiencing significant counter-transference, but I certainly wanted to help him survive with every fiber of my being. I was fearful for him and his family, and of how it would be for me if he killed himself but was able to stay effectively in my clinical mind most of the time. I came to believe that his difficulties were situational, not based in mental illness, although by any criteria, he was depressed. He did not see a future for himself. He came to see me without fail on Sunday mornings, despite his belief that there was no point to therapy. He grudgingly admitted that it was good to have somebody to talk to; he told me later the only useful thing I ever said to him was that if he was going to stop his medication, which he did, then he had to start doing a lot of aerobic exercise.

The treatment truly consisted of building a human connection, known of course as the therapeutic relationship, and working to instill hope. He tested my intellect for weeks, then deemed me an acceptable person to have in his life. I attempted to utilize some CBT techniques with him, but he rejected them. He just wanted to talk, so talk we did. We explored what he could do with himself, what kind of adult he wanted to be, what kind of woman he wanted to be with. He remained suicidal for a few months, but in typical analytical Sam-style, he thought that he should wait and see how things went. He gradually stopped coming, but he texts me from time to time when he's done well in a race. I would be surprised if he became suicidal again; he knows now that life problems need not be fatal. He dropped out of school, found a trade he likes, is coaching rugby, saving money, and perhaps most importantly, working out and running marathons, and says he is not depressed. His was a good case to be my first direct service suicidal client after my son's death. Sam is a physics and math person, and emotional language does not come easily to him. It worked for both of us to come at this problem intellectually; there was not a lot of affect management, neither his nor mine.

Case 2: Tyler

Thirteen years after the death of my son, a colleague referred a mom, Audrey, to me for therapy, and parent guidance, as her 20-year-old son was reportedly depressed and struggling. I began meeting sporadically with the mom in March; she did not want a regular appointment. Her son was finishing up his junior year at an Ivy League college. She reported that her son, Tyler, had for the last several years reported that he suffered from bouts of depression, which he apparently had been self-medicating with alcohol and marijuana. She spoke of him with love and pride. He was funny and outgoing, an excellent student, had many friends, a seemingly charmed upper-middle class life, and very supportive and loving parents.

Audrey was afraid for his future, as he seemed agitated and unhappy. He had a psychiatrist in the city where he attended college, and he had been put on an antidepressant, the effects of which were unclear. I saw Audrey two times, and she and her husband, Peter, once to discuss how they could get support for themselves and their son, and to discuss parenting strategies. Tyler had outbursts of rage, primarily at his siblings, when he was home. He was easily provoked by seemingly benign comments by family members. Tyler at this time did not have his own therapist but had had a few in the past. The importance of Tyler having his own therapist was discussed at length with his parents, and they agreed that when he returned to school, he would begin therapy again, to which Tyler agreed.

Tyler's parents seemed reluctant to believe that Tyler had a significant substance abuse problem. I had difficulty tolerating the denial, as all the signs were there, signs with which I am very familiar. Tyler came with his parents to see me one time before he returned to school, so that, in his mother's words, "You can see what an amazing kid he is." His parents had been working to identify a therapist for him there, and he was looking forward to beginning therapy again. He would also be re-connecting with his psychiatrist, who he had been in touch with over the summer.

During this session, he was discussing how depressed and angry he felt, while having difficulty identifying specific reasons. He was articulate and forthcoming. He was able to discuss with his parents how they could support him. He minimized his substance use, and it was clear that his parents desperately wanted to believe that he had "cut way back" over the summer. I asked him if he ever had suicidal thoughts, and he confirmed that he had passive suicidal ideation, without intent or plan. He reported that he wished that he "would wake up dead," as he was tired of feeling "horrible" all the time. He said this was the first time he had expressed this, and his parents were understandably shocked and fearful. He was adamant that he had no intention of hurting himself and promised his parents they had nothing to worry about.

He returned to college, a senior, began work with a therapist, and managed the semester apparently well. He and his siblings came home for the holidays, and one evening he and his brother got into a verbal argument that escalated into shouting. Mom came running and was drawn into the conflict. After the boys had calmed down, she said she was going for a walk, and asked her husband to keep an eye on Tyler. When she returned from her 15-minute walk, she went to Tyler's room to check on him, and found him hanging in his closet.

How I found out was a call from his father from the ambulance, in the middle of a birthday dinner at my house, saying his son was dead, and what was he supposed to do for his family. He asked if I would come over to the house the next day and meet with the family. This phone call was extremely difficult; it was difficult to process what I was hearing, and for the next 24 hours I had flashbacks of the phone call I had received from a police officer about my own son.

In the next week, I spent many hours, at the parents' request, at their house meeting with various combinations of family members. They were flattened by shock, worry, shame, guilt, and despair. The work with them consisted of listening, reframing, and more listening. It was difficult, but the family was extremely appreciative and told me that they found the visits very helpful. I felt honored to be a support for them, and once the flashbacks subsided after a few days, I was able to be fully present. It gave me a different kind of understanding of what it must have been like for my friends to be at my house and to support me when R. died.

An unexpected challenge presented itself; I found it excruciatingly difficult to discuss money. They paid me directly, and I found myself feeling unable to accept money from them, for this extremely intimate and grave work. I, on the advice of a colleague, broached the topic directly, and explained it in just that way to Tyler's mom. She very kindly told me she understood what the dilemma had been for me, yet nonetheless, I was to accept payment, which of course, I did.

The theme of "No one can possibly understand what this is like" began to present itself in these sessions. After much thought and consultation with a colleague from my supervision group, I decided to disclose to Tyler's parents that I had had a son Tyler's age who killed himself. They both expressed appreciation for letting them know and had no questions. It was eventually agreed that the father would seek his own treatment, as he and his wife were dealing with their son's death in entirely different and not particularly compatible ways. He liked his new therapist and said that she was very businesslike and did not push him to talk about feelings. He soon insisted that all the family members see her. Around 2 months after Tyler's death, I had not heard from the family in a couple of weeks, so I called the other therapist to see how things were going with the father, and she told me that the entire family was now seeing her, individually, and together as a family. There was no opportunity for closure with me and the family.

I wonder if the self-disclosure had anything to do with their decision, which the therapist maintained was at the insistence of the father. Perhaps they wondered if I would be able to manage their grief. I had let them know that my son's death was a long time ago, and that I would have referred them to another therapist after Tyler's death if I thought I would not be able to be helpful to them. The other therapist told me that they had found the disclosure very reassuring, but I wonder if the family knowing about my own loss made them think if I lost my own son, how could I handle the pain from their loss? Or maybe they worried that it would be so evocative for me I would not be able to focus on their tragedy. I'll likely never know.

Case 3: Ted

This case involved a man in his late 40s I had been seeing for several years at the agency. He had come for therapy following the death of his wife from cancer, now 5 years ago. They have three children, two of them with significant medical problems. He was requesting support for grief after his wife's death and the challenges of now being a single parent. He lives with several extended family members with problems of their own. He has a history of abuse and neglect in his youth. He is very much a black-and-white thinker, which has presented some challenges in therapy. Like the suicidal young man in the first case, he does not respond well to CBT techniques, because to him his irrational thoughts are completely rational, with no room for exploration. Despite his resistance to what he calls "therapy stuff," therapy with him has been straightforward and effective; we have a particularly positive therapeutic alliance. It was an easy case until he made a major and out-of-character decision that threw his entire family into disarray, alienating his children. He got himself into a "rock-and-a-hard-place" situation, and, because of his rigid thinking, could not see any way out. He completely rejected my suggestions that there could be solutions, as I truly believed there were. In one session he stated that he was acutely suicidal. I knew he had a gun at home; he said he had a plan, but he declined to tell me what it was. I asked him if, when he went home, he would take his gun to the police station and turn it in, and he said he would not. While we were talking, I was thinking about how to call 911 without him bolting from the office. I let him know that since he had disclosed actual intent to kill himself, that I had the responsibility of keeping him safe by whatever means were required. He replied that he knew that, but that he would not go to the hospital or a higher level of care under any circumstances.

In contrast to the instance of self-disclosure in the previous example, which was carefully thought out over several days, I made a decision in the moment to tell him that I had experience with the death of a parent by suicide. I provided no further detail, except that I knew what it was like. He was attentive and listening. The next intervention was to help him imagine, one by one, for each of his children, what it would be like to hear of his death, and what it would mean for them going forward in their life. I used very graphic, yet realistic examples. In the midst of this, I began to cry, not sobbing, but tears overflowing. So did he. I was fully conscious of the fact that I was, in that moment, trying to save his life. It was the most intense session I have ever experienced, to the point of having an extremely brief episode of depersonalization, watching the two of us hunched over the table in my office. At the end of my verbal imaginings of the devastation of his family, we sat in silence for 10 minutes. He then said, "Okay, I see I can't kill myself, so I guess I have to start thinking of solutions." It felt like a miracle.

I do not believe this approach would work with everyone, but I felt that I knew my client. He left the office with a promise that he was not going to kill himself, and because he is seemingly incapable of guile, I believed him. He has now solved his problem, through no small effort, and he and his family are safe and stable. I asked him in the session 2 weeks after what he thought about what we called our "cry-fest." He said that he did not think that without my telling him I had lost a parent to suicide that he would be alive. He also said that by my tears, he knew that I was truly trying to help him. If he had not ultimately responded the way he had, I would have called 911 and had a 72-hour hold instituted.

This was an instance where the self-disclosure was a positive, but I will always consider very carefully how and when to do so. I generally am conservative about self-disclosure. While the decision to disclose was made quickly, I was fairly certain it was the right thing to do. The countertransference in that session was powerful, and while I felt at the time I did not do a good job of managing my own emotions, it is likely that my tears were, in fact, important and meaningful to the client. I do not generally have rescue fantasies, but certainly this was a rescue mission. I was very fortunate that this ended the way it did, as I took a risk. I discussed the session with two trusted colleagues, truthfully, hoping for reassurance about the self-disclosure and the tears.

Issues of self-disclosure, countertransference, and emotional management are likely to surface in any situation in which the therapist has lived experience of the challenges a client is working on. The reactions of therapists can mirror those of survivors when a client kills him- or herself or of family members when one sits in a room with a person who is contemplating suicide. The parallel process in supervision also can be notable, in terms of feelings of helplessness and despair on the part of the therapist who is dealing with life-and-death situations. As with any challenging clinical process, good supervision is important, and critical in cases with very high risk. Ultimately, having successfully worked with suicidal clients and with suicide survivors has helped me realize how far I have come in my own journey of healing.

Reflection Questions

- What are your thoughts about self-disclosure in cases such as these?
- Why do you think there is such stigma around suicide?
- What are your thoughts about suicide?
- What would it take for you to feel that you would be able to work with suicidal clients?
- How do you feel about a therapist displaying emotion, such as crying, in a session?

KolKatta's Burning Ghats: The Power of Personal Ritual in Addressing Historical Trauma

Mark Smith, PhD, LCSW, Barry University, Miami, Florida

Mark Smith PhD, LCSW is an Associate Professor at Barry University School of Social Work, Miami Shores, Florida teaching in the masters and doctoral programs. His areas of interest include social work education and pedagogy, trauma responsive clinical interventions, narrative practice, group work, grief work, affirmative LGBT, family therapy, anti-racist, anti-oppressive practice, clinical supervision and qualitative research.

A little over one year ago my life partner, spouse, and closest companion died. We were together for 28 years, but only married for the last 5 after it became legal. What precipitated his final stage was a fall, cellulitis, a hospital stay of 3 weeks, followed by 4 weeks in a rehabilitation facility, and eventually back home with hospice. On his 86th birthday I arranged a small party for him at the rehabilitation center with a few friends and Ms. Millie, his beloved beagle, whom I snuck in. Later that evening, after we had tucked him into bed for the night, he said he had something important to tell me. *I want you to get me out of here. I want to go back to our home and have hospice take over. Yes, I know what that means, and I want you to be okay with my decision. I'm just so tired; I just don't see the point of continuing. Please do this for me. So I did. It seemed surreal that the hospice social worker who came to W's room to do the assessment and intake was a former student of mine.* About a month later W took his last breath, and a year of being reshaped by grief began.

FIGURE 3.6. Warren Crane, Brazil 2012

After he died nothing seemed real. I carried out my responsibilities and functioned normally, apparently, but there were great lapses of judgment and serious cognitive impairment. I managed to lose five cell phones over the year. I was unable to file my taxes that spring and had to get several extensions. I kept overdrawing my bank account. Twice I showed up to teach my classes on the wrong day. I lost my keys about once a week. I was unable to keep up with e-mails and text messages. I often forgot to eat. I would catch myself staring at a wall for 30 minutes or more. I would climb into my car and not know where I was going or why. Looking back over this year of grieving and reflecting on my experiences, several observations are articulated. These observations are presented from the perspective of one who has survived the early years of grief and healing. "Case information" about my situation is provided, along with a sketch of some key intersections of personal and public identities. The importance of honoring cultural contexts and personal grief processes, particularly when one's lived experiences have been dismissed or discredited, is illustrated. Finally, a new understanding of the importance of personal ritual is described.

Case Details and a Disclaimer

The inherent problems involved in reporting self-case studies are acknowledged. This chapter is not meant to suggest a new practice model, but to report personal observations that may be important to other contemporary workers.

W and I enjoyed a quirky, improbable relationship. Perhaps the greatest difference between us was age: W was 86 when he died; I was 63. W was retired from Broadway theater; I was a social worker with a private practice and professor of clinical practice in a school of social work. During his last months it seemed everywhere I turned, grief was being talked about and processed. The clients I saw in my private practice, the students I taught, and the interns I supervised seemed to all be dealing with significant loss or trauma. In my supervision practice, most of the interns were working in addiction treatment. Each week they came to supervision seeking emotional and professional support as the result of having to grieve yet another young client's death from heroin/fentanyl overdose. During this same period, I was teaching a master's-level course on trauma and resiliency. Like my clinical supervisees, students consistently reported feeling overwhelmed with their clients' narratives of trauma and loss.

In the clinical social work classes I teach, I emphasize the surprising power of grief and the way it manages to disassemble and transform lives. I tell about clients who were top-level, highly accomplished professionals whose lives dissolved into almost catatonic status. In the classroom, we talked about the symptoms of functional struggles that grieving clients are likely to exhibit, for example the inability to remember to pay bills; daily struggles to get up, shower, and get dressed for work; maintaining poor nutrition and/or hygiene; difficulty concentrating or completing tasks; and unintentionally instigating interpersonal conflict that often damaged key relationships (Stillion & Attig, 2014; Worden, 2018). In my classes, students talk about how similar these symptoms are to major DSM-5 diagnoses (American Psychiatric Association, 2013). I stress the importance of helping grief-stricken clients first talk about and process possible meanings the loss might suggest. Then I stress the importance of anticipating the impact of the loss on one's basic life functions. We brainstorm ideas for helping clients reestablish regular daily schedules in order to restore a sense of personal agency and self-efficacy (Worden, 2018). And as a long-term devotee of social group work, I emphasize the magic and power of groups in restoring a sense of connection and membership in a community (Price, Dinas, Dunn, & Winterowd, 1995).

When students begin discussing community and social membership, inevitably the issues of racism, cultural norms, cultural oppression, and historical trauma arise. My own grief process brought to my attention the importance of honoring family and cultural legacies regarding grief, especially legacies of historical injustice and political and religious oppression (Bolton & Camp, 1987; Heart, Chase, Elkins, & Altschul, 2011). Observing the reactions of W's friends to his death illustrated the impact the early HIV/AIDS period continues to have in older LGBT communities. When W died, I also experienced a powerful recollection of the fear, denial, helplessness, and outrage that was part the early AIDS pandemic. We had both lived through a time when it was not unusual to have one half of one's close friends and associates die over the course of 2 or 3 years. W lived in New York City and was working in the theater during the 1980s and 1990s. The theater community, like many artistic communities, was decimated by HIV/AIDS. In New York, as in Los Angeles, San Francisco, Miami, and other urban centers, the ongoing cumulative loss of close friends and lovers was massive, disorienting, and unremitting. Equally traumatizing was the virulent dominant social narrative about gay men and AIDS. One encountered frequent messages supporting the need to "exterminate" HIV-positive individuals, or quarantine and sequester gays away from society. There was a constant chorus of extremist hate, fearmongering, and stigma.

While the current generation has grown up with AIDS always a reality in their lives, and greater social acceptance and effective treatments are more available, social stigma still exists. The association of AIDS with gay men still persists. For example, only recently have federal statutes regulating blood collection and transfusion allow men who have sex with men to donate blood, despite their known and testable HIV status. For many older gay men who lived through these times, the trauma legacy continues to have an impact. It shows up in the way many older gay men still approach the prospect of hospitalization. In the early days of HIV/AIDS the expectation was that if you were admitted into the hospital it was to die. What continues to live on as part of the cultural memory and legacy of HIV/AIDS in the gay community is the collective memory of those who died alone, shame ridden, without support, and undergoing what was often a horrific dying process. I was just becoming a social worker in the late 1980s in San Francisco and watched as the pile on of devastating loss upon loss produced a population of zombies, numb with unspeakable terror, grief, and shame. Another traumatic memory is the fact most newspapers would not publish obituaries of gay men who died of AIDS. Religious institutions would not host funerals or memorial services for people known to be gay or to have died of AIDS. The memory of that time when the death of so many gay men went without public acknowledgment still influences expectations and norms around deaths (Oram,Bartholomew, & Landolt, 2004). Without family, without church or synagogue, without the supportive structure of religious rituals, gay men often gathered for almost secret memorial services. Thirty years later W's friends spoke in whispers about his dying. They wondered whether I would bother to have a memorial service. They cautiously asked if there were any angry family members who might be flying in. Public expression of and social acknowledgment of mourning ensures better community connection and a greater likelihood of healthy processing of grief.

Stigmatized and oppressed communities often develop covert codes for sharing information with each other while remaining under the radar of the dominant culture. Language, rituals, and shared beliefs provide a means for allowing individuals to feel connected and supported. Cultural practices universally act to buffer members from adverse situations and provide a range of culturally prescribed coping strategies. When W died he was surrounded by a group of young gay men of diverse cultural origins, mostly Cuban and Colombian, who had been hired as caregivers for the past few years. Following W's death, my actions, or my failure to act by not arranging a religious ceremony or funeral, was shocking to these young men because I was not following what they felt were powerfully prescribed social actions. Josiah, who is Cuban, insisted I should engage a local *santera* in a Santeria ceremony to help ensure W's safe passage in the afterworld. Ernie, a young man from Colombia, was upset that I did not sit with the body for a full day with invited family and friends and cook comforting foods for all to share. Recognizing that individuals from diverse cultures engage in distinct approaches to grief along with distinct rituals that help the aggrieved process their loss, clinicians should always explore the influence of different cultural practices rather than assume the dominant culture's practices are universal (Barnhill, 2011; Bolton & Camp, 1987; Running, Woodward, & Girard, 2008).

Guiding client, supervisee, and student inquiries into their own personal and cultural contexts for processing grief did not ensure that I would do so for myself. Soon after W's death I hid behind my academic status at the university as an excuse not to have to personally engage in the same self-examination

I expected of others. Soon after W's death I believed I was doing perfectly fine. In fact, I felt somewhat embarrassed that I did not feel sadder and emptier. The realization that I was not handling loss very well came as a surprise about 4 months later.

My journey with grief this past year has taught me several things that are now important in my practice. First, my personal experience reminded me of the importance of assisting grieving clients improve daily functioning. The ability to have a tangible indicator of healing based on concrete behaviors can be empowering. Second, the importance of encouraging supportive interpersonal connections and membership in communities of support was reinforced. Third, the importance of honoring personal and cultural practices around grief, especially any unique practices associated with subjugated and discredited groups. The third realization that emerged from my year of grief is the power of ritual.

Ritual provides a metaphor and set of embodied actions for representing and getting through significant life transitions. Ritual is usually a socially prescribed and endorsed sequence of symbolic actions that represent the culture's intrinsic values and beliefs. From a bio-neurological perceptive, when the body is allowed to work through or enact unresolved conflicts, integration is possible (O'Connor, 2013). However, when grief is marginalized, discredited, and generally excluded from socially endorsed rituals and community practices, personally constructed rituals and practices should be encouraged (Running, Woodward, & Girard, 2008). It is crucial that social work education programs encourage students to be adept at recognizing and critiquing existing social structures that impede equal membership in society. For example, after learning about Kübler-Ross's grief model, students could be invited to question the degree to which this model fits with their own cultural backgrounds and familiar practices.

CULTURAL CONTEXT

In India, ghats exist in towns along the Ganges and other sacred rivers where sections of riverfront steps lead down to the river banks. These steps or ghats become sites of various social, commercial, and religious transactions. One the most important cultural/religious ceremonies is the Hindu rite of Antyesti, or the cremation of the dead. While practices vary among sects, generally the body of the deceased is washed, wrapped in white cloth, or if the dead person is a man or a widow, a red cloth. A Tilak (red, yellow or white mark) is usually placed on the forehead. The dead person's body is carried to the cremation ground near a river or water by family and friends and placed on a pyre with feet facing south.

Several years before W's final year, we had a conversation about what his final wishes were. He was adamant that there was to be no funeral, that he wanted to be cremated, and that he wanted his ashes mixed with mine. The plastic box with his ashes still sits on the top shelf in my office. Last year, when I was in Kolkatta, India, I spent most of the 1-year anniversary of his death at the burning ghats along the Ganges. I had contracted with a driver to pick me up at 4:00 a.m. so I could be at the massive indescribable flower market when it opened. I bought 28 yellow roses, his favorite, one for each of the years we were together. I also bought eight lotus flowers, one for each of the decades of his life. All day I watched families arrive in station wagons and trucks and unload the body of a family member wrapped in white or yellow cloth with incense and flowers scattered over them. Then the family would wait together for their turn at the wooden pyres or at the government-run electric ovens, which were faster and cheaper. When given the final remains, the ashes, the family members would take turns reverently scattering them at the edge of the river, some accompanied by little boats of incense and flowers. When I was ready, I spoke words of acknowledgment and gratitude for each year we had together and tossed in one yellow rose. Then, for each of his decades (eight), I tossed in a lotus flower, and watched the blossoms drift down the Ganges. This small private ritual, enacted on the 1-year anniversary of W's death, has brought more peace than I imagined. I returned to the United States unafraid and slightly joyous, ready to begin constructing a newly formed identity and re-engaging in life.

Reflection Questions for Students

1. What rituals and grieving practices are parts of your family's tradition?
2. What are some ways you might respectfully inquire about a client's belief system and spiritual practices regarding death and loss?
3. For those who have legacies influenced by historical trauma and oppression, how might grief ceremonies and rituals serve as a way to express strength, meaning, and hope for the community?
4. What might be a meaningful ritual or memory practice you would like to have as part of your own funeral?

References

American Psychiatric Association. (2013). *Diagnostic and statistical manual of mental disorders* (5th ed.). Washington, DC: Author.

Barnhill, J. J. (2011). Giving meaning to grief: The role of rituals and stories in coping with sudden family loss. *Graduate Theses and Dissertations*. Retrieved from http://scholarcommons.usf.edu/etd/2996

Bolton, C., & Camp, D. J. (1987). Funeral rituals and the facilitation of grief work. *OMEGA: Journal of Death and Dying, 17*(4) 343–352. doi:/10.2190/VDHT-MFRC-LY7L-EMN7

Heart, M. Y., Chase, J., Elkins, J., & Altschul, D. B. (2011). Historical trauma among indigenous peoples of the Americas: Concepts, research, and clinical considerations. *Journal of Psychoactive Drugs, 43*(4), 282–290.

O'Connor, M. F. (2013). Physiological mechanisms and the neurobiology of complicated grief. In M. Stroebe, H. Schut, & J. van de Bout, (Eds.) *Complicated grief: Scientific foundations for health care professionals.* (pp. 205–217). New York, NY: Routledge.

Oram, D., Bartholomew, K., & Landolt, M. (2004). Coping with multiple AIDS-related loss among gay men, *Journal of Gay & Lesbian Social Services, 16*:2, 59-72, DOI: 10.1300/J041v16n02_04

Price, G. E., Dinas, P., Dunn, C., & Winterowd, C. (1995). Group work with clients experiencing grieving: Moving from theory to practice. *Journal for Specialists in Group Work, 20*(3), 159–167. doi:10.1080/01933929508411340

Running, A., Woodward, T., & Girard, D. (2008). Ritual: The final expression of care. *International Journal of Nursing Care, 14*(4), 303–307. doi.org/10.1111/j.1440-172X.2008.00703.x

Stillion, J. M., & Attig, T. (2014). *Death, dying, and bereavement: Contemporary perspectives, institutions, and practices.* New York, NY: Springer.

Worden, J. W. (2018). *Grief counseling and grief therapy: A handbook for the mental health practitioner,* (5th ed.). New York, NY: Springer.

Not Your Average Fairy Tale: Grief and Loss as a School Social Worker

Kelly Zinn, MSW, Lumberton Township School District, New Jersey

Kelly is a licensed social worker in New Jersey and New York and a certified school social worker in New Jersey. Presently, Kelly is in her second year of the Rutgers University DSW program, and in the process of obtaining her LCSW in New Jersey. Kelly earned her MSW at State University of New York, Stony Brook. Throughout Kelly's career in social work, her focus has been working with children and families. She has worked as the coordinator of a support group program for families that experience sexual abuse and as a therapist in a treatment foster care program. For the past 13 years, Kelly has been a school social worker, providing student support through small group and individual counseling, crisis work and child study team case management. Kelly is committed to the mentorship of social work students and her research interests include creating trauma-sensitive schools and improving stability for children in foster care. She can be reached at ktz7@scarletmail.rutgers.edu

I was 20 years old when I met my husband in Disney World. We were both participating in the Disney College Program, and our assigned rooms happened to be across the hall from one another. I could tell he was special from the start—funny, kind, and full of life. We became fast friends and within a few months we started dating. We got married at 28 and settled into our newlywed life, content to live out our own version of happily ever after.

A few short years later the unexpected happened. At age 32 my husband, Rich, was diagnosed with anaplastic astrocytoma, Grade 3—an inoperable, malignant brain tumor. Rich faced cancer with a positive attitude and a determination that he would win. Rich went into remission just 7 months after diagnosis and remained in remission for the next 4 years. During that time, we lived—we traveled, spent time with family and friends, started our own family—and it was not until the last few weeks of his life that Rich's health began to steadily decline. We also grieved during that time, for loss of the life we had planned. All the possibility that had stretched before us seemed to have been yanked away. After the diagnosis we became inundated with doctor appointments, medication schedules, and concerns about side effects; everything seemed risky and unsafe. I was nervous to be away from Rich; I did not want to leave him alone for even a few hours to go to work. We were grateful that he tolerated his treatment well, but he was disappointed to have to take an indefinite leave from his job. These new circumstances changed the way we approached life. We were angry at how our life had become consumed by cancer, and we struggled to reconcile that this *was* our life now.

At initial diagnosis, my mom had asked the doctors about our chances at having children. At the time, I thought it was pointless; there was no possibility of a family or anything resembling the life we had planned for anymore. Within a year of the diagnosis Rich was in remission and had a few clear MRIs, and we began to hope we could keep the cancer at bay indefinitely. We revisited the idea of starting a family. Due to Rich's chemotherapy and radiation treatments, we had to pursue in-vitro fertilization. I became pregnant, and we were elated. I had a miscarriage and we were distraught. It was grief on top of grief; how could this be happening? It was so unfair. We moved on, we continued to live—after all, we had each other. Another year passed, remission continued, and eventually my husband had been without treatments for long enough for us to try naturally to have children. Within 16 months we had two children, but 1 month after the birth of our second child my husband's second brain tumor was diagnosed.

FIGURE 3.7. Rich Zinn, shown here moments after ringing a bell to celebrate his final radiation treatment.

It sounds odd to say that I was surprised when Rich died; after all, he had brain cancer—had I been delusional? But I was not alone. Family members, friends, and even his doctors were all amazed by Rich's overall health throughout his disease. On our first visit with one oncologist, the doctor said that, after looking at his MRI, he could not believe how well Rich was functioning. Days before he passed, we all met with his medical team and advocated for him to receive a new, non-invasive treatment, and the doctors allowed it. I clearly recall one evening very close to the end of his life, after Rich had a particularly bad seizure, I was talking to my parents and my father encouraged me, "Don't count that guy out just yet." We all lived by the old adage, "Where there is life, there is hope." And when the time came, we were all in shock.

I remember the day so clearly. Rich was in the ICU, having had a trach tube put in just days before to help him breathe. On the last day of his life, I went home after having been at the hospital all night, and I was exhausted. While our baby girls napped, I decided to get some rest too. Then the phone rang. It was my father-in-law; I needed to get back to the hospital. I was filled with dread on the drive over. When I arrived, the resident was waiting outside Rich's room and she said, "I'm sorry, there's nothing else we can do." My worst fear realized. It was so difficult to believe that my strong and positive husband—who had fought cancer with such tenacity and bravery—had reached the end of his road. Throughout this rollercoaster of illness hope had always prevailed; indeed, we were only 9 days into a new treatment. I could not fathom this reality, the inevitability now inescapable. There were decisions to be made and since Rich was on a ventilator, we were able to keep him alive until everyone could come say goodbye. He passed peacefully, just a few minutes after the ventilator was turned off. It wasn't until I returned to our home—for the first time truly without him—that I felt the weight of all that had come to pass in the last 12 hours. My partner was gone; I was a widow and a solo parent. My parents were there, my dad holding me as I cried, and it hit me that my own children would never be held by their father again. Mentally and emotionally drained, I finally slept. When I woke it was hard to accept that I did not get to go to the hospital. Instead it was time to make funeral arrangements. To say I felt sad and angry would be an understatement. What saw me through those first days were my relationships—with family, friends, and most of all our daughters, who were pure light in this devastating darkness—and the need to honor Rich's life by thoughtfully planning his services. I took comfort in making a playlist of his favorite songs and creating picture boards with loved ones, reminiscing about the good times as we worked. Writing his eulogy was therapeutic in a way, as it was my chance to pay public tribute to the awesome man I was lucky to share a life with.

Allowing family and friends to fully be there for me—to prepare meals, to take care of my children, to listen, or just be present—is how I survived those dark days.

Although Rich had cancer we had never prepared for his death. At the time it seemed that doing so was an admission that his disease was terminal, and we were not ready for that. Moreover, the end was so quick, and Rich was not coherent, so we never got the chance. I work in a school, and Rich died on the last day of the school year, giving me time before I had to return to work. I spent that summer running away from our home, visiting family, continuing with a beach trip that we had planned, doing whatever I could to keep moving until I had exhausted myself enough to sleep.

I had been a school social worker for 9 years. I was used to the rhythm of the school year, always ready to get back into a routine after the welcome respite of summer, but that year, of course, was different. The summer break gave me time to process, time to grieve, time to begin to pick up the pieces and move forward. However, I was nervous and anxious about returning to work. I was not certain how I would handle simple questions about my summer from the students, or even sympathy from the staff. In those first days and weeks back at work I relied on the support of the school counselor, who had been my colleague and friend for several years. I have always considered myself to be very reflective as a clinician, but now I worried that my judgement was skewed. Taking time to process student counseling sessions with the school counselor or my supervisor helped me to be aware of how my grief was impacting my practice. Personally, I was also seeing a therapist who I spoke with about my return to work, and I processed my feelings about work situations in therapy. I found therapy to be an essential piece of self-care, as a helping professional who is also grieving. In therapy, I had the opportunity to focus directly on my grief. To speak freely, without concern for how it might affect others. This was important because grief can be a lonely process. When you lose someone, who was loved by many and in different ways, it can be challenging to share the depth of your grief with others who are also grieving. This is not to say that I couldn't go to our family and friends; I could, and I did. What makes therapy different is the individual nature; in therapy I could unpack my feelings in a way that was only about me, and I found that to be helpful in my healing process. Therapy also reinforced the importance of taking care of myself, a trait that can be lost on people in helping professions. While we are well equipped to help others, we sometimes struggle to help ourselves. Participation in the therapeutic process, as a client, enriched my understanding of the necessity of self-care.

The school setting presents clients with issues that run the gamut, and grief and loss were no exception. Furthermore, cancer is so common. Prior to my husband's death, there were instances in which I would disclose his condition at appropriate times—usually when talking with parents who were going through treatment—in an effort to provide hope and encouragement. After Rich passed, I would freeze at the mere mention of cancer. In the first year following my loss, I worked with several students who were dealing with the loss of parent, whether through death, divorce, or incarceration. The students about to be discussed are unidentifiable; their anonymity is assured by changes to several descriptive characteristics. This work was challenging, especially with one young child whose father had been incarcerated and ceased to communicate with the family, rejecting visitation and not acknowledging letters.

Ashley was a 7-year-old student, presenting with extreme behaviors including physical aggression and elopement. I initially became involved because of the behaviors that were disrupting Ashley's academic progress, as well as having a detrimental effect on the learning environment in the classroom.

Ashley's teacher and the school administrators were frustrated with these behaviors. Ashley was added to my caseload, and I began working with her in a small group. After a particularly concerning incident, during which Ashley eloped from the building and ran into the street, we held a meeting with her mother. She explained that she was working to get Ashley help, but that Ashley had been very angry since her father's incarceration, and that this anger had increased since her father had ceased communication and refused visitation with the family.

As we built a relationship, Ashley would request to stay after group to speak privately and take breaks from class in my office. She began to draw pictures that led to discussions about her father. Ashley expressed that she was angry with her father, first for having become incarcerated, and then for cutting off communication. She would say things like, "He could talk to me, but he doesn't want to; why?" In the wake of my grief, I found that I was angry with this father—that I had never even met—too. Indeed, how could he and why would he? Did he not know about all the fathers who are taken too soon? Why was my husband taken away when there were fathers who were choosing to opt out of parenting?

Engaging in frequent self-reflection was absolutely necessary in working with Ashley. At first, it was challenging for me to reconcile that my reaction was directly related to my grief. I was sure that I was experienced enough to parcel out my grief and not let it affect my work. Surely, I would be angry on this child's behalf if my husband were still alive. But something was nagging in the back of my mind—was that true? Perhaps my visceral reaction to this situation was related to my own loss. After all, clinicians are still human. Once I acknowledged the connection between my reaction and my loss, I was able to consider—and seek supervision around—how this realization was informing my practice with this child. Additionally, Ashley was dealing with disenfranchised grief, as her father was gone from her life yet still alive. This grief was complicated by the fact that her father was incarcerated, which created feelings of shame. Ashley struggled to speak with her mother about her feelings, for fear of upsetting her mother. Shame connected to her father's incarceration made her reluctant to speak with other trusted adults as well.

While Ashley's situation raised feelings of anger and frustration, another student caused me to reflect on my grief in a different—and, for me, frightening—way. Martin, a 12-year-old male student, came to talk with me one day. Martin was not on my caseload, but his assigned counselor was out on leave, so I had been working with him. Martin had recently lost his father after a long illness. His mother—who had also suffered from a long-term illness—had passed several years prior, and he was now dealing with being an orphan. Even though Martin had moved in with his older sister and her family, he was feeling anger toward his deceased parents. "Why did they have me?" he questioned, "They knew they were sick." It was a very difficult moment for me, something I struggled with personally embodied in a child I was working with. I had often wondered if my own children would someday feel angry with me or find fault in our decision to start a family after a cancer diagnosis. I had processed these feelings in therapy, talked about them with family members and friends, written explanatory letters to my girls, and truly believed I had come to terms with the feelings—until Martin was sitting in front of me, questioning his own parents. I struggled through the session and felt relief when the other counselor returned from leave and I could transfer Martin back to her caseload.

Through my work as a school social worker I have learned and transformed as a clinician. Much like grief, this transformation is a continuous process of self-reflection and growth. Grief does not end.

It changes, and you change, but it never ceases. As a clinician, I find that my continued experience with grieving has helped me to gain a deeper understanding of my clients and their experiences, and to be more compassionate. At times, I still struggle when a client presents concerns that seem insignificant to me; however, I am now quick to revisit these instances in supervision or remind myself that everyone is in their own place and clinicians need to honor where clients are on their journey.

Supervision and peer support have been invaluable tools for me. Self-reflection is extremely important; but beyond this it is necessary to discuss, describe, and receive feedback on counseling sessions. I recall one instance where I immediately texted my supervisor after a session because I wanted to discuss my feelings and reaction. When we are grieving, it is important to seek extra support. Reaching out to supervisors and trusted peers is good clinical practice and an important piece of self-care.

Questions for Reflection

- Think about the connections between your clients and your own grief. What potential is there for crossover between your grieving process and your clients'? How can you relate to their experience?
- Grief comes in all different forms. What losses have you experienced (include significant deaths, and other—perhaps disenfranchised—forms of grief)? How might these losses impact your work?
- What do you do for self-care? What practices might you add?
- When might it be necessary to consider transferring a client to another clinician?

Traumatic Pet Loss and the Clinician

Katherine Compitus, MSEd, LCSW, MA, DSW, New York University, New York City, New York NYU

FIGURE 3.8. Katherine Compitus

Katherine Compitus is a bilingual licensed clinical social worker in New York and a doctoral candidate in clinical social work at New York University. Her research focuses primarily on disorganized attachment and the human animal bond. She is especially interested in crisis intervention and working with trauma survivors; she is a certified family trauma therapist and trained in EMDR. Katherine was a teacher prior to becoming a social worker and has over 18 years' experience working with children and families. Katherine is currently an adjunct lecturer at New York University, Fordham University, and Columbia University. She is also the founder and chairman of Surrey Hills Sanctuary, a nonprofit organization providing veterinary social work services. Katherine has an MSW from NYU and also an MSEd (education) and an MA (biopsychology) from Hunter College. Early in her social work career Katherine was a grief counselor for pet loss at the Animal Medical Center. Special thanks to Milagros Sanchez-Nester for her mentorship and guidance in the preparation of this writing. Katherine can be reached at kog206@nyu.edu or kcompitus@gmail.com.

It is important to acknowledge how important my black Labrador Retriever, Morgan, was in my life. I adopted her at only 8 weeks old and when I had just received my first master's degree. I had had pets my entire life, but I was very allergic to dogs as a child and, despite always wanting a dog, I could never go near them. It was only as an adult that I realized that had outgrown my allergy and I was no longer allergic to dogs. It was very soon after this that I adopted Morgan. When Morgan was only 1 year old both she and my sister's 2-year-old dog became very sick. We don't know what happened, but within days my sister's dog died in the hospital. Morgan spent over a week in the hospital. She wouldn't eat or drink. We had to secure special medicine for human chemotherapy patients and, after a few days, she slowly began to recover. For the rest of her life, when she would sleep deeply, I would become concerned and check that she was breathing (to her annoyance). Morgan's well-being became my purpose in life

FIGURE 3.9. Morgan, beloved dog of the author, greatly loved and missed.

and I adopted another dog, Angie, as a companion for Morgan. We opened a dog daycare so that our dogs would have a safe place to play and we moved to a larger house so that the dogs would have more room to play. Morgan passed away just months before her 12th birthday, but I had been dreading this loss for most of her life.

Morgan had what we thought was an asthma attack on Christmas Day, so we rushed her to the hospital. I had suspected cancer for months, but our regular vet kept telling me that I was paranoid, and I had no proof. The veterinarian at the hospital, on Christmas Eve, took X-rays of her chest and a few hours later, on Christmas Day, called us back to say that she had a cancer that had already metastasized to her lungs. We took Morgan to an oncologist, and they ran tests; we did everything humanly possible to save her, but it was too late. One week after the initial diagnosis Morgan was in the hospital, again. I went to visit her and told her I loved her. She gave out a cry, collapsed, and was gone. And as everyone celebrated the new year, I started the descent into a deep clinical depression that would last for months and would forever affect the trajectory of my life.

It is important to note that Morgan came into my life at a period of growth and change, when I really craved a stabilizing influence. I was no longer a student and I was moving out of my parents' home into my own apartment. Mahler (1972) examined the separation-individuation phase of toddlers. The child must go out on its own and establish itself as an independent individual. The child cannot do this successfully if he or she does not already have a secure base (parents) to return to. My parents are good people, but we always had a bit of a tumultuous relationship. Having Morgan with me at this point in my life was key; she became the secure base that I could always depend on to love and protect me (Ainsworth, 1991). Most people see their own companion animals as family member who often provides an unconditional positive regard and nonjudgmental relationship that is often lacking in other humans (Field, Orsini, Gavish, & Packman, 2009). In fact, people often turn to their pets to comfort them in their time of grief (Kurdek, 2008, 2009). But at the time when I needed Morgan to comfort me, she was no longer there.

When Morgan passed away, I had been a social worker for several years but primarily worked in the nonprofit sector. I had previously dabbled in animal-assisted therapy (AAT) and had done my first social work internship (for the master's degree) doing AAT with pediatric patients at a local hospital. For my second social work internship, I had worked as a grief counselor for pet loss at a large animal hospital. I worked there 4 days per week, for over 7 months. So, when Morgan passed away, I thought that, since I had clinical experience with the subject, I would be able to cope well with my own loss. I utilized rationalization as a coping technique, reminding myself that I had pets that had passed away before, mostly recently my 15-year-old cat, Eros, who passed away on Thanksgiving from a heart attack and exactly 1 year before our other cat passed from cancer on New Year's Day. I saw these losses as independent, not cumulative, despite what I knew to be true. (All loss is cumulative, especially when they happen so closely in time and to ones you love so dearly.) But I used rationalization as a way to cope with Morgan's death and I was fine, for about 6 weeks. My husband remarked on how calm I was, and I told him that, as a former grief counselor I understood that nobody lives forever and I had done everything in my power to save her. I told him that I am a clinician; I knew how to cope better than the average person. However, Carmack (2003) explains that the loss of a pet can be very traumatic, and can be severe enough in intensity and duration to cause serious psychological distress. And one day, out of the blue, I began to cry hysterically and I did not stop for over a month. I could not get off the sofa; I could not eat or sleep. I had to stop working at my nonprofit, since I was unable to work at a job or even take care of my own activities of daily living. All I could do at the time was to cry and to hurt.

The death of a pet is what is often called a "disenfranchised loss," which may result in others being less supportive and understanding of the loss (Carmack, 2003; Packman, Field, Carmack, Ronen, 2011). Often this is due to the lack of understanding of the depth of the bond that forms between humans and their companion animals. We frequently hear that someone should quickly get a new pet when one has passed; however, it is unlikely to hear that we should replace a deceased child with a new one immediately. It is this disenfranchisement that often leaves bereaved pet guardians with a lack of societal and familial support in their time of need. There were many people in my life who tried to be supportive but simply trivialized my pain. Some asked when I would be finished grieving, some suggested that I immediately adopt a new dog, some simply told me to get over it. Even those who wanted to be supportive were often unaware of how to support someone who is grieving the loss of a pet. With limited support, I fell deeper and deeper in grief and I had no idea how to help myself recover.

It was 6 weeks before the shock wore off and I became clinically depressed, but it was only 2 weeks before my husband encouraged me to return to therapy, because he was concerned that I was unable to function. I had suicidal ideation (without intent), which is common among the bereaved, who often want to be reunited with the deceased loved one. It was the combination of therapy, time, and the support of my husband and other pets that helped me recover from my clinical depression. Our other dogs, Boston and Angie, were an immense comfort to me at this time. Boston was especially aware of my grief and he refused to get off of my lap while I was depressed. He constantly laid his 93-pound body on top of me or next to me, providing both tactile stimulation and also a literal stabilizing presence. He was never trained to do this; he appeared to intuitively know what I needed to comfort me. Although my dogs, and my husband, tried to comfort me, still they were not Morgan and I had to process the loss that I felt before I could connect again with anyone else.

I began to see my therapist twice a week to explore my feelings of loss and how they related to my childhood attachment issues. I began to involve myself in more self-care and adaptive coping techniques such as attending yoga classes, spending time with friends, and taking my dogs on long walks. I tried "floating," a sensory deprivation tank (the idea of which terrified me because I would be alone with my feelings, but actually was very comforting), and I began to regularly visit my local Buddhist temple to practice mindfulness meditation. I also read extensively on death and loss, especially Buddhist literature on death and dying and scientific research on reincarnation (Rinpoche, 2012; Weiss, 2012). I am a spiritual but not religious person and in order to heal I was forced to develop my own beliefs about what happens to a being after death. I needed to know that even in death that Morgan was at peace and safe. Finally, started wearing a memorial necklace that contained Morgan's DNA inside (extracted and placed into amber). This was my transitional object, which can be described as a physical manifestation of an emotional connection (Winnicott, 1986). When I wear the memorial necklace I feel empowered and revived; I feel that, in some small way, I have reconnected with my secure attachment figure again and I can safely navigate the world.

After 6 months away, I finally returned to work, but I began a new job working in the psychiatric emergency room of a small hospital. It had always been interested in crisis intervention but I felt that I now had a deeper understanding of what it felt like to actually be the one in crisis. With this new insight I felt that I could more easily understand the needs of others in crisis. While working at the hospital, I came upon a man whose cockatiel had recently died. He was so distraught at the passing of his bird, at the loss of his beloved family member, that he attempted to hang himself. He reported that the bird was his primary source of support and he did not want to live without his bird. Of course, it was difficult for me to work with this patient, due to the counter-transference that I felt. I shared his pain, but I did not know enough about him to compare my relationship with Morgan to his relationship with his bird. But I still felt a great deal of compassion for this man. Some of the other staff members mocked the patient, stating that it was only a bird and not worth killing himself. I felt very hurt by their remarks and I made sure to discuss with them that the support from his bird (who was a talking bird) was extremely important to this patient. Perhaps he had learned to rely on this bird as his primary source of support and without his bird he felt extremely lost and without any adaptive coping mechanisms. In self-psychology we call this a self-object. An animal that serves as a self-object may be providing a person with a sense of cohesion or support (Blazina, Boyra, & Shen-Miller, 2011). Without that self-object, the person no longer knows where he or she fits in the world. Kohut explained that a self-object will provide validation to a person and will help him or her connect to the world (Kohut, 1984). I could personally understand how the loss of his bird caused this man to feel that his connection to the entire world had been lost.

It is unfortunate that pet loss is still marginalized by both laypeople and clinicians. Although there is no definitive explanation why some people are more or less understanding about pet loss, we can hypothesize why some clinicians continue to marginalize this type of grief. Cultural beliefs may cause clinicians to bring their personal biases into their work. Some cultures firmly believe that animals belong outside the home and are seen as tools to help people survive (livestock, herding dogs, etc.), rather than as family members. However, clinicians should always be aware of their own biases and a culturally competent clinician will not let his or her own beliefs cloud his or her therapeutic judgement. Alternately, clinicians may be affected by the culture of his or her agency or institution. If a clinician is working in a toxic, invalidating environment where he or she feels unsupported or unappreciated, he or she may, in turn, be more dismissive and less understanding of clients' feelings. I believe that the dismissive behavior that I witnessed at the hospital was a direct result of the culture and climate of that agency. This is common in hospitals, where pets are often overlooked as a source of support and are rarely (if ever) asked about during intakes or initial assessments. I also believe that clinicians' own personal experiences and relationships with animals may also cloud their judgement when working with pet loss. Some clinicians may not want to empathize with clients who are grieving, because they will have to acknowledge that they may also grieve the loss of a pet in the future. To acknowledge the client's feelings would mean clinicians would have to acknowledge their own potential for future pain. Clinicians may be scared to acknowledge their own vulnerability, their own attachments and dependence on an animal, or they may just not want to seem vulnerable to other staff and clinicians. To mourn the loss of a pet may seem overemotional to those who do not understand the attachment and, in an attempt to remain professional, they may be trying to avoid this perceived weakness. Finally, some clinicians simply may not connect with animals in the same way as their clients. They may not have a deep and lasting relationship with their own pets and, therefore, are unable to understand when faced with a client who has an attachment that they are unfamiliar with. It is clinicians' own biases and fears that often prevent them from helping clients who are experiencing the loss of a pet. When we speak of cultural competence, we should also discuss value-based cultural competence. Clinicians should be aware that, even if they have different values from their client, their client's experiences are still valid (also known as constructive realism). Clinicians who are able to consider their client's values as valid and real are those who are more able to understand experiences different from their own. Therefore, clinicians who share similar values to their clients, who have a similar relationship with their own pets, may be best suited to counsel clients who are grieving the loss of a cherished pet.

Sadly, 6 months after Morgan passed away, Angie was diagnosed with cancer. However, our experience with Angie was entirely different. The doctors were able to cut the tumor out and over the next year and a half, Angie went to chemo treatments monthly. We changed her diet and started also seeing a holistic Eastern medicine veterinarian. Above all, we paid close attention to her quality of life. We created a "bucket list" for her that included taking her to the beach and feeding her some of her favorite foods. We did everything we could do help Angie. The original prognosis given was that Angie would live for 2 months. With intensive treatment and care, she lived another year and a half. She was also almost 12 years old when she passed away. We had a veterinarian come to our home and spread out blankets on our front lawn where Angie laid down. We hugged her and sang songs to her as the veterinarian helped her peacefully pass away. For us, Angie's passing was deliberate and peaceful. She was no longer in pain. Aside from the most obvious differences in their cases, the most important difference between the passing of Morgan and Angie was the time spent in preparation of their death. With Morgan, I had no time to prepare. I had always assumed that she would be in my life and I took this for granted. When she passed I was in shock because I was unable to believe that it was real. With Angie, I was prepared for her passing. I appreciated every moment spent with her, and I deliberately paid attention to the many details about her (such as how soft her fur felt, how she yawned, etc.), so that I could forever remember who she was.

After working for several years in the psychiatric emergency room, I returned to school to pursue my doctorate in clinical social work at New York University. I also took additional courses and became certified in a number of trauma-informed treatment options including TG-CBT, certified family trauma, EMDR and hypnotherapy. I voraciously read everything I could find on trauma, grief, and loss. The way that I coped with the loss of Morgan was to throw myself into my work. I utilized intellectualization as a coping technique; if I could understand what trauma is, why I was grieving and what happens when loved ones die, I could feel more comfortable with the idea of death. My current work focuses on the human-animal bond (HAB) and attachment theory. I study HAB in all its forms including disaster relief, homelessness, domestic violence, and clinical applications such as animal-assisted therapy and psychiatric service dogs. I have become very driven and, when asked, I explain that my work is an adaptive coping technique to help me work through my pain.

It has been 5 years since Morgan passed and I have not yet slowed down. The grief has transformed me into a full-time academic, an AAT clinician, an educator who teaches about the physical and mental health benefits of the human-animal bond. I worked extensively with one of my other dogs to establish him as a therapy dog; he has now been approved by Pet Partners (formerly the Delta Society) to officially work as a therapy dog. I continue to incorporate animal-assisted therapy into my work with pediatric and adolescent trauma survivors. The clients are more quickly to view our sessions as a safe "holding environment" (Winnicott, 1986) and are more quickly to establish a rapport when the therapy dog is in the room. In addition, the clients may begin to view the therapy animal as providing that "safe base" that they so dearly need (Bowlby, 1982). The loss of a loved one can throw a person into a state of disequilibrium and, as a franchised grief, society is (unfortunately) less supportive during times of pet loss. As clinicians we must examine the connection and importance of each individual to each loss; it is not our job to assume how that loss should be felt. Rather, we should support our clients through any loss of a supportive figure in their lives. The death of Morgan profoundly changed my life. To ignore the transformative power of animals and their bond to people would mean overlooking a significant source of strength for people. To ignore the influence of that loss would do our clients an injustice. As a clinician, we should always start where the client is at, even if that means recognizing a loss that is unfamiliar to us.

Reflection Questions

1. How does the author define her relationship with her pet? How is her personal definition of the relationship relevant to the grieving process?
2. Was the loss an expected loss or a sudden loss? How does the location of the pet's death (at home, in a hospital, in transit to the hospital, etc.) affect the grief process?
3. Is guilt always associated with grief and loss? When is guilt more likely to be present in bereavement?
4. How does a strong support network help the grieving process in a disenfranchised loss?
5. How do established beliefs about death and life after death help people who are grieving? How can we help those who have ambiguous (or unestablished) beliefs about death?
6. How can other pets comfort people who are grieving the loss of a pet (or a human)?
7. How does a person's attachment style affect his or her grieving process?

References

Ainsworth, M. D. S. (2006). Attachments and other affectional bonds across the life cycle. In *Attachment across the life cycle* (pp. 41–59). Routledge, New York, NY

Blazina, C., Boyra, G., & Shen-Miller, D. S. (2011). *The psychology of the human-animal bond.* New York, NY: Springer.

Bowlby, J. (1982). *Attachment and loss. Vol. 1: Attachment* (2nd ed). New York, NY: Basic Books.

Carmack, B. J. (2003). *Grieving the death of a pet.* Minneapolis, MN: Augsburg Books.

Field, N. P., Orsini, L., Gavish, R., & Packman, W. (2009). Role of attachment in response to pet loss. *Death Studies, 33*(4), 332–355. doi:10.1080/07481180802705783.

Kohut, H. (1984). *How does analysis cure?* A. Goldberg (Ed.). Chicago, IL: University of Chicago Press. Kurdek, L. A. (2008). Pet dogs as attachment figures. *Journal of Social and Personal Relationships, 25*(2), 247–266.

Kurdek, L. A. (2009). Pet dogs as attachment figures for adult owners. *Journal of Family Psychology, 23*(4), 439–446.

Mahler, M. S. (1972). On the first three subphases of the separation-individuation process. *International Journal of Psycho-Analysis, 53*(3), 333–338.

Packman, W., Field, N. P., Carmack, B. J., & Ronen, R. (2011). Continuing bonds and psychosocial adjustment in pet loss. *Journal of Loss and Trauma, 16*(4), 341–357. doi:10.1080/15325024.2011.572046

Rinpoche, S. (2012). *The Tibetan book of living and dying: A spiritual classic from one of the foremost interpreters of Tibetan Buddhism to the West.* New York, NY: Random House.

Weiss, B. L. (2012). *Many lives, many masters: The true story of a prominent psychiatrist, His Yo.* New York, NY: Simon and Schuster.

Winnicott, D. W. (1986). Transitional objects and transitional phenomena. *In L. Caldwell & H. T. Robinson, The Collected Works of D. W. Wincott, Vol. 9 (pp. 265–288)* . New York, NY: Oxford University Press.

Grief and Grieving as a Grief Counselor: The Loss of My Parents

Luella A. Loudenback, Ed.D., LICSW, CT Lewis-Clark State College, Lewiston, Idaho

FIGURE 3.10. Luella A. Loudenback

Luella A. Loudenback, MSW, LICSW, CT, lives in Tacoma, Washington, and has worked as a clinical social worker for 23 years, particularly in hospice for the last 15 years. She recently returned to school to pursue a doctorate in educational leadership to prepare new social workers for professional practice. She and her husband Aaron have six children and four grandchildren. She can be reached at loudenbackluella1011@gmail.com.

Introduction

Walter and McCoyd (2016) stated that because the death of a parent or parents is universal and expected, it might not be considered highly disruptive for an adult in middle adulthood. Because it is expected, parent loss may be socially minimized; thus, according to Walter and McCoyd (2016), if parental grief is not attended to, it can result in a disenfranchised grief experience. This writing is informed by my compounded, complex grief experience related to the deaths of my parents, early in my career as a clinical hospice social worker.

I have spent the better part of my career counseling grieving people. My personal story and healing narrative inform this writing. I will share my loss history and discuss the compounded and complex nature of my grief experience related to the deaths of my parents. I will share what I experienced and discuss the impact of living my grief process while I worked in clinical practice in hospice and bereavement services, counseling people who were experiencing their own grief. I will identify ways to mitigate transference and countertransference from exposure to vicarious trauma and other peoples' suffering and discuss self-care as a way to maintain resiliency for sustainable practice in the counseling of the grieving client.

My Loss History

My loss history began long before the deaths of the sick and old in my family. My father was a violent, abusive alcoholic and my mother was his primary target when he was in a drunken rage. This exposure to violence resulted in the fundamental loss of a safe and secure childhood and has influenced the rest of my life. Growing up in an alcoholic family, I was determined to live a different kind of life. I left home as a young adult, unconsciously angry and living a pseudo-independent life, typical of the avoidant dismissive attached persona (Worden, 2009). I couldn't have characterized or articulated my way of relating to the world and other people at that time; however, in retrospect, with time and doing my own grief work, I can frame it now as a way to make sense of it and to share my story.

I believed that education was the path to that life. I did not know what I did not know, and education was the start of creating my own life and experiences. While I carried the pain and grief of a traumatized childhood, I did the best I could with my personal and professional life and my growing family. As a result of my education and professional trainings, I understood that to heal my historical loss, I would need more than the information and content that I found in course curriculum. I needed to do some therapeutic work.

In a therapeutic setting, I was able to identify the grief from my childhood and find ways to forgive my parents and to heal. I understood that the healing I sought was deeper than knowing that I needed it. I participated in individual and group therapeutic and reflective work. As the child of an alcoholic, I was also introduced to the 12-step recovery process and the spiritual healing therein.

The confluence of interventions, support programs, and services for healing and growth opened my heart. I understood I needed to heal from trauma exposure and that I needed to grieve that my parents were who they were, human and fallible. Given the professional direction I was taking, it was imperative that I learned that grief is more than an emotional response to the death of a person. It is the pain of loss on many levels.

Levin (2005) cautioned that unattended sorrow narrows the path of a person's life. I began to understand that the paradox of grief work is, according to Skovholt and Trotter-Mathison (2016), about learning to live one's life in the context of the losses that have been experienced, however those losses are defined.

The context of my family dynamics was complex. I understood the disease of addiction, co-dependence, mental illness, family systems, and grief theory from an academic perspective, yet knowing at a cogntive level was far more straightforward than integrating the knowledge and experiencing healing in my heart, healing that would repair my family relationships and help me to construct my own life, values, and belief systems. It is that healing that inspired my commitment to grief work as a field of professional practice. I was called to it. I understood that if I could heal, anyone could. I understood you couldn't get time with your person back and how important it is to do the work of healing before someone dies to mitigate the grief after death.

I had gone to school, found my way to personal therapeutic work, raised my children, and undertook a career as a social worker. My father got sober, and my parents remained committed to each other until his death. It was through the death of my parents that the continuum of healing would become more personal and relevant to the here and now in my career.

FIGURE 3.11. Luella Loudenback's parents

Healing and forgiveness with my parents was in some way a parallel process to my professional career and development. My first social work role after my graduate studies was with veterans in long-term care. I began to see my parents differently and became committed to repairing those relationships and letting go of the hurt I held on to. While I did not realize it at the time, my father's death, the subsequent death of my mother, and my ongoing emotional healing would transform my approach to family, friends, and professional practice.

Case Study

My father died before I started working in hospice. For years, he struggled with a chronic respiratory illness that impacted his ability to breathe. He repeatedly refused to go into hospice services and consequently was hospitalized multiple times for respiratory distress and anxiety. He was always fighting for his life. I would get pleading calls. "Your father is in the hospital, and you need to be here." I would dutifully go home (I lived hundreds of miles away by then) to see him, and so he could see me. I'd been working as a social worker in long-term care with veterans and my understanding of some of what my father had experienced as a GI helped me see him differently. I had forgiven him for the years of abuse exposure and understood that time with him was precious; being there was important.

Because I had found some measure of healing and forgiveness and I knew that I wouldn't get this time back with him or with my mother (she was his caregiver by now), I realized a sense of urgency. I did not ever want to look back at my life and my relationships with them with regret that I wasn't there for them in the ways that I could be. Frankly, that was the easy part.

I saw my father in June 2001, in the hospital, on oxygen, and swollen from steroid medications that are given to relax the bronchial airway. He had stabilized after a 3-day stay and was preparing to be discharged home. That was the last time I saw him alive; little did I know that in less than 30 days he would be dead. He died at age 67, 2 years before I began working in hospice care. I remember the call like it was yesterday. I had this keen perception of energy passing through the room and a powerful sense of calm at the same time. Shortly after learning of my father's death, I experienced what I describe as an out-of-body experience. It was surreal, like the twilight zone, a collision of my reality with that of the rest of the world. I did not return home for the service. I had just been there, after all, and decided to return at another time to scatter his ashes. I remained at work, life as usual.

I have said that I understood that after a person dies, however that happens, you don't get that time back. When someone you love goes into hospice services, there is, in general, time to prepare for the death, time to say what hasn't been said, to ask for and or offer forgiveness. I have seen this again and again in hospice and bereavement work. The sorrow of the death of a person is often more intense when someone has not said "I love you," "I forgive you," "Please forgive me," or "I will be okay." It is the unfinished conversations that keep people up at night. Moreover, for those people who have experienced the death of a loved one suddenly or unexpectedly, grief can be more complicated. These were the griefs that, as I witnessed them, again and again, motivated my commitment to my ongoing grief work, so that I might be kinder, softer, more understanding, and more compassionate with my people.

I recall finding peace in knowing my father was no longer suffering, consistent with how Corr, Nabe, and Corr (2009) suggested a young- to middle-adult might respond in the wake of the death of a parent. Bowlby (1980) described putting up a protective shell, a result of problematic attachment, as a way of coping. I may also have experienced what Walter and McCoyd (2016) described as a dual process, being able to function in day-to-day life while grieving. In my case, these were not mutually exclusive. I began to contemplate my mortality (Walter & McCoyd, 2016) and to reevaluate my priorities and dreams. Suddenly I saw the world differently; this influenced how I treated my children, my friends, and my mother, which is also typical in the wake of the death of a parent (Walter & McCoyd, 2016). Moving through the experience of my father's death, in fact, inspired me professionally to go in a new direction, into end-of-life social work.

Within 2 years of my father's death, I was called to hospice work where facing the pain of others' grief was never far from my own. In the first years of that clinical work, I participated in 2 years of training through a course called the Sacred Art of Living in Bend, Oregon. The foundation of the training is the identification and transformation of spiritual pain (Groves & Groves, 2002). The focus of the program was to learn, as clinicians, staff, and caregivers, to identify the pain that people experience as they prepare to die, to consider the origins of the pain, and to work with the dying person to mitigate the pain so that he or she might find healing and a more peaceful death. The practical application of this approach to spiritual and emotional healing in no small way changed my life.

The 2-year course was specific to life, death, healing, grief, self, and relationships. I discovered through that process that there is healing from grief related to all manner of loss and, beyond that, hope for a joyful life. Clinically, this process provided me with the language and capacity to ask about and articulate what I previously had been unable to do in my personal and professional life. I gained a heightened sense of importance to find healing in my relationship with my mother. I would not get this time back; it was time to say what needed to be said, to ask the hard questions, do what needed to be done and to forgive and heal. Moreover, I wanted to truly be the person who helped others navigate the pain of grief and offer the hope for healing, to be a conduit of hope to others who might be suffering in their grief.

This newfound drive grounded me as daughter, mother, sister, friend, and grief counselor. My resolve solidified, having transformed much of my childhood grief, I could offer testimony of hope for finding healing with people who were hopelessly lost in their grief. I could be a messenger that the pain would change and that lives and hearts could heal. I had worked in hospice for 3 years when my mother died.

I always felt honored when people sought grief support and education from me personally or in the program that I coordinated for many years in my community. I had done very powerful and transformative healing work, which had informed my capacity to be present for the pain of others. Because of this, work, I was able to find healing with my mother and joy at being able to be present for her and my family when they needed me. I had no regrets because I had done my work with her before she died. My training and personal experiences with both my parents prepared me with an inherent willingness to listen to the individual narratives of the bereaved; I could listen without judgment, encourage the healing process, and provide hope that they too could find their way.

I have always called mother loss "the one great loss." Corr and colleagues (2009) describe the complexities of healing from parent loss as being more complicated when things are left unsaid or business unfinished. Mothers teach us who we are in the world, how to be. Good, bad, or indifferent, there is a grief response when a mother dies. In more complicated relationships, unfinished relationship issues, grief can be more complex healing and peace may be harder to find (Walter & McCoyd, 2016). This was not the case for me with my grief related to losing my mother.

I had lived through the death of my father, and my mother had been dancing with death since I was 14 years old. She was given months to live at that time and, despite being plagued with baldness and other chronic conditions from toxic cancer treatments, she survived. Our family always recognized this as a gift because the medical community predicted her death before she turned 40. She was 67 when she died.

Because of her history with illness, my mother was monitored regularly for recurrent cancer and secondary illnesses that might present themselves. At age 66 she was diagnosed with stage four colon cancer. Too far gone, there was little that could be done other than to keep her comfortable and safe and prepare for a peaceful death—all with which I was familiar as a hospice social worker. I often found myself taking on the role of a social worker with her, my siblings, and medical personnel. I traveled home to see her in February 2005 and spent 10 days with her. This provided respite for my sister from the hands-on care she was providing, common when family members live nearby. This time was essential to our relationship. My education, training, and spiritual healing allowed me to be with her in intimate and purposeful ways. I was committed to making the experience meaningful for both of us. I got to ask the hard questions about her life as a child, and mother; about decisions she had made, and other long unasked questions about our family. I got to know her, really know her. Because this was my time to ask and share, I let her get to know me too. She died in June of that year.

Only having been a hospice social worker for 3 years at the time of her death, I was still learning about life balance and self-care. The time after my mother's death took a toll on me emotionally and spiritually, but because we had done good "work" together before her death, I had no regrets. I understood the importance of the relationship work before her death. Having been present to that experience was a bridge to healing after her death, and I leaned into it (Meagher & Balk, 2013). Not that I did not grieve; I did: While my heart was broken, there was no unfinished business. I had to feel my feelings and mourn the death of my mother; I couldn't just pick up the phone to get her doughnut recipe. I also had to mourn the deaths of both of my parents, for new grief melds with older grief. And their deaths repositioned me in the world and in my family. I had to learn how I fit in, in those places and spaces that had been buffered by them. I also understood that this was normal.

Moreover, I had to get on with the business of life. It was tricky to balance the day-to-day grief work with clients while being profoundly sad. In the context of a complex family history and the compounded grief, I saw everything differently. I had come face to face with the mortality of my family and, inherently, my own, and the finite nature of life (Walter & McCoyd, 2016). I had to learn what would trigger my grief (Skovholt & Trotter-Mathison, 2016) and prepare to take care of myself while still being present to support others, which is why it is so important that grief counseling professionals find ways to take care of themselves in the process of helping others.

On Being a Grieving Grief Counselor

Most of my professional career has been spent counseling people who are in grief. What I know for sure is that grief is unique, individual, and highly contextual to one's life, relationship, and experiences with someone who has died. Despite the plethora of information about the experience of grief or perhaps because of it, as a culture we do little to allow for the grieving process, often leaving our grieving friends and neighbors to cope in isolation (Cable, 1998). Unless someone has experienced the death of someone or has had a similar loss, it is unlikely that the experience will be truly understood. Perhaps because it is painful to witness and people perceive an inability to help (Bowlby, 1980), for whatever reasons, there seems to be an inability to fully appreciate the personal grief experience as a unique, individual, and emotional process in a consistent and meaningful way. Harvard-trained theologian Stephen Jenkinson characterizes our culture as grief illiterate, adding that we have no language for what happens in grief (Hoffner, 2015).

In the early years of my career as a hospice social worker, I learned the language of grief by immersion. Daily, I was actively and intimately involved with patients and families who were living with the knowledge that at some point, perhaps at any moment, death would come, entering their hearts and their homes, forever changing their lives. I loved hospice work, the experience of being present with people who fear the unknown of the inevitable, being able to be the strong one because the pain was not mine. It was easy to offer compassion and support because I understood it and I understood my role—the familiar detachment of an outsider, there without personal emotional involvement—to allow each of them to express their feelings in whatever way they might.

It was a strange juxtaposition, to experience my grief and to be there for others. I learned to situate myself as the compassionate professional. I learned to compartmentalize my work, to mind my healing heart by learning to identify my triggers (Skovholt & Trotter-Mathison, 2016) such as smells, songs, and similar diagnoses, and to take tender care of myself at those times. I had to remind myself daily that the pain of others was and is not my pain, and I found strength from my healing to be able to do that. There is a fine balance between being professional and tender.

Several years after my mother's death, I moved into bereavement services as an educational counselor and transitioned into the formal role of being a full-time grief counselor and organizing grief services for hospice. Every day I made outreach calls, counseled individuals and families, facilitated support groups, and coordinated a grief support program with upwards of 800 bereaved individuals at any given time. I became acutely aware of the need for balance to sustain in this work.

The role of the social worker, counselor, or other practitioner in grief work is vital. Grief counselors are there for people in grief when the rest of the world is unable to, for whatever reason. Because each person has a unique threshold for tolerating the pain of others, it is important to find ways to sustain in this work.

Recommendations for Sustaining in Grief Work

Grieving is a process. It takes time. It is not a prescriptive experience. It is from this place of knowing that I make recommendations to clinicians working with or preparing to work with people who are in grief and who are suffering from loss related to death or other some other type of loss experience so that they might sustain in this area of practice.

First and foremost, I encourage clinicians to do their own healing or therapy work. Some academic programs require this; I encourage it. Worden (2009) recommends a proactive approach to prepare counselors by having them actively face their loss history. This is a way to deal with unresolved issues and to explore resources that are available to people in grief. The process of doing personal therapy work can prepare and sensitize individuals to work with clients who are in pain. This also can mitigate the risk of transference and countertransference when clinicians work with people who seek support. Healing work for clinicians can provide protective factors to deal with the grief of others.

Second, it is essential to practice appropriate boundary setting. Learning to set boundaries is also a skill to help minimize the risk of transference and countertransference. To know where a counselor's role begins and ends and where the client's experience begins and ends is essential in counseling and therapeutic work. Doing client-focused work is not the place for clinicians to work out their personal issues. This should be done in a setting that fits the clinician, in supervision, with peers, or other supports to process any feelings that come up. If a clinician cannot maintain appropriate boundaries, according to Worden (2009), it is not only compassionate, but responsible to refer a client to someone else.

Third, do not assume anything about the client's grief experience or emotional process. No one can ever really know how another person feels; no one knows what is best for someone else who is in pain and despair. Much of what I have spent years doing with grieving people is re-educating them about what grief is and what it is not. Myths such as, "You'll get over it," "He or she is in a better place," and "I understand how you feel," can hurt a grieving person more than help.

One of the biggest assumptions that people make is related to grief support groups. I received calls all the time saying, "My sister thinks I need a group" or "My cousin went to a group." I would have to ask, "Well, what do you think you need?" to help conversation unfold. Not everybody is suited for group work for any number of reasons. Perhaps they are introverted, or more private about sharing their experiences; perhaps there are underlying mental health issues that would preclude them from engaging in a group context in a meaningful way without being disruptive to others; perhaps it's too soon after a death; and, most importantly, perhaps being exposed to multiple loss narratives could re-traumatize the person.

What works to help one person cope may not work for another. When you assume you know what another is feeling, the person and his or her experience can become devalued and minimized, and his or her pain can become compounded. It is important to understand that culture can also impact a person's grief response and his or her interest or willingness to reach our for or accept support. Additionally, within families, each person has his or her own grief response. Every individual has a unique, personal response to loss. Accordingly, it is important to be armed with as much knowledge as possible about grief theory and cultural and faith orientations and to remember that grief is a healthy, reasonable emotional response to death (Corr et al., 2009; Doka & Davidson, 1998; Worden, 2009).

Grief is not a pathological experience but an individual, personal, and intimate process influenced by variables that are a part of each grievers' experiences and relationships. In his attachment theory and stages of grief model, Bowlby (1980) describes grief as instinctual, adaptable, and valuable to the bereaved. Grief in itself can be complicated. Grief is not something to get over; it is not linear or time-oriented. It is messy, awkward, and painful. Understanding that grief is normal does not preclude the clinician's risk of burnout or being vicariously traumatized. Each of us has a threshold for tolerating others' pain; thus, we all must find ways to take care of ourselves.

The assumption that a grief counselor should know everything about grief is a misbelief; and it is a setup for expectations that will invariably leave the grief counsleor feeling inadequate. Because each person's grief is unique, clinicians cannot know or anticipate a person's experience. Moreover, an unreasonable drive to always know what to say can impact a clinician's self-perception. There is nothing wrong with not knowing what to say. One way that I navigate unknown differences, whether they are cultural, racial/ethnic, faith based, or most importantly, loss types such as a parent, spouse, or child loss, protracted hospice deaths, or sudden deaths related to suicide or homicide, is to be honest.

I am the first one to say "I don't know what to say." I encourage clinicians to own the not knowing and to be honest about it. Supporting people in grief is often more about listening, allowing for them to say whatever they need to, without judgment. People want and need to be heard and to release the pain, even if for a moment.

Finally, I encourage clinicians to take care of themselves (Skovholt & Trotter-Mathiason, 2016), whatever that means to them. Only they can identify what they need to have a balanced life. Balance in the physical, spiritual, emotional, and social parts of life is fundamental to sustainability in this work. They should learn to give themselves the compassion, kindness, gentleness, and understanding that they will give to the people who seek their counsel.

Doing grief work with heartbroken people is the most rewarding work I have ever done, and it can take a toll. I hope that sharing my history, the narrative of my grief experience related to the death of my parents, and how I have sustained in my work, is helpful. There are many ways to practice self-care and to guard against transference, counter-transference, and burnout—much more than could be covered, here. I hope that what I have shared, that which I consider important, will serve others along the way.

Questions for Discussion

1. Discuss the myths about grief and the process of healing that might put someone at risk for having a complicated grief experience.
2. Imagine that you are offering grief support to a grieving family. There are several adult children of a man who has died on hospice. There is reported conflict between two of his children and each of them voices tension with the other when you speak with them. Discuss your plan for support as the bereavement counselor. How would you navigate grief support for two daughters who have individually responded to your outreach?
3. In small groups, identify and discuss what you will do to practice self-care to sustain in your role as a social worker. (While bubble baths and chamomile tea are fine, go deeper and be reflective about what restores your spirit.)
4. Role-play in pairs: One person is the grief counselor, the other a bereaved person who is distraught. How would you respond? After 10 minutes or so, switch roles and then debrief the experience. Be mindful of what was helpful and not helpful to you when you were in the role of the bereaved. After a break, debrief the experience in a larger group.

References

Bowlby, J. (1980). *Attachment and loss: Loss, sadness, and depression* (Vol. 3). New York, NY: Basic Books.

Cable, D. G. (1998). Grief in the American culture. In K. J. Doka & J. D. Davidson (Eds.), *Living with grief. Who we are, how we grieve* (pp. 61–70). New York, NY: Routledge.

Corr, C. A., Nabe, C. M., & Corr, D. M. (2009). *Death and dying, life and living.* Belmont, CA: Wadsworth.

Doka, K. J., & Davidson, J. D. (Eds.) (1998). *Living with grief. Who we are, how we grieve.* New York, NY: Routledge.

Groves, R. F., & Groves, M. L. (2002). *Sacred art of dying. Unit 1: Diagnosing and addressing spiritual pain* (3rd ed.). Bend, OR: Sacred Art of Living Center.

Hoffner, E. (2015). As we lay dying. Steven Jenkinson on how we deny our mortality. *The Sun*, 476. Retrieved from https://www.thesunmagazine.org/issues/476/as-we-lay-dying

Levin, S., (2005). *Unattended sorrow: Recovering from loss and reviving the heart*. Emmaus, PA: Rodale.

Meagher, D. K., & Balk, D. E. (Eds.) (2013). *Handbook of thanatology: The essential body of knowledge for the study of death, dying, and bereavement*. New York, NY: Routledge.

Skovholt, T. M., & Trotter-Mathison, M. (2016). *The resilient practitioner: Burnout and compassion fatigue prevention and self-care strategies for the helping professions*. New York, NY: Routledge.

Walter, C. A., & McCoyd, J. L. (2016). *Grief and loss across the lifespan: A biopsychosocial perspective*. New York, NY: Springer.

Worden, J. W. (2009). *Grief counseling and grief therapy: A handbook for the mental health practitioner* (5th ed.). New York, NY: Springer.

Multiple Loss: A Home to Natural Disaster and the Sudden Loss of a Parent

Kathleen Werner, PhD, LSW, ASW-G, CCM, Hackensack Meridian Health-Southern Ocean Medical Center New Jersey

FIGURE 3.12. Kathleen Werner

Kathleen Werner is a licensed social worker who has been practicing in the hospital and post-acute care setting for over 7 years and has recently become an adjunct professor in New Jersey. She received her PhD in social work from Adelphi University in 2018 and her MSW from Stockton University in 2011. In addition, Kathleen has received certifications in advanced social work in gerontology (ASW-G) and case management (CCM). Her research focus is on the use of evidence-based practices to treat substance use disorders and her most recent research was focused on social workers' knowledge, attitudes, and use of evidence-based practices for the treatment of substance use disorders in older adults. She hopes to expand this research to all substance abuse treatment professionals.

Framing the Loss

In the fall of 2012, I was working part time as a hospital social worker near the coastal community where I lived in southern New Jersey. I was also commuting 3 hours each way twice a week up to Adelphi University in New York where I was a second-year full-time PhD student. While the workload was heavy, I was juggling it all with the help of my understanding family, friends, and coworkers. Maintaining a 3.5 GPA finally seemed easy when I was interested in the material I was learning.

The first 2 months of the semester breezed by; I was checking items off my assignment to-do list and moving easily through my work during the last week of October when I received the first notification of tropical storm Sandy heading up the eastern seaboard with the potential to impact coastal New Jersey. While I did not have time to be worried, the notifications became warnings, and I was forced to put homework on hold while I prepared my tired old beach house for the worst. Not long after I refocused on my schoolwork, I received notice that the storm had surpassed hurricane status, become a superstorm, and made a sharp turn toward New Jersey. Voluntary evacuations became mandatory. I did what any tired, stressed, and level-headed PhD student would do: packed two oversized plastic bins with textbooks and a small bag with clothing and evacuated to my parents' home just a few miles inland. The superstorm wasn't changing course, and what would occur over the next 24 hours was something I never could have imagined or prepared for.

The Primary Loss

Later that evening superstorm Sandy made landfall, and had I stayed in my own home I would have been swimming through 5 feet of water on the first floor and my car would have floated away. While for a moment I felt relieved, the relief did not last, as the tidal floods and relentless rains began to fill the lagoons behind my parents' house. Despite their house being several miles inland, just after midnight, over three feet of water made its way into their house. My car was filled with salt water, my childhood photos and books were floating in the bedroom I grew up in. The place where I sought shelter from the storm and everything in it was waterlogged and destroyed.

In the days following superstorm Sandy everything was a blur. Just days earlier, every free minute I had was spent studying; now, every free minute was spent tearing out wet sheetrock and emptying the contents of my home into dumpsters, only stopping for meals when a volunteer appeared at our doorstep with one. Despite all of my best efforts to salvage some of my favorite items and memories from the home, the damage was extensive and profound. Until October 29, 2012 I had felt like a successful independent woman capable of overcoming any obstacle in my path. But now, the necessities that I took for granted were gone. No car, no Internet, no bed, and no place to wash the few clothes I had left. I became reliant on the charity of others. I realized how many people experience life like this every day with or without a storm.

Despite feeling like my world had just ended, life around me was still moving at full speed, and I had to quickly buy a car, return to work, and get back to my commute to the classroom in order to not lose my job or my course credits. At the hospital I spent my work days helping others recover from the physical and emotional effects of the storm while not giving myself the time to process my own experiences. After work, I would spend late nights awake catching up on homework anywhere I could find electricity and Internet. I mustered the strength to power through, to complete all my assignments, and finished the semester up strong. I finally saw the light at the end of the tunnel.

While normalcy was still a world away, I had adjusted to my temporary living situation and was ready to celebrate the semester break and holiday season with my family and friends. That Christmas was the most memorable to date—our Christmas tree was spray painted on the exposed insulation in the walls and gifts included sheet rock, new work gloves, and masks donated from local charities. We celebrated health, and happiness, and family.

FIGURE 3.13. Theodore (Ted) Werner, retired social worker

The Secondary Loss

Just as I started to see a hope and light ahead, my father was unexpectedly admitted to the hospital where I worked the day after Christmas for a gastrointestinal bleed. My coworkers were now caring for my father. I was working in the same building helping others get back on their feet while the ground was falling out below mine. Just as my spring semester was beginning, due to complications, worsening conditions, and an extensive cardiac medical history that was making treatment more difficult, my dad was transferred to a Maryland hospital over 3 hours away where he could be treated by a team of specialists. I put countless miles on my new car driving from New Jersey to New York for school, back to New Jersey for work, then down to Maryland visit my dad while new doctors worked tirelessly to pinpoint and treat the source of an unknown infection.

Despite all treatments and efforts by the doctors, on February 10, 2013, in the wake of losing my house, my car, all my material goods, and my priceless keepsakes to superstorm Sandy, I lost my father to a systemic septic infection that he fought hard against for nearly six weeks. Prior to his illness, I thought the hardest days were behind me. I was broken and destroyed. It felt like I was thrown from the emotional rollercoaster I had been riding for nearly 4 months.

I remember calling my manager at the hospital and the program director at school and informing them. I remember dragging myself back into work and classes days after the funeral services. I remember being offered a leave of absence, but I was so close to this doctorate I could taste it. Just days before my dad died, I completed my final competency exam and I only needed five more courses to officially complete the program. So, I refocused on the goals knowing that my biggest supporter would not be there to see me through this on this journey.

Professional Impact

The summer of 2013 things finally started looking up again. I finally moved back into my home after nearly 7 months and I finished my last course requirements, feeling like I could breathe again. But it was only then, as the summer ended, that I finally had time to process the last year of my life. The physical things that I lost in superstorm Sandy, the things that broke me and devastated me, were now just things. I had lost my father, my inspiration, my biggest fan, and I only now had the time, energy, and emotional capacity to finally mourn. It took a long time to realize that I wasn't healing.

The impact was visible in both my personal and professional lives. I shut down, gained weight, lost motivation, put up emotional barriers between the people and family still left in my life, and forgot about my goals. At work, I saw it when I would become angry with families forcing treatments on their elderly loved ones because they were not ready for hospice. I would think, "You should feel lucky you had as much time as you did" or "I lost my dad when he was only 62 years old; you shouldn't complain about losing your parents when they are 95 years old." I saw it when I became judgmental of patients who resorted to or relapsed on drugs and alcohol because of a bad day while I managed to stay clean despite all that I had endured. My empathy and compassion for the patients and their families was fading. I was no longer the social worker I once was; instead, I lost focus of the inherent values, beliefs, and ethics central to being a social worker.

Self-Care Recommendations

It has not been an easy journey to heal on my own for I'd lost my focus, my drive, and my passion. I was so busy just trying stay busy and be distracted from everything I was also ignoring the ongoing responsibilities and requirements I still needed to fulfill to obtain my PhD. I saw the thing I fought so hard for in the aftermath of not one but two traumatic events slipping away from me, and I knew I needed to fight for it again. But this time I realized I could not do it alone. I had to stop and ask for help.

This time I asked my family not only support and encourage me to move onward with my journey, but also with help with the basics: I could not keep juggling work, my dissertation, and managing my house alone. I started by asking for help with everyday tasks like dishes, laundry, and grocery shopping. I cut back some of the extra hours I was working at the hospital. I dedicated more time each week to my dissertation and to myself.

By handing off responsibility and recognizing I was giving too much of my time to work, I was able to focus not only on my education, but also on the self-care I had been neglecting for far too long. I rejoined the gym, I started participating in social activities with friends again, I made time to relax. Taking this time to refocus, I was able to restore my sense of self, successfully complete my PhD program, and regain the skills I needed to be able to treat and help my patients with and open heart and an open mind.

Social workers and social work students often learn about and teach about self-care, but few take the time to practice what they preach. My advice to anyone who experiences trauma or works with clients who have: Take the time to make sure you and your clients are getting all of the care needed to maintain a healthy outlook on life.

Reflection Questions

1. What does the concept of "home" mean to you?
2. How do you imagine multiple and unexpected levels of trauma may impact your interactions with clients?
3. For you, what does it mean to be on autopilot, and how might you catch yourself from not processing your traumatic experiences?
4. What hobbies or activities could you include in your personal life to help prevent compassion fatigue and maintain your integrity as an ethical social worker? How can you learn to practice what you preach?

Winter Melting

Jean Toner, MSW, PhD, Arizona State University, Flagstaff, Arizona

FIGURE 3.14. Jean Toner

Jean Toner, MSW, PhD is an instructor in Arizona State University's Online MSW Program. She formerly was an associate professor in the Department of Sociology, Anthropology, and Social Work at Central Michigan University. Prior to her positions in higher education, she practiced in communities and agencies in clinical and administrative positions, and currently serves her home community of Flagstaff, Arizona, in a variety of voluntary commitments. She has a passion for hiking, camping, and stargazing in her beloved southwestern canyonlands and mesas. Jean Toner may be reached at jmtoner@asu.edu.

Content warning: Please note that this section of the chapter includes a discussion of sexual assault.

I don't remember the first act of violation, nor do I remember the last. I have spotty memories of the years in between (often terror-laden flashes of visual or aural representations). Recollecting has been an uneven and unbalanced process, and utterly incomplete. It has been slow. I don't have a narrative. But my body remembers; my body is the narrative.

There was intervening relief in later years. I stole my parents' beer. I stole their cigarettes. It was my relief and my resistance. They were too impaired to notice. I got demerits from a nun because I smelled bad. Bathing was not a dependable practice in my house, and not necessarily safe. I used talcum powder in my hair because I heard it cut the oil. Mostly I just pretended nothing happened the night before. I tried to block it out when the girls laughed at me on the bus.

There were some good times. My family went camping during the summers. We (unwittingly) covered much of the same territory as the Lewis and Clark expedition. I later learned that their historic expedition, like my family's, was an act of domination and that it laid a path for violent oppression. I did not know that attempted genocide had been perpetrated across the Western landscape, but I do remember feeling what I know today to be deep cellular grief at the Little Bighorn. I was about 10 years old.

In later years it would seem to me that there were concentric circles of triumph and suffering ... nesting states of me, my family, my neighborhoods, the landscape beyond ... all moving out in concentric circles. I did not necessarily know the word or the meaning of resilience, but looking back I know I lived it. I had escape hatches, painting, reading, excelling in school (unnoticed at home), writing, and accepting a welcome into homes of friends. I trace these trails through escape hatches with profound gratitude. They got me through unspoken pain and bewilderment. Those trails through escape hatches enabled me to be here now and speaking.

Intervention/Self-Care/Healing

Today I know that I have suffered from an array of complex traumatic stress disorders (Courtois & Ford, 2009). Although labeled as disorder, it is truly a form of profound loss. In trauma, we suffer loss of safety, loss of predictability in our daily lives, loss of connectedness to the present moment, loss of the ability to stay in our bodies, loss of a sense of what is real and what is not real. Other losses include loss of happiness, loss of confidence in self and in the world around us, loss of trust in self and others. Given that complex traumatic stress is at its core about loss, I will refer to the phenomenon as complex traumatic stress *responses*, rather than disorders. Words matter, and the word *responses* better captures the dynamic response to loss as one of resilience and one that demonstrates the adaptive capacity of the array of defensive responses to unspeakable psycho-physical insult.

The phenomenon of complex traumatic stress does not fit neatly into one diagnostic category, such as PTSD (post-traumatic stress disorder) (Courtois & Ford, 2009). In addition to complex traumatic stress, the phenomenon is referred to as developmental trauma disorder, which contextualizes responses to abuse within developmental stages (van der Kolk, 2014). The phenomenon includes responses that involve anxiety, vigilance, dissociation, personality structures, thought disordering, and the originating, reacting, and attendant neural processes. Complex trauma response/developmental trauma is not traceable to a discreet event or confined to a discreet array of psychological responses. Its complexity is the very essence of variable defenses, energetic discharges, somatization, and occasional delusional interpretations of events. Complex trauma response is born of long-term interpersonal abuse, coupled with absence of protection or reality check. Surviving such a pervasive and unnatural state requires an enormously complex defensive response.

My description of the process of coming to terms with the true nature of my history will follow the three-stage recovery model developed by Judith L. Herman (1992) in her seminal work first published in the early 1990s. Her brilliance in understanding the sequela created by maltreatment, and her understanding of what is needed to effectively treat the consequences of relational abuses, continues today to be a guide for recovering from complex traumatic stress/developmental trauma. She describes the first stage as establishing safety, the second stage as remembrance and mourning, and the third stage as reconnection and expansion of positive social connections (Herman 1992).

Coming Into Awareness: Naming and Creating Safety

The first stage began for me with getting sober. I had joined my parents in practicing alcoholism and added in other forms of drug abuse. It was difficult to name myself an alcoholic because I was not "as bad" as my father or mother. I was also 30-plus years younger and had not had as much time to ravage my body when I got sober at age 28. Coming to terms with that basic admission of alcoholism opened an inner door that was characterized by intrusive and horrific memory flashes, nightmares, and a level of mistrust that sometimes bordered on paranoia. At the time I could have been diagnosed with multiple DSM illnesses and disorders, but the truth was, and is, that I was suffering from the unnamed complex of responses—physical, emotional, and mental—resulting from child abuse.

Fortunately, caring and corrective relationships guided me to help. In the years of early recovery, the presence of caring relationships, coupled with psychotherapy, allowed me to slowly begin to tell my stories. The combination of a supportive community and the safety derived from a powerful psycho-spiritual belief system allowed the arduous process of discovery and un-covery to proceed.

I gradually learned to trust. Much of my recovery involved writing. I have been a diarist since around the age of 10. My diary was my best friend. "She" was the outlet for my anguish and bewilderment and the repository of my deepest longings. This practice of writing was steadying and hopeful and continued to be a central recovery practice. Other recovery practices in stage 1 of healing included membership in recovery networks, women's support groups, and rediscovering my connection with nature and its capacity to heal.

In the later years of this early stage, I was encouraged by a counselor to consider becoming a counselor myself; she believed I had a gift for it. As I began my professional training, my understanding of myself became more layered: I could observe and name the responses I was studying as ones I had adopted as an adjustment to unnatural acts and conditions. The fact that there was a name for what I experienced gave me hope for deeper recovery and partially neutralized the shame. I began to understand that shame—that sense of being irredeemably flawed—was born of lies I was told about personal worthlessness coupled with the invisibility born of neglect.

Remembrance and Mourning

My professional training took me through an undergraduate degree and substance abuse counselor training and would later take me through an MSW program. My work in the early years of my career was in substance abuse services. While there were some invitations for counter-transference, there were more opportunities for identification. I identified as an alcoholic in recovery and was able to join with clients from that perspective. I believe there may have been some blind spots, particularly around the potentially deadly impact of domestic violence. But for the most part, my recovery from child abuse seemed to be a separate process from my professional engagement as a substance abuse counselor.

That changed. I moved from the community within which I got sober to a tiny rural coastal community in the southern region of the United States. There were no substance abuse counselor jobs for me. There was a job available in Child Protective Services (CPS), and I accepted the job offer. It was at this point where my traumatic history intersected with my professional social work. I can best characterize the next 2-and-a-half years as a descent into darkness with no guide or signposts. My community was gone, my trusted others were not in my life on a daily basis, and I no longer had the support of a therapeutic community. I deeply regretted the decision to move but did not see a way out (this is, itself, a symptom of complex trauma/developmental trauma). When having to investigate a report of child abuse, I feared that behind every door I knocked on, stood my father. I was terrified.

The first part of my brain to go to sleep in the midst of trauma was the speech center. I lost my voice. In losing my voice, I lost the ability I had developed to make sense of events and people and situations. My world was collapsing, and it did not make sense. I kept showing up for my job, trying to "be good." I walked through what felt like a half-life (it was dissociation) and lost touch with how I was appearing to the world outside of myself. Any sense of identity was failing. Fortunately, some caring and alert coworkers intervened. There was the nurse in the County Health Department ("Jean, you have to get some help; you are depressed") and the social services agency's contract child psychologist ("It is time for you to leave this work and get some help"). I am grateful for their intervention. I have no idea in hindsight if I hurt clients. I hope not. Fortunately, I worked with excellent social workers who stepped in as I was failing.

This decompensation led me to stage 2, remembrance and mourning. I moved to a metropolitan area close to the rural coastal home community and found a "therapist for the therapists" who skillfully led me through this stage of healing. This stage involved making space for the process of allowing my body's story to emerge in the absence of a cognitive narrative. The vulnerability and confusion of discovering a deeper level of injury (that felt like *damage*) was frightening, but also freeing. Some of the activities and encounters contributing to this deeper level of healing included expressive arts as the following:

- Re-engagement with my poetry (knowing from years of writing that the muses tell truths that my conscious mind can hide)
- Journaling
- Drawing and coloring feelings that had no words
- Drawing and coloring memories that had no cognitive narrative

I gained a deeper appreciation for the harm done to me in childhood, gained a starker view of the reality of the years of abuse and neglect, and developed a greater appreciation for the resilience that upheld me throughout those years, and for the angels (families of my friends) who had been put in my path. The most significant growth during this stage came through my connections with other "wounded healers," along with people who did not carry the same scars but were able to enter into the experience and language of healing from complex trauma. I was not alone or an oddity. Connecting with complex trauma practitioners and completing graduate school affirmed my voice and worth.

This stage took me through mourning the losses sustained from a painful childhood. The losses were many: loss of safety, loss of certainty, loss of worth, loss of coherence and predictability, loss of voice, absence of love, absence of connection, sense of helplessness. The recognition of loss led me into grieving the losses and the absences. I discovered grief to be the deeper level of healing following affect stabilization. I found grief is as complex as trauma. My response to the core issues of loss prior to recovery, and often in recovery, was to "be strong." "Being strong" was actually a coping strategy that separated me from my trauma and prevented me from being vulnerable or authentic. I learned to trust on a deeper level. These were profound and reorganizing realizations. I was able to grieve, to connect and learn, to experience rage, then let go of it.

I came out of that time of powerful healing—remembrance and mourning—a calmer, less frightened, less anxious, and less driven person, with greater skills in affect management. Eventually, I returned to the coastal rural community and opened a private practice. As the only clinical social worker within 60 miles, my practice was busy. It was during those years that I developed the skill of consciously listening to clients with my whole body. This is a gift of trauma recovery. As I sat with another, with my whole body listening, there was a vibratory response of "I hear you," "I get it." I had integrated affect management skills and mindfulness, so was acutely aware of any emerging responses I may have experienced and could deal with any triggering immediately and in an effective manner. I learned to pace myself in order to maintain that level of intensity and intimacy. I could not see more than six clients a day, and no more than 20 per week. I guarded my schedule that allowed 3 days off per week (at a minimum). I blended fun/play, physical activity, and soothing practices in my self-care regimen. Some examples of activities that worked for me included weight training, walking and hiking, golf, empty time in nature, bird watching, and sitting on the beach and listening to the sounds of sea and wind. Staying grounded and connected with my body and with our great Mother Earth enabled me to maintain balance and energy. I gradually developed a supportive network of safe friends that required driving some distances to get-togethers, but to this day are sustaining relationships.

Reconnection and Expansion of Social Networks

Changes in my life prompted a move from the rural coastal South to the high desert, mesas, and canyonlands of the southwest. Herman's third state of trauma recovery was well underway in the networks and relationships I had forged in the coastal community. I carried them with me (as I continued to carry friends with me from high school days, the "angel families"). I did not feel alone stepping out into the southwest. My clinical skills and my ability to listen with my whole body seemed intact. But I was discovering I wanted something else. I wanted to take my years of clinical practice and pass on those skills as an educator. Fully in stage three of healing, I was able to forge new relationships in both professional and social arenas. Those new relationships joined with relationships I brought with me from earlier homes. There was a sense of richness and fulfillment during those years and an enormous sense of agency and accomplishment in successfully completing my doctoral studies and securing a tenure-track appointment at a university in the Midwest.

The new job required relocation, so once again I had to immediately begin the process of building new relationships. The most critical recovery requirement, from my experience, was and is supportive, caring relationships. I needed to affirm my identity, as a "wounded healer" and trauma survivor/thriver, held in a web of relationships that affirmed who I am and supported finding out who I could be as an emerging teacher and scholar. In the midst of fulfillment and a sense of agency and stability, a serendipitous relationship catapulted me back into feelings of the child who lived in my parents' house. I share this fact because I discovered that there exists within me a dormant fracturing that can reexpress itself even after years of recovery and years of being able to share my vulnerability and recovery when partnering in healing with others. I knew what to do: Find a trauma therapist, write, write, write, walk on the earth and gain strength and healing from the earth, engage in soothing and affect management practices, and most critically maintain connection with others. I did those things. Identity and stability and fulfillment returned, but with a recognition that complex trauma creates conditions of fragility, even after long periods of healing. I also learned that fragility is an invitation to deeper encountering with history and self. I wrote this poem during that time:

winter moon –

full and haloed …

I need no reminder

of cold, but do remember

that ice and deep sleep

can save a child.

FIGURE 3.15.

The skills I have acquired over the years, reaching out, connecting with supportive and caring social circles, speaking my truth, remembering that I am not my trauma, and working with my arousal system through mindfulness, yoga, and meditation, end up enhancing my life and make me more available to others. Working out of the ice and deep sleep that saved this child is its own gift—a gift for sharing.

Concluding Thoughts

History can be destiny but does not have to be. History can be the navigating force in a path of healing. That path of healing can be shared with others; we can be "wounded healers." But we must do our own work first and forever. We must attend to our own recovery, walk through the terror, pick up shards of history and fashion them into the vessel that encases all of who we are. We can discover that we can live our possibilities, not our limitations. We can accept our occasional relapses and pick ourselves up again and reconnect. We can reconnect with healthy boundaries that we have learned and developed as we have strengthened in our identity, our sense of self. When I lived at the beach, I would find "broken" whelk shells. Waves had battered and shattered their outer shell and left exposed the spiral inner core. I called them "dancer shells." The exquisite inner core appeared to be pirouetting—demonstrating inner strength, persistence, and unique beauty. Wounded healers are like the dancer shells living at the nexus of power, history, and renewal, poised for celebration within our singularly beautiful web of connection.

Some Questions to Ponder

1. What feelings were you aware of in your body as you read this story? What does that awareness teach you about your own history or attitudes or beliefs regarding the connection between personal wounding and the choice to enter a clinical career?
2. Have you known a "wounded healer" and what have you learned from that person? If you are a wounded healer, what self-care practices do you believe you will find most helpful?

References

Courtois, C. A. & Ford, J. D. (2009). *Treating complex traumatic stress disorders: Scientific foundations and therapeutic models.* New York, NY: Guilford.

Herman, J. L. (1992). *Trauma and recovery: The aftermath of violence—from domestic abuse to political terror.* New York, NY: Basic Books.

Van der Kolk, B. (2014). *The body keeps the score: Brain, mind, and body in the healing Of trauma.* New York, NY: Penguin.

The Loss of Your Brother

Dylesia Barner, MSW, LCSW, Existence, Consciousness, Bliss Counseling, Psychotherapy & Wellness Center, Portsmouth, Virginia

FIGURE 3.16. Dylesia Barner

Dylesia Barner, LCSW is an author, speaker, and entrepreneur from Portsmouth, Virginia. She graduated from Old Dominion University in 2011 with a bachelor of science in communication and Norfolk State University in 2013 with a master of social work. She is currently a doctor of social work student at Millersville University. Dylesia owns Existence, Consciousness, Bliss Counseling, Psychotherapy, and Wellness Center, a mental health practice located in Nashville, Tennessee. She is also the founder and president of Trap Therapist, a platform connecting mental health professionals from urban, low-income backgrounds with one another and with clients from marginalized communities. Passionate about using transparency to humanize therapists in a way that breaks mental health stigma, Dylesia regularly creates conversations around emotional healing, breaking generational curses, and the differences that exist within minority subcultures. She has traveled as far as to Europe to deliver presentations to practitioners and laypersons on topics such as spiritual abuse, a form of religious trauma that often impacts vulnerable populations. In 2012, Dylesia published her first book *Encouragement at Your Fingertips: 365 Days of Inspiration.* She continues to develop self-help and Christian devotional content through her website dylesiabarner.com.

In February 2015, I lost my 21-year old brother in a fatal car accident. A pre-licensed social worker at the time, I had recently been laid off from a community mental health agency and was struggling to make ends meet by working part time as a private practice resident. Certain that losing my main source of income without warning would be the lowest point in my new year, I woke up one Sunday morning to find that things had gotten worse. Several "PLEASE CALL SOMETHING HAS HAPPENED TO TREY" text message notifications from my little sister preceded the worst news not only of 2015, but of my life. I was over 500 miles away from my dead brother and mourning family, and about 4 hours into a reality that did not include him. "Dead" was a word I'd learned early in life, but it had never felt as finite as it did in the moment it was used in a sentence that included my brother's name.

Nearly 2 years before Trey would take his last breath, I packed my leather-seated, non-air conditioned 1995 Honda Accord and drove over 8 hours in the blistering mid-May heat from Portsmouth, Virginia, to Atlanta, Georgia, to start a new life. Just days before, I'd graduated with a master of social work degree—an educational feat that I, a first-generation college student, was exceptionally proud of. The long drive was filled with memories and tears as I mourned the people, places, and things I was leaving behind. "I knew you'd be the one to abandon us"—the last statement I'd heard from one of my parents before I left home for undergrad—haunted me as I was certain the belief that upward mobility is likened to betrayal had been intensified by my decision to leave home. I would return a mere two times before my brother's death, and during each of my visits he would be as cool, calm, and collected as I'd always known him to be, a laid-back man caught between three contentious women (my mom, my sister, and I). Trey had close relationships with each of us, but due to my aversion for how unstable our relationships with one another were, I missed my opportunity to connect with him, to make memories with him, and—so regret would have me believe—to save him from dying.

Trey was the middle child, born almost exactly 3 years after me. I remember him being my first enemy—for taking my "only child" status—and my first friend—for being a live-in sharer of the experiences I had previously faced alone. We did not get much time together before our younger sister was born a year later. Being so close in age, the two of them quickly connected and grew up practically inseparable and often mistaken for twins. The differences between me and them became more obvious as we grew older and my age, paternal family, and interests impacted how I experienced life. Early on, we'd play church together and slide down the stairs on cardboard boxes, but as time went on, I became the outsider. I loved books and remember one time opening my bedroom door and having an avalanche of them collapse on me. "Nerd girl! Nerd girl!" my brother and sister screamed while pointing and laughing. They were typical annoying little siblings and I was an easy target.

As we entered adulthood, my sister and I became closer. She began to explore what it meant to be a woman and, other than our mother, I was her only example. She'd steal my clothes and dress like me, visit me on campus when I went to college, and share all her secrets with me. My brother became distant to each of us as he entered manhood. Leading up to what I'd later know were the years before his death, he became a source of encouragement for m,– a hype man and a sounding board to bounce ideas off. His technical savviness made him my go to for filming important events, developing digital mediums to promote my various projects, and deejaying/creating party playlists. He was lighthearted and trailblazing—a self-taught pianist and rapper who others turned to for comedic relief, television and computer repair, and belief … *in their dreams and ability to connect with God.* Trey had a front-row seat to the dysfunction that periodically unfolded between my mom and I, my sister and my mom, and my sister and I, but he rarely commented or got involved, almost as if he was rising above it in hopes of influencing us to do the same. I hadn't realized that his reaction to our turmoil was foreshadowing. *One day he would rise above us.*

Traumatically losing my little brother impacted me in so many ways. Emotionally and psychologically, I battled with depression, guilt, and anxiety. I spent the days after his death experiencing somatic symptoms such as headaches, fatigue, and cold sweats prompted by mental pictures of him laying alone on a freezing, wet interstate. In between two romantic relationships, I found that neither satisfied my longing for comfort, so I began using alcohol and random sex to cope. When I returned to work 3 weeks later, I was warmly greeted by colleagues who offered grief support and as needed coverage for my caseload, but due to the amount of time I'd spent out of work and the lack of full-time positions available at the practice, I was financially forced to re-enter the job market. In late March, I transitioned into a hospice social work position, which offered a generous compensation package that I couldn't afford to turn down. Caring for myself became even more difficult as I was then responsible for helping others through the death and dying process by providing grief counseling, illness education, and placement services to hospice patients and impacted family members. I also participated in the on-call social worker rotation, responding to after-hours medical emergencies and deaths.

Most of my clients were older, middle- and upper-class Caucasian American adults with terminal illnesses, but despite the many demographic factors that separated them from my brother, countertransference was impossible to escape. I regularly found myself wondering if the death of a loved one was easier with warning than it was without, and how different life would have been for both of us if my brother would have lived to be the age my patients were. Although I was sensitive to the struggles they and their families faced, I found it hard not to compare my scenario with my clients'. This made me empathic yet envious and caused doing work that made me feel helpful yet less fortunate than those I was assisting difficult. For starters, I was a 24-year-old Black woman living alone in a redeveloped community in Atlanta known for being the location of a popular rapper's drug house. My patients lived in multi-story homes on the outskirts of the city and were often paying out-of-pocket for hospice treatment, which included physician care, medication, nursing, social work, and chaplaincy services. Our obvious differences were compounded by the fact that they'd been granted several decades of life beyond what my brother would ever see. I'm not certain I would have paid as much attention to how little we related to each other if I hadn't been in a season of longing for Trey to be granted as full of a life as they had. He died without children, lacking a career, and having never traveled more than 4 hours outside of the area we grew up in. He never flew on a plane, never owned an apartment, and never graduated college. Knowing that his potential and life were cut short made showing unconditional positive regard to patients who grieved the idea that they may not see their 100th birthday hard. It was particularly difficult to be understanding toward those who faced terminal conditions that were a result of poor habits and choices. "If only Trey could have those years" played in my mind over and over in those situations. After 4 months of fearing that my personal experiences were preventing me from showing up like my patients needed me to, I was tasked with propping up a stiff, dead body as the on-call nurse cleaned it. Shortly after that encounter, I put my 2 weeks' notice in.

As I write this, 3 months separate me from the 4-year anniversary of my brother's death. A lot has happened in the time since he and I last spoke: I'm licensed, married, own a private practice, and founded Trap Therapist, a company that connects mental health professionals from urban, low-income backgrounds with potential clients from marginalized communities. I'm also able to share details about my grieving process without breaking down. Shortly after leaving the hospice agency, I began going to therapy and continue to do so weekly. I received eye movement desensitization and reprocessing (EMDR) therapy to unpack the traumas of being a member of a dysfunctional family, growing up in distressed communities, losing my brother, and all the disturbing events that have occurred before, between, and after. While EMDR is often associated with post-traumatic stress disorder (PTSD) treatment after experiences such as military combat, it can be helpful for victims of physical assault, rape, car accidents, and other traumatic events. Using my knowledge as a clinician to consider my adverse childhood experiences (ACEs) alongside the traumas I have directly/indirectly witnessed led me to determine I met the criteria for PTSD. Upon realizing that I did, I sought out a mental health professional who offered affordable EMDR to help me begin another phase of my healing journey. The first experience we addressed was my brother's death. At the time, I'd been experiencing upsetting memories, nightmares, emotional distress, and physical reactivity. Recognizing that I was having nightmares related to my brother's death at a more frequent rate than I had before was what prompted me to begin processing it instead of other traumas. At least once a week, my sleep was interrupted by disturbing dreams of him dying in different ways. On occasions, I witnessed him be murdered, commit suicide, and die accidently. In some of the dreams, I would also die. This resulted in me waking up with heart palpitations, in cold sweats, and having difficulty breathing or controlling racing thoughts. As a result of my first EMDR session, the image I associated with his death (him laying alone on a freezing, wet interstate) became distant and foggy and my physical (shivering, shortness of breath) and emotional/mental (anxiety, depression, guilt/feelings of responsibility) reactions decreased tremendously. I also stopped having nightmares about him dying.

Other forms of self-care and restoration I've relied on to heal from my brother's death and other trauma include spiritual comfort achieved through regular church attendance, prayer, Bible and devotional reading, and meditation. Additionally, I deep breathe, exercise, journal, and use tools such as a stress ball to relieve the tension I experience during moments of anxiety often caused by triggers such as car rides in the passenger seat and my husband driving long distances without me. Although I participate in professional peer support groups, these strategies also play a large role in my ability to manage issues of counter-transference, vicarious trauma, and burnout that I experience in my career.

When I reflect on how ineffectively I initially coped with the loss of my brother and consider how heavy the warfare work I do as a clinician is, I am inspired to live a life that emphasizes healing even when there doesn't seem to be anything to heal from. Consequently, I'd encourage students and professionals to take a prevention approach to self-care and restoration rather than a treatment approach. More specifically, to prioritize protecting well-being and happiness before periods of stress ensue. This can be accomplished by including self-care activities in your regular routine instead of relying on them only during moments of hardship. I often describe self-care to my clients and colleagues as a bank account: If your balance is high, you're less likely to overdraft during moments when more is being withdrawn than deposited. As clinicians and students of therapy, it is our job to guard ourselves against the outcomes of poor mental hygiene habits such as low motivation, exhaustion, cynicism, and poor job performance. This can only be done if we develop a self-care regimen and commit to sticking to it no matter how busy we are or "okay" we feel. Engaging in self-care is like saving for a rainy day.

Reflection Questions

1. What is the most important thing I learned personally as a result of reading this chapter? Professionally?
2. What diversity factors/experiences do I present with that may impact my ability to sit with clients who differ from me?
3. Based on my personal experiences, what types of clients may be the most difficult for me to give unconditional positive regard and understanding to?
4. Are there personal issues I have that could benefit from therapy? If so, what are they?
5. Do I have any reservations about seeing a therapist? If so, what are they?
6. What do I do now to take care of myself?
7. What self-care activities am I willing to add to my weekly routine?

When My Body Betrayed Me: Falling Through My Identity and Into Myalgic Encephalomyelitis or Chronic Fatigue Syndrome

Jemel Aguilar, PhD, LCSW, Southern Connecticut State University, New Haven, Connecticut

FIGURE 3.17. Jemel Aguilar

Jemel Aguilar, PhD, LCSW is on faculty at Southern Connecticut State University. Dr. Aguilar has conducted extensive research on HIV among ethnic minorities and published students in prominent journals such as *Social Work in Public Health, Journal of HIV/AIDS and Social Services,* and *Journal of Community Practice.* Dr. Aguilar also provides clinical social work services to children, adolescents ,and adults who have experienced trauma. He is currently extending his research into Myalgic Encephalomyletis/Chronic Fatigue Syndrome.

Who Am I?

I did not always want to be a social worker. In the 1980s, I thought I might have a chance to be a computer scientist or maybe an actor. But smoldering under the city streets was a virus. On June 5, 1981 the U.S. Centers for Disease Control published a report about a strange pneumonia infecting five gay men. Around the same time as the Centers for Disease Control report about the strange pneumonia, the U.S. Drug Enforcement Agency was contending with large shipments a cocaine powder coming into the United States. The large shipments of cocaine powder flooded the market and drug dealers converted the powder into a solid form of cocaine that became known as crack. I remember sitting at a table in a public library hearing crackling sounds coming from a tablebehind me; someone was smoking crack in the public library. While I was not aware of the importance of these reports to my life, these events shaped my future work including college and graduate school, including committing myself to pursuing a doctoral degree in social welfare.

Over the next 10 years I participated in the efforts of a group of people to address that means of what became human immunodeficiency syndrome (HIV). I started my work by picking up prescriptions and delivering them to those who could not leave their house, assisting people who are sometimes friends and family with the attending doctors' appointments, understanding what the doctors were trying to tell them about their disease, and coordinating the multiple appointments that included immunologists, infectious disease specialists, and eventually HIV specialists. I did not have a direction at this time. Many people would decide to go to college, work for the City of New York, or have some other plan. I did not. So, I followed the pack to college while working full-time.

In my HIV organization, I was surrounded by educated people. I worked with medical doctors, social workers, public health managers, and nurses. We collectively strove to alleviate the devastation that HIV wrought on our community, all the while waiting and hoping for a cure. At graduation, my colleagues encouraged me to further my education because, as they believed, one day the epidemic of HIV would end and an education would be vital in the post-AIDS era. I wondered what that era would be like after the explosion of death that surrounded me. Who would I be after working with so many people that died?

Following their guidance, I pursued a bachelor's degree to progress in my agency and learn skills that could further my work with people with HIV. I grew into roles such as case manager, outreach coordinator, AIDS educator, or legislative advocate all the while obtaining an education. Once I had the courage, I decided to apply for a master's degree in either social work or public health because I worked with people who held these degrees and they suggested that I could do the academic work given my professional experience. Their reverence for education countered mine in that I was unfamiliar with the college environment and chose a human development undergraduate degree because that simply "made sense." The degree was, in my opinion, "just a piece of paper" so I could continue working in the field of HIV at a higher wage.

I remember standing on a street corner with friends discussing where a person's funeral was to be held. We were going through the list of funeral homes and remembering which friend, neighbor, colleague, or client had their funeral service in particular funeral homes. I remember counting over 256 people we had buried over the tenure. I was only 22 years old by this time. Deaths due to complications associated with AIDS, rational suicide, and drug overdose were common ways that I closed cases. The number of deaths I encountered at this age did not strike me as odd. Life, at that time, was about staving off death as long as possible in hopes of a treatment or a cure that we hoped was around the corner.

During my college education I thought, given my work in HIV, that I would take a course on death and dying. My colleagues and supervisor suggested that I consider taking a different course, given our work and that this course might be "too close to home." I liked the professor and it filled a requirement, so I remember questioning what the "big deal" was with this course because—I now regret saying—"What does death and dying have to do with my work? I am a case manager." The instructor introduced concepts and death and dying across cultures with relevant cultural definitions, mores, and funeral practices. My chest tightened as I sat in class, the room started to get hot, and on break I moved my seat, letting my friends know that I thought I was having problems breathing and "it must be the dust from the heater." Over the next several classes, we reviewed prominent mass deaths in world history including African slavery, Hiroshima, reports of the Khmer Rouge Killing fields, and the Jamestown and the Peoples Temple. When brought into contemporary mass deaths and specifically HIV, my chest started to tighten and I had trouble breathing. The health professional at the college health center asked a few questions about my family health history and then suggested that I had adult onset asthma, gave me a rescue inhaler, and I returned to class. The next set of classes involved applying cultural concepts of death to our own lives by first creating a timeline of our lives up to our own death. My peers in the class described long lives that included children, grandchildren, houses, cars, and other things that to them represented a full life. I sat quietly in the class thinking that it must be odd that they could do and achieve all of these goals by the time they were to 24. Twenty-four is when I assumed I would be dead by disease or violence.

SEE ME! This was what my professor handwrote at the end of my timeline of my life. "Why did not I get a grade?" I thought to myself peering around and seeing that my peers all had grades. "I must be a bad student" was my next thought. I nervously walked into my professor's office during his office hours and braced myself for his recommendation that I quit school and find a job. He sat across from me with his eyes fixed and said, "Do you think that everyone believes they will die at 24?" He then reviewed what we had learned and said that like many of the people who grew up during times of mass deaths, this experience was atypical and not a defining feature of who I am. Then he asked me the question that nagged at me for years to come, "Who are you outside of the world of HIV?"

Jacob and the Lost Clinical Social Worker

I met Jacob for his first appointment on a wintry Friday afternoon. Jacob found me through a website and called me because he was having trouble in his daily life. At our first meeting Jacob described feeling "nervous" and wanting some help to feel better about himself. Jacob was a 30-year-old Latino male who reportedly "smoked too much pot." Jacob appeared to me as if he had just smoked pot before entering my office, although I did not smell it and he denied smoking before the appointment. Jacob said that he really wanted help but that he was at a loss for what to do. I asked Jacob what was his family life was like. Jacob had reported that he was one of three children born to parents who were still together at the time of the interview. Jacob's family reflected most of the families I had seen in the area where my office is located. My office is located in a suburban town 30 miles outside of a small city. The families in this town are middle and upper-middle class with small pockets of poor populations. Most of the families had two-parent households with kids who enjoyed the benefits of living a suburban life. These benefits included cars at their disposal, lots of free time, and sometimes drug and alcohol use, along with other risky sexual behavior. Jacob is not much different from the kids in these neighborhoods.

Jacob was in a relationship, worked part time, and reported spending most of his time in his basement apartment in the building that his parents owned. He started smoking pot about 9 years ago after a funeral in which he buried his brother's best friend. Jacob said that he grew up with his brother's best friend and the friend was like an older brother. At the funeral, he was so overcome that a friend offered him a "bar"[1] to "calm down and chill." Jacob said that he liked feeling chill but did not like the idea of taking medications that were for someone else, so his brother introduced him to "smoking weed." Smoking weed, Jacob said, helped him stop thinking about "bad thoughts" and he was able to just "be present," so he continued. His bad thoughts were mostly about the video of his sister's suicide and her final moments—a video that she sent him before she died. Jacob says that people have commented on his marijuana use recently, most notably his father. He reports that his father recently completed 2 years of sobriety and decided to talk to Jacob about smoking marijuana every day. Jacob says that be believes that his father stopped using drugs after his brother and cousin completed suicide last year. When pressed further, Jacob indicated that 10 people he is close to died by suicide in the last 9 years.

In some ways I related to Jacob in that he, like me, reflected the common elements of his neighborhood while trying to seek out different ways of being in the world. We differed in our economic

1 A slang term for Xanax.

circumstances in that Jacob was clearly upper-middle class, while I did not grow up with the financial security that Jacob's family had. We both, however, has significant risks that laid the groundwork for potential harms that could change the trajectory of the rest of our lives. Jacob sought assistance outside his family and his neighborhood in the form of psychotherapy for what he described as his "nervousness." When pressed further about his family, Jacob indicated that his two siblings had passed away within a year of each other. As he described the death of his two siblings in detail Jacobs facial expression did not change or show any hint of sadness.

At this point in my career, I had been a clinical social worker who specialized in treating traumatic reactions to life events such as the sudden onset of chronic disease, exposure to violence, or sudden death of a loved one. I remember my first impression of Jacob was that he seemed divorced from the world around him, like me. He would look at me during the initial interaction, but there seemed to be no spirit or life behind his eyes. Something about Jacob seemed lost, like he did not know where or who he was anymore, not in a dissociative sense but as if he misplaced such a big part of himself; now he is trying to find it. Watching Jacob maintaining a flat affect while describing the overdose of his brother and the suicide of his sister within a 2-year period reminded me of my flat reaction to speaking about the 256 deaths that I dealt with as a case manager in an HIV organization. In some ways the Jacob who sat before me was similar to who I became as an HIV counselor. Even now, I typically discuss death with little to no affect. As things changed and I could no longer do the emotional work of HIV care, I found myself lost, unsure of what to do next. Despite pursuing an education to prepare for the post-AIDS era that had not come, I was unsure what to do next, until I fell ill.

Identity Change

I was driving home from the gym that is 10 minutes from my house, after my usual workout with my personal trainer. I hated working out, but I was trying to lose weight that crept up on me over the years of sitting at desks completing research projects, poor eating habits, and growing health problems. These were typical CrossFit training regimens that I successfully followed for a few months. I was losing weight and my resting heart rate was at about 60 bpm, which is good for a person in his or her 40s. I had struggled with losing weight for a couple of years and I decided that I would make a more concerted effort after my most recent bout with asthma, sleep apnea, and a few random lung infections. I had been getting sick so much that my friend gave me a magnet to describe my life, which said "I finally got my head together and my body fell apart." For a few years I had been dealing with infections and my allergist suggested that my allergies were getting worse, but that day driving home from the gym I felt different, tired—so tired that I had to pull over in a parking lot near the gym to rest for a while.

My routine had been the same as any other day at the gym, but today felt different. After resting in a shopping center parking lot for an hour, I grabbed a cup of coffee from the grocery store and drove the rest of the way home. At home, I was still tired so I decided to take a nap. It was 10:00 a.m. so I planned to sleep for an hour or two and then go to work and get some things done from my ever-growing to-do list. I set the timer on my alarm clock for 2 hours, thinking that would be enough time to rest and get to work. I laid down, comfortable in my bed, and slept for hours. This pattern continued for a few weeks. After several weeks of going to training sessions and then sleeping for 6 to 8 hours afterward, I spoke to my trainer to ask if this change in energy level was a "rough patch" and he indicated that this was not usual and suggested that I get another physical just to make sure everything was okay. My medical doctor quipped, "You just need to lose more weight and people your age slow down physically. It will pass."

Something still did not feel right, so a close friend suggested to seek out a naturopath. I did because I was not convinced by the flippant "you are fat and old" diagnosis of my medical doctor. The first session with my naturopathic doctor was surprising when she said, "Something is attacking your immune system." Blood tests revealed an elevated level of Epstein-Barr virus, but I had "mono" before and I thought that it was not supposed to reactivate. The medical research literature I found indicated that reactivated Epstein-Barr virus is linked to a little-known epidemic called Myalgic Encephalomyelitis or chronic fatigue syndrome (Johnson, 1996).

Resurrection

Every day is like resurrection. In the morning, I lay in bed sensing where in my body the "fever" is located; the fever is the term that I use to for the sensation that I have an elevated temperature in part of my body. The fever is typically an omen for how my health will be that day. Fevers in the morning mean a day of unrelenting fatigue, muscle pain, brain fog, and a long day of accomplishing very little. Naps during the day do not resolve the fatigue or lessen the muscle pain. Taking acetaminophen and naproxen for the pain results in stomach cramps; that is more discomfort. As I go to bed, I typically feel fevers in my legs. The fever precedes the pain. In the morning the fevers cooccur along with the pain. Sometimes as I lay in bed scanning my body to determine the physical obstacles that I will have to manage that day, my mind drifts back to the days when I would complain to myself that the alarm went off too early or when I would feel tired after a long day's work and wish that I could lay in bed all day and watch television. Now that I work and then quickly return to my bed to receive some relief from the supine position, I wish that I could be back where my life used to be.

I miss hanging out with friends at local events, going from work to dinner parties, or traveling to events that I was interested in attending such as conferences or talks. Now, 2 hours of social time means at least 2 hours of sleep afterward. Work days are interspersed with laying down and the gross, and I assume unsanitary, carpet of my office so that I, in the supine position, decrease the energy use and lessen the 5:00 p.m. nap time that I need to ensure that I will recover enough the next day to return to work. I take 13 medications a day to prevent, protect, or treat illnesses in the environment that most people's immune system simply fights off with ease. Sneezes or cough near me can lead me to a "crash," which is a severe episode of ME/CFS, including chronic fatigue, pain, and orthostatic intolerance, and brain fog, further stressing my already fragile immune system.

I use Twitter and Facebook groups for people living with Myalgic Encephalomyelitis/chronic fatigue syndrome to connect with people who live with the same symptoms and ambiguity that I do, vent my frustrations at the disease, and ask for support from people who understand what it is like to live with a drastic change after one incident; for me, like many others, it was a virus. In these groups, we share ideas, medications reactions, treatment options, news about ME/CFS research or politics, and most importantly fatigue jokes. One day I realized that I felt connected to these electronic faces and we shared something challenging and special.

While contending with the therapeutic questions posed by my clients, I struggle with ME/CFS symptoms and questions about who I was now that I had changed my life to fit this disease. Do I have a disability or, as some of my social justice colleagues noted, am I a person with a disability? Should

I quit my university post and take a less stressful position so that I decrease the strain on my body and health? Should I maintain my position at the university and stop practicing with clients so that I can lessen the strain, but could I financial stability to afford that decrease in pay? Can I really work with clients when I worried about my own symptoms? The questions were sometimes similar to the questions that my clients asked of themselves and me as the therapist. Would the noted parallel process between me the client interfere or help the client-practitioner interaction (Ganzer, 2007; Ganzer & Ornstein, 1999)? Could I use my experiences with ME/CFS in my work with clients (Ganzer, 2007)?

Post-Traumatic Stress Disorder and Myalgic Encephalomyelitis/ Chronic Fatigue Syndrome

I have Myalgic Encephalomyelitis/chronic fatigue syndrome (ME/CFS) a condition in which I experience post-exertional malaise, irritable bowel, unrefreshing sleep, difficulty finding words, postural tachycardia, muscle pain, and generalized weakness daily (Anderson, Jason, & Hlavaty, 2014; Jason et al., 1998; Johnson, 1996). While a definitive causal agent for ME/CFS has yet to be identified, the prevailing theory that has some epidemiological evidence is that a virus attacks that body and results in metabolic physiological changes that produce 20 different types of symptoms including fatigue-related symptoms such as post-exertional malaise, unrefreshing sleep or fatigue; cognitive difficulties such as difficulty with memory, finding words, and multitasking; pain-related symptoms such as facial pain, headaches, nerve pain and tingling, generalized weakness, bone, muscle, and joint pain, atypical chest pain, non-specific abdominal pain, dysmenorrhea; as well as other symptoms like sore throat, tinnitus, poor circulation, sensitivity to light, temperature, sound and chemicals, dizziness, postural tachycardia, or orthostatic hypotension (Jason et al., 1998; Johnson, 1996; Myhill, 2017). The onset of my illness is linked to a viral infection in 1998 and the symptoms slowly developed over time, yet I, and medical and mental health professionals, mistakenly attributed the symptoms to other diseases such as post-traumatic stress disorder or pre-diabetes, developmental processes such as aging, or the need for dietary changes and weight loss. To manage my symptoms, I take six supplements and five medications daily, pace my activities to prevent post-exertional malaise, and take lots of naps throughout the day. Coping with the ups and downs of this disease is a challenge in that I cannot work or live at the pace that I used to. I spend little time with my friends because I cannot exert myself without consequences that confine me to bed for hours for what I learned is an unrest, an unrefreshing nap. The widespread isolation coupled with the pain, malaise, and other symptoms lead me to research literature on ME/CFS so that I could learn about this disorder and identify ways to cope with the disease. Unlike PTSD, there are no effective treatments for ME/CFS, only suggestions on ways to manage individual symptoms and many snake oil sellers touting cures. I questioned if I could continue being a social worker and academic if I struggle with exertional malaise, pain, and fatigue. Who am I if I am not an academic? I have this thought many times throughout the day as I climb into bed for a 3-hour unrest.

I realized that I needed help, so I started participating in a time-limited supervision group for independently licensed mental health providers. The group featured eight to 10 clinical social workers who wanted to improve their practice in specific ways that included learning new techniques to engage reluctant clients, ensure that personal and professional boundaries were in place with clients who were struggling with problems that the clinician was dealing with at the time, or those newbies who wanted to continue receiving supervision until their confidence was adequately developed. The clinician leading this supervision was gifted and her background placed her in the relational social work. In this camp, the relational framework suggests that the characteristics of the therapist enter into the therapeutic relationship (Ganzer, 2007). As campers, we were tasked with identifying aspects of our current client interactions in which aspects of ourselveswere entering into the therapeutic relationship. At the time, I wondered how I could facilitate healing work when I had not yet lived traumas that my clients had experienced.

And now, I was dealing with a new disease. The group pushed me to "look deeper" and the fatigued part of me questioned whether this would be useful or another hole in my "energy bucket" (Myhill, 2017). Falling back on my early research training, I developed a series of matrices to compare characteristics of my clients and myself, as well as their and my symptomology. Looking deeper lead to the realization that I was going through a crisis of identity, accepting a loss of who I was, and searching for meaning in this new life with as a person with Myalgic Encephalomyelitis/chronic fatigue syndrome. Do I now have to admit to other people and myself that I have problems like the clients who sit on my couch? Does this mean I am not a good social worker because I am struggling, or resisting, accepting a debilitating disease in my life?

FIGURE 3.18. Life post-24

Therapist and Clients

My client and I have similarities in our experiences of our individual illnesses and situations. We both had a suddenness to the onset of our individual illness. Jacob's family member's first exposure to death was the unexpected overdose of a close friend of the family. After this overdose and within a few months after the death, several others died every few months for the next 5 years. I thought I was making improvements in many aspects of my life including weight management, which should have indicated that I was getting better. We thought our lives were headed in a particular direction and then that direction changed. Now each of us, in our own ways, must redirect our attention from our daily lives toward managing our respective situations—the intrusive thoughts, the loneliness, the fears, and the symptoms. Our lives, thus, have been significantly intruded upon by our current situations and so time, energy, and effort must be redistributed to accommodate these new aspects of our lives. We are no longer the people we thought we were or hoped to be; we are now different.

Reflection Questions

1. What does the concept of health mean to you? What does the concept of illness mean to you?
2. What connection do you see between the author and his client Jacob? Based on the story he has shared, how would you frame your work with Jacob?
3. How do you quantify the construct of the loss of health? What does the loss of physical and social status mean in behavioral health practice?

References

Anderson, V. R., Jason, L. A., & Hlavaty, L. E. (2014). A qualitative natural historysStudy of ME/CFS in the community. *Health Care for Women International, 35*(1), 3–26. doi:10.1080/07399332.2012.684816

Ganzer, C. (2007). The use of self from a relational perspective. *Clinical Social Work Journal, 35*(2), 117–123. doi:10.1007/s10615-007-0078-4

Ganzer, C., & Ornstein, E. D. (1999). Beyond parallel process: Relational perspectives on field instruction. *Clinical Social Work Journal, 27*(3), 231–247.

Jason, L. A., Richman, J. A., Friedberg, Wagner, L., Taylor, R., & Jordan, K. M. (1998). More on the biopsychosocial model of chronic fatigue syndrome. *American Psychologist, 53*(9), 1081–1082. doi:10.1037/0003-066X.53.9.1081

Johnson, H. (1996). *Osler's web: Inside the labyrinth of the chronic fatigue syndrome epidemic.* New York, NY: Crown.

Myhill, S. (2017). *Diagnosis and treatment of chronic fatigue syndrome and Myalgic Encephalitis: It's mitochondria not hypochondria* (1st ed.). White River Junction, CT: Chelsea Green.

Resick, P. A., Monson, C. M., & Chard, K. M. (2017). *Cognitive processing therapy for PTSD: A comprehensive manual.* New York, NY: Guilford.

Learning to Love My Mother

Alex Redcay, PhD, LCSW, co-editor
Millersville University, Lancaster, Pennsylvania

FIGURE 3.19. Alex Redcay

When my coauthor, Beth, and I met, both of my parents had died a couple of years before. Beth and I wanted to collaborate on a project, so we shared stories of our dead parents (only her father at the time) and thought developing this book was needed and important for clinical students. Saying the phrase "dead parent" may sound harsh to the reader, but I use these words intentionally. Working part time in disaster psychology and emergency management has taught me that. You never want the loved one of the deceased to be confused when you use abstract terminology such as "passed away," "gone," or "no longer here." In disaster psychology you need to be clear in your language, and the word *dead* is clear, concise, and definitive. Although, in a cultural context the word dead may be confusing or offensive (see chapter 3).

Conversely though, my mother's slow death over 10-plus years was anything but definitive and concise. My mother died in her 50s from liver failure that was caused by prolonged alcohol misuse, drug use, and hepatitis. I have been ashamed of this detail and have never shared it publicly until now.

FIGURE 3.20. Carol Ann Shanaman Redcay Nickeson, 2013

I was raised by my maternal grandfather on a central Pennsylvania farm of 50 acres. My older sister describes our childhood as idyllic. My mother was more of a distant aunt who would visit randomly. We have very strong aunts and uncles in my family, so I do not feel that I missed anything in terms of parental figures. I had no strong feelings either way toward my mother for most of my life; instead my feelings were more of apathetic disinterest. However, the knowledge that my mother chose drugs and alcohol over raising my sister and I was present in my history, but it felt like a story I read about someone else's life. As an adult, now I understand the nature of addiction being a brain disease, not a free choice. Addiction is a compulsion that can only be arrested, never cured. Disease or choice, some people recover while others die. "We are people in the grip of a continuing and progressive illness whose ends are always the same: jails, institutions, and death" is frequently said in Alcoholic Anonymous (AA) meetings. My mother participated in each: jails, institutions, and eventually death. Recovery is always possible but for my mother, the consequences of her use were inescapable. She went on to have three more children but did not finishing raising them before she died.

She became sick a decade ago before her death, but the illness was not a daily concern. My mother would periodically vomit blood that would fill a small trash can and would be rushed to the hospital for emergency surgery. As your liver fails, the body builds up ammonia, which can cause confusion, slurring speech, and stumbling and can lead to a coma. She was prescribed Lactulose, which reduces the ammonia in the body and is expected to prolong life. My mother would inconsistently take this medication due to the severe side effects of terrible flatulence and diarrhea. Due to her failure to be compliant with this medication or her periodic relapse of alcohol use, she ended up in the hospital more than a few times. Typically, she would start off unconscious or in a coma but would always recover. The doctors would nag her about taking the medication consistently and she would fiercely complain that she hated the medication and she wanted to stop it. Others would complain about the smell making her feel worse.

For many years, my mother and I lived in different states and I traveled quite a bit, so we were not physically or emotionally close. When I met my wife, who was born and raised in Guatemala, she was shocked by my American coldness toward my mother. We frequently argued about her enmeshment (or closeness) with her mother and my coldness (or indifference) toward mine. Eventually, she convinced me that I should demonstrate love and care for my mother. So, we began to drive to Pennsylvania on a regular basis to visit her and I learned how to love my mother genuinely.

Due to her illness, her body would bloat and shrink 50 pounds, so my wife and I would take her shopping every year. She had trouble walking and moving around, so I had to help her get dressed and undressed in the changing rooms. Sometimes I was too quick because I wanted her embarrassment to end but this physically hurt her. She would yelp in pain and I would apologize. We began to celebrate her birthday or Mother's Day at Red Lobster or Olive Garden, her absolute favorite restaurants. She would worry that it was too expensive but she would always order the biggest meal and savor every bite. She expressed her sincere gratitude for the celebration like it may never happen again. I began to take care of things for her, going through her mail that was piled up around her house, paying the bills and managing her finances because all her bills were late. Occasionally, she would get arrested for public drunkenness and I would attend the court hearing and plead with the judge to not make her pay the fine because she only had Social Security for income. She lived in public housing, had food stamps, did not have a car or any possessions of value. Her home was messy and she hoarded things. Many weeks she could not afford groceries or her medication. Somehow, my wife loved my mother more than I could and taught me how to love her, honestly, despite her flaws.

My youngest sibling was still living with her at the time, so we were able to spend good quality time together. He was having so much trouble in school. My mother thought asking a child to read books was child abuse, so she never wanted him to do his homework. As a consequence, he was failing nearly every subject. I attended school meetings for 2 years in a row, sympathizing with the teacher and trying to convince my mother to get him to do his homework. In one of our last arguments, I begged my mom to let him live with someone else—anyone else. I yelled at her that she was a terrible parent and for once in her life could she please think about someone other than herself. I was mad and yelled and cried. I felt guiltily for saying things that would hurt her but part of me, wanted to hurt her. I guess I was mad about all the things that came before. I did not want her to destroy his life (too?). A few weeks later, she sent my brother to live with his father several states away. This was an incredibly hard decision for her because she loved him more than anything and to let him go was one of the most painful sacrifices of her life. I was relieved that he was not living with her but devastated that she did not pick a relative within the same state so we could maintain a relationship to him. We never spoke about it afterwards. I never said thank you, never said sorry, never explained. Within a year, she was dead.

I received a call from a relative that my mother was in the hospital again. I was out of state helping a friend with a personal emergency so I did not call my mother right away. Eventually, I made it back home and began to drive back and forth to Pennsylvania again, visiting her in the hospital. A relative kept insisting that she was going to die immediately but this particular relative had made these claims before and my mother always recovered. I discovered that hospice was involved, but at the time, I did not know what that meant. I had a few visits with my mother but talked about nothing of consequence. Another sibling just had a baby so he brought the baby to visit our mother and they had a nice visit. My mother asked me to take her outside so she could feel the fresh air.

The nursing home she was in smelled absolutely awful. Since she was regularly forced to take Lactulose and could not move easily, she would have explosive diarrhea all over her bed, and the nursing home only cleaned up most of it. When I would arrive, I found fecal matter on the sheets, the nurse call button, the light switches. I felt terrified. It was an awful moment when you realize how vulnerable people who are older and in poverty can be, how vulnerable I could be eventually. Poverty led her to the nursing home with poop on the sheets. I politely requested that the nursing staff resolve the "poop" issue and they did. This was "resolved" by sending in two enormous men to change my mother's diaper and using a lift to move her like a cow. Without permission, like an infant, they pulled down her pants and washed her most private areas, put another diaper on her, and redressed her. I was horrified. Afterward, she told me that she has refused to take showers because she did not want these men touching her any more than they already did. I understood.

The staff would often forget to bring her food and then argue with me that they did. I quietly informed them that I sat in her room for 6 hours and no one came by with food—no one even came to the room. So, when she asked me to take her outside, I was happy to do so. She could no longer walk, so it took great effort to move her from the bed to the wheelchair and also caused her pain. I rushed, struggling to manage her weight, and pinched her leg in the hinge of the chair, causing her to scream. I can still hear, feel the pain that I caused her. I wheeled her around for a while but every door we tried to get out was locked like a prison for old people. My mother repeatedly said, "Never mind, just take me back to the room," but I refused. I couldn't fail in the one task she gave me. We finally found a door requiring a code, but there were no staff around to give us the passcode. Eventually, we got the code and my wife, my mother, and I sat outside in a little courtyard overlooking some grass and the red brick walls of the building. She was cold, so we maneuvered the wheelchair so she faced the warm midday sun. She closed her eyes and smiled. My wife and I sat talking as my mother fell in and out of consciousness. She was sleeping so much at the time. After about 20 minutes she said that she loved sitting in the warm sun but she was tired now and wanted to return to bed.

It took a week or two for me to meet with the hospice worker who explained that when Hospice is involved, that means the person only has 6 months left to live. Your mother only has a few weeks left.

A few weeks left to live? I was in disbelief. I drove home, read through all the hospice materials. The documents recommended that you think carefully about the last few conversations including asking questions about her childhood, about family history, and what her final words will be to her children, her family. So, I drove back. I had all my questions ready and prepared for the end. She was unconscious, when I arrived, and she never woke up again. I was never able to have the final conversation. I never asked her final words. All my questions remained unanswered.

I sat next to her for about 16 hours every day after that. I put thick lotion on her dry cracked feet. I put a moist sponge to her lips to give her some water. The nursing staff put in a catheter and at my request stopped giving her Lactulose. They cautioned me that this would speed up her death but I just wanted the explosive diarrhea to stop and to prevent the intrusion and humiliation that came with the two enormous men cleaning my mother's most intimate parts. The nursing staff would come in the room and examine her toes, fingers, skin, assessing how close she was to death. They would come, examine, and then leave, never telling me their assessment. When they predicted that she had less than 3 days left to live, they would transfer her to a hospice facility. They gave us the deadline of 3 days. If she did not die within 3 days, then they would transfer her back to this nursing home with the poop on the sheets.

The hospice facility where we spent the last 3.5 days of her life was perfect. It was like a beautiful hotel or resort. We had a patio, a small dining room area, and even a sofa to sleep on. This was incredible when compared to the nursing home. They had nurses, social workers, pastoral staff, each who kept asking me if I was okay, which was annoying. What did they want me to say? Fantastic? One noted that I appeared young and asked the age of my mother. When I said in her 50s, she realized that I was probably in my 30s, and she became visibly upset. She asked about my father, hoping to cheer herself up, but he was dead too. Orphaned in my 30s. It is a strange feeling to realize that you are now the keeper of the family memories. I was now responsible to share the stories with my younger family members. All my parents, and grandparents are dead. I should have paid attention more.

I hardly left my mother's side. My wife insisted that I go home to shower but I refused. Perhaps I had hoped that she would wake up again and talk to me. I wanted to be there; I needed to be there for the moment she died. I did not want her to be alone, not even for a minute. I did not want her to feel abandoned, or forgotten, or unloved, despite everything. No one should feel that way at the end. I wrote, I read books, I talked to her when the nursing staff came to do some procedure. They would roll her over, poke her, assess. My wife sang and read stories to her, and prayed. On the second day, my mother started making awful sounds of suffocating, drowning, or being unable to breath. It went on and on for hours. It was awful, unbearable to hear someone suffocating and to not be able to do anything. I felt like I was going to lose my mind. I pleaded with several of the nurses to do something, anything at all. They all insisted that she could breathe just fine. I had no confidence that they actually had any idea what this might feel like to her. I had to help her. Finally, one suggested a particular medication on the third day, but he cautioned me that it may hasten her death. He probably did not realize that they gave us a 3 day death deadline. A hastened death or the slow torture of suffocation and drowning in her own saliva? Not a hard decision but one that I have reflected on over and over since.

That night, we laid down to go to sleep and I sat listening to my mother's loud breathing. It was significantly better which made me feel calm but still loud, like snoring. I worried about the fourth day. If she did not die, would they send her back to the poopy nursing home? When they said 3 days, did they mean 72 hours or 3 business days? I started drifting in and out of sleep, thinking, worrying, dreaming in the quiet. I sat up when I realized it was quiet. I turned on the light and stared at my mother observing her carefully for any sign of movement, breath, or life. My wife told me to get a nurse. I obeyed. The nurse came in and confirmed that she was dead. The nurse called the coroner and gave me a long speech about what happens next, but I zoned out. I felt outside of my own body as his voice droned on. My wife and I sat and cried for a while. We left messages for relatives, packed her belongings, and felt relieved. As we walked away from her body, I wanted to rush out of the building. I could not bear to be present when the coroner came to collect the remains.

The next day, I felt restless, irritable and discontent. I just did not know what to do with myself. I had spent so much time with my mother, what should I do now? My wife kept asking me what I wanted but I could not articulate it. The only words that came to mind was, "go." I just wanted to get out, go away, leave. She suggested a road trip. My mother's memorial service was in 3 weeks so I had nothing but emptiness until then. So we drove north with what felt like my mother's presence in the backseat. We traveled through New England and ended up in Montreal, Canada. I imagined that my mother enjoyed the journey. We stayed with a friend my wife knew from Guatemala. The friend only spoke French and Spanish, while my wife only spoke Spanish and English and I only spoke English. So every conversation was either a 5 step translation (French to Spanish to English to Spanish to French) or I sat "alone" in my own thoughts. The first bit of joy I felt was looking at her glass cutting board. It had bright yellow sunflowers and a perfect blue sky. It captured my mind and I could not let it go. I stared at it for so long wondering/wishing that my mother existed in a space like that now. I made the mistake of saying how beautiful it was and in typical Guatemalan custom, this meant our friend had to give it to me and I must accept the glass cutting board gift. When my restlessness subsided, we made our way back home.

I cried nearly every day for months. I withdrew, stepped down, quit all my professional and personal obligations, I mostly sat alone in my home from August to November in a fog, vacillating between numbness and hysteria. Friends reached out, I ignored them. I had my wife talk to everyone and field all phone calls. Every TV show or movie I watched seemed to have a mother who died and I would become inconsolable. However, my reclusion helped me. When I encountered people, they said things that caused me greater pain. One woman whose mother was still alive told me with a wave of the hand, "You'll get over it." I felt like she punched me in the gut. I was speechless and angry. A few weeks later, that women's mother died and as a result her brother died by suicide. I could not be mad at her, because we do not understand how to handle other people's grief. We say all the wrong things, as therapists and as friends.

If I did go outside, I could not make it through without crying. I had a job interview in October; I cried before I went in and again when I left but apparently they did not notice because I was hired. In November, I started working at a prestigious partial hospital program for individuals who were trying to recover from drugs and alcohol. Working in substance abuse was not new to me as I had worked for 20 years in the field. However, this time was different. I was supposed to help people recover from drugs and alcohol when my own mother just failed and died. Despite all my years of experience, I could not save my own mother. I felt like I was holding my breath trying not to cry. It was a struggle trying to keep my personal life private and be a good therapist in this setting.

It became more difficult when the staff or clients reminded me of my mother. So many people seemed to reflect different sides of my mother, her anger, laughter, smile or inappropriate jokes. I never shared why my mother died with any staff nor clients. I think when this information is shared, then the conversation becomes about me, not them. Therapy is about clients, not because they have more needs or more problems than me, but because it is simply time set apart for them. I did not share with the staff either because I feared their judgement. We had an intern who was openly in recovery from drugs and alcohol and I heard my colleagues judging him. I could not imagine what they would say about me or my mother. Despite my privacy, this workplace taught me a tremendous amount about good clinical work. My colleagues and former supervisors are still good friends and excellent therapists.

What Helped

Grieving Alone and Writing

I just wanted to be free to bear my grief alone. I knew that my emotions would cause others to react and then I had to deal with their reactions to my emotions. How exhausting! So, I spent a lot of time alone, crying as much as I needed. I did not hide or hold back when I was alone. Instead, I just let grief come. I wrote out thousands of words, stories, memories. I wrote for 3 days straight when I was in hospice; I could not leave where I was, yet it was hard to stay, and writing made staying with my dying mother bearable. I traveled to Santa Cruz, Guatemala, for 5 weeks alone. I spent the majority of the time in isolation, writing, reading, thinking. I was alone with my thoughts and my own words until I could bear to be with people.

Memorial Service

My mother was cremated so there was no funeral, burial, church service, or grave, etc. We organized a memorial service 3 weeks after her death and only immediate family members came. I spoke at the service and prepared a video of pictures and music of her life. I found so many wonderful pictures and took a family survey of my mother's favorite music. As the photos crossed the screen, her favorite songs played. My mother had five children over 25 years so we each have different or similar memories of her, regardless of whether she raised us or not. I talked to each one and asked what were their favorite memories. I identified the memories we shared and told the story of her life at the service. Afterward, even her siblings said that they learned so much and felt really glad that they came. This act of love gave me peace.

The Apartment

I cleaned out her apartment, which at times was excruciatingly painful. The act of erasure. Extinction. The person that is no longer. When someone dies, it is over—forever. Then begins the erasure of their life by throwing all their possessions in the garbage. Of course, we kept things that felt important. My mother collected angels and snow globes. I collected all the angels together and asked each of her children to pick one to remember her by. But it was the elimination of her that stuck with me. At what point do I delete her phone number? What do I do with her underwear?

You have a window into the most personal items of someone's life: her bathroom soap, her hairbrush with hair remaining, the toothbrush. How would you feel if someone rummaged through all your stuff? That is what happens when you die. It was awful, but it helped me. It was another chance to say goodbye, over and over and over again. I kept so many things because I just could not bring myself to throw them away—even if it was junk. The things were a part of her and her presence remained.

Rituals

For the first few years after her death, I would pull out all the boxes of my mother's things and go through them on the anniversary. I would hold each item and determine if I could give it away that year. With each year, certain items became easier to give away, and so I parted with them, but only when it felt right. Now I only have one box left. For the first few years, we continued to celebrate her birthday and Mother's Day at her favorite restaurants. I almost imagined that she was with us in spirit.

My Wife

My wife is the most loving person I have ever known. She is warm, patient, and fierce. She knew that the right decision for me was to learn to love my mother before she died and I did. This love caused me greater pain at her death, but I am at peace (mostly) with all of the final decisions. I will be forever grateful for her for insisting on her perspective and not giving up in the face of my stubbornness.

Recommendation to Clinicians

1. Stop asking how we are feeling. I'm terrible; my mother's dying. Make statements. Ask us to tell you stories about our loved one. Just listen. Be present without rushing off to your next task.
2. Remind us to leave every loved one with nothing left unsaid or questions left unanswered because we never really know if this conversation will be the last one. Do not plan for the "last conversation"; coach us that any conversation may be the last one.
3. Prepare us for the exhaustion, for the hysterical crying, for the numbness. Encourage us to just let all the emotions come.
4. Prepare us for the erasure of a life.
5. Encourage us to have rituals even if we think it is silly.
6. Push us to trust our instincts about whether to isolate or to be with people, to hoard possessions or to throw them out.
7. Stay open and mindful when we tell you stories about explosive diarrhea or trash cans filled with blood. Don't change the subject even if it is awkward, gross, or uncomfortable. Don't react. Set your feelings aside. Hold the space firmly. We need to talk about it all without being censored or having to worry about your feelings about our grief.

Credit

CHAPTER FOUR

Religion and Culture

Working With loss Through the Lens of Culture and Faith

Panagiotis Pentaris, PhD, University of Greenwich, London, England

Panagiotis is a Senior Lecturer for the Department of Psychology, Social Work and Counselling at the University of Greenwich. He is also a Postdoc Research Fellow for the Faiths & Civil Society Unit at Goldsmiths, University of London. Panagiotis is a thanatologist, as well as a qualified social worker (nationally and internationally) with specialty in hospice social work, as well as clinical social work in end of life care. His research stretches from death policies to professional practice, while he has recently completed a large-scale UK-national project about religion, belief and spirituality in end of life care practice; he has devised a model of religious literacy in end of life care, which is currently being introduced to policy makers, while it already informs training and development of palliative professionals in hospice care. Panagiotis has written widely about the intersection of religion and death and is focusing on professional practice and policy in these areas. He is also a Trustee Member for the Independent Academic Research Studies (IARS) International Institute, and a Country Representative for the International Peace Centre Africa, while he acts as an international advocate for LGBTQ rights and dying and grief.

The concept of loss remains one of the most pertinent themes in a clinician's life. Clinicians work with individuals or larger systems when in crisis, and the latter is often the outcome of a loss, whatever the type. Individuals who experience a loss respond to it emotionally; in other words, they grieve (Izard, 2013). This section highlights the unique nature of both loss and grief. It does so by emphasizing the need to *interpret* a person's lived experiences of loss and grief prior to being adequately equipped to work with them. Both concepts are understood via the lenses of *culture* and *religion*; and these terms are used here more loosely, as follows. Drawing on Van Gennep (1961), culture refers to shared ideas, beliefs, and traditions, as well as one's lifestyle and way of understanding life, as well as acting on it. Religion, on the other hand, is used here to refer to a series of choices or belief systems or the lack of which people nowadays identify with. The concept, for the purposes of this chapter, includes religion, faith, belief, spirituality, nonreligion, secular beliefs, atheism and agnosticism, as well as lack of any of these, informed by Davie's (2013) explorations about the presence of religion in contemporary societies.

If we follow the logic that every person experiences losses in life and look at psychological research that suggests that each developmental stage in human growth is accompanied by a loss and a crisis (see Walter & McCoyd, 2015), and, thus, grief, then we might suggest that the experience is unifying (i.e., same or similar for all). However, abundant work to date (e.g., Scheider, Sneath, & Waynick, 2012) has shown that this suggestion is far from reality. What is it then that makes one's experiences of loss and grief so unique?

Culture and religion are both significant indicators of one's interpretations of life and/or death. Often, where science is lacking, tradition, rituals, or faith come to answer questions related to death. When one is approaching the end of life, they tend to prioritize what is concerning to them (Noyes, 1980), and often the most concerning items are pertinent to pain, often related to existential queries. When working with individuals who understand their experience via the lens of their culture, it is paramount that clinicians dedicate a fair amount of time to comprehend this. In other words, per professional values and principles, across disciplines, show empathy (e.g., British Association for Counselling and Psychotherapy). However, attempting what anthropologists call the *anthropological paradox* (Roheim, 1950) (i.e., understanding one's experience via a subjective lens) is a very difficult task and often impossible to attain. Yet, there are ways in which a clinician can come closer to this goal. The concepts of *cultural competence* and *cultural humility* have come to illuminate some of these.

Kohli, Huber, and Faul (2010) describe cultural competence as a process which "engages the development of abilities and skills to respect differences and effectively interact with individuals from different backgrounds" (p. 257). This process is never ending and requires self-awareness and perceptiveness (Pentaris, 2019a). Until recently, the term was used to refer to race, ethnicity, and culture. Yet, some professional associations (National Association of Social Workers (NASW, 2015); Australian Association of Social Workers (AASW, 2013) have already expanded this pallet and include religion or belief, gender, and sexual orientation when discussing the need for cultural competence.

Charleston, Gajewska-De Mattos, and Chapman (2017) and Garneau and Pepin (2015) have highlighted that cultural competence may only be understood in the context in which one is attempting to exercise it. It is the growing understanding of diversity in a particular context, which assists with advancing culturally sensitive and appropriate practice. Professional standards about ethical practice (e.g., NASW, 2015) explicitly suggest that professionals, including clinicians, have an ethical responsibility to exercise cultural competence. In the process, it is imperative that professionals engage in activities that enhance cultural self-awareness (Pentaris, 2019b) (i.e., an in-depth understanding of own culture and appreciation of this impacts on the way one *makes sense of the world*).

It is evident from the little information available in this section that achieving cultural competence is neither easy nor linear as a process—more of an iterative process—which, despite the recommendations that a clinician's cultural views should be set aside, it is an impossibility to do so (Boyle & Springer, 2001) and, therefore, the possibility for cultural competence is questionable altogether. Yan and Wong (2005) identified that the model of cultural competence requires the capacity to suspend own beliefs and values, which contradicts their own individuality and use of self in practice. Instead, the authors recommended the "dialogic self," to suggest that cultural competence is the product of the interaction between the subjectivity of the clinician and the client.

A separate concept, and possibly more effective and adaptable to a wide range of situations, is cultural humility (Hook, Davis, Owen, Worthington, & Utsey, 2013). While cultural competence focuses on the interactions with the *other*, cultural humility is centered on the professional. The concept explores both intrapersonal and interpersonal dimensions of the clinician and highlights the need to develop a sense of humility (i.e., lack of superiority; for example, one culture versus another). This suggestion is paramount, especially considering power dynamics in the professional-client relationship and the professional intent to enable clients to be empowered while adapting to their loss and befriending their grief.

While both models of cultural competence and cultural humility encompass, in their descriptions of religion and belief, the latter has been distinguished from the former, increasingly (Pentaris, 2014; 2019b). This said, the concept of religious literacy is introduced (Dinham & Francis, 2015; see Pentaris, 2019b for places in which the concept has been explored) to provide context and a model toward a more religiously and spiritually sensitive practice. Religious literacy is a fluid notion, as are cultural competence and cultural humility, and can only be understood in the context in which it is exercised or applied (Dinham & Francis, 2015). The concept of religious literacy provides to clinicians the space for a well-balanced professional attitude toward working with loss and grief in a religiously diverse environment (Pentaris, 2019a), while it helps distinguish culture and religion to better understand the probability that they are not connected (Foucault, 1999/2013).

According to Pentaris (2019a), religious literacy requires advancement in two areas: first, engagement with traditions, religions, and beliefs, and next, the development of understanding of religion and belief as themes and their role in the context of practicing with loss and grief. Further, a value-based approach is necessary in order to develop religious literacy. This approach consists of self-awareness, self-understanding, interpersonal skills, and empathy (Pentaris, 2019a). In other words, religious literacy identifies the need to develop knowledge, skills, and abilities to work with individuals for whom their religion, faith, or spirituality are important, in contemporary societies where religion and belief continuously change their role in the public (Davie, 2013).

These are but a few of the models or concepts that aid clinicians to advance their capacities when working with loss and grief; subjects that are highly subjectified by the person's worldview; informed by culture and religion. There are many more tools to use in clinical practice—especially concerning the measurement of spiritual needs and spirituality, such as Frick, Riedner, Fegg, Hauf, and Borasio (2006) and Puchalski and Romer (2000), yet this section's aim is not to list and appraise all those tools. To the contrary, the purpose is to put emphasis on the need, for clinicians who work with loss and grief, to engage with further activities that will enhance their capacities when working with people with different views from their own. The first step in this process, as described by the religious literacy concept, is the acquisition of new knowledge about different traditions, religions, and cultures, which will become the basis for developing understanding and comprehending the context of a client's lived experience. The following chapters introduce some key religious and cultural views about death, loss, and grief, as well as information about how such worldviews impact practices and perceptions about death and the afterlife, which can aid clinicians in their journey to religiously and culturally sensitive practice.

Sections in this part of the book refer to perceptions about death and grief and discuss the various types of loss while examining death and loss via different cultural and/or religious lenses. The reader should not take this knowledge as one that can be generalized, but own the responsibility to understand the information when placed in any given context. The information should, in other words, be approached deductively, and clinicians should allow themselves the opportunity to learn from this anew and not simply test it against their current knowledge and/or assumptions about knowledge.

Reflection Questions

1. How do you understand your own culture and how far do you think it impacts on your lived experiences?
2. Would you suggest that every person from the same culture or religion as yourself presents the same worldview about similar situations? Please explore.
3. Is it possible to demonstrate empathy when working with clients, if you lack an understanding of how one makes sense (interprets) of one's experience?

References

Australian Association of Social Workers (AASW). (2013). *Practice standards.* Retrieved from https://www.aasw.asn.au/document/item/4551

Boyle, D. P., & Springer, A. (2001). Toward a cultural competence measure for social work with specific populations. *Journal of Ethnic and Cultural Diversity in Social Work, 9*(3–4), 53–71.

Charleston, B., Gajewska-De Mattos, H., & Chapman, M. (2017). Cross-cultural competence in the context of NGOs: Bridging the gap between "knowing" and "doing." *The International Journal of Human Resource Management*, 29(21), 3068–3092. doi:10.1080/09585192.2016.1276469

Davie, G. (2013). *The sociology of religion: A critical agenda.* Thousand Oaks, CA: SAGE.

Dinham, A., & Francis, M. (Eds.) (2015). *Religious literacy in policy and practice.* Bristol, UK: Policy Press.

Foucault, M. (1999/2013). *Religion and culture.* New York, NY: Routledge.

Frick, E., Riedner, C., Fegg, M. J., Hauf, S., & Borasio, G. D. (2006). A clinical interview assessing cancer patients' spiritual needs and preferences. *European Journal of Cancer Care, 15*(3), 238–243.

Garneau, A. B., & Pepin, J. (2015). Cultural competence: A constructivist definition. *Journal of Transcultural Nursing, 26*(1), 9–15.

Hook, J. N., Davis, D. E., Owen, J., Worthington Jr., E. L. & Utsey, S. O. (2013). Cultural humility: Measuring openness to culturally diverse clients. *Journal of Counseling Psychology, 60*(3), 353–366.

Izard, C. E. (2013). *Human emotions.* London, UK: Springer.

Kohli, H. K., Huber, R., & Faul, A. C. (2010). Historical and theoretical development of culturally competent social work practice. *Journal of Teaching in Social Work, 30*(3), 252–271.

National Association of Social Workers. (2015). *NASW standards for cultural competence in social work practice.* Retrieved from https://www.socialworkers.org/LinkClick.aspx?fileticket=7dVckZAYUmk%3d&portalid=0

Noyes R., Jr. (1980). Attitude change following near-death experiences. *Psychiatry, 43*(3), 234–242.

Pentaris, P. (2014). Religion, secularism, and professional practice. *Studia Sociologica, 6*(1), 99–109.

Pentaris, P. (2019a). *Religious literacy in hospice care: Challenges and controversies.* London, UK: Routledge.

Pentaris, P. (2019b). Religion, belief and spirituality in healthcare. In S. Gehlert & T. Browne (Eds.), *Handbook of health social work* (3rd ed.) Hoboken, NJ: Wiley.

Puchalski, C., & Romer, A. L. (2000). Taking a spiritual history allows clinicians to understand patients more fully. *Journal of Palliative Medicine, 3*(1), 129–137.

Roheim, G. (1950). *Psychoanalysis and anthropology: Culture, personality and the unconscious.* Oxford, UK: International Universities Press.

Scheider, D. M., Sneath, L., & Waynick, T. C. (2012). Grief and loss. In D. K. Snyder & C. M. Monson (Eds.) *Couple-based interventions for military and veteran families: A practitioner's guide* (pp. 260–285). New York, NY: Guilford.

Van Gennep, A. (1961. *The rites of passage.* Chicago, IL: University of Chicago Press.

Walter, C. A., & McCoyd, J. L. (2015). *Grief and loss across the lifespan: A biopsychosocial perspective.* London, UK: Springer.

Yan, M. C. & Wong, Y. L. R. (2005). Rethinking self-awareness in cultural competence: Toward a dialogic self in cross-cultural social work. *Families in Society: The Journal of Contemporary Social Services, 86*(2), 181–188.

Concept of Death in Hinduism: Implications for Therapeutic Process

Apurvakumar Pandya, PhD, MA, Indian Institute of Public Health Gandhinagar, Gujarat, India
Tripti Kathuria, PhD, MSc, Maharaja Sayajirao University of Baroda, Vadodara, India

FIGURE 4.1. Apurvakumar Pandya

Apurva-Kumar Pandya is a registered rehabilitation psychologist in India. Currently he is working as a scientist at Regional Resource Centre for Health Technology Assessment, Indian Institute of Public Health Gandhinagar (IIPH-G) and as a psychologist providing counseling services to post-graduate students of an institution. He has more than 12 years of experience working in the field of HIV prevention, research, program management, and preventive counselling services for youth; vulnerable children in need of care and protection and children in juvenile homes; and lesbian, gay, bisexual, transgender, and Hijra populations. While dealing with clients having chronic health conditions such HIV/AIDS, cancer, as well as clients with same-sex sexual identities, transgender, transsexual, and hijra individuals going through grief, concepts of death have been common issues he encountered during therapeutic process. Each client's experience of chronic disease and reaction to near-death experiences is greatly affected by the culture, religious and spiritual notions, as well as practices. This lead him review the concept of death/end-of-life issues in the Hindu religion very closely, from the clients as well as practitioners' perspective within given sociocultural context.

FIGURE 4.2. Tripti Kathuria

Tripti Kathuria is an assistant professor (temporary) at the Department of Human Development and Family Studies, the Maharaja Sayajirao University of Baroda and is also pursuing doctoral research from the same university. Prior to joining the department, she worked as a counselor at Vidya Global School in Meerut, Uttar Pradesh. She teaches post-graduate courses on guidance and counseling and research methodology and supervises practicum course. She has dealt with students having suicidal tendencies where she explored how students with these tendencies conceptualize death and how the same the religious concepts around death help overcome suicidal thoughts. In addition to this, her areas of research interests include emotion socialization of children, guidance and counseling, identity development, and yoga.

Introduction

Inclusion of spirituality and religion in therapeutic process has been a relatively recent development (Mizock, Millner & Russinova, 2012; Post & Wade, 2009). Professional and scientific psychology during the 20th century intentionally excluded issues of religion or spirituality from psychotherapy (Gorsuch & Miller, 1999; Plante, 2007). Moreover, the positive association between religious and spiritual issues and mental health was rarely mentioned. Some scholars, however, have pointed out that these are ancient practices filtered over hundreds of years from the collective experience of the community, that in fact have a high degree of efficacy at the practical and everyday level (Day, 2010; Hamilton, 2017, Hoy, & Worden, 2013, Manickam, & Sahya, 2004). Recently scholars, clinicians, and psychotherapists have started understanding religion and spirituality for better mental health outcomes (Brewer-Smyth & Koenig, 2014; Fallot, 2008; Hoy, & Worden, 2013) and hence growing efforts to incorporate spiritual perspectives in the context of psychotherapy (Klaasen, Graham, & Young, 2009; Mizock, Millner, & Russinova, 2012) are evident.

Within the broader health perspective, the aspect of religion and spirituality cannot be ignored. Ignoring religious concepts of death and relevant practices may create barriers between clinicians and clients (Day, 2010; Sperry & Shafranske, 2005), which could compromise the therapeutic relationship necessary for successful health outcomes. Awareness and sensitivity to cultural diversity begins with acknowledging religious and spiritual practices (Hage, Hopson, Siegel, Payton, & DeFanti, 2011). Religious beliefs and practices contribute to clients' coping strategies, psychological well-being, successful coping, and resilience (Blando, 2006; Brewer-Smyth, & Koenig, 2014; Faigin & Pargament, 2011; Klaasen, Graham, & Young, 2009). The therapeutic process can be counterproductive when religious and spiritual issues are integrated into therapeutic process (Richards & Bergin, 2005; Young, Wiggins-Frame, & Cashwell, 2007). Becoming sensitive to clients' concepts of death and relevant practices show acceptance and respect for the client, which in turn increase trust and elevates the therapeutic alliance.

This section provides a brief overview of Hinduism, discusses concept of death, meaning of death, and rituals related to death. At the end, the authors present implications for facilitating the therapeutic process.

Methodology

Authors reviewed Indian as well as international literature on the concept of death in Hinduism and its therapeutic relevance. Keywords used were *concept of death in Hinduism, meaning of death in Hinduism, death-related rituals in Hinduism*, and *concept of death in counseling and psychotherapy*. Google scholar and PubMed were used for researching relevant articles. Between the years 2008 and 2018, 593 articles addressing the theme from a variety of theoretical and empirical perspectives were found and 14 articles were selected for the appraisal after reviewing abstracts. While reviewing, authors realized the need to understand perspectives of individuals, Hindu priests, clients who have availed counseling services in the past 6 months, and psychologists who deal with issues of grief, bereavement, and end-of-life issues on death and rituals related to death. In this vein, the first author has conducted rapid telephone interviews with 23 Hindu clients, two practicing psychologists, and three priests to understand their conceptualization of death, meaning of death, and practices popularly followed to deal with death and terminal illness. Data was translated, coded, and analyzed using thematic content analysis (Vaismoradi, Jones, Turunen, & Snelgrove, 2016).

Hinduism: An Overview

Hinduism is the world's oldest living faith; it can be traced back to 4,000 years ago and is third largest religion, practiced primarily in the Indian subcontinent. Hindus are spread in many countries around the world, including by substantially large populations in southern and southeast Asia, Europe, the United Kingdom, Africa, North America, and Australia. The Hindu faith has numerous schools of thought, without any founder, organizational hierarchy, structure, and central administration. Hinduism is defined by its social system and life-centered philosophical, religious, and ethical approach (Bowker, 2000). Hinduism as a way of life upholds the principles of virtuous and true living (Thillainathan, 2009).

The Hindu religion is also known as *Sanatan Dharma*, which translates to Eternal Spiritual Path. Hindu beliefs, rituals, and religious practices emanate from a wide collection of philosophical literature and scriptures including the Vedas, the Upanishads, the Bhagavad Gita, Samhitas, Darshan Shastra, and the epics Ramayana and the Mahabharata. The Hindu belief is nonexclusive, which accepts all other faiths and religious paths, for example, *Rig Veda* (one of the four vedas) says that "God or Truth is one and wise people refer to it by many names."

Concept of Death in Hinduism

Death is frequently mentioned in many *Upanishads*, the *Samhitas* and *Bhagavad Gita*. These scriptures describe that the mind and body are subject to death and destruction, while the soul is eternal and indestructible. Death is a temporary cessation of physical activity. The body is subject to death, hunger, and decay, while soul (*atma*) is immortal and indestructible. The *atma* is reborn many times. Bhagavad Gita explains this concept as follows:

> *As a man casts off his worn-out clothes and takes on other new ones, so does the embodied soul cast off his worn-out bodies and enters other new.*
>
> Bhagavad Gita 2:22

According to *Bhagavad Gita*, chapter 2, stanza 27, death is an inevitable. The soul can move nearer the ultimate release from rebirth, *moksha*.

> *For sure is the death of all that comes to birth, sure is the birth of all that dies. So in a matter that no one can prevent thou hast no cause to grieve.*
>
> Bhagavad Gita 2:27

The ultimate goal of the life is to attain *Moksha*: subsume with great *atman* and free from the cycle of birth and death. *Karma* (deeds) decides the course of a soul to Moksha. *Karma* is the law of cause and effect, which teaches that all actions have corresponding results. Three types of *Karma* are explained in Hindu scriptures:

- *Sanchita karma*: The karma credited from previous lives
- *Paapa*: Sinful actions in the past and present that cause suffering
- *Agami karma*: The actions that are performed in the present life and which will affect the future

Hinduism approaches the end of life with good and bad death and emphasis on good karma (good deeds) and rituals to achieve peaceful death (Hamilton, 2017; Sharma, Jagdish, Anusha, & Bharti, 2013).

Ending life is not acceptable to Hindus, unless they took their lives as self-sacrifice or attain self-knowledge and accept *Samadhi*. The first historic emperor of India, Chandragupta Maurya, who in the last phase of his life traveled south and fasted for 40 days in a cave to end his life. Hindu tradition proposes to renounce the social life and adapt *Sanyasa ashrama* in the last phase of his life to attain *Moksha* (liberation). The Indian warriors believed to be fought valiantly with the sole objective of dying while fighting and going to the heaven of warriors (*vira-svargam*). It was also common for the wives of warriors to commit ritual suicide when their husbands died in the wars. This tradition eventually resulted into the practice of Sati custom and Johar among Rajput women, which is abolished now. Suicide is acceptable under extraordinary circumstances. Hindu traditions and customs do not permit killing of any kind and suicide is no exception. *Yajur Veda* explains this as follows:

> *The one who tries to escape from the trials of life by committing suicide will suffer even more in the next life.*
>
> Yajur Veda 40–43

Beliefs About Death: Source of Meaning Hindus Assigned to Their Lives

Authors have analyzed beliefs related to death and rituals from 28 participants which are categorized as follows:

Death is natural; no one can delay it. Death is inevitable. Those who live have to die one day. The time of death is determined by one's destiny that no one can change. Pain, illness, and suffering are results of past *karma* deeds or deeds of previous lives. Future lives are influenced by how one faces illness, disability, and/or death. According to the *Vedas*, the world in which we live is a mortal world. The Supreme Brahman, who was originally a non-being, manifested as a supreme being in the world. Supreme Brahman is also known as *Isvara*, God, or *Param Atman* (supreme soul). People with these beliefs are often open to accept illness. Gautam and Jain (2010) highlighted that Hindu patients tend to accept the diagnosis of cancer rather easily compared to others.

It is a tradition to read Gita when death is anticipated to help the individual accept the death in a more gracious manner (Gautam & Jain, 2010). The concept of "स्थितप्रज्ञ" (sthit-pragna), remaining detached from pleasure and sorrow, denotes that when mind is unaffected by losses and gains, it represents the peaceful state of the mind. One of the Neeti Shlokas says, "It is not your duty to grieve the past nor should you worry about the future. Only he, who lives the present and thinks about the present is a wise man," and this saying can help a depressed patient worrying about a recent loss. Bhagawad Gita says in the second chapter, stanza 22, "[A]s you remove torn clothes and wear new ones *atma* also leave[s] and occupies new bodies." This helps clients as well as significant others to accept death (Balodhi, & Keshavan, 2011).

There is no start or end of life. According to Hindu mythology, the soul goes through different lives, experiencing death multiple times to attain the *Moksha* liberation from the cycle of death and birth. Gautam and Nijhawan (1987) found in their study that the concept of death in Hindu clients is based on philosophy of *Gita* where soul is considered as immortal and has significant impact on the easy acceptance of the diagnosis and the planning for the rest of the life. Gita's chapter 2, stanza 23 says, "[T]he soul can never be cut to pieces by any weapon, nor burned by fire, nor washed away by floods nor moistened by water, nor withered by the wind." Further in 27th stanza of chapter 2 Bhagwat Gita says, "[E]verything born must die, everything dead must get born again and you should not worry about these events."

There is one place called *Swarg* (heaven) and one place called *Narak* (hell). Soul after death is assigned either *Swarg* or *Narak* according to deeds, karma, until they take their next birth. *Yama,* popularly believed to be the god of death, is probably the one, like a shrewd accountant, who keeps track of the good and the bad deeds, devoid of feeling or judgement, and sends the soul accordingly to its deserving place.

The deceased first resides in *Pitrulok,* until designated the next place of accommodation, and until eventually they take the next birth. Hinduism talk about three worlds, Swarglok, Pitrulok, and Yamlok. *Pitrulok* is the world where all ancestors reside who watch over us. *Yamlok* is above the *Pitrulok. Swarglok* is on the top of the *Yamlok.* Shraddh (after death ritual spread over the year, 10th day, 12th day, 13th day, 1-year rituals) helps souls to travel through pitrulok, and yamalok to new birth or liberation. Soul with good karma goes to *swarglok.*

Thoughts at the time of death determine the next birth. The state of mind at the time of death, like predominant thoughts and desires, decides the place (*swarglok, heaven or pitrulok, place of ancestors or narklok, hell*) where the soul will reside and re-birth. For example, a person thinking of his family and children at the time of his death will go to the *pirtulok* and will be born again in that family. A person with negative or evil thoughts or desires will go to the *narklok* and suffer in the hands of evil. If a person is thinking of God at the time of his death, he will go to the *swarglok,* the highest world. Souls cannot take anything except samskaras (tendencies). The Bhagvad Gita says, "[Y]ou worry about events you are not supposed, and speak like a learned man, wise people do not worry about things that are perishable, or immortal." It is advised to take name of the God while dying, *Maafi* forgive people, *prayaschit* (confess) all sins, and *jaap* (meditate God's name), *daan* (give gifts or help the needy) to cleanse soul from *Maya* desire and remain detached (Balodhi, & Keshavan, 2011).

Devotion and trust in God ease the pain and bring peaceful death. Trust or faith remains the most important elements of Hindu life. Trust is also a very important part of the therapeutic relationship. Chapter 18 of Bhagwad Gita says, "[L]eave everything and trust me, I will rescue you from all the problems, Do not Worry." It further says in chapter 10, stanza 22, "I am the mind; and in living beings I am the living force [consciousness]. I am Omnipotent, and Omnipresent" (Balodhi, & Keshavan, 2011, p. 301). This directs Hindu followers to pray and believe that God is there.

Karma or deeds play an important part. The next birth is also decided on the karma of the previous birth where there are ample chances for improvement. Therefore, Hindus are believed to engage in good deeds. In Hinduism there is no particular judgment day. In fact, every day persons' actions are weighed and *paap (de-merit)* and *punya (merit)* keeps accumulating according to your deeds (Bhargava, Kumar & Gupta, 2017). Therefore, emphasis is on earning *punya* from good deeds. The legend of *Savitri* (an ancient character) provides the framework to deal with loss in psychotherapy (Chadda, & Deb, 2013; Bhargava, Kumar & Gupta, 2017). Further, the concepts of *karma* and *dharma* are very useful in the psychotherapy (Balodhi, & Keshavan, 2011).

Good deeds accumulate *punya* and bad deeds result into *paap*. Hinduism put emphasis on *karma* in life. Present life is the result of *karma* earned in the past life and the future life is determined by our current deeds. Good actions (pious activities) create *punya-karma*, while sinful deeds result in *paap-karma* and accordingly go to the *swarglok*, *pitrulok*, or *narklok*. There are 10 activities suggested to earn *punya*: (1) helping the needy by providing assistance in getting rid of material suffering, (2) promoting spiritual development, (3) respect for elders and ones in higher position, (4) charity, (5) giving something away to worthy people, (6) cleanliness of body and mind, (7) observance of holidays, (8) Vratas (e.g. fasting as an offering to various deities), (9) mortality (e.g. forgiveness, gratitude, truthfulness etc), and (10) taking care of domestic animals (e.g cows are compared to mother).

***Moksha* (liberation) is the ultimate goal of life.** The cycle of births and rebirths is seemingly never ending; however, it can be escaped through *Moksha (liberation)*. *Moksha* is attaining self-knowledge and obtaining freedom from *desire*. Once moksha is attained, a soul is subsumed with supreme soul (*Paramatma*) or God and is free from the cycle of death and birth. *Moksha* metaphorically means abandoning desire one by one until you are left with nothing. *Moksha* is attained through *yoga*, *jap* (chant), and *karma* (good deeds).

True devotees follow rituals to get rid of problems. Hinduism is rich in rituals to have a peaceful death and achieve liberation. The most prominent rituals related to death are daily puja, prayers, bhajans, daan, and shraddh. Various religious rituals are carried out to build relationship with the Divine and bring peace to the soul. Religious practices and rituals have been associated with various positive outcomes including resilience and coping (Worthington, 2011). Hindu rituals provide an opportunity for catharsis, for people to confront their grief, interact with it, accept it, and have the courage to move on both in personal and spiritual life. These practices also can promote a sense of security and ease anxiety and loneliness.

***Atma* soul is eternal and does not die.** It is beyond birth and death. It's not the soul but the body that dies. The soul travels from one body to another and is eternal. Persons are the absolute knower and observer of the soul and the body. Since all species experience the cycle of birth and death, humans tend to perceive death as death of self. Wise people are thosee who view the self as a separate entity from the body and constantly remain the "knower and observer" of the body.

Practices Related to Death

Rituals before death. The rituals represent practices to prolong death and attain *moksha* (liberation). Primarily these practices emphasize good deeds, yoga, and rituals to have painless death and attain liberation.

Good deeds. The karma is the cause of rebirth and human suffering and no one can escape from the consequences of actions. Pious deeds result in good karma and secure the place in heaven or the ancestral world, where souls can stay and avoid the mortal world and death until their karma is fully exhausted. Besides this, by performing meritorious actions one can secure better life in the next birth. Good karma can be gained by performing rituals and obligatory duties.

Yoga. The purpose of yoga is to obtain immortality. The practice of yoga ensures detachments from desires by training the mind, ensuring better health and peace. Yoga practices, retraining of the mind and the senses, breathing techniques, and postures purify the mind, soul, and body. The advanced practices of yoga result in inner transformation and cleansing of the karmas whereby a person becomes liberated from the mortal life forever. Hinduism prescribes several other forms of yoga, namely *samkhya yoga, rajayoga, hatha yoga, karma yoga, sanyasa yoga, bhakti yoga, karma sanyasa yoga, dhyana yoga,* and so, which are equally effective in achieving self-transformation and liberation. Many mental health professionals consider yoga as a complementary psychotherapy and use it as a treatment modality (Anodea, 2016; Manickam & Sahya, 2004; Weintraub, 2012).

Rituals. Neither the first nor the second approach helps humans escape from the cycle of births and death. Rituals help persons become pure, attain liberation, and enter the world of *Brahman* as a free soul (*mukta*).

Rituals while dying. The atmosphere around the dying person is created peacefully. The holy book *Gita* (Hindu scripture) and religious *mantra* is recited to strengthen the person's mind and provide comfort. A family member chants the mantra, *Aum Namo Narayana* or *Aum Nama Sivaya* softly in the right ear of a dying or deceased person.

Rituals at the moment of death. Religious chanting before and after death is continuously offered by family, friends, and priests. Immediately after death, priests or family members pour (*River Ganga*) water drops into mouth of deceased. Water of *Ganga is* considered holy. The body is laid on the cot or the ground with the head facing south at the home's entry gate, reflecting a return to the lap of Mother Earth. Holy ash or sandal paste is applied to the forehead, and a white cloth is tied under the chin and over the top of the head. The thumbs are tied together, as are the big toes. The lamp is kept lit near the head and incense is burned. A widow places her wedding pendant around her husband's neck, signifying her enduring tie to him. The coffin is then closed. Relatives bid farewell and sing sacred hymns and devotional songs (*bhajans*) at the side of the body. The body is lifted by four people to cremation, which is commonly done on day of death, with the exception or fetuses or children under age 2 and Sanyasis bodies, which are buried without any rituals observed.

Cremation. The act of cremation is considered *antyesthi*, the ultimate sacrifice in human life. It purifies the soul from the impurities of the body by the fire. Traditionally, only men were allowed to go to the cremation site; however, with time, now women, in some communities, too go to the cremation site and perform rituals. The body is placed on the pyre, covered with wood, and offered incense and ghee. The chief mourner lights the pyre and leaves the cremation grounds.

Returning home, all bathe and clean the house. Twelve hours after the cremation, the chief mourner returns to the cremation site to collect the remains: ashes and small pieces of white bones. Ashes and pieces of bones are carried and deposed in the Ganges river or placed in an auspicious river or the ocean either on the 13th day or any day within a year. Some communities observed for 13 days wherein family and close relatives of the deceased do not visit others' homes and cook food at home. It is a norm that neighbors and relatives bring daily meals to relieve the burden during mourning days. The family doesn't celebrate or attend any festivals and temples, visit priests, or take part in marriages or any social functions for the period up to one year. These observances are optional in case of the death of friends, teachers, or students. In Hinduism, mourning is never suppressed or denied; however, scriptures encourage joyous release. It is believed that the departed soul is acutely conscious of emotional forces directed at him or her. Prolonged grieving can hold him or her in earthly consciousness, inhibiting full transition to the heaven worlds. Therefore, performing *rituals, prayers, daan, and good deeds* are emphasized for the peace of departed soul.

First memorial. On the third day relatives gather at the home of deceased person. A photograph of the deceased is placed, a lamp is lit and incense is burned. Relatives offer prayers for the soul and offer condolences to the family of the deceased. This is the time when all relatives and neighbors visit the home and provide support to the family of deceased as it is considered *punya karma* to receive blessings from ancestors.

Thirteenth day of memorial. On the 13th day, a memorial service is held at home or at holy place or on the Bank of the Ganga or any holy river. The place of the puja is thoroughly cleansed to remove all impurities in the home or at the place. A hindu priest (*Brahmin or Maharaj*) performs the *Shraddh.* He prepares *sapindikarana,* making one big pinda (ball from boiled rice), which represents the deceased, and three small pindas, representing ancestors (deceased father, grandfather and great-grandfather). The large pinda is cut into three pieces and assimilated with three small ones to ritually unite the soul with the ancestors. These three *pinda* are offered prayers. The *pindas* are fed to the crows, to a cow, or thrown in a river for the fish. Some perform this rite on the 11th or 12th day after cremation. Others perform it twice: on the 11th, 12th, or 13th day and after one year. Once the first *sapindikarana* is completed, the ritual impurity ends and the soul can travel from *yamalok* to *pitrulok* peacefully. Some communities perform *shraddh* every month for the peace of the soul.

Shraddh: One-year memorial. *Shraddh* is usually performed on the first anniversary of the death of the deceased. A priest conducts the *shraddh* rites in the home, offering *pinda* to the ancestors. This ceremony is done once and some do it yearly, as long as the family wants to perform. It is now common in India to observe *shraddh* for ancestors just prior to the yearly Navaratri[1] festival.

Authors' Reflections on the Concept of Death and Its Usage in Therapeutic Conversations

According to Hinduism, the soul is born again and again on earth in different bodies. It is also called reincarnation and a cyclic existence (McClelland, 2018). Re-birth of soul continues until it reunites with the supreme source, popularly known as *Param Brahma* or *Parmatma* and attains *moksha* (i.e., salvation, where cycle of birth comes to an end). Intent and actions impact how one dies and reincarnates. Good intent and actions create positive causes leading to dignified death and a good life after

1 Navratri denotes to "nine nights," a Hindu festival to Goddess Durga or Amba Mata. Various Hindu sects celebrate Navratri differently; however, the common theme is the battle and victory of good over evil. Over 9 days, devotees observe, fast, and offer prayers. This is considered an auspicious day and ancestors travel on the earth. It is considered the best time to offer prayers and pinda to receive blessings from ancestors.

death while bad intent and actions cause negative tendencies in life and attract bad life after death. Therefore, the primary goal of life, according to Hindu philosophy of existence, is to attain a dignified death and attempt to attain salvation.

This concept is applied during therapeutic conversations with clients having suicidal ideation. Once excerpt from a client pursuing 12 years of schooling in India is as follows:

> Clinician: What made you think of suicide?
>
> Client: I fear the exam. I am sure that I will fail the board exam and not able to face the consequences.
>
> Clinician: You reached to the 12th class, which means that you have taken many exams already. If you find suicide as the last resort, then you won't be re-born after death and then you have to take exam again from the first class.
>
> Client: Haa [Yes], then I need to appear for exams again and will face fear again.
>
> Clinician: What is better for you do right now?
>
> Client: [thinking] How can I face the exam and overcome fear?

The purpose of this counseling case was to encourage the student to reflect on his fears and deal with them. We present another case depicting how concepts of Hinduism in therapeutic processes facilitate change in clients' lives.

Case Story

This case is of a young Indian woman, 27 years old, Piya (pseudonym), who lost her husband unexpectedly. Piya is well educated with her master's degree in computer science. She met her late husband, Rahul (pseudonym), in her undergraduate college, and they were in a relationship for 5 years before they decided to marry each other. Getting married to a person of her choice was not difficult in their case (not very common in small town of north India) since they belonged to same community. She had her first boy child who is around 2-and-half years old. She always wanted to be homemaker and take care of the family. She was not at all ambitious for her career. She was happy with living life as she wanted and was content with life.

After 3 years of their marriage, Piya and her husband went out to celebrate a New Year's party (on December 31, 2015). While returning home, Rahul complained of a stomach ache and everyone in family tried home remedies, which is common practice in India, assuming it might be result of over-eating or alcohol. However, it did not help, so finally they decided to seek medical help. While they were on the way to visit the doctor, Rahul left his body, an utter shock for Piya and her in-laws. She was not able to accept an untimely, unexpected death and had difficulty sleeping. She was not able to do day-to-day work, felt lonely and scared to go in her own room, and was concerned about the future of her son, leading to panic attacks. She was advised to consult a psychiatrist and was on anti-anxiety medication. She was annoyed with people's sympathy, their perception of a single mother, and advice from others for re-marriage was discouraging, making her more anxious.

After her husband's death she soon joined one school as a computer teacher to divert her mind, where she consulted a school counselor. She emptied herself and the counselor encouraged her to express her emotions—sadness, fear, questions, gratitude—through poems and write-ups. The counselor moved her attention toward shifts in her writings: poems and write-ups moving from sadness, fears, and "Why me?" questions to showing gratefulness toward God for the support from her in-laws, encouragements from the family even in the absence of her husband, daily prayers, and worships. More importantly, she, for the first time, discovered the creative writer inside her. She then started writing more about strengths and faith in God. At the same time, her sister-in-law (late husband's sister who is settled in United States), suggested for her to join a Buddhism group in her town that meets every month and chants in alliance. She started chanting every day, in addition to her daily prayers and worships, with a purpose to achieve her goals: become a creative writer/poet, aspire to a career, and attain happiness. She focused her life on creating a good cause for a better life with prayers, chanting, and rituals, which is in Hinduism is good *karma*. Her faith in life and God rebuilt and she gained courage to dream and pursue her dream. Consequently, she got her visa for higher education studies in the United States on the date of her husband's death anniversary, which she considered his will for her to settle abroad.

Reflections on the Case Story

Counseling intervention and religious ritual has played an important role in overcoming her grief, identifying her life goals, and pursuing them tirelessly. Counseling sessions only comprised of listening to her, reading her poems and sharing counselors' reflections on what she has shared. Her faith, inculcated through counseling process and engagements in rituals (prayers, chanting, and worship), gave her new direction. During the counseling sessions, the psychiatrist evaluated her case and tapered the drug dose and gradually stopped medication.

Implications for the Therapeutic Process

Hinduism represents diversity and inclusiveness with multiples sects within the faith and allows individuals to practice as they desire. Therefore, there would be personal and cultural variations, making it difficult to provide prescriptive rules that apply to all. With Hindu beliefs of *karma* and reincarnation, Hindu clients tend to accept difficult circumstances and comply with the instructions of health care providers easily (Gautam & Jain, 2010; Reddy, 2012). However, clinicians need to understand clients' beliefs, acceptance of current situation, level of religious observance, spiritual goals, diet, and religious as well as spiritual practices as steps for building alliance. Clinicians can take a spiritual history, examining changes in faith and levels of commitment, core religious and spiritual beliefs about death and dying, level of connection with religious/spiritual communities, personal spiritual practices, and the relation of spiritual life to goals of well-being (Fallot, 2008).

Death is recognized in Hinduism as a central problem of the human being and all rituals and spiritual practices are meant to achieve peaceful death and immortality. Discussion on the natural inevitability of birth and death of life cycle, immortality of soul, and deeds otherwise create the risk of shame and public defame (Manickam, 2010). Therefore, it is crucial to remove guilt and fear and engage the mind constructively. Spiritual concepts of *karma* and *dharma* help clients deal with death and dying positively. Here, the discussion on rituals to cleanse the soul may be useful.

Hindu culture emphasizes the power and capabilities of the individual self and how the person alone is responsible for his or her actions, growth or otherwise. Clinicians could harness and utilize these techniques and accommodate the Hindu meditative and contemplative approach with its emphasis on an interior life. Emphasis could be placed on inner resources and a heightened self-control of will. Healthy practices can be encouraged, for example, breathing exercises (*pranayama*), meditation, and chants (*jaap*) are good strategies to help clients calm their mind, accept illness, and reduce overthinking or worries related to disease and death; yoga can be helpful to improve physical movement and mental alertness; recitation *of mantras* or devotional songs or reading of the Holy book, *Shrimad Bhagawad Gita*, and other scriptures, can restore faith. Charity (*daan*) can be very useful if a client is loaded with the guilt of bad karma, which resulted in the illness or dying situation.

Conclusion

Various schools of thoughts in Hinduism present the importance of the soul, the ultimate aim of attaining *moksha,* and the requirement of living virtuously in order to be prepared for a death. A significant body of literature reflected that recognizing and integrating religious beliefs can hold many benefits. Understanding religious beliefs of death, rituals related to death in Hinduism can facilitate therapeutic conversations and interactions with Hindu clients. Inclusion of cultural, spiritual, and religious issues in therapy for Hindu clients offers valuable opportunities to provide spiritual support in the individual's journey of recovery and dealing with chronic diseases.

References

Anodea, J. (2016). *Chakra yoga*. Woodbury, MN: Llewellyn.

Balodhi, J. P., & Keshavan, M. S. (2011). Bhagavad gita and psychotherapy. *Asian Journal of Psychiatry, 17*(4), 300–302.

Bhargava, R., Kumar, N., & Gupta, A. (2017). Indian perspective on psychotherapy: Cultural issues. *Journal of Contemporary Psychotherapy, 47*(2), 95–103.

Blanch, A. (2007). Integrating religion and spirituality in mental health: The promise and the challenge. *Psychiatric Rehabilitation Journal, 30*(4), 251–260.

Blando, J. (2006). Spirituality, religion, and counseling. *Counseling and Human Development, 39*(2), 1–14.

Bowker, J. (2000). *Hinduism. The concise oxford dictionary of world religions.* Oxford, UK: Oxford University Press.

Brewer-Smyth, K., & Koenig, H. G. (2014). Could spirituality and religion promote stress resilience in survivors of childhood trauma? *Issues in Mental Health Nursing, 35*(4), 251–256.

Cashwell, C. S., & Young, J. S. (2011). *Integrating spirituality in counseling: A guide to competent practice* (2nd ed.). Alexandria, VA: American Counseling Association.

Cashwell, C. S., Young, J. S., Crockett, J., Fulton, C., Giordano, A., Tate, N., … & Wyatt, L. (2013). Clinical behaviors for addressing religious/spiritual issues: Do we practice what we preach? *Counseling and Values, 58*(1), 45–58.

Chadda, R. K., & Deb, K. S. (2013). Indian family systems, collectivistic society and psychotherapy. *Indian Journal of Psychiatry, 55*(2), 299–309.

Day, J. M. (2010). Religion, spirituality, and positive psychology in adulthood: A developmental view. *Journal of Adult Development, 17*(4), 215–229.

Faigin, C., & Pargament, K. I. (2011). Strengthened by the spirit: Religion, spirituality, and resilience through adulthood and aging. *Resilience in Aging*, 163–180.

Fallot, R. D. (2008). Spirituality and religion. In K. T. Mueser. & D.V. Jeste (Eds.) *Clinical handbook of schizophrenia* (pp. 592–603). New York, NY: Guilford.

Gautam, S., & Jain, N. (2010). Indian culture and psychiatry. *Indian Journal of Psychiatry, 52*(1), 309–313.

Gautam, S., & Nijhawan, M. (1987). Communicating with cancer patients. *British Journal of Psychiatry, 150*(6), 760–764.

Gorsuch, R. L.; Miller, W.R. (1999). Assessing spirituality. In Miller, W.R., (Ed)., Integrating spirituality into treatment: Resources for practitioners. (pp. 47–64). Washington, DC: American Psychological Association.

Hage, S., Hopson, A., Siegel, M., Payton, G., & DeFanti, E. (2011). Multicultural training in spirituality: An interdisciplinary review. *Counselling, 50*(3), 217–234.

Hamilton, I. (2017). Indian philosophical foundations of spirituality at the end of life. *Mortality: Promoting the Interdisciplinary Study of Death and Dying,* 1–13.

Hoy, W., & Worden, J. (2013). *Do funerals matter?* New York, NY: Routledge.

Klaasen, D., Graham, M., & Young, R. (2009). Spiritual/religious coping as intentional activity: An action theoretical perspective. *Archive of Psychology Religion, 31*(3), 3–33.

Kübler-Ross, E. (2009). *On death and dying: What the dying have to teach doctors, nurses, clergy and their own families.* Taylor & Francis.

Manickam, L. S. S. (2010). Psychotherapy in India. *Indian Journal of Psychiatry, 52*(1), 366–370.

Manickam, L. S. S (2004). Sahya: The concept in Indian philosophical psychology and its contemporary relevance. In K. Joshi & M. Cornelissen (Eds.) Yoga and Indian approaches to psychology. (pp. 427–435). New-Delhi: Centre for the Study of Civilizations.

McClelland, N. C. (2018), Encyclopedia of Reincarnation and Karma, McFarland, pp.24–25, p.321. ISBN 978-0786448517

Mizock, L., Millner, U. C., & Russinova, Z. (2012). Spiritual and religious issues in psychotherapy with schizophrenia: Cultural implications and implementation. *Religions, 3*(1), 82–98.

Plante, T. G. (2007). Integrating spirituality and psychotherapy: Ethical issues and principles to consider. *Journal of Clinical Psychology, 63*(9), 891–902.

Post, B. C., & Wade, N. G. (2009). Religion and spirituality in psychotherapy: A practice-friendly review of research. *Journal of Clinical Psychology, 65*(2), 131–146.

Reddy, M. S. (2012). Psychotherapy: Insights from Bhagavad Gita. *Indian Journal of Psychological Medicine, 34*(1), 100–104.

Richards, S. P., & Bergin, A. E. (2005). *A spiritual strategy for counseling and psychotherapy.* Washington, DC: American Psychological Association

Sharma, H., Jagdish, V., Anusha, P., & Bharti, S. (2013). End-of-life care: Indian perspective. *Indian Journal of Psychiatry,*55(2), 293–298.

Sperry, L., & Shafranske, E. P. (2005). *Spiritually oriented psychotherapy.* Washington, DC: American Psychological Association.

Surya, N. C., & Jayaram, S. S. (1968). Some basic considerations in the practice of psychotherapy in the Indian setting. *Indian Journal of Psychiatry, 4*, 153–156.

Thillainathan, N. (2009). Rogers to reincarnation: Counseling people of the Hindu faith. *Psychotherapy in Australia, 15*(4), 51–52.

Vaismoradi, M., Jones, J., Turunen, H., & Snelgrove, S. (2016). Theme development in qualitative content analysis and thematic analysis. *Journal of Nursing Education and Practice, 6*(5), 100–110.

Weintraub, A. (2012). *Yoga skills for therapists: Effective practices for mood management.* New York, NY: Norton.

Worthington, E. L. (2011). Integration of spirituality and religion in psychotherapy. In J. C. Norcross., G. R. VandenBos & D. K. Freedheim (Eds), *History of psychotherapy: Continuity and change* (2nd ed) (pp. 533–543). Washington, DC: American Psychological Association.

Young, J. S., Wiggins-Frame, M., & Cashwell, C. S. (2007). Spirituality and counselor competence: A national survey of American Counseling Association members. Journal of Counseling & Development, 85(1), 47–52.

Faith, Vow, and Practice: Dealing With Grief and Death in Chinese Buddhism

Wei Wu Tan, PhD, University of Melbourne, Australia

Wei Wu Tan is a Social Work PhD student and researcher at the University of Melbourne, Australia, doing research in child protection systems and social service programs. He is also involved in teaching research methodology and implementation science. Wei has a PhD in physics and has previously done research in atmospheric science. Prior to pursuing his second PhD at Melbourne, he was a high school principal in Malaysia for six years. Wei also has extensive experience in Buddhist studies and translations. He is interested in exploring how the insights of Buddhism and Social Work can enrich each other. In 2004, when Wei was working in the US as a researcher, his father passed away in a car accident in Malaysia. Seeing how his mother came to term with her loss prompted him to think more deeply about death and grieving, eventually leading to his participation in this book project.

FIGURE 4.3. Wei Wu Tan

Introduction

I still vividly remember the day when I received an unexpected phone call from my mom in late November 2004. It was early in the morning on a Saturday and I was making preparations to serve as the interpreter in a Buddhist meditation retreat in upstate New York over the Thanksgiving holidays. Sitting on the curb in front of a hospital mortuary in Malaysia, my mom called to tell me that my dad had just passed away in an accident. While walking to his car after attending a wedding banquet, he was hit by a motorcycle traveling against the traffic. I have never heard mom sound so distraught; an immense sense of sadness was transmitted thousands of miles across the continents as she broke the news to me, crying uncontrollably.

The incident was made worse since my mom and dad had received invitations to two events that evening and decided to each attend one, separately. For mom, there was probably also a sense of guilt and "what if," in addition to tremendous grief and loss. I could only console my mom and immediately arranged for a flight home. From the moment I learned of the news and through the 22-hour journey home from New York City to Malaysia, in accordance with my Buddhist practice, I silently chanted the name of Amitabha Buddha continuously, to help my dad move on to the ideal destination of rebirth as taught in Chinese Buddhism—the Western Pure Land of Amitabha Buddha.

My action on that journey home and through that episode of loss had its basis on the internalization of Buddhist philosophy of life, the practice of Buddhist mindfulness meditation, as well as faith-based Buddhist teachings. For many adherents of Chinese Buddhism who do not practice meditation, they would most likely rely on faith in Amitabha Buddha and practices associated with this faith when facing their own death and the death of loved ones. This is the subject matter of this section.

A brief overview of Buddhist traditions, Chinese Buddhist's view on death, and Buddhist cosmology is first presented to provide a historical and intellectual grounding for death and grieving-related issues.

Buddhist Traditions

Buddhism can be broadly classified into the southern tradition and the northern tradition (e.g. Gethin, R., 1998). The former includes the Burmese, Cambodian, Laotian, Sri Lankan, and Thai Buddhist traditions and is also known as the Theravada tradition or tradition of the elders. The latter includes the Chinese, Japanese, Korean, Tibetan, and Vietnamese Buddhist traditions and is also known as the Mahayana tradition or tradition of great vehicle. Buddhism practiced in the West today is informed by these diverse sources.

The foundational teachings of Buddhism, as taught in all traditions, are recorded in two sets of largely overlapping scriptures, one preserved in the ancient Pali language and the other in the Chinese language. Portions of this material are also preserved in the Tibetan language (Gethin, R., 1998). The former is called the Nikayas and is the major component of the canon of the southern tradition; the latter is called the Agamas and comprises a small part of the canons of the northern tradition. These core teachings entail understanding the causes of sufferings and engaging in practices to transcend sufferings.

The differences between the southern tradition and the northern tradition lie mainly in the former adhering to the foundational teachings as recorded in the Pali Canon while the latter emphasizes the bodhisattva ideal—the archetype of compassionate beings who work selflessly and tirelessly to alleviate sufferings of others—in addition to the foundational teachings. A large body of scriptures expounding the bodhisattva ideal comprise the most important part of the canons of the northern tradition. It is believed in the northern tradition that all sentient beings have the capacity to become a buddha and may realize that potential by living the bodhisattva way of life.

All Buddhist traditions venerate a buddha not as a god but as a compassionate being who has attained complete and perfect enlightenment and teaches what he has realized to help others transcend sufferings (Chan Master Sheng Yen, 2007). The southern tradition speaks mainly about the historical buddha on Earth, Shakyamuni Buddha. However, the northern tradition teaches that in addition to our world system, there is an infinite number of world systems across the universe, with innumerable buddhas whose salvific power is accessible to all. The most famous among these is Amitabha Buddha: the Buddha of Infinite Light.

Teachings on Death in Chinese Buddhism

Cyclic Existence

To understand practices associated with faith in Amitabha Buddha, one must first understand the teachings on death and thus the doctrine of cyclic existence in Chinese Buddhism. Cyclic existence is an important doctrine that underpins foundational Buddhist beliefs and practices. Shakyamuni Buddha taught that all sentient beings, including human beings, are trapped in cyclic existences characterized by pervasive un-satisfactoriness or suffering. This pervasive un-satisfactoriness essentially boils down to our attachment to the notion of an unchanging and permanent self. The ultimate objective of Buddhist practice is to realize selflessness and insubstantiality of all phenomena. With this realization, suffering is transcended, and one attains liberation.

Attaining such a realization takes innumerable lifetimes of practice. All along, one is reborn time and again, in an unceasing chain of cyclic existences. When the life force expires for a sentient being at the end of a particular lifetime, one will be reborn into one of the six planes of existence: hell, hungry ghosts, animals, human beings, demigods, and heavenly beings, depending mainly on the karma one has accumulated and on the habitual tendency and conditions of one's state of mind at the moment of death. If one's karma is strong, in the sense of having lived a particularly unethical or a very ethical life, it would propel one to be reborn either into the three relatively unfortunate planes of hell, hungry ghosts, and animals, or into the three relatively fortunate planes of human beings, demigods, and heavenly beings. If the karma one has accumulated is relatively weak (e.g., in the case of someone whose actions have neither been very harmful nor benevolent, rebirth will depend on one's habitual tendency or the mind state when one passes away) (Chan Master Sheng Yen & Gildow, 2007).

The Intermediate State Between Death and Rebirth

Buddhist practices for the dead are intimately related to the existence of an intermediate period between death and rebirth. In the southern tradition, it is generally taught that all rebirths are instantaneous, with no intermediate state. In the northern tradition, which includes Chinese Buddhism, Japanese Buddhism, Korean Buddhism, Tibetan Buddhism, and Vietnamese Buddhism, the existence of an intermediate state between death and rebirth is a common teaching.

This intermediate state may be short or long, but it generally lasts up to 49 days (Chan Master Sheng Yen & Gildow, 2007; Goss & Klass, 1997), with seven critical intervals of 7 days. Since the karmic force, which will ultimately bring about the next rebirth, is not fully shaped during the intermediate state, such a state is an opportune period of influence where practitioners, especially accomplished masters and survivors of the deceased, may engage in practices to help the deceased attain a better rebirth. In Chinese Buddhism, this often takes the practice of reciting or chanting the name of Amitabha Buddha and reciting a scripture named the Amitabha Sutra. This practice is a means of connecting with the salvific power of Amitabha Buddha. It is essentially a prayer without an explicit content of praying, much as the invocation of the name of Jesus Christ is a prayer without an explicit content that connects one to God for Orthodox Christians, for it is said in the Amitabha Sutra that those who focus single-mindedly on Amitabha Buddha through his name will be connected to his salvific power and assured of rebirth in his Pure Land.

Buddhist Cosmology, the Western Pure Land, and Amitabha Buddha

Buddhist Cosmology

In a previous section, it is mentioned that scriptures in the northern tradition teach that there is an infinite number of world systems across the universe, with innumerable buddhas whose salvific power is accessible to all. World systems that are free of sufferings are called Pure Land. Pure Lands are shaped by the efforts and merits of a buddha through incalculable eons of practicing the bodhisattva vows. This can be understood using the analogy of a paradise where everybody lives a bountiful life in perfect harmony; the paradise is shaped through the great wisdom and tireless compassionate efforts of its great leader and founder, in accordance with his or her vision. Albeit in Buddhist cosmology, the vision of Pure Land is realized not in one lifetime, but through incalculable lifetimes of efforts.

The Western Pure Land and Amitabha Buddha

According to scriptures such as Amitabha Sutra, Sutra on the Buddha of Infinite Life, and Sutra on the Contemplation of Amitabha Buddha (Inagaki & Stewart, 1995), the Western Pure Land presided by Amitabha Buddha has one of the most conducive environments for cultivating compassion and wisdom, thus enabling one to transcend all sufferings and develop altruistic capability. Therefore, in Chinese Buddhism, it is generally encouraged that practitioners should aspire to be reborn in the Western Pure Land. Upon being reborn there, one would practice until one would no longer regress on the path of compassion and wisdom and then go on to fulfill one's bodhisattva practices wherever one is needed. As a result, chanting the name of Amitabha Buddha and seeking rebirth in the Western Pure Land have become two of the most popular forms of practice in Chinese Buddhism.

Three prerequisites underpin the quest for rebirth in Amitabha Buddha's Pure Land: faith, vow, and practice (Jones, 2003). One must first learn about Amitabha Buddha and the Western Pure Land and generate faith in Amitabha Buddha. With a firm faith, one aspires to seek rebirth in the Western Pure Land, vowing to be reborn there. Finally, one engages in practices that will bring about the fulfillment of this aspiration. Such practices, including cultivating one-minded chanting or recitation of Amitabha Buddha's name, are based mainly on the three scriptures mentioned in the beginning of this subsection. They are normally referred to as Pure Land practices.

Preparing for Death

The renowned contemporary teacher Chan Master Sheng Yen taught that death is not an occasion of sorrow, neither is it an occasion of joy. Rather, it is an occasion for solemn Buddhist practices. This places death, grieving, and rebirth within the larger context of Buddhist practices—the cultivation of compassion and wisdom to transcend sufferings for oneself and others. Without a steadfast practice, and viewing death, loss, and grief as part of it, a mere belief in ideas such as rebirth would most likely not be adequate to protect one against death anxiety and alleviate grief (Hui & Coleman, 2012). How then, do Buddhist practitioners prepare for death?

In general, lay Buddhist practitioners rely on upholding the five precepts—not killing, not stealing, not engaging in sexual misconducts, not lying, and not taking intoxicants—as well as practicing good deeds to achieve a favorable rebirth upon death. Some practitioners may also engage in meditation practices to achieve stability of mind and to realize experiential insights on selflessness and insubstantiality of phenomena. Many Chinese Buddhists engage in Pure Land practices. Together with the internalization of Buddhist philosophy of impermanence and letting go, these practices would prepare people to face their own death and the death of their loved ones.

Assisted Chanting

In Pure Land Buddhism, attaining rebirth in the Western Pure Land of Amitabha Buddha is the paramount objective of practice. To this end, practitioners often conduct group sessions where Amitabha Buddha's name is chanted. Such group chanting sessions are also used as a means of preparing the terminally ill and the dying for the final moments of life. In this context, chanting of Amitabha

Buddha's name, whether carried out by an individual or a group in the company of the patient, is termed assisted chanting or recitation.

Assisted chanting can in many ways be viewed as a component of palliative or hospice care in Chinese Buddhism (Hui & Leung, 2012). Pure Land practitioners visit the home of a patient to carry out practice sessions, often with both the patient and the family involved. The purpose of these sessions is to help the patient establish stable mindfulness of Amitabha Buddha. It is believed that at the final moments of life, if the patient can be mindful of Amitabha Buddha, to the extent of being able to single-mindedly focus on Amitabha Buddha through his name, rebirth in the Western Pure Land will be assured.

The power of assisted chanting lies in the fact that if the patient is left alone, it is difficult for him or her to maintain single-minded focus on Amitabha Buddha. The company of fellow practitioners and family in chanting assists the patient in maintaining focus. An audio chanting device is often used so that the patient can listen to the chanting non-stop. In addition, a sermon based on the teaching of the intermediate state and on Amitabha Buddha's Pure Land may also be administered by a group leader. It delineates what the patient may encounter at the moments around death and gives advice on the proper course of action that the patient should take. It also extols the supremacy of Amitabha Buddha's Pure Land and encourages the deceased to seek rebirth there.

In addition to helping the dying, assisted chanting also provides the opportunity for family members to participate in a ritual that is perceived to be highly beneficial to their loved ones. Such participation is important in helping the surviving family members deal with the sense of grief and loss, especially if they also share the faith in Amitabha Buddha.

Religious Practices After Clinical Death

As mentioned earlier, the intermediate state is believed to last up to 49 days. This state is an opportune period to influence the rebirth of the deceased. It is believed that at the time of clinical death, subtle consciousness of the deceased remains. Free of the burden of the coarse body, in this conscious state, one becomes very sensitive. The consciousness of the deceased generally will still be attached to the body and thus will be aware, with heightened sensitivity, of the body and what happens in the surrounding.

Family members are often advised against displaying intense emotions of attachment to the deceased and are encouraged to engage in practices that will help their loved one move on. The common recommendation is for them to conduct assisted chanting for their loved one for a critical period, which lasts at least 8 hours, and ideally up to 12 hours after clinical death. Within this critical period, it is also advised that the body of the deceased be left untouched.

After the critical period, the body of the deceased can be cleaned and the undertaker will be called in to provide funeral services. The timing of funeral services depends on social norms and limitations in service facilities. For example, in Hong Kong, funerals may be held only weeks or even months after clinical death due to inadequate funeral and crematorial facilities. In Malaysia and Singapore, Buddhist funerals services are started hours after clinical death and usually last 3 or 5 days. During the funeral, monks and nuns may be invited to perform daily rituals of varying durations that include reciting of scriptures and chanting. In the past, family members were mostly passive participants in such rituals. They would follow the procedural instructions of the presiding monastics in kneeling and prostrating. Recitations were carried out by the monastics, and the family members were merely required to be present.

In contrast, many contemporary masters encourage family members to play a more active role in the funeral service by joining to chant Amitabha Buddha's name (Chan Master Sheng Yen, 2017). When the scripture recitation is done, liturgical books may also be provided so that the family members can recite along or at least understand what is being recited. Sermons on the intermediate state, a particular scripture, Amitabha Buddha and the Pure Land, or the subject of life and death may also be given.

Such an approach has transformed the death ritual into a bona fide spiritual practice with a number of benefits. First of all, in conjunction with the teaching that the deceased is still very much attached to the body and loved ones, active participation of family members in chanting, scriptural recitation, and sermons would lessen this attachment and, conversely, their own attachment to the deceased. Secondly, by actively participating in the rituals to help the deceased move on, the survivors transform their grief into something positive.

Dealing With Grief

For the survivors, engaging in practices that can help their loved one attain a better rebirth or even a rebirth in the Western Pure Land is an important source of comfort. Grief may thus be transformed into hope.

In this light, survivors often continue to engage in practices after the funeral. Some continue to engage monks or nuns to provide ritual services every 7 days, up to 49 days. Some may make a vow to go on vegetarian diets for 49 days or even longer. Such a diet is in accord with the precepts of not harming sentient beings and is viewed as compassionate and meritorious. Many people continue to engage in group practices long after the funeral services. Such group sessions serve both the function of religious practices and social support.

Ultimately, the process of grieving can be summed up with the teachings of Chan Master Sheng Yen. He taught that there are four steps for handling adversity: facing it, accepting it, dealing with it, and letting it go (Chan Master Sheng Yen, 2011). Instead of denying the death of love ones or our grief, we face it and accept it. For people who have established a steadfast daily practice, there would have been an internalization of teachings such as impermanence and those on living and dying. This helps one face the death of loved ones and may shorten the phase of denial, leading to acceptance. One then engages in practices such as those prescribed in the Pure Land teachings. Not only do these practices bring a sense of hope in helping the deceased move on, they also strengthen the mental health of the survivors, making it easier for them to let go.

Recommendations for Clinicians

Based on the description on how Buddhists engaging in Pure Land practices of Chinese Buddhism view and deal with death, loss, and grief, a few recommendations for clinicians can be drawn.

First of all, it is important for clinicians to learn about the clients' practice tradition. Many Chinese who identify themselves as Buddhists actually observe a mixture of Buddhist, Taoist, and shamanistic practices. Only by learning about their actual practices and beliefs would a clinician be able to offer the most pertinent supports.

Second, for Buddhists who have an established Pure Land practice, it is good if clinicians can help facilitate the opportunity for clients to hold relevant ritualistic practices in the hospital. For example, upon clinical death, family members should be given an opportunity to engage in silent chanting practices surrounding the deceased before the body is moved. Although it may not be possible to do this for 8 hours, as prescribed by orthodox practices, the opportunity to do so may play an important role in helping survivors transform their grief or even guilt. If the body has to be moved within 8 hours, it is important to do so respectfully, allowing the survivors or even the medical personnel to communicate with the deceased that this is happening. Such communications may also entail telling the deceased to let go of the attachment to the body and that the medical personnel are moving the body out of goodwill. The purpose is to encourage a sense of gratitude to replace any sense of anger that may arise when the body is moved.

Third, for those who have a comfortable home environment, clinicians can encourage family members to have their loved one home in the final days. A comfortable home environment is more conducive to spiritual practices for both the dying and family members. If returning home is not possible, a second option is to transfer the patient to a hospice care facility, which may be more conducive to spiritual practices.

Final Reflections

While my mom was not active in religious practice before my dad's fatal accident, she joined a Pure Land chanting group after my dad passed away and practiced with the group weekly during the 49-day period. This has no doubt been critical in helping her recover from the loss. However, that alone is not enough. After my dad's funeral, my aunt moved in to stay with mom so that she would not be alone. I moved back to Malaysia 7 months later, after tendering my resignation and completing my project at work. Mom's active social life also played an important part. In fact, family support and other social supports are just as important as one's religious faith and practice. They are perhaps akin to the legs of a three-legged stool and are all critical in facilitating a stable process of overcoming grief and loss.

Reflecting on my own experience, I realize that I have been able to let go of grief more easily than most people around me since I was a teenager. My first experience with the loss of a loved one was the death of my grandmother. In her final years, my grandma was seriously ill with diabetes and hypertension, with her condition getting progressively worse after a heart attack. She was very dear to me, and when she was bed-ridden, I had tried to stay by her side whenever I could. One day, her condition got so bad that we all believed she would pass away and gathered around her while she lied in bed. I still remember hearing her words that it was good to have me as a grandson. She did not pass away that day. When she did, I was in school and was informed of her death through a phone call to the principal's office. I remember that I did not feel overly sad and did not cry throughout the funeral. Perhaps it was a sense of having done what I could and seeing her passing as a relief from prolonged suffering that I was able to let go more easily than others. I was 16 years old.

In contrast, my dad was healthy and died in an accident. Presumably, I would have a stronger and more prolonged sense of grief. However, I was much older at that time and had been practicing Buddhism seriously for more than 6 years, including studying Buddhist philosophy and practicing meditation. I also had the blessing of studying with and serving as an interpreter for Chan Master Sheng Yen. What I remember of my feelings speaking to my mom on the phone was not an overwhelming sense of loss but a sense of duty toward my mom, knowing how distressful it was for her. I knew immediately that I would go back to Malaysia for good to be with her. I could not recall having a very strong and prolonged sense of grief and loss.

My reaction to my dad's death was perhaps a reflection of my internalization of the teachings on impermanence. Because everything is impermanent, we love and cherish those around us the best we can in the present moment, for we do not know when impermanence will make us part. Because everything is impermanent, change is the natural order and loss is to be expected. Because everything is impermanent, we may dwell at peace with hope in hard times, knowing that even hell is impermanent.

Such internalization, together with my meditation practice, and my belief in rebirths, which could be shaped by our own intentions and actions, led to a relatively calm mind state and led me to immediately engage in Pure Land practices for my dad, continuously through the long journey home from New York City to Malaysia.

I have taken the verse of impermanence from a scripture titled Diamond Sutra (Watson, 2010) to heart and am still learning to contemplate it more deeply:

> All composite phenomena
>
> Are like dreams, illusions, bubbles and shadows
>
> Like dews and lightning
>
> Thus shall we contemplate them (p. 96)
>
> May love and the ability to let go arise from such a contemplation.

References

Chan Master Sheng Yen, & Gildow, D. (2007). *Orthodox Chinese Buddhism: A contemporary chan master's answers to common questions.* Elmhurst, NY: Dharma Drum Publications.

Chan Master Sheng Yen. (2011). The four steps for handling a problem. *Living in the 21st century: A Buddhist view.* Taiwan, China: Sheng Yen Education Foundation. Retrieved from http://ebooks.dila.edu.tw/books/n/DDM_en_9-16

Chan Master Sheng Yen. (2017). *Common questions in the practice of Buddhism.* New York, NY: Sheng Yen Education Foundation. Retrieved from http://www.108wisdom.org/html/OTH_05.pdf

Gethin, R. (1998). *The foundations of Buddhism.* Oxford, UK: Oxford University Press.

Goss, R. E., & Klass D. (1997). Tibetan Buddhism and the Resolution of Grief: The Bardo-Thodol for the Dying and the Grieving. *Death Studies, 21*(4), 377–395. doi:10.1080/074811897201895

Hui, V. K. Y. & Coleman, P. G. (2012). Do reincarnation beliefs protect older adult Chinese Buddhists against personal death anxiety? *Death Studies, 36*(10), 949–958. doi:10.1080/07481187.2011.617490

Hui, E. C., & Leung, D. C. (2012). Chinese religions and hospice care. In H. Coward & K. I. Stajduhar (Eds.), *Religious understandings of a good death in hospice palliative care* (pp. 145–164). Albany, NY: SUNY Press.

Inagaki, H., & Stewart, H. (1995). *The three Pure Land sutras: A study and translation from Chinese.* Kyoto, Japan: Nagata Bunshado.

Jones, C. B. (2003). Foundations of ethics and practice in Chinese Pure Land Buddhism. *Journal of Buddhist Ethics, 10,* 1–20.

Watson, B. (2010). The diamond sutra. *The Eastern Buddhist, 41*(1), 67–100.

Grief and Mourning in the Jewish Tradition

Josh Fischel, PhD, Millersville University, Lancaster, PA

Josh Fischel has written on topics in American Jewish popular culture. His research interests include American pragmatism, American intellectual history, as well as the intersection between 20th century continental thought and the work of John Dewey, William James, and Charles Peirce. Currently, he's at work on what he hopes turns into a manuscript on the thought of John Dewey and William James.

FIGURE 4.4. Josh Fischel

Grief and Mourning in the Jewish Tradition

This section attempts to provide an overview of the Jewish response to the experience of grief and trauma. Of course, a loss of a home by fire, being laid off from a job, or any number of life-altering events in an individual's life can induce these emotional responses. However, this section will focus primarily on the Jewish mourning rituals surrounding the death of a loved one.

It should be noted that religious rituals not only root and tie individual experience to cosmological significance, it also ensures that the individual, especially during periods of life transitions like the death of a loved one, is supported and fully integrated into the social network of the religious community. This is crucially important because, in Peter Berger's (1990) words, "Death radically puts in question the taken-for-granted, "business as usual" attitude in which one exists in everyday life" (p. 43). By tearing out the foundation of ordinary experience, death puts into question the norms and practices of the lived experience of the bereaved. It throws one into a dizzying state that Arnold Van Gennep has referred to as liminal (Van Gennep, 1961). Those who experience this liminal state find themselves "betwixt and between the positions assigned and arrayed by law, custom, convention, and ceremonial" (Turner, 1969, p. 95). To transition out of this state of liminality requires elaborate ritual processes that mark the meaning of this transitional stage in one's life and allow for the establishment of new norms and conventions that will reintegrate the individual back into the community, albeit with new obligations and responsibilities. In the case of the death of a loved one in the Jewish tradition, this is realized through the year-long process of mourning to which we now turn.

The Meaning of Death

Before entering into a discussion of Jewish mourning rituals, it would be helpful first to look at two primary ways that the Jewish tradition has come to think about death. First, Jews understand death to be a natural part of the cycle of life (Rubin, 2014). As it is written in the *Tanakh* (תַּנַ"ךְ), the Jewish Bible, in Psalm 144:4, "Man is like a puff of wind, his days like a fleeting shadow." It is telling that, while Judaism does have some notion of the afterlife, it is not nearly as central to the practice of the individual Jew as it would be for a Christian or Muslim (Diamant, 1998). In Judaism, the emphasis is on the sanctification of this world. Secondly, the universality of death and suffering is something that cannot be fully understood (Rubin, 2014). Judaism is a religion first and foremost of religious *practice*, embodied in the manner one follows a life of the Halakah (הֲלָכָה) or Jewish law, as outlined in the Torah (תּוֹרָה): the first five books of the Jewish Bible. As Eugene Borowitz (1952) has noted, God, from the Jewish perspective, is more interested in us acting and living the life of the Torah (תּוֹרָה) than in gaining specific knowledge or understanding of the nature of God's essence.

These perspectives on the meaning of death also signal the fact that Judaism is a religion that places far greater importance on events than on places. In short, it is religion of time that attempts to sanctify the significant moments of life (Heschel, 2005). The following discussion of Jewish mourning rituals should be understood in this light.

From Death to Burial

We can begin by noting that the Halakah (הֲלָכָה) describes two distinct phases that the bereaved will pass through during his or her period of mourning. The first stage, referred to in Hebrew as *Aninut* (אנינות), or period of deep suffering, runs from the death of a loved one (a parent, child, sibling) to interment. It is also important to point out that Judaism requires that once death occurs, the deceased is never left alone until interment. During this stage, great care is taken to respect the dignity of the deceased. To this end, Judaism requires that the deceased is provided a quick and dignified burial. Generally, this entails a burial that takes place within 24 hours of death. Once the bereaved, known as *onen* (אוֹנֵן) in Hebrew, becomes aware of the death, they will spend much of their time prior to the funeral in a flurry of activity. After contacting the funeral director, they will visit the funeral home, pick out a coffin, contact relatives, and deal with any other arrangements that are required. The *onen* (אוֹנֵן), of course, is in a deep state of grief and sorrow during these early moments after the death of a loved one, so it is often the case that the synagogue (Jewish place of worship), not the bereaved, helps to facilitate any formalities necessary leading up to funeral. During this period, the *onen* ((אוֹנֵן) is not permitted to shave (for males), get their hair cut, nor bathe. In addition, Torah study is forbidden, as is going to work and any other forms of social interaction, such as going to a party or athletic event (Lamm, 2000).

The culmination of *Aninut* (אנינות) takes place at the *levayah* (לְוָיָה), the Hebrew word for funeral. While it's traditionally the case that a rabbi (Jewish religious leader/teacher) leads the funeral service, it is not required by Jewish law. If circumstances warranted and no rabbi was present to lead the funeral, it would still take place under the collective leadership of the family and Jewish community of which the family are members. The family and the Jewish community are ultimately responsible for burying the deceased not the rabbi. (Diamant, 1998). In this sense, the secular idea of a "private" funeral goes against Jewish tradition. It is also not the goal of the Jewish funeral to provide comfort for the bereaved, however much it might do so. The goal of the Jewish funeral, in Anita Diamant's (1998) words, "is a confrontation with the finality of death" (p. 70).

The Funeral

Jewish funeral services traditionally have two parts, one service taking place at the synagogue and another at the site of interment. Today, however, it is not uncommon to have one graveside service that combines the liturgy of both services (Lamm, 2000). The two most significant moments in the synagogue service are the *Kriyah* (קריעה) ritual and the presentation of the eulogy. *Kriyah* (קריעה) is a Hebrew word that means tear. This ritual has its origin in the book of Genesis, where the patriarch Jacob tore his garment when he believed that his son Jacob had died. Before the service begins, the family of the deceased commonly meets with the rabbi who discusses with them the meaning of the *Kriyah* (קריעה). Afterward, the family members proceed to tear the fabric of their garments above the heart (Lamm, 2000). It is more common today for the funeral home to provide a black ribbon, symbolic of the deep pain and separation felt by the bereaved between themselves and the deceased, rather than a formal tear of one's clothing. And indeed, this is what I experienced when my grandparents and uncle passed away recently. Prior to the funeral service, we went to a private room in the funeral home and the rabbi gave each us a ribbon to wear. This ribbon is then worn for part of *avelut* (אֲבֵלוּת), the second period of the Jewish mourning process, which begins at the moment of interment. The centerpiece of the actual synagogue service is the eulogy. Jewish eulogies are meant to extoll the contributions the deceased have made to the world. They should not be presented in a manner that exaggerates the character of the deceased nor attempt to airbrush the flaws or shortcomings of the person. However, the Jewish tradition is adamant in the belief that every person has some sort of intrinsic value. The eulogy should reflect that belief. Who gives the eulogy? It is usually family members, simply because they knew the deceased best. If the bereaved are not in a state to do so, the rabbi will do so instead.

The Significance of the Kaddish Prayer

If the eulogy is the centerpiece of the synagogue service, then the prayer of kaddish (קדיש) is the centerpiece of the interment (or burial) service (Diamant, 1998). The kaddish (קדיש) is one of the oldest and most significant prayers in the Jewish liturgy. It is said during morning and evening services, at holidays, as well as, of course, at the "emotional peak" of the burial service (Diamant, 1998). There are five different versions of this prayer. And while it is true that the "burial kaddish" was traditionally said at graveside (and often still is by Jews), today many Jews have replaced it with the more familiar mourner's kaddish (Diamant, 1998). Following is the mourner's kaddish, its transliteration, along with an English translation.

Yit'ga'dal v'yit'ka'desh sh'meh ra'bah.	יִתְגַּדַּל וְיִתְקַדַּשׁ שְׁמֵהּ רַבָּא.
B'ol'ma di v'rai khir'u'teh,	בְּעָלְמָא דִּי בְרָא כִרְעוּתֵהּ,
V'yam'likh mal'khu'teh b'ha'yey'khon uv'yo'mei'khon	וְיַמְלִיךְ מַלְכוּתֵהּ בְּחַיֵּיכוֹן וּבְיוֹמֵיכוֹן
Uv'cha'yey d'khol beyt Yis'ra'el,	וּבְחַיֵּי דְכָל בֵּית יִשְׂרָאֵל,
Ba'a'ga'la u'viz'man ka'riv, v'im'ru a'men.	בַּעֲגָלָא וּבִזְמַן קָרִיב, וְאִמְרוּ אָמֵן.
Y'hey sh'meh ra'ba m'va'rakh l'o'lam ul'al'mey al'maya.	יְהֵא שְׁמֵהּ רַבָּא מְבָרַךְ לְעָלַם וּלְעָלְמֵי עָלְמַיָּא.
Yit'ba'rakh v'yish'ta'bach v'yit'pa'ar v'yit'ro'mam	יִתְבָּרַךְ וְיִשְׁתַּבַּח וְיִתְפָּאַר וְיִתְרוֹמַם
V'yit'na'seh v'yit'ha'dar v'yit'a'leh v'yit'ha'lal	וְיִתְנַשֵּׂא וְיִתְהַדָּר וְיִתְעַלֶּה וְיִתְהַלָּל
Sh'meh d'kud'sha b'rikh hu,	שְׁמֵהּ דְּקֻדְשָׁא בְּרִיךְ הוּא,
L'el'la min kol bir'kha'ta	לְעֵלָּא מִן כָּל בִּרְכָתָא
V'shi'ra'ta tush'b'cha'ta v'ne'che'ma'ta,	וְשִׁירָתָא תֻּשְׁבְּחָתָא וְנֶחֱמָתָא,
Da'a'mi'ran b'ol'ma v'im'ru a'men.	דַּאֲמִירָן בְּעָלְמָא, וְאִמְרוּ אָמֵן.
Y'he sh'la'ma r'ba' min sh'ma'ya,	יְהֵא שְׁלָמָא רַבָּא מִן שְׁמַיָּא,
V'cha'yim to'vim a'ley'nu v'al kol Yis'rael,	וְחַיִּים טוֹבִים עָלֵינוּ וְעַל כָּל יִשְׂרָאֵל,
V'im'ru a'men.	וְאִמְרוּ אָמֵן.
O'seh sha'lom bim'ro'mav, hu ya'a'seh sha'lom	עֹשֶׂה שָׁלוֹם בִּמְרוֹמָיו, הוּא יַעֲשֶׂה שָׁלוֹם
A'ley'nu v'al kol Yis'ra'el, l'im'ru a'men.	עָלֵינוּ וְעַל כָּל יִשְׂרָאֵל, וְאִמְרוּ אָמֵן.

Glorified and sanctified be God's great name throughout the world

which He has created according to His will.

May He establish His kingdom in your lifetime and during your days, and within the life of the entire House of Israel, speedily and soon; and say, Amen. May His great name be blessed forever and to all eternity. Blessed and praised, glorified and exalted, extolled and honored, adored and lauded be the name of the Holy One, blessed be He, beyond all the blessings and hymns, praises and consolations that are ever spoken in the world; and say, Amen.

May there be abundant peace from heaven, and life, for us

and for all Israel; and say, Amen. He who creates peace in His celestial heights, may He create peace for us and for all Israel;

and say, Amen.

The mourner's kaddish, according to Maurice Lamm (2000), has two critical functions. First, it provides psychological comfort to the bereaved (Lamm, 2000). Secondly, it has a pedagogical function, in that it teaches the mourner lessons about the nature of life and death, and how evil in this world can and will be overcome (Lamm, 2000). Importantly, prior to the kaddish being said, the *onen* (אוֹנֵן) is declared by the rabbi, for the first time, to be formally in the state of mourning. This change in status of the bereaved is one more step in the process of transitioning from one stage of life to another—shaped, governed, and guided by the mourning rituals.

The 7 Days of Sitting Shiva

As the bereaved are now officially acknowledged as mourners, they enter into the second period of Jewish mourning rituals, the *avelut* (אֲבֵלוּת). This second period begins once the kaddish is said prior to interment of the deceased and runs until the end of the first year. The first 7 days, mirroring the time of creation outlined in the first book of the Torah, is the period known as "sitting shiva" (Fishbane, 1989). *Shiva* (שבעה), in Hebrew literally means seven. It is during the *shiva* (שבעה) that the mourners begin to come to terms with their loss. As the family of the deceased exit the gravesite they walk with their backs to the grave, symbolic of a new phase in the ritual process, which turns from a focus on the deceased to the mourner (Lamm, 2000).

Upon returning from the funeral, mourners wash their hands and take off their shoes prior to entering the home, both of which signify the change in focus of the mourner from burying the dead to that of grieving for them (Diamant, 1998). Once completed and they enter the home, they are served a "meal of comfort" that is provided by friends and more distant relatives. The *shiva* (שבעה) is a space for mourners to begin to come to terms (for the first time) with their loss, and to do so in the context of family, friends, and others from the Jewish community. *Shiva* (שבעה) is not then exclusively a private affair. In fact, it is an obligation in Judaism that neighbors and others from the Jewish community come visit with the bereaved. Throughout the 7 days of sitting *shiva* (שבעה), moreover, the mourners adjust the physical position of their bodies to match their emotional state. As such, those sitting *shiva* (שבעה) will sit lower to the ground (if not on the floor) on wooden benches or chairs to symbolize their grief and mourning (Lamm, 2000). In addition, work is not permitted, nor studying the Torah. Those prohibitions outlined during the pre-burial stage are still operative during the *shiva* (שבעה). Jewish law proscribes no exit ritual from the 7 days of sitting *shiva*. However, Krentzman (1986) notes that among North American Jews, the formal end of sitting *shiva* is often accompanied by the bereaved taking a walk around the block of their neighborhood. This walk, in addition, has come to symbolize the mourner beginning the process of rejoining the larger community. In my experience of sitting *shiva*, my family did not perform this exit ritual. After the 7 days of sitting *shiva*, we quickly transitioned to the mourning practices of the month of *Sheloshim* (שלושים).

The Month of Sheloshim

The 7 days of sitting *shiva* (שבעה) is followed by the 30-day period of *sheloshim* (שלושים), which literally means thirty. This period begins at the end of the *shiva* and is considered completed 30 days from the time of burial. After *Sheloshim* (שלושים) it is the year-long period Yud-bet-chodesh (י"ב חודש), which translates into English as 12 months, which begins at the end of the 30 days of *Sheloshim* (שלושים) and continues for an additional 11 months. During the period of *sheloshim* (שלושים), the mourner begins to reintegrate oneself into the norms and practices of everyday life. While there still is more need for mourning and coming to grips with the finality of a loved one's death, slowly the mourner begins again to take on life's responsibilities. Still, the bereaved are required to say the kaddish daily. It should be noted that this period also begins the resumption of enjoying some of life's pleasures, such a playing with one's children or reading or studying the Torah (Diamant, 1998). Other kinds of pleasures, like going to a concert, sporting event, or going to a movie, are still not taken up again by the bereaved during this period (Diamant, 1998). For instance, when my grandmother died, my father neither listened to any music, watched any television, nor shaved. Only with the end of the month of *Sheloshim* (שלושים) did he resume shaving and commenced watching television. He did not, however, listen to any music until the *yahrzeit.*

The Yahrzeit

The completion of the *Sheloshim* (שלושים) ends the required mourning observances for everyone except for those mourning the death of a parent. If a parent has died, then mourning continues for an additional 11 months. The bereaved continues to say Kaddish on a daily basis, as the bereaved are still in a state of mourning and need this time for further reckoning of their loved one's passing. In addition, it is common for some to decide that they can also honor their loved ones by contributing to charity. The year-long mourning process ends with the anniversary of the death of the deceased. For Jews, this anniversary is called the *yahrzeit,* a Yiddish word that translates as "a year's time." The *yahrzeit* is a particularly painful moment for the mourners, in that it often brings back the rush of emotions that initially emerged when the mourners first learned of their loved one's death. At the anniversary of the death, a 24-hour candle is lit in remembrance. Each year, subsequently, Jews will mark the *yahrzeit* of the deceased. Unlike in Christianity, the unveiling of the headstone doesn't take place until a year after the completion of the mourning process, which concludes with the first *yahrzeit.* Many Jews will also take this time to visit their loved one's grave. Because the location of the burial is in relative proximity to where my family lives, each year we visit my grandmother during her *yahrzeit.* While my grandfather is buried in Sunrise, Florida, a 22-hour drive from where most of my immediate family resides, when any of us are close by his gravesite, we will visit even if it is not on the date of his *yahrzeit.* In addition, after mourning is complete, Jews will also attend what is called a Yizkor ((יזכור) service, which takes place on the high holidays of Rosh Hashanah and Yom Kippur, as well as on Passover and Sukkot. *Yizkor* (יזכור) is a Hebrew word that means remembrance, and it is the primary memorial service that Jews attend who have suffered the death of a loved one.

Recommendations for Clinicians

Those clinicians working with Jewish families who have experienced a death should be aware of where their client is on this year-long process of mourning, be it sitting *shiva,* the following month of *Sheloshim* (שלושים) or the subsequent year of mourning that concludes in the *yahrzeit.* Each phase of this intricate mourning process imposes different demands on the mourner to which clinicians should familiarize themselves. For instance, during the period of sitting *shiva,* clinicians should not have the expectations that regular appointments with their client will kept, and that reaching out to them, however well intentioned, should wait until the *shiva* is complete. In this regard, they should also understand that in the Jewish tradition there is an important difference between the death of a parent and the death of a sibling or other relative. While most Jews will adhere to the basic elements and obligations the bereaved have toward the deceased as outlined in the *Halakah* (הֲלָכָה), individual Jews will differ in how strictly they follow the various niceties of these practices. For instance, both my uncle and my grandmother passed away within 6 months of one another. While my uncle was given a traditional funeral, there was no period of sitting *shiva* or *Sheloshim* (שלושים) that was observed. On the other hand, my grandmother's family observed all of the pre-burial, burial, and post-burial rituals of mourning outlined in Jewish tradition and law. These kinds of individual differences are also something clinicians should take note of when working with families from the Jewish tradition. In addition, clinicians working with Jewish families should also be aware of community resources that they can consult (especially if they are not familiar with Judaism) and other resources that may be of help to their client. And finally, in the case of new clients who are grieving, clinicians should take measures to create an environment of trust between themselves and the mourner, so that over time clients, if they feel so compelled, will feel comfortable discussing their grief with the clinician.

FIGURE 4.5. Miriam Fischel

FIGURE 4.6. Robert Lipkin

Questions

1. Even the most well-intentioned practitioner of any of the caring professions are occasionally subject to bias toward clients who are of a different ethnicity, religious background, or socio-economic status. What might you do as a clinician to reduce this likelihood with a Jewish client or that of someone coming from a different religious tradition other than your own who is working his or her way through the process of mourning a loved one?
2. How might your knowledge of the grief that results from various forms of trauma (natural and social disasters, war, etc.) be of help with the grief of a Jewish client who has lost a loved one?
3. What resources might be helpful in the development of a treatment plan for a Jewish client who is in the process of mourning?
4. How might your own experience of mourning be of help in working with a Jewish client who has experienced the death of a loved one?

References

Berger, P. L. (1990). *The sacred canopy*. New York, NY: Anchor Books.

Borowitz, E. B. (1952). *Understanding Judaism*. New York, NY: UAHC Press.

Diamant, A. (1998). *Saying Kaddish*. New York, NY: Schoken Books.

Fishbane, S. (1989). Jewish mourning rites: A process of resocialization. *Anthropologica, 31*(1), 65–84.

Heschel, A. J. (2005). *The sabbath*. New York, NY: Farrar, Straus, and Giroux.

Krentzman, M. (1986). *Jewish laws and customs and mourning*. Montreal, Canada: Kehila Consultants.

Lamm, M. (2000). *The Jewish way in death and mourning.* Middle Village, NY: Jonathan David
Mourner's Kaddish. (n.d.). Retrieved from https://bje.org.au/course/judaism/jewish-prayer/kaddish/
Rubin, S. S. (2014). Loss and Mourning in the Jewish Tradition. *Omega: Journal of Death and Dying, 70*(1), 79–98.
(1985). *Tanakh: The holy scriptures* (1st ed.). New York, NY: Jewish Publication Society.
Turner, V. (1969). *The ritual process: Structure and anti-structure.* Chicago, IL: Aldine.
Van Gennep, A. (1961). *The rites of passage.* Chicago, IL: University of Chicago Press.

Islamic Processes for Managing Grief, Loss, and Death

Sameena Azhar, PhD, LCSW, MPH, Fordham University, New York, NY

FIGURE 4.7. Sameena Azhar

FIGURE 4.8. Rafathunnisa Begum (1924–2018) and Khadim Hussain Qureshi (1911–1954), Hyderabad, India circa 1950

Sameena Azhar has more than 15 years of clinical and research experience in the fields of mental health, substance abuse, and HIV care. She is currently an assistant professor at Fordham University's Graduate School of Social Service. For her dissertation research, Sameena conducted a mixed methods study of people living with HIV in Hyderabad, India. Over the course of 3 years of fieldwork, she examined the intersections between HIV stigma, gender, depression, and medical care utilization among cisgender women and hijra/third gender women living with HIV. Her research has been funded through the Council on Social Work Education's Minority Fellowship Program, Ford Foundation, the University of Chicago's Center for the Study of Gender and Sexuality, and the Foreign Language and Area Studies Fellowship in Urdu through the U.S. Department of Education. Sameena is currently working with a team of Asian American researchers on a qualitative analysis of the #ThisIs2016 hashtag, which has archived more than 5,000 tweets of experiences of microaggression, prejudice, and discrimination against Asian Americans. Sameena also plays jazz piano and grows orchids.

This section seeks to review the Islamic processes of managing grief, loss, and death. Grief can be caused by a number of sources, including the end of a marriage from divorce or separation; the death of a child, parent, spouse, or other loved one; the loss of personal property or wealth, perhaps from a fire, earthquake, or financial hardship; or the loss of physical or mental abilities of one's self or others through illness or injury. This section will review the various ways in which Muslim communities address grief and loss, paying particular attention to the Islamic traditions and rituals regarding death and bereavement.

As Amer and Ahmed (2013) note, there is great diversity within the multicultural identities of Muslim communities. Because Islam is a global religion, there are cultural nuances to these traditions that differ widely by region and custom. Because the experience of lived Islam is so diverse in its practice, making generalizations about processes regarding the management of grief, loss, and death can become complex (Venhorst, 2012).

The two main denominations within Islam are Sunnis and Shias; there are multiple smaller communities within each of these two main branches. Within both Sunnis and Shias, there are various *madhhab* (مذاهب) or schools of thought within Islamic jurisprudence (*fiqh* الفِقْه) that help guide Muslims through various laws and customs. Within Sunnis, the major *madhhab* include the Hanafi, Maliki, Shafi'I, and Hanbali traditions. Within the Shias, the major *madhhab* are the Jafaris, the Batiniyyah, the Ismaelis, the Sufis, and the Zaydis (Welton, 2006).

Muslims are the majority in several parts of the globe, namely in Middle Eastern and North African countries, which are predominantly Arabic speaking (Algeria, Bahrain, the Comoros Islands, Djibouti, Egypt, Iraq, Jordan, Kuwait, Lebanon, Libya, Morocco, Mauritania, Oman, Palestine, Qatar, Saudi Arabia, Somalia, Sudan, Syria, Tunisia, the United Arab Emirates, Yemen); in sub-Saharan African countries (Burkina Faso, Chad, Eritrea, Gambia, Guinnea, Mali, Mauritania, Niger, Nigeria, Senegal, Sierra Leone, Somalia, Western Sahara); in South Asian countries (Afghanistan, Bangladesh, Iran, Pakistan, Maldives); in Southeast Asian countries (Brunei, Malaysia, Indonesia), and in Eastern Europe and Central Asia (Azerbaijan, Iran, Kazakhstan, Kosovo, Krygyzstan, Serbia, Turkey, Turkmenistan, Tajikistan, Uzbekistan). Muslim minority groups also exist throughout Western Europe, East Asia, North and South America, and Australia.

There are notable differences in how Islam is practiced across different groups, regions, cultures, and denominations. As such, clinicians need to avoid stereotyping Islamic culture as monolithic, but also need to avoid the pitfalls of ignoring shared cultural traditions across Muslim communities. In this section, I will first provide an overview of general practices regarding grief and loss in Muslim communities with a focus on death and bereavement. Then I will describe in detail the various steps that traditionally occur within Muslim communities, preceding and following death.

Grief and Loss in Islam

Grief is socially constructed through an intersubjective meaning-making process that is accomplished primarily by constructing narratives (Neimeyer, 2001). Death and the rituals surrounding it both reflect social values and are important in shaping them (Geertz, 1973). Rituals regarding grief or loss play an important role in completing the mourning process by addressing the emotional needs of the bereaved (Hunter, 2007) and providing a sense of closure. As Durkheim (1965) notes, the dead are collective representations that mediate cultural notions of mortality and reinforce social identity. By understanding a community's relationship with the dead, we are able to better understand cultural notions regarding the meaning of death, and by proxy the meaning of life. Through an understanding of death rituals, we are also able to understand cultural notions regarding existence, justice, and morality. In many societies, the experience of death often induces a reflection on one's own life and a re-evaluation of one's experiences and priorities.

Generally Islamic scholarship regards the nature of grief as a private experience. The rituals surrounding the dead body serve as a means of maintaining social, religious, institutional, and political structures (Abu-Rabia & Khalil, 2012). Research on Palestinian Muslims in Israel indicates that public displays of grief, including memorial services or eulogies, are discouraged in funerals (Yasien-Esmael & Rubin, 2005). These beliefs about the parameters for public grieving are influential in the emotional response expected by the bereaved. Rituals serve to structure the response of the grieving and may serve to reduce the anxiety and confusion that often accompanies loss. At the same time, deviances from these death rituals are sometimes seen as being risky, perhaps for the dead person's salvation or perhaps for potential misfortunes that could be incurred by the family left behind (Rosenblatt, 2001).

Most of the beliefs surrounding death and its rituals mimic Islam's Judeo-Christian theological origins. Islam's central text is the Quran and each chapter within the Quran is called a *surat* (سورة). God or Allah is referred to in the Quran without the use of gendered pronouns like "he" and "she," but rather the gender neutral and plural pronoun of "we." In the Quran, death is viewed as impermanent, a transition from the physical world to the spiritual world. Surat Taha (20:55) of the Quran states, "From it [this very earth] We created you, and into it [the same earth] We will return you, and from it We will bring you once again" (The Quran, 2009). In Islam, death is seen to be a change of the soul from a mortal existence to an immortal, spiritual life (Sarhill, LeGrand, Islambouli, Davis, & Walsh, 2001).

In Islam, mankind is not believed to have power or control over death; Allah is seen to have an active influence on the progress of life and the timing of death. Surat An-Nahl of the Quran (16:70) states, "God created you; then he takes you away" (The Quran, 2009). Similarly, Surat Al Nisaa (4:78) of the Quran states, "Wherever you may be, death will catch up with you, even if you were in fortified towers" (The Quran, 2009). In the same vein, Surat Qaf (50:19) of the Quran states, "The daze of death has come in truth. This is what you were trying to escape" (The Quran, 2009). Death is seen as being the inevitable and final bodily phase in the longer trajectory of the existence of one's soul. Following the same depiction of death, Surat Waqia (56:60) of the Quran states, "We have decreed death among you, and We will not be outstripped." Under Islamic views, though the body of the person is thought to have passed at the time of death, the soul of the person lives on.

According to one of the sayings of Prophet Muhammad, known as *hadith* (حديث), "Death is the bridge that leads the beloved to his lover" (Al-Qurtubi, 1997). As death is ultimately seen to be in the hands of God, committing suicide is forbidden. Islam teaches that following death the deceased enters a waiting period for all souls called Al Barzakh (البرزخ). *Al Barzakh* in Arabic means separator or barrier and refers to the life in the grave, which marks the wall between this world and the afterlife. Along with all souls, the dead person will ultimately face a day of judgment before Allah when his or her soul will be prescribed his or her fate in the afterlife, namely either going to heaven (*Jannat* جنة) or to hell (*Jahannum* جهنم).

Preceding Death

If death is known to be immanent because of illness or injury, in the hours or days leading up to the individual's passing, the family often gathers around the body of the sick person and prays for the salvation of his or her soul. The dying person and those surrounding this person often repeat a declaration of *iman* or faith إيمان)) known as the *Shahada*: "Lā'ilāha 'illā llāh muḥammadun rasūlu Allāh (لَا إِلٰهَ إِلَّا ٱللهُ مُحَمَّدٌ رَسُولُ ٱللهِ), meaning "There is no God but Allah and Muhammad is the Messenger of Allah."

At the moment of death, or shortly following it, Muslims will often say Takbir, which is the statement, Allahu Akbar (الله أكبر), meaning God is the greatest.

Once the person has passed, Muslims often recite this passage from the Quran: "Inna lillahi wa inna ilayhi raji'un" (إِنَّا لِلَّهِ وَإِنَّـا إِلَيْهِ رَاجِعُونَ), which translates as "We belong to God and truly to Him we shall return" (The Quran, 2009; Al Baqarah 2:156). This prayer (*dua* دُعَاء) is known in Arabic as Al stirja. Following death, the body is often straightened out; the eyes are closed; the hands are crossed over the chest in a position similar to the standing position in prayer; and the mouth and feet are bound (Gilanshah, 1993). Up until the moment of the burial, it is customary to not the leave the body alone; someone sits with the corpse at all times. In South Asian communities, a light or candle is often also left on or burns through the night, often even after the corpse has been removed from the room, to signal to the deceased that they have not been forgotten and to ease their transition into the other world.

Washing of the Body

Muslims are traditionally buried in a cemetery, not cremated. Muslims do not practice cremation because of their belief that the body must remain whole (Beaty, 2015). It is customary to bury the body immediately, sometimes even the same day, and in no longer a period than 3 days following the death (Karmali, 2008). This may be rooted in a belief that the soul is thought to be waiting until the burial in order to begin the process of judgment.

Prior to the burial, the same gendered members of the family of the deceased participate in a ritual washing of the body called *ghusl* (غسل). *Fiqh* provides guidance on who should do the washing and detailed instructions for how to conduct the bathing of the body (Venhorst, 2012). Generally, male members of the deceased's family wash a male corpse and females wash a female corpse, with the exception of the husband, wife, or parents of young children.

While the particulars of this process may slightly vary, washing of the body generally begins with a cleansing of the perineum, a scrubbing of the limbs, then the completion of *wudhu* (الوضوء), the ablution that is performed by Muslims prior to prayer. *Wudhu* entails the washing of the hands, face, arms, and feet, each three times. The water used for ablution may be mixed with perfumed oils, herbs, rose water, lotus, or camphor (Venhorst, 2012). Following the bathing of the body, the corpse is shrouded in a simple, white, seamless cloth called a *kafaan* (كافان), similar to what Muslims wear during the Hajj pilgrimage to Mecca. The meaning of having all Muslims wear the same, simple cloth in their burial emphasizes the universal mortality of mankind and how material possessions will not be able to be taken into the afterlife.

Some of these actions accompanying death and dying rituals are considered by Muslims to be *sunnah* (سنة). *Sunnah* refers to those actions that mimic those of Prophet Muhammad and are therefore considered a preferred action. Many of these recommended actions are reported through the sayings of Prophet Muhammad, known as *hadith* (Duderija, 2007). For men, it is considered *sunnah* that a man be shrouded in three pieces of cloth: the *izar* (ازار), a loin cloth extending from the head to the feet; a *qamis* (قميص), an upper garment extending from the shoulders to the feet; and the *lifafah* (لفافه) or chador, a long piece of cloth extending from the head to the feet. Women should be shrouded in five cloths: the *izar, qamis, lifafah*, plus the (*khimar* خِمَار) around her head, and a fifth cloth binding the chest.

No jewelry, ornate clothes, make-up or other décor is provided to the body. Embalming fluid or other means of preserving the body, including laying the body in aboveground mausoleums, are prohibited. In the community of Muslim Americans in the Minnesota/Minneapolis region, Saudi Muslims have been invited to teach Muslim converts on the process of correctly washing the body (Gilanshah, 1993).

Organ donation remains a controversial issue among Muslims but has been both forbidden and supported by both Sunni and Shia religious scholars (Hedayat, 2006; Raza & Hedayat, 2004). In Iran, for example, there is general public resistance to organ removal, despite clear rulings from religious leaders to the contrary (Reza & Hedayat, 2004). Some religious authorities have waived family permission and allowed cadaver organ removal even if the deceased person had not made a declaration for organ donation. In such cases, scholars have exempted physicians from paying a legal penalty for removing organs. Another case in which organ donation has been allowed is when the deceased person has made a declaration that money obtained from the recipient be spent to pay his or her debts or for public welfare and that the organ be used to save a life (Reza & Hedayat, 2004).

Prayer for the Deceased

The next major rite following the cleansing of the corpse is the completion of the funeral prayer, called *salat-ul-janazah*. This prayer is typically performed near the dead body of the Muslim in an Islamic place of worship, known as a *mosque* or a *masjid*, following the afternoon prayer called *zuhr*. The funeral prayer consists of quietly reciting the first chapter of the Quran, Al Fatiha, followed by two shorter *duas*. Unlike the five daily prayers, this prayer does not involve any bending (*ruku* رُكوع) or prostrating (*sajdah* (سجدة). The person remains standing for the entirety of the short prayer. During this prayer, the congregation (*jummat* جمعة) prays for the forgiveness of the sins of the deceased. Following the prayer, family members may gather in groups to complete a rosary (*tasbeeh* تَسْبِيْح) where they continue to silently repeat prayers for the deceased. The 36th chapter of the Quran, Surat Yaseen, is often recited during these gatherings (Hasan & Salam, 2007).

Burial of the Body

The next part of the funeral process is the burial of the body, typically in a graveyard where other Muslims are also buried. Prior to earth being placed over the corpse, a religious leader (*imam* إمَام) is often asked to recite a sermon (*khutbah* خطبة) at the burial site. Graves and cemeteries are not meant to be elaborately decorated or marked as it is seen to be an affront to the modesty expected of Muslims. Because of this belief in simplicity, elaborate monuments on grave sites are discouraged; simple graves are preferred (Venhorst, 2012). The depth of the grave is recommended to be greater than the height of the person. Traditionally, the body is buried directly into the ground, without a coffin. In modern times, many states/countries have public health laws that prohibit the direct burial of the body in the ground, so this practice has often been modified. If a coffin is to be used, a simple wooden one is preferred, with the body laid on its right side with the face in the direction of the *qibla* (قِبْلَة). The *qibla* is the direction toward Mecca in which all Muslims pray. Mecca is also the city to which all Muslims are expected to make a pilgrimage, called hajj (حَجّ), at least once in their lifetime. Praying toward Mecca and making a pilgrimage to Mecca reinforces a universal experience for all Muslims across the world and connotes a unity in the Muslim community (*ummah* أمة)). Laying the body in this position of the *qibla* again reinforces the dead person's commitment to Islamic beliefs. In some

Muslim communities, family members and friends take turns throwing a handful of earth over the dead body.

In Palestine, during the mourning period, relatives dye their shirts, head veils, and handkerchiefs blue or black with indigo (Abu-Rabia & Khalil, 2012). In South Asian Muslim communities, the color of funeral-goers is white. In South Asian funerals, the spouse of the deceased, especially if a woman, traditionally wears white for several days or even months following the death. Similar to Hindu South Asian traditions, following the passing of her husband, some widowed women elect to wear white for the remainder of their lives. In South Asian cultures, the color white symbolizes asceticism and death. Therefore, wearing white often connotes a detachment from worldly pleasures and happiness.

In Muslim customs, loud crying or wailing is often discouraged at the funeral or burial site, particularly when this crying is done by women (Abu-Lughod, 1993). Tears divulge the existence of religiously defined cultural norms (Jones, 2012). Muslim women were traditionally advised to avoid even being present at the burial site to discourage loud wailing or spectacular moaning. The ideology behind why women were traditionally not permitted at funerals varies. One interpretation is that the mourning expressed by women may be distressful or sorrowful for the dead to witness. The barring of excessive grief reactions are prohibited because Islam teaches that the deceased will suffer emotionally and this may detract from their ability to make the final transition to the afterlife (Yasein-Esmail & Rubin, 2005). Another interpretation argues that public wailing was forbidden because it was seen to be ostentatious and was making a show (*jahr*) of one's worship (Jones, 2012).

Various schools of Islamic thought (Hanafi, Shafi'i, and Hanbali) disapprove of the participation of women in funeral processions, referring to gendered cultural traditions regarding these rituals. The practice of public wailing or crying is seen by some Islamic scholars to be impious. However, it does not seem that these traditions are rooted in any explicit reference to the Quran, but reflect historically gendered traditions in *fiqh*. This disapproval of public grieving may be because lamenting is seen as recognizing the finality of life whereas religious belief indicates that the deceased is not gone, but is now in another, eternal world. Similarly, women in many Muslim communities are discouraged from visiting the gravesite as their lamentations are thought to disturb the dead.

It is important to note that there are gendered, hierarchical undertones to these traditions. Although this practice of gender segregation and stifling of emotional response has been challenged by contemporary Islamic scholars, particularly for the ways in which it may bottle up emotions of grief and loss, the practice still remains quite common throughout Muslim communities. Some modern Muslim communities do allow women to attend the funeral prayer and burial services, though these practices vary widely.

One of the functions of these narratives regarding the impermissibility of public lamentation is to monitor expressions of grief. All societies have rules for how grief is to be publicly displayed (Walter, 1999). Structure can help individuals cope with grief, particularly traumatic loss. These Islamic rules of conduct provide parameters for the bereaved and give some sense of structure or purpose to the ambiguous process of bereavement. On the other hand, not allowing the bereaved to express their grief may also hinder their ability to find closure in the loss and disable them from moving past the loss.

Even with the admonishment from certain Islamic schools of thought, many Muslim cultures have longstanding traditions of public grieving. These traditions are again modified by gender where women are afforded the opportunity for more emotional responses than men. For example, in Egyptian culture, funeral lamenting of women occurs in unison and is referred to as *yatabko* (Abu-Lughod, 1993). Egyptian Muslim women in the 19th century would cry together in lamentation and would even invite other women to join them. These women were known as *naddabat* and would publicly wail while beating to a tambourine (Abu-Rabia & Khalil, 2012). In Guinnea-Bissou, Mandinga women are often more accepting of the practice of public lamentation than Mandinga men; some women even considered it a social responsibility to publicly mourn the loss of the dead through loud and dramatic wailing (Johnson, 2009). Bedoin women in the Sinai have been known to dishevel their hair, throw earth on their heads, tear at their clothes, and scratch their faces (Abu-Rabia & Khalil, 2012). From a clinical perspective, one might view the process of collective lamenting as reinforcing social bonds between those left behind. Collective lamenting may assist families from recovering from the loss through unified action with others.

Visiting the Gravesite and Commemorating the Death

Some Muslim cultures pay respect to the dead by visiting their grave or making prayers on their behalf. However, such practices have been forbidden by Wahhabi scholars. The reformed Wahhabi school of Islamic thought is derived from the broader Salafi tradition and comprises a conservative minority of Muslims originating from the Najd region of the Arabian Peninsula (Farquhar, 2016). Wahhabism is the official state-sponsored interpretation of Islam under the Kingdom of Saudi Arabia and also influences religious laws and social policies throughout the Persian Gulf, namely in Qatar and the United Arab Emirates. Because of the centrality of the importance of the cities of Mecca and Medina in Islam, both of which are located in Saudi Arabia, Wahhabism has been exported to many other parts of the Muslim world through the instruction of scholars at the Islamic University of Medina (Farquhar, 2016).

Under Wahhabi interpretations of Islam, any interaction with the dead or veneration of ancestors or saints became seen to be problematic, a reprehensible innovation *bid'ah* (بدعة) (Klass & Goss, 2003). Under Wahhabi interpretations, the practice of visiting or praying near graves, called *ziyarat* (زيارة), became considered *shirk* (شرك), the sacrilegious practice of ascribing divine capabilities to humans, an act which is considered a blasphemy to the faith. Wahhabi Muslims also oppose the use of music or poetry to venerate God, saints (*imams*), the dead, or one's ancestors—practices that have historically occurred across a variety of cultural contexts within the Islamic diaspora, particularly among Sufis.

Following the burial, Muslim cultures vary by region in their traditions for praying for the dead. Typically, family and friends are expected to grieve for a period of 3 days from the announcement of the death. This period is meant to demarcate the limitations of excessive grieving and help families move on past the loss. For the widow, the length of the mourning or "waiting" period, referred to as *iddah* (العدة), is substantially longer. The *iddah* for the widow typically lasts for 4 months and 10 days. During this period, the widow usually stays at home while family and friends take care of her basic needs, such as food and household tasks. During this period, she is also not allowed to remarry. Under certain Arabic traditions, she is also barred from leaving the home or wearing fancy clothes or jewelry in public (Abu-Rabia & Khalil, 2012).

Following the initial mourning period of 40 days, many South Asian Muslim communities hold a gathering of family and friends, called a Khatm al-Qurān (ختم القرآن), where the Quran is recited from beginning to end with the intention that the spiritual reward (*sawaab* ثواب) from this recitation benefit the soul of the deceased person. The purpose of the gathering is for the absolution or forgiveness of the sins of the deceased, which in Urdu is known as *magfirat* (مغفرت). Folklore indicates that during these 40 days, the soul is still wandering in a purgatory-like phase.

The period of 40 days makes recurring appearances throughout Biblical and Quranic scripture as a symbolic period of testing, trial, probation. Noah's ark floated through the flood for 40 days. Moses lived 40 years in Egypt and 40 years in the desert before he led the Israelites out of Egypt and across the Red Sea. Moses was also on Mount Sinai for 40 days and nights, on two separate occasions. The first three kings of Israel, Saul, David, and Solomon, each ruled for 40 years. Jesus was resurrected after 40 days. In addition to being recognized by some Muslim communities, customs regarding a ritual service for the bereaved at the marking of 40 days are also followed by Eastern Orthodox Christians and Filipino Catholics; Orthodox Jews hold a similar service 30 days after the death (*sheloshim*).

The marking of this timeframe of 40 days can provide a sense of formal closure to the grieving process and signals to the bereaved that a path has been made toward their coping with the loss and reintegrating into society. In rural Pakistan, followers of the Barelavi school of thought, heavily influenced by Sufism, believe that these rituals following death, especially recitation of the Quran and offering food to neighbors and the poor in the community, will help the dead on their journey to the other world (Suhail, Jamil, Oyebode & Ajmal, 2011). Some Pakistani British Muslims reported gaining comfort in collectively reading the Quran and being in a community during this mourning period (Hussein & Oyebode, 2009). However, others found the process to be intrusive and that the time of grief was treated as a social occasion (Hussein & Oyebode, 2009).

In some Muslim communities, prayer gatherings may continue to be scheduled on the annual anniversary of the individual's passing. In a study of South Asian Shia Muslims in America, faith-based activities, such as more regularly visiting and praying at the mosque, were reported to provide comfort and strength to families (Karmali, 2008). British Pakistani Muslims reported continuing to maintain relationships with the deceased through communication in their dreams, remembering their lost ones through storytelling, following the example of the deceased, or keeping mementos or objects possessed by the dead (Hussein & Oyebode, 2009). With many of these traditions, it becomes difficult to differentiate between folklore, superstition, and religion. Islamic rituals have been adapted in a number of cultural environments, leading to a wide range in tradition and norms. Examining death ritual practices in Kuwait, Iqbal (2011) argues that traditional, religious, and private ways of dealing with death in Islam have been modernized under the same commercialization and efficiency making as prescribed by the fast-food model of McDonald's.

To reiterate this diversity within Muslim rituals regarding death, even the practice of commemorating the death anniversary at 40 days is not universally accepted among Muslims. For example, the Shafi'i school of Islamic thought strictly forbids such commemorations of the mourning period (Ashry, 2018) and disallows prayers for the dead. This variability in tradition reinforces the notion that Islamic practices are not uniform throughout the ummah, but vary substantially by region and by Islamic school of thought.

Recommendations for Clinical Practice

Clinicians working with Muslim individuals and families dealing with death, bereavement, grief, or loss should be familiar with these traditions, particularly in regard to the various gendered ways in which traditions are upheld. For example, a younger, female therapist may be working with a Muslim family where the elderly Muslim husband has recently lost his wife to breast cancer. The therapist should be careful in providing grief counseling to the bereaved as there are often normative, cultural rules of conduct for Muslim interactions between men and women, as well as norms for social interactions between older and younger people. In other words, a clinician of the same gender may be more appropriate for counseling in these circumstances. It is important as clinicians to respect these cultural traditions, even if we do not personally agree with all of these practices. This is not to say that female clinicians can never work with Muslim male clients, or vice versa, but that the clinician should take care to ensure that this arrangement is comfortable and acceptable for clients and their families.

When dealing with female clients, it is also important to not fall into the portrayal of Muslim women, particularly immigrant women, as being oppressed by patriarchal cultures and lacking in agency (Kristiansen, Younis, Hassani, & Sheikh, 2016). Such portrayals of Muslim women as being forced to wear a head scarf (*hijab*) and not being afforded independence from their husbands are stereotypical caricatures. As clinicians, we should make every effort to avoid the replication of such dehumanizing and inaccurate depictions of Muslim women.

In conclusion, cultural patterns of grieving offer a process of distilling the complexity, contradictions, and ambiguity surrounding death (Rosenblatt, 2001). Regardless of gender, ethnicity, or age, individuals in the grieving process will utilize a number of coping strategies to manage loss, including feelings of blame, attaching positive meaning to the loss, seeking social support, and avoiding family interaction (Neimeyer, 2004). For clinicians dealing with any individual or family that is grieving, it is important to note that no fixed trajectory exists for the process of coping with loss. Individuals will vary widely in experiencing anger, sadness, denial, avoidance, and even relief regarding the loss. Individuals may also have multiple ways of managing death and may offer one reaction in public and another in private (Rosenblatt, 2001).

From a social constructionist perspective, the bereaved participates in a network of interacting individuals, families, groups, institutions, and ways of thinking to make meaning of reality (Rosenblatt, 2001). Research conducted in Muslim majority societies, such as Turkey, has demonstrated how religion shapes the rationalization of death for the bereaved within a transcendental framework (Beaty, 2015). Islamic frameworks constitute a source of meaning and comfort by posing illness, injury, and death as predetermined moments in life by God, potentially helping to ease the pain of loss for the bereaved. Nonetheless, across the world, societies, including Muslim ones, differ greatly in what they regard as normal grief (Kleinman, 2012). As such, clinical practitioners should take care not to make assumptions about their Muslim clients, but rather ask them about grieving processes in their own communities. This form of cultural humility and exchange will be beneficial in being able to more fully assist Muslim individuals and families through the process of grieving.

References

Abu-Rabia, A., & Khalil, N. (2012). Mourning Palestine: Death and grief rituals. *Anthropology of the Middle East, 7*(2), 1–18.

Abu-Lughod, L. (1993). Islam and the gendered discourses of death. *International Journal of Middle East Studies, 25*(2), 187–205.

Al-Qurtubi, I. M. A. A. (2008). *Kitaab Al-Tadhkirah bi Ahwal al-Mawta wa Umur al-Akhirah*. Allentown, PA: Dar Al-Minhaj.

Amer, M. M., & Ahmed, S. (2013). Islam, Muslims, and mental health. In S. Ahmed & M. M. (Eds.), *Counseling Muslims* (pp. 23–34). New York, NY: Routledge.

Ashry, Z. H. (2018). *Death crossing the bridge to the hereafter.* Kuwait: IPC Islam Presentation Committee. Retrieved from https://www.muslim-library.com/dl/books/English_Death_Crossing_the_Bridge_to_the_Hereafter.pdf

Beaty, D. D. (2015). Approaches to death and dying: A cultural comparison of Turkey and the United States. *OMEGA: Journal of Death and Dying, 70*(3), 301–316.

Duderija, A. (2007). Islamic groups and their world-views and identities: Neo-Traditional Salafis and Progressive Muslims. *Arab Law Quarterly*, 21(4), 341–363.

Durkheim, E. (1965). *The elementary forms of the religious life.* J. W. Swain (Trans.). New York, NY: The Free Press.

Farquhar, M. (2016). *Circuits of faith: Migration, education, and the Wahhabi mission.* Palo Alto, CA: Stanford University Press.

Geertz, C. (1973). *The interpretation of cultures.* New York, NY: Basic Books.

Gilanshah, F. (1993). Islamic customs regarding death. In D.P. Irish, K.F. Lundquist & V.J. Nelsen. (Eds.), *Ethnic variations in Dying, Death, and Grief: Diversity in Universality*, 137–145. New York: Routledge.

Hasan, I. Y., & Salaam, Y. (2007). Faith and Islamic issues at the end of life. In C. M. Puchalski, (Ed.), *A time for listening and caring: Spirituality and the care of the chronically ill and dying* (pp. 183–192). New York, NY: Oxford University Press.

Hedayat, K. (2006). When the spirit leaves: Childhood death, grieving, and bereavement in Islam. *Journal of Palliative Medicine, 9*(6), 1282–1291.

Hunter, J. (2007). Bereavement: An incomplete rite of passage. *Omega: Journal of Death & Dying, 56*(2), 153–173.

Hussein, H., & Oyebode, J. R. (2009). Influences of religion and culture on continuing bonds in a sample of British Muslims of Pakistani origin. *Death Studies, 33*(10), 890–912.

Iqbal, Z. (2011). McDonaldization, Islamic teachings, and funerary practices in Kuwait. *OMEGA: Journal of Death and Dying, 63*(1), 95–112.

Itani, T. (Trans.). (2009). *The Quran.* CreateSpace. Retrieved from https:clearquran.com

Johnson, M. C. (2009). Death and the left hand: Islam, gender, and "proper" Mandinga funerary custom in Guinea-Bissau and Portugal. *African Studies Review, 52*(2), 93–117.

Jones, L. G. (2012). "He cried and made others cry": Crying as a sign of pietistic authenticity or deception in medieval Islamic preaching. In E. Gertsman (Ed.), *Crying in the Middle Ages* (pp. 132–165). New York, NY: Routledge.

Karmali, A. S. (2008). *Role of religious community support among bereaved South Asian Muslim children living in America.* (Doctoral dissertation). Retrieved from ProQuest. (Accession No. 3318655).

Klass, D., & Goss, R. (2003). The politics of grief and continuing bonds with the dead: The cases of Maoist China and Wahhabi Islam. *Death Studies, 27*(9), 787–811.

Kleinman, A. (2012). Culture, bereavement, and psychiatry. *The Lancet, 379*(9816), 608–609.

Kristiansen, M., Younis, T., Hassani, A., & Sheikh, A. (2016). Experiencing loss: A Muslim widow's bereavement narrative. *Journal of Religion and Health, 55*(1), 226–240.

Neimeyer, R. (Ed.) (2001). *Meaning reconstruction and the experience of loss.* Washington, DC: American Psychological Association.

Neimeyer, R. A. (2004). Research on grief and bereavement: Evolution and revolution. *Death Studies, 28*(6), 489–575.

Raza, M., & Hedayat, K. M. (2004). Some sociocultural aspects of cadaver organ donation: Recent rulings from the scholars of Iran. *Transplantation Proceedings,* 36, 2888–2890.

Rosenblatt, P. C. (2001). A social constructionist perspective on cultural differences in grief. In M. S. Stroebe, R. O. Hansson, W. Stroebe, & H. Schut (Eds.), *Handbook of Bereavement Research: Consequences, Coping, and Care*, 285–300. Washington, DC, US: American Psychological Association.

Sarhill, N., LeGrand, S., Islambouli, R., Davis, M. P., & Walsh, D. (2001). The terminally ill Muslim: Death and dying from the Muslim perspective. *American Journal of Hospice and Palliative Medicine, 18*(4), 251–255.

Suhail, K., Jamil, N., Oyebode, J., & Ajmal, M. A. (2011). Continuing bonds in bereaved Pakistani Muslims: Effects of culture and religion. *Death Studies, 35*(1), 22–41.

Venhorst, C. (2012). Islamic death rituals in a small town context in the Netherlands: Explorations of a common praxis for professionals. *Omega: Journal of Death and Dying, 65*(1), 1–10.

Walter, T. (1999). *On bereavement: The culture of grief.* Buckingham, UK: Open University Press.

Welton, M. D. (2006). The origins and evolution of Islamic law. *The Middle East Journal, 60*(1), 180.

Yasien-Esmail, H., & Rubin, S.S. (2005). The meaning structures of Muslim bereavements in Israel: Religious traditions, mourning practices, and human experience. *Deaf Studies, 29*(6), 495–518.

Working With Grief in Secular Clients

Hayley Twyman Brack, MA, LPC, University of Central Oklahoma

Hayley Twyman Brack holds a master's degree in Counseling Psychology from the University of Central Oklahoma. As a mental health therapist and member of the Secular Therapy Project, Ms. Twyman Brack provides evidenced-based mental health treatment for clients primarily working through trauma, grief, and religious/secular related issues. Ms. Twyman Brack also leads continuing education seminars for mental health clinicians on best practice in serving secular clients and the ethical treatment and mandated reporting in cases of sexting and dating on social media. In addition to counseling and lecturing, Ms. Twyman Brack frequently works as a freelance writer, secular wedding officiant, and podcaster.

FIGURE 4.9. Hayley Twyman-Brack

Mackenzie O'Mealey, MA, LPC-C

Mackenzie O'Mealey attained a master's degree in counseling psychology from the University of Central Oklahoma and provides mental health counseling as a Licensed Professional Counselor Candidate at Seasons of Change Behavioral Health Services, Inc. in Edmond, Oklahoma. As a registered provider for the Secular Therapy Project, Ms. O'Mealey provides evidence-based mental health treatment services for secular clients working through such issues as depression, anxiety, relational conflict, trauma, or grief. Ms. O'Mealey has presented educational seminars to mental health professionals on the ethical concerns and unique needs of secular clients in counseling. Ms. O'Mealey also passionately advocates for ethical, evidence-based, affirming mental health services for LGBTQIA+ individuals and allies.

FIGURE 4.10. Mackenzie O'Mealey

Caleb W. Lack, PhD, University of Central Oklahoma

Dr. Caleb Lack is a Professor of Psychology and clinical psychologist at the University of Central Oklahoma. He is the author or editor of six book and over 50 scientific publications, many of which focus on the anxiety and obsessive-compulsive and related disorders or critical thinking. He teaches a variety of courses related to the evidence-based treatment of behavioral and emotional problems, as well as how to become a better critical thinker. Dr. Lack is also the Director of the Secular Therapy Project (STP), an arm of Recovering from Religion. The goal of the STP is to connect non-religious persons seeking mental health treatment with secular, evidence-based providers. He frequently writes for the public on secular and psychological issues via blogs on the Skeptic Ink Network and for the Center for Inquiry.

FIGURE 4.11. Caleb W. Lack, PhD, University of Central Oklahoma

Grief is a typical response to the loss or death of a loved one and generally affects the thoughts, emotions, and behaviors of the person experiencing it. Though grief is a normal response to loss, approximately 10–15% of grieving individuals experience problematic grief (Center for Complicated Grief [CCG], 2017). When delivering treatment to a secular or nonreligious client, cultural considerations like degrees of belief in a deity and philosophical stance may be important to understand and incorporate into treatment. Though empirical research of the secular and nonreligious experience of grief is scarce, the body of research is growing and informative. However, in all treatment it is important to tailor treatment to take the client's idiosyncratic experience into consideration via an appropriate case formulation.

Degrees of Belief

The nonreligious—often called the "nones" or "religiously unaffiliated"—are those who report no particular religious affiliation but who can and do and hold varying degrees of disbelief in a god or gods. The "nones" includes atheists, agnostics, deists, secular humanists, and the unaffiliated. Atheists are those who do not believe in the existence of a god or gods. Agnostics believe that the existence of any deity or the supernatural are unknown or unknowable. Deists are those who believe in a non-interventional god, one who is responsible for the creation of life but does not intervene afterward. Secular humanism is a philosophical stance that embraces human reason, social justice, and philosophical naturalism while rejecting religion and other dogmatic systems of beliefs or morals. Secular can also be used as an adjective synonymous to nonreligious.

On the opposite end of the belief spectrum are those who identify as religious or religiously affiliated. Somewhere between "religious" and "agnostic" on the belief spectrum are those who identify as "spiritual" but not religious. Spiritual individuals have varying degrees of belief in a god, deity, "higher power," or otherwise supernatural force influencing human existence but do not prescribe to any religious institution or dogma (Lipka & Gecewicz, 2017). This group, as with the nonreligious, is an especially heterogenous group, with each individual holding idiosyncratic belief systems. As with any client, clinicians should take great care to avoid generalizations, assumptions, or stereotypes about spiritual and nonreligious clients. An evidence-based case formulation approach to treatment (discussed later in this chapter) is an effective method of avoiding these damages. Informing that formulation should be an understanding of the available research on the nonreligious community's mental health needs.

Research on the "Nones"

Although there has been a spike in research on the nonreligious in the last decade, research on their clinical needs is still limited (Sahker, 2016). The available research on mental health in the nonreligious community examines the effects of nonbelief on well-being and the compatibility of clinician and client's beliefs (D'Andrea & Sprenger, 2007). Psychological well-being appears to be mediated by social support and confidence in beliefs, whether religious or nonreligious (Herzbrun, 1999). In other words, well-being is positively correlated with social support and confidence in beliefs, rather than the specific content of those beliefs. Compatibility of beliefs in the therapeutic relationship appears to favor matching clinician and client beliefs, but it is not crucial to the outcome of the counseling process (Richards & Davison, 1989).

Empirical research on grief in the nonreligious community is even more sparse than research on the overall clinical needs of the nonreligious. In a comparative case study analysis, Wilkinson and Coleman (2010) found no significant differences in efficacy of coping with loss between religious and nonreligious participants, suggesting that strength of beliefs may contribute more to efficacious coping than the content of beliefs. In a recent study, Sawyer (2017) compared coping outcomes in grief between atheists and believers. He found that believers experienced significantly more positive changes and post-traumatic growth as a result of the loss than atheists. However, believers also experienced significantly more complicated grief and psychological distress than atheists. This may be due to believers experiencing distress in response to the loss (e.g., anger at god or attempting to find reasons for the loss) while also perhaps finding comfort in the concept of an afterlife (Sawyer, 2017).

In the experience of this author (CWL), there appears to be no single "secular" response to the death of a loved one. Instead, one's response is driven by numerous factors, including prior and/or current religious beliefs, current attitudes toward death, personal mental health, the relationship one had with the deceased, and a host of other factors. For example, in my own life I have lost friends, family, and even students across the past 20 years. Reflecting on these, my responses to each varied greatly across time, based on where I was in my personal beliefs at the time and what the person who died believed.

When I was an undergraduate and had a good friend my own age die unexpectedly, I was much more agnostic in my belief system and not far removed from my Southern Baptist background. My response was first shock (as it was for many of us, as he was only 21 at the time), followed by anger at, well, everything. Anger that if there was a god of some kind that he had let this happen to my friend, anger that if there wasn't then he had died for zero reason, anger that I would likely never get to see him again. He had a relatively traditional Protestant Christian funeral, which made sense because he strongly identified with a particular denomination and was very active in his church. A few years later, when I was describing myself more as an atheist, I remember going to the funeral of a former boss of mine who I absolutely adored and who was not herself a religious person. Her funeral, however, was held in a church and was 85% focused on sermonizing and using her death as means to try and convert people to "the Lord." My anger then was a righteous fury that the passing of this woman whom I cared for so much was being used for (what I viewed as) cheap scare tactics and that who she was and what she believed was being thrust to the wayside.

As I have aged, I describe myself as a scientific skeptic and a secular humanist. When a nontraditional student of mine passed from cancer in the middle of her graduate program, my anger was replaced with sadness and acceptance. I visited her in the hospital during her final days, spoke (and cried) at her funeral, and met with her family. Being more secure in the lack of afterlife led me to focus more on her life, her accomplishments, and the positive memories we all had about her, and much less on the fact that she was no longer with us. There wasn't anger at some potential deity anymore, but a focus on those of us who were still here and how she lived on through our memories of her and the genes passed to her children and grandchildren.

Despite limited research on the clinical needs of grieving secular individuals, clinicians can still provide evidence-based, affirming grief counseling by utilizing the case formulation approach, as illustrated in the following case study. The case formulation approach to psychotherapy combines the use of evidence-based practices with the client's specific symptom etiology (Persons, 2012). Being that the multifaceted secular identity is idiosyncratic to our clients, it is important to tailor the treatment of grief to the individual. Just as the 21-year-old Caleb would have needed different interventions for his grief than the 37-year-old Caleb, each secular client you work with will need to be carefully assessed. The case formulation method calls for the clinician to take into consideration the client's unique history and personal experience of grief in order to develop a hypothesis for how the client's symptoms both developed and have been maintained.

Case Study

A 45-year-old man, Mr. Smith, was referred for services due to complicated grief after his wife was killed in a car accident. At intake, it is discovered that though his wife's accident occurred more than 2 years before, he has not yet removed any of her belongings from the home and has even gone so far as to continue to pay for her cellphone number to remain active. Mr. Smith reports that "it is easier to act like she is alive than to deal with her death" and that as an atheist he is "jealous of the Christians, because at least they think they'll see their family again." He also expressed concerns that if he removes his wife's name from bills or belongings from the home, that he will forget her and it "will be like she never existed." However, he then expressed fear that if he doesn't remove her belongings, he will "never move on with life."

Mr. Smith's reports suggest he is experiencing avoidance symptoms. For example, he states he will begin the task of calling to remove her number from his phone bill but will become too overwhelmed with emotion during the phone call with the service provider to complete the removal. He reports that this leads him to hang up and avoid attempting to complete the task for weeks or months at a time due to his reportedly overwhelming emotions. With this historical information, it can be hypothesized that his anxiety about forgetting his wife has led to the avoidance of certain tasks. As he engages in these avoidance behaviors, the belief he holds about not being able to "move on" after his wife's death is reinforced and then maintained.

Once the clinician and Mr. Smith together identified the mechanisms maintaining the symptoms, a treatment plan was created. In the case formulation approach, evidence-based interventions for grief are tailored to the client's individual symptomatology. Evidence-based treatment of grief consists of psychoeducation about the grief process, coping with distressing emotions, grief narratives, systematic exposure to reminders, future planning, and remembering the lost loved one (CCG, 2017). Importantly, not every client experiences the same etiology, which is why once an individual's symptoms are identified, the needed interventions are incorporated as necessary (Persons, 2012).

In this case study, the man reported being "jealous" of those who believe in an afterlife. This is because he believes "Christians" will find peace in thinking they'll see their loved ones again in heaven, while he, an atheist, fears that he will deny his wife's existence if he "moves on." This dichotomous thinking appears to lead the man to experience distress, as well as avoid tasks. Therefore, part of treatment may incorporate cognitive restructuring to challenge the belief that planning for the future and removing her items means forgetting her existence, as well as systematic exposure to reminders of his wife to decrease overwhelming distress he experiences when attempting to remove them.

Along with creating a treatment plan that caters to the individual's grief, it is important to continue to monitor symptoms throughout the therapeutic process to address and attempt to avoid treatment failure. If it is discovered that a particular intervention is not contributing to a decrease in symptoms, the case formulation approach posits that the clinician should collect information from the client to determine what is contributing to poor outcomes. A variety of confounds may affect the efficacy of the treatment process, including poor rapport between client and clinician, nonadherence to treatment, and intervention failure. It is important to collect data and continuously check in with the client throughout the therapeutic process to make sure the interventions are indeed efficacious (Persons, 2012).

After development of the formulation and treatment, then sharing it with Mr. Smith and getting his feedback, therapy began. However, the clinician noted that 2 months into treatment Mr. Smith was reporting little decrease in avoidance symptoms. Upon examination, Mr. Smith revealed that he did not trust that the clinician could help him "get better." The man believed that as an atheist he would never "get over" his grief because he did not think he could recover from her death without the "comfort that she's in heaven." Thus, the man reported he had not been motivated to engage in homework assignments aimed at the systematic desensitization to reminders of his wife because he saw treatment as "hopeless."

The clinician hypothesized that not only was the client ill-informed about the grief treatment process, but also that rapport may need to be strengthened to increase treatment compliance. The clinician then spent two sessions providing psychoeducation revolving around normalizing the grief symptom development and treatment process, all while empathizing with Mr. Smith's feelings of distress. After these sessions, he was more consistent in completing his homework assignments and eventually reported a decrease in his subjective units of distress when it came to removing his wife's name from bills. The clinician added to Mr. Smith's case formulation that clinician rapport, as well as psychoeducation aimed at normalization, are both vital components to clients' adherence to treatment.

Case formulation is an integrative process that attempts to tailor evidenced-based practices to the client's individual experience. But, as illustrated, in order to do so it is important to create and maintain rapport with the client throughout so that treatment may be a collaborative experience. Clients may seek services from mental health professionals, but it is the clients themselves who are the experts of their own bereavement etiology (Persons, 2012).

Conclusions

Secular and nonreligious clients vary greatly in degrees of disbelief in deities. Some, like atheists, may completely deny the existence of a god or gods, while spiritual persons tend to hold supernatural beliefs while often refraining from identifying with a religion. Research on the clinical needs of nonreligious clients experiencing grief or bereavement is limited, but growing. Sawyer (2017) found that atheists experience less complicated grief and psychological distress than believers in deities but report less post-traumatic growth after a death. Though research is leading to a greater understanding of the secular person's experience after a death, it is important to apply treatment in an individualized manner. The case formulation approach allows clinicians to achieve this by combining evidence-based practices with the client's own unique history and symptomology, while objectively monitoring progress throughout treatment.

Mental health professionals are obligated by ethical standards to avoid allowing personal biases enter the therapeutic process. If clinicians find themselves unable to do so, it is important that the client is referred. This is especially pertinent for the understudied, heterogeneous demographic of the nonreligious. Facilitating grief and bereavement treatment with these individuals must take into account their idiosyncratic experiences and beliefs.

Further Reading

- The Grief Beyond Belief support network offers a library on understanding grief and secular celebrations of life. Go to www.griefbeyondbelief.org/library for this extensive resource.
- For secular individuals experiencing bereavement, the Secular Therapy Project offers a database of vetted mental health clinicians who employ evidenced-based, secular therapeutic practices. Go to www.seculartherapy.org for more information.
- Humanists UK is a charity that provides support networks, literature, and other resources in hopes of expanding the understanding of humanism and secularism. For information on practicalities and considerations for secular funerals, go to www.humanism.org.uk/ceremonies.
- For further reading on providing support to secular individuals experiencing grief, we recommend *The Secular Grief Support Handbook* by Rebecca Hensler, founder of Grief Beyond Belief.
- For resources helpful in explaining death in a secular manner to young children, we recommend *I Miss You: A First Look at Death* by Pat Thomas.

Discussion Questions

1. A client is suffering from a terminal illness and is beginning to explore end-of-life care and wishes for their funeral. While the client identifies as agnostic, he reports valuing the ceremonial funeral traditions of their former Catholic faith, but without the belief in God. How do you explore these values with the client?

2. How do you identify and explore the belief system and grief practices of secular clients without bringing your own beliefs into the therapy environment?
3. Your client has recently lost a brother to cancer. The client reports that the brother was known by the extended family to be an atheist, yet loved ones held the funeral in a church and included Biblical passages in the ceremony. Your client reports feeling too angry to grieve. Why might they feel angry? How do you explore and validate these feelings without allowing the client to ruminate?
4. Have you ever been to a funeral that consisted of grief practices and rituals that varied from your own traditions? What thoughts or questions did you have? What did you learn? How did you honor the deceased within their own cultural practices? If you have not been to a funeral with traditions that varied from your own, take time to research the grief practices of a belief system unlike your own. How would you honor the deceased within their own cultural practices?
5. Your client was raised in the Methodist faith for the majority of her life, but for the last 7 years has gone through the deconversion process and reports identifying as an atheist. However, upon the death of her spouse she reports experiencing a reemergence of questioning her belief system. The client is unaware if her questioning is due to a reemergence of her belief in the Christian God or uncertainty of the afterlife. How do you explore and validate your client's questioning without allowing your own beliefs to interfere with the therapeutic process?
6. What are some common misconceptions about secular clients? What may be harmful to say to a grieving secular client? Why?

References

Center for Complicated Grief. (2017). *Complicated grief overview.* Retrieved from https://complicatedgrief.columbia.edu/professionals/complicated-grief-professionals/overview/

D'Andrea, L. M., & Sprenger, J. (2007). Atheism and nonspirituality as diversity issues in counseling. *Counseling and Values, 51*(2), 149–158.

Herzbrun, M. B. (1999). Loss of faith: A qualitative analysis of Jewish nonbelievers. *Counseling and Values, 43*(2), 129–141.

Lipka, M., & Gecewicz, C. (2017, September 6). More Americans now say they're spiritual but not religious. *Pew Research Center.* Retrieved from http://www.pewresearch.org/fact-tank/2017/09/06/more-americans-now-say-theyre-spiritual-but-not-religious/

Persons, J. B. (2012). *The case formulation approach to cognitive-behavior therapy.* New York, NY: The Guilford Press.

Richards, P. S., & Davison, M. L. (1989). The effects of theistic and atheistic counselor values on client trust: A multidimensional scaling analysis. *Counseling and Values, 33*(2), 109–120.

Sahker, E. (2016). Therapy with the nonreligious: Ethical and clinical considerations. *Professional Psychology: Research and Practice, 47*(4), 295–302.

Sawyer, J. S. (2017). *Grieving without God: Comparing posttraumatic growth, complicated grief, and psychological distress in believers and atheists during bereavement.* New York, NY: Columbia University Press.

Wilkinson, P. J., & Coleman, P. G. (2010). Strong beliefs and coping in old age: A case-based comparison of atheism and religious faith. *Ageing & Society, 30*(2), 337–361.

Grief, Loss, and Bereavement: Traditions, Customs, Ceremonies, and Rituals Among Kenyans

Wanja Ogongi, PhD, LSW, Millersville University, Lancaster, PA

Born and raised in Kenya, Dr. Wanja Ogongi is an Assistant Professor at Millersville University School of Social Work. She graduated from the University of Nairobi with her B.A, earned her MSW at West Chester University of PA and her PhD in Social Work at Widener University. Dr. Ogongi teaches a variety of courses in the BSW and MSW programs. Her areas of teaching include HBSE, Social Work Macro Practice and Social Work Field Education. Dr Ogongi has practiced social work professionally in the areas of International Human Rights (focus on women and children), Child Welfare, Refugees and Unaccompanied Minors, and Medical Social Work. Her areas of interest for research and presentation include Women empowerment, Social and Community Development, International Social Work, and Issues affecting the African Diaspora in the United States.

FIGURE 4.12. Wanja Ogongi

Kenyans as Africans

A congruent and authentic understanding of death, grief, and bereavement among Kenyans must take into consideration the cultural experiences and philosophies of the African people that govern life, death, dying, and the afterlife, for these factors influence individual experiences (Baloyi & Makobe-Rabothata, 2014). There are several aspects of the African worldview and philosophy (Mbiti, 1969) that influence the concept of death and bereavement processes of individuals of African descent and that are distinct from the mainstream Western/American conceptualizations of human behavior. This section provides a general overview of how Kenyans conceive and deal with death, grief, and bereavement, as well as the meanings and significance attributed to this phenomenon. It should be noted that Kenyans are not a homogenous group with the same bereavement, mourning, and grieving customs, practices, and rituals, as the country is a constellation of 43 distinct communities whose traditions and cultural and spiritual beliefs sometimes differ but also have similarities. The term *community* here is utilized to refer to what Westerners may refer as a "tribe" (a group of people who share a language, customs, traditions, and way of life). That said, some of the overarching shared beliefs, customs, and practices regarding the nature of life, illness, death, bereavement, and remembrance of the dead that are commonly shared among the many different communities that comprise modern-day Kenya and Africa in general will be discussed. The chapter will locate grief and loss death in the larger African epistemological paradigm and worldview as the underlying philosophy that is central to understanding, interpreting, and making meaning of many of the customs, practices, and rituals that govern bereavement and mourning among Kenyans.

African Epistemology and Beliefs on Life and the Hereafter

Before we can begin to appreciate death and bereavement customs and practices among Kenyans, we must locate the discussion within the African conceptualization and understanding of the nature of life, existence, the universe, religion, and spirituality.

Nature of Life and the Universe

According to African cosmology, the universe is made up of a complexity of visible and invisible aspects that encompasses natural and supernatural beings and is experienced through the natural and supernatural senses (Musana, 2018). African philosophy as rooted within the African culture is therefore much more epistemologically metaphysical and spiritual in nature, unlike many Western traditions or philosophies that place emphasis only on what can be proven empirically or observed and experienced through the five senses, namely hearing, seeing, feeling, tasting, and smelling (Ekanem, 2012). Traditionally, among Africans, it is believed that the universe was created by the creator, even though mythologies differ on how exactly this creation took place (Mbiti, 1969). This creation consists of two realities: a visible and invisible realm, and the existential base and idealism of African philosophy is therefore to coexist with nature and the world. Therefore, African views of the universe and life in general are profoundly religious and spiritual in nature, and the physical and nonphysical (spiritual) universe is considered permanent, eternal, and unending (Mbiti, 1969). Many African religious scholars have emphasized that Africans conceptualize "the invisible spiritual universe as a unit with the physical or visible, that, these two realms intermingle and dovetail into each other so much that it is not easy, or even necessary, at times to draw the distinction or separate them" (Mbiti, 1990, p. 74).

Perspectives on Life, Death, and Spirits

The general understanding among Africans is that there is an inextricable spiritual connection between the visible and invisible aspects of the world within which we live. Further, God/Creator holds utmost and absolute power and influence over the physical world; then there are the spirits who are seen to be able to easily transcend the boundaries between the physical and spiritual worlds. In simple terms, according to traditional African views, the universe is occupied by God/Creator, spirits, human beings, animals, plants, and minerals. God is perceived as the creator of all that exists in the visible and non-visible world, and spirits have a status between God and human beings (Mbiti, 1990). God is further viewed as the ruler of both of these worlds; in this creation, he is viewed as immanent and benevolent, and life is the greatest gift he has given to the human and nonhuman creation (Kinoti, 2010). Additionally, God is viewed as occupying the invisible or spiritual realms of the world but is represented in several ways by his creation in the physical world as well. Among the Gikuyu people, God is believed to carry out periodic inspections of the physical world from and will bring blessing or punishment depending on people's deeds (Kenyatta, 1938; Kinoti, 2010). In most African cultures, spirits generally are viewed as the ontological existence between man and God. Spirits (including those of departed humans) are seen as occupying a powerful position between humans and God and being higher in rank and power than human beings who are still living. They are seen as being able to have an influence on the living as well as those in the spirit world, including ancestors and God, and therefore more powerful than living humans. However, Kenyans speak of spirits (especially those of their recently departed) in human terms and treat them as if they have the same human characteristics they occupied when they lived. For example, someone might say "I just spoke to my grandfather" rather than "The spirit of my departed grandfather is speaking to me." As a clinician, how would you react to a client expressing sentiments about communicating and interacting with a dead relative? What tools would you utilize to distinguish between these beliefs and what is considered in the West "delusional or hallucinatory" behavior?

According to many African beliefs, a human being is made up of a physical visible body as well as an invisible spirit or soul. The spirit is what remains of a human being once he or she dies physically and exits the physical world. Because the physical and spiritual world are interconnected and in constant interaction with each other, the spirits of departed humans are believed to continue to exist and often appear to their kin (and sometimes non-kin) who are still living. They are believed to be more powerful than human beings and able to influence the lives of those they have left behind, as they straddle the physical world which we occupy, as well as the spiritual world within which the creator resides.

Death as an Expected Transition/Rite of Passage

As a result of the conceptualizations of the physical and spiritual worlds as interconnected, death is accompanied by a series of practices and performance of rituals that are meant to maintain the connection between the departing persons and the living, while ensuring a smooth transition for the soul/spirit of the departed to the spiritual world. Death is not feared, but rather greatly respected. In many of the communities that occupy Kenya today, as it is in many African communities, death is seen as serving as the mode of transition or transportation of the essence or spirit of a person from the one realm (physical tangible world) to the other (spiritual invisible world) (Baloyi & Makobe-Rabothata, 2014; Kenyatta, 1938; Mbiti, 1969). As such, death is treated as a rite of passage, a natural transition of the human spirit or human essence from the visible physical to the invisible spiritual realms of our world (Baloyi & Makobe-Rabothata, 2014; Kenyatta, 1938; Mbiti, 1969). This perception differs from the Western perspective where life is viewed as consisting of discrete developmental stages starting with conception and ending with death, with death marking the end stage of life when the dead person ceases to exist (Baloyi, 2014). In addition, the death of the physical body is not viewed with the finality that I've seen my American counterparts view it with, as can be witnessed in the manner with which deceased people are treated as well as in the mourning and burial rituals and rites, which continue for years after the actual physical death of the individual has occurred. Many Kenyans therefore approach death as an expected transition from one state of being to another, just as they do any of the other important rites of passages such as birth, transition to adulthood, marriage, starting a family, entering old age, and so on. As a result, Kenyans talk about death casually in all everyday conversations, as you would about a wedding, work, or birth of a child. It's not unusual to hear Kenyans speak jokingly about their own expected death and/or that of others as well as what they anticipate or wish to happen when they die. Because much of the time my classes involve discussions, this manner of speaking about death will often slip and I joke about death in my classes and my American students always appear startled or shocked about how I talk about it. For example, I've been known to often say that "nobody leaves this life alive; that I expect to die someday and any day is as good as any other." Among Kenyans, this manner of speech about life and death is common and happens all the time. It is rare to attend a gathering of Kenyans and not hear conversations about death and dying.

Spirits of the Departed (aka the Living Dead)

African culture recognized two categories of spirits: those that were created by God/Creator as such and those that were once human and occupied a human body but have now passed on to the spirit world (Mbiti, 1990). Spirits that were created as such are further classified into good and bad spirits; they occupy and had certain powers and limitations and carryout certain duties according to the position they occupy (Kinoti, 2010). They could, for example, punish one who intentionally destroys trees because they are affiliated with the environment, or punish a member who breaks the moral code. In the African worldview, people who have most recently physically departed from our world, and who are otherwise still alive in the memories of those who knew them in life, are generally known as the living dead (they are still alive in people's memories as well as alive in the world of the spirits). For example, among the Gikuyu community of Kenya (of which this author is a member) three types of the class of spirits that were once human are recognized and acknowledged. These include the living dead who are recently departed family members, of whom one's parents are the most important, and two other groups of spirits that relate to the clan and the Gikuyu nation as a whole (Kenyatta, 1938; Mbiti, 1990). When one dies, his or her spirit was believed to possess the character he or she had when they lived, and a good person with wisdom and counsel continues to be tapped beyond the grave as it had been before he or she died (Kinoti, 2010). A bad spirit, on the other hand, continues to bother the living relatives, and rituals are often performed to rid the family of such spirits, which then means these individuals would become forgotten and abandoned and no rituals to acknowledge or appease them are performed. Everyone strives to be of good character as a result.

The living dead spirits are highly regarded and will often receive offerings of food and libations from their living relatives in order to maintain oneness between them and the living and maintain harmony between the physical and the spirit world. The Gikuyu community believe that the spirits of the dead, like those of the living human being, can be pleased or displeased by the behavior of an individual, a family group, or age group (Kenyatta, 1938). In all Kenyan communities, as it is among most Africans, it's considered critically important to appease these spirits and bring them into harmony with the living; otherwise they cause havoc, illness, and misfortune in the lives of their living relatives if they are displeased. In order to establish and maintain good relations, spirits require the same courtesies that they would have been accorded if they were still living.

Rituals to Acknowledge the Living Dead

There are a variety of rituals that may somewhat vary from one community to another, but beliefs about the importance of maintaining relations between the living and spirits (especially those of recently deceased relatives) are common, real, and powerful. These rituals include pouring libations of beer, wine, milk, water, and even tea and coffee, as well as offerings of bits and pieces of food. Because the physical and spiritual are interconnected, these rituals are conducted everywhere and anywhere (not necessarily where one is buried). It is commonplace to observe individuals pour a libation on the ground before they start to eat or drink, to reestablish that connection with their living dead. These ritual offerings are often accompanied by words in the form of prayers, invocations, or even instructions to the departed as they are viewed as the link between the physical and spiritual world in which God and other spirits dwell (Mbiti, 1990).

For as long as the living dead are remembered by one or more individuals who are still living, they are considered to be in a state of personal immortality (Mbiti, 1990) and are commemorated by relatives through offerings of bits of food, libations, as well as carrying out instructions they may have given when still alive or when they appear to their loved ones. Their process of dying is really not complete as they are still part of their human families and fresh in people's memories, but they are also the closest links to the world of the spirits since they straddle both worlds (Mbiti, 1990). The view of a spirit of a person as immortal means he or she is seen as living on forever.

The living dead are believed to have the ability to appear or visit their living relatives from time to time and to be able to punish and/or influence the lives of those they've left behind. These appearances to the living are enjoyed and welcomed to an extent; however, they may also be treated with trepidation and fear when they happen too often, as this is seen as a sign that the they may be displeased about something that their living relatives are doing, or for not following instructions they may have given when they were still alive. It is therefore not unusual to hear individuals of Kenyan descent not only talk about their recently departed in both past as well as present tense as if they are still there, but to also report encounters with them. A "Western-oriented" clinician ought to follow up and encourage conversations on this topic, as this can often be a great indicator of unresolved grief and/or psychological distress that the individual maybe experiencing. The manner and language with which the departed are spoken about are a much more reliable indicator than the descriptions of an "emotion or feeling," as most Kenyan and African cultures do not consider or even name emotions and feelings. In many instances, individuals, when encouraged to talk about the living dead, and their interpretations of how they perceived their relationship with them will, even know exactly what needs to be done if they seem bothered by the appearances of their living dead (many a times, this will be some kind of ritual that may need to be done, completion of an act the departed relative may have instructed them to complete, and/or many of the other customs that may have been skipped that need to be completed to bring the individual psychic relief). When the very last person in the family and/or community who may have known a departed person dies, then he or she is considered as having completely transitioned to the world of the ancestors and he or she has completed the journey to join the spirit world.

Despite these perceptions of death as a transition to the spiritual world, when death occurs, community members will often come up with explanations of what has caused the death. Premature death or illness that interfered with the natural course of life and led to an early demise from the world is/was considered a bad thing and seen as a result of evil spirits, and/or magic (Kenyatta, 1938; Mbiti, 1969). These views persist today, even with the adoption of Christianity, and even within the Kenyan immigrant community in the United States. Some communities readily accept the explanation of a medical cause of the death, whereas some blame mystical or magical powers that are believed to have been utilized to cause the death. Some of these communities, such as the Tiriki, Abanyole, and AbaGusii communities, do not readily accept a medical or natural explanation even when presented with evidence, but will attribute the occurrence of the medical or natural death to be as a result of a metaphysical act of an evil person or spirit (Alembi, 2002). A clinician who is utilizing a culturally sensitive lens ought to check into the narratives of explanations of causes of death, as this is an area that can cause significant psychological distress for some individuals and require remedies in the form of rituals and ceremonies. Additionally, one should solicit explanations and solutions with an open mind from the individual as to what could be done to bring relief, as there is always a solution regardless of the explanations provided for a death. Ignoring these explanations or the need for ceremonies and rituals can get in the way of being able to effectively treat this population.

Customs, Rituals, and Practices During and After Death

With this conceptual background in mind, let's now look at the specific rituals and practices among Kenyans when a death occurs. Kenyans, like most Africans, are brought up in communal environments with a strong sense of belongingness, interconnectedness and relatedness to others, resulting in a strong sense of obligation and responsibility to a large set of individuals within the community/ies in which they live (Ekore & Lanre-Abass, 2016). As a result, what happens to the individual happens to the entire group, and whatever happens to the whole group happens to the individual. The lines between what is individual and what's communal are often so blurred that it can sometimes be difficult to draw a line between individual and collective experiences. This concept applies to all aspects of community life including death, mourning, and grief. After a death has occurred, a spokesperson will automatically take on the responsibility of informing the community that there's been a death. In many instances, this individual is a close friend of the family or an elder and not a family member because the assumption is that the immediate family members are too grief stricken that they cannot be burdened with the frivolous responsibilities required in planning and organizing mourning and burial events that need to follow. Furthermore, it's the responsibility of the community to take on all of the responsibilities that pertain to the burial. The immediate family members of the deceased are regarded as having no strength to do anything during this period of time and therefore the other members of the community, neighbors, distant family members, friends, and relatives, must help make the necessary arrangements for the burial and funeral ceremonies (Baloyi, 2014; Maboea, 2002). One has to remember that African families are extensive, are constantly evolving, and their boundaries are more fluid than in the West. They will include biological and nonbiological members who consider themselves kin for one reason or another.

Immediately following a death announcement, community members will gather at the home of the departed to support the family. Further, life and time seem to come to a standstill in the community after the occurrence of a death to acknowledge the gap left by the departed community member; this is especially noticeable in rural areas of Kenya. The manner in which community members gather varies from one community to another. Among the Gikuyu, community members will quietly trickle into the home; this period is accompanied by lots of silence, a solemn mood ,and lots of reflections and talk in hushed tones. There are quiet conversations about what may have led to the death, about the person who has departed, and very little public expression of grief maybe witnessed in the form of crying or other outward behavior during this period (there will be crying during the actual funeral). Among other communities in Kenya, this is not the case. Communities such as the Luo, AbaGusii, and certain groups of the Abaluhya are very expressive in their mourning, with women wailing and crying loudly and the men chanting and wailing. These forms of outward mourning practices are meant to express anger at death for robbing them of a family and/or community member. Men in these communities will be seen carrying sticks or clubs, which they use to strike the ground as they wail and chant after a death occurs, especially one of an elder (Alembi, 2002; Hoy, 2012). These collective mourning rituals and practices are geared toward providing support to the individuals directly affected by the death, such as family members, to help them deal with the loss of their beloved, as well as create a collective acknowledgment of the loss, shock, and other feelings that accompany death and loss. Many Americans are not accustomed to these outward and vivacious expressions of grief and sorrow and may easily mislabel it as unhealthy. This author remembers an incidence during an internship at a children's hospital where an African family accompanied by a sizeable group of community members who lost a child and they broke into loud crying and wailing, with the women throwing themselves on the floor, as is custom in many parts of Africa. The medical providers labeled this behavior as unhealthy and discussed contact with child welfare as the family had other children who were "witnessing this behavior" and contacted social work. When the social worker and this author arrived, they were able to provide information and education in reference to interpretations of this behavior, which obviously did not warrant a report to child welfare.

The Burden of Funeral and Related Expenses

Among Kenyans, all funeral and burial expenses (which often times run into thousands of dollars or Kenyan shillings) as well as ample social support is provided to the family of the departed, and it's very rare that the bereaved family is expected to contribute financially. For Kenyans living in the United States, the community forms a committee that prepares a budget of the funeral and any related expenses and informs the community. Community members will then individually contribute monies toward this budget depending on their own financial ability and the perceived level of need. The budget for Kenyans in the United States is normally inclusive of food expenses needed to feed community members during the mourning period, travel expenses to and from Kenya, as well a couple of months of rent and/or bills for the bereaved family to allow them enough time to grieve without having to worry about their everyday expenses. Within Kenya, in many cases, these monies will include paying off bigger debts the departed may have owed (such as hospital bills if they had been sick and spent time in a hospital).

The amount of financial aid provided to the families varies and is dependent on the level of involvement and connection the individual and his or her immediate family have had in the community. If they are known to attend most if not all community events, financially/emotionally/socially contribute, and are heavily invested in the affairs of other Kenyans, contributions can range from $20,000 to fifty $50,000. If, on the other hand, the family is not very involved in the affairs of others, then the contributions are sometimes just enough to cover the actual cost of burial/funeral. Nonetheless, no Kenyan family is left to cater to these expenses on its own, regardless of financial or social standing in the community. Therefore, the more faithful an individual is at attending other community events such as funerals and weddings, the more likely it is that others will help when a member of their own family dies or they are in need. There is an unwritten rule that an individual ought to give to the community and spend time cultivating a relationship with the community in order for the community to extend its assistance when individual needs arise. This is simply summed up in the African philosophy of Ubuntu: "I am because we are, and because we are, therefore I am" (Mbiti, 1969, p. 109).

During the period immediately following the death and through the funeral and several days, weeks, and/or months after the burial, the immediate family members are never left alone; community members will stay at the home 24 hours a day to provide support. Nights are spent singing and talking, and even though people may take turns to nod off, there is a core group of people who stay awake throughout the night until a few days after the burial ceremony has occurred. Many of the songs or dirges sung during burial and funeral ceremonies are ephemeral and composed specifically for each individual and only relate to him or her and who he or she was perceived to be as a person (Alembi, 2002; Asatsa & Gichuho, 2014). Among the Abanyole, there are dance performances during the night performed by specific groups such as boys, men, or women. Within these groups, there may be more categories of groups such as married men with at least one child, young women who are ready for marriage, among others, as well as certain songs that include everyone. These dirges and songs have a celebratory tone to help guide those present at the time toward a collective feeling and expression of grief and loss (Alembi, 2002). Most funeral dirges are simple and spontaneous and are sung at specific points to emphasize pertinent points or to recount the life of the departed, tell his or her story, or simply express a variety of feelings the singer is experiencing. As it is with many Kenyan songs, dirges are sung in a question-and-response style.

A dirge I sing about my mom:
Gikuu nikiandunya maitu wakwa *(death has robbed me)*
Woi woi … ndirarira na kieha *(I'm crying due to the great sadness I feel)*
Mweri ithatu mweri wa gatano *(on the third day of the fifth month)*
Riua rikiratha, maitu Wambui ndarionire … *(when the sun rose, my mom Wambui did not see it rise)*
Iiriii iiriii; iiriiii, iriiiii
Woi woi, woi woi Ndirarira na kieha *(I'm crying in sadness)*
Ndaririkana maitu wambui … woi woi *(when I remember my mom Wambui)*
Ndaririkana ati niandiga woi woi … woi woi *(knowing she has left me)*

I then insert words about who she was, our lineage, and what happened when she died and go on and on until my sadness feels like it's lifting. Even though these dirges are spontaneously composed, families tend to remember them and will sing them over and over for some years.

Funeral and Burial Attendance Obligations

If the departed was a parent of older children who have their own homes, the expectation is that these siblings travel home immediately to be with their families following the death and will only return to their own homesteads several days after the actual burial and interment ceremony has occurred (which in many cases in Kenya is a process that takes no less than 2 weeks). Even in the case of children or relatives who may be living in far-off communities or outside the country, the expectation is that they leave immediately to be with the rest of the family. Funerals are big social events among Kenyans, and for many Africans, they are viewed as a uniting factor that brings people together to pay tribute to the deceased and provide the family left behind with emotional and social support (Baloyi, 2014). Many people will gather to offer support in the form of condolences and contributions; others will offer to prepare meals and take care of guests, clean up, dig the grave, provide utensils and seats, and so on. Further, funeral attendance is an obligation for family members and the community as a whole. It is not unusual for bodies to be kept frozen in the mortuary or funeral home for several weeks while funeral preparations are being made and while relatives living in far-off lands are awaited. In addition, funeral preparations require time, effort, and people, and it is common for all other activities to be completely suspended in the community to enable everyone to participate in the funeral ceremonies. Inability to attend the funeral ceremony or missing parts of it causes significant emotional and psychological distress among many Kenyans. Participation in the collective grieving and mourning ceremonies is considered extremely important, and if an individual misses out on any of it, it brings significant psychological pain for years; this is remembered not only by the individual but also becomes a community memory that "so and so missed the funeral of this and this relative." Within Kenya itself, employers are very understanding of this expectation and will automatically grant extended paid leave to an employee when he or she has experienced a death. During this time, the employee is paid 100% of his or her salary, and his or her work colleagues will often travel long distances to attend the funeral ceremonies as well. The amount of leave varies depending on the relationship with the deceased, as well as the needs and flexibility of the employer (but it is rarely less than 3 weeks). It's important to remember that African culture conceives and perceives death as a grieving process, which is not restricted to time, and therefore there is no set standard of how much time an individual requires; this is constantly negotiated and renegotiated to accommodate personal needs.

Death is treated with utmost respect, importance, and care, probably even more than any of the other rites of passage or developmental stages, in my opinion. The obligations of funeral attendance and work pose great difficulties for many Kenyan immigrants in the United States. Most of them do not feel that death is treated in the same seriousness and weight by their American counterparts, that Americans are too casual about death, and the amount of time individuals are allocated (if at all) to deal with loss is ridiculously insufficient. Most companies will provide just 3 days for bereavement, which to Kenyans is laughable, especially when they are so far away from home. Additionally, because many of us grew up in close-knit communal environments, we have close ties with many individuals in the community, many of whom we consider parents and who we might be even closer to than our own biological parents. The American emphasis on the biological nuclear family and the ability to get time off from work only for deaths that occur in the nuclear family poses significant challenges for many Kenyan and other African immigrants in the Diaspora. As a result, it is not uncommon for Kenyan immigrants to quit their job when a death occurs and start all over when they return from home, which makes it essential for them to have sufficient community financial support.

Burial Rituals, Ceremonies, and Customs

The burial rituals and customs may differ from community to community. However, because of the earlier stated African connection between the living and the dead, the burial practices dictate that the individual be buried on ancestral land where his or her ancestors are buried. Burial in public cemeteries is greatly frowned upon, and so is cremation or other forms of disposal of the body. As such, it is a common practice among Kenyan immigrants to collectively raise thousands of dollars to transport bodies of the dead home, as well as cater for the flights of their relatives. There are varying mourning rituals performed for a deceased person, which are sometimes dependent on the position he or she occupied in life and his or her age at death. For example, among the Abanyole (a patrilineal community), siring sons for the continuity of the family and community is greatly valued (Alembi, 2002). As a result, men who have sired at least one son receive elaborate ceremonies with lots of singing, dancing, and celebration as well as very public expressions of grief compared to women or men who did not have sons (Alembi, 2002). Among the Gikuyu people of Central Kenya, on the other hand, (a matrilineal community), women, especially when they are older and die a natural death, are heavily grieved by the entire community. The funeral ceremonies of older women start at or before dawn and end after sunset and are accompanied by long speeches from community and family members who tell and retell every single detail about the departed individual.

Among the AbaGusii, the individual must be buried right outside his or her house. In many of the communities, the body of the deceased is brought home the day prior to the burial/funeral ceremony to allow people ample time to bid them goodbye. Among the AbaGusii, the person will be placed in the living room in a casket and community members will come in to view the body and bid the person farewell. During these viewings, it is commonplace to witness crying and wailing, as well as some standing and talking to the departed person to express their sadness and anger at the death. Children are involved in all aspects of grief and mourning customs and rituals and are not shielded from any of it; they are provided ample opportunities to talk and express their feelings and will often participate in all aspects of planning and funeral services. In many communities, it's considered important to appease the dead through elaborate funeral ceremonies to avoid angering them, which would in turn lead to the dead haunting the family and community. A Western clinician should seek to understand how the individual processes the burial and funeral ceremony, as it can be another area that can cause significant distress. Funeral and burial ceremonies including the interment are conducted by the family and community from begin to end and are open to all community and non-community members including children. In addition, many burial ceremonies are an all-day affair that is accompanied by many speeches from family members as well as a variety of scripted rituals depending on the community (especially if the deceased was an elder). Private funeral rites do not exist in our communities and many of us are baffled by American funeral rituals that exclude the community members. It is not necessary for an African to know someone in order to attend his or her funeral. When a death occurs, even at workplaces with relatives of colleagues, we expect to not only be involved in funeral arrangements but also be able to go to the funeral ceremonies.

Recent Personal Experiences With Death

When I recently lost one of my advisees, I was heartbroken, grief stricken, and extremely sad due to several issues involving how it happened, as well as what happened after. This was a young woman in her freshman year whose future held much promise, according to me. This particular death event hit me extremely hard emotionally for several reasons. First, I found myself engulfed in extreme sorrow and thoughts about what this beautiful young woman could have experienced in life that led her to this kind of departure from the world (she died by suicide). I felt that as a society we had failed her. Whereas this might sound unrealistic to an individual who was brought up with Western values where individuals are viewed as having autonomy over their lives and actions, my African sense of interconnectedness and belonging meant that I viewed this as a collective action that resulted in such an unfortunate end rather than an individual action. The "I" and "We" in my world are so intricately interwoven and entangled that the actions and responsibilities of the individual to the community and vice versa are impossible to unravel and separate. There was a sense of total loss: She was young and had not had much opportunity to create a legacy and leave a mark on the world. As discussed, when one dies in old age and has the opportunity to make an impact on the world, the community preserves the memory of such an individual in many ways such as naming children after him or her, creating songs, incorporating him or her into oral histories that are passed from one generation to another, as well as performing ceremonies and rituals that commemorate him or her for many years after the physical departure. A death by suicide in the African culture in the first place is viewed as a premature and unnecessary death. Because this particular death happened to a young woman, she did not have time in this life to contribute in a manner for the community to preserve her memory. So, unlike many other deaths I have experienced where I feel there is some sort of mark or legacy that the individual left of the world and therefore will always be remembered, I felt that this young woman was really truly dead. It was extremely difficult to come to terms with the thought of a human spirit who had walked with us just to disappear and be gone completely and forever. It brought a feeling of such total and complete loss.

The other factor about this death that affected my grief related to what happened after the news of her death became known to me and those around me. Kenyans and Africans in general view human life and all that pertains to it as extremely valuable, sacred, and precious. This value of human life is easily visible in the African philosophy and great emphasis on *personhood or humanness*, as described by African scholars such as Mbiti (1969, 1990). As such, human life is valued beyond mere physical existence (Musana, 2018), and this background provides a basis for most of the ceremonies that take place from the time one dies to the end of the mourning period (Iteyo, 2009). As explained in an earlier section, a human life is made up of the physical visible body and an invisible spiritual essence. At death, the physical body perishes, but the spirit/essence of the person remains; he or she retains the individual identity and continues to live within his or her families and communities, therefore occupying the interconnected invisible world (but still present in the physical world, nonetheless). When a person transitions from the physical to the invisible spiritual world, the community pauses to acknowledge his or her existence and the gap he or she has left behind, celebrate his or her life, commune with each other, and perform rituals and ceremonies to mourn the departed as a community, not just the family involved.

With this in mind, when I went to work the next business day after the death of my advisee, I was there early with the expectation that there was going to be some kind of communal gathering to acknowledge and talk about the death for me, colleagues, classmates, and the university community in general. To my surprise, there was nothing going on; in fact, I remember going to see a colleague I had been communicating with the entire weekend and the greeting to me was "Hey, what's up?" to which my response was "What's up? One of our students died!" I was pretty shocked and truthfully hurt; I found myself thinking, "A human being just died, and people are just going on as if nothing happened."

It was extremely upsetting that the world did not pause even for a minute to pay tribute to this young beautiful human being who just left us. This lack of acknowledgement, announcement of her death, communal gathering and acknowledgement, and conversations about her made me feel as if her life had meant nothing to those around me. So, I spoke to a couple of colleagues and told them how upset I was about this. When a university wide e-mail was finally sent that included a number to our employee services as well as student counseling, I got angry and frustrated; I felt that this action communicated that this was a personal/individual occurrence and problem to be dealt with individually with a counselor, not with the support of the rest of the community. There were no immediate opportunities for people to gather and talk about their feelings of grief and loss. This made me worry about the rest of the student body in which this young lady had belonged. Counselors were brought in to speak to students who shared the same classes; to me, again, this kind of isolation was hard to understand: What was to happen to all the other students who would read the story in the paper or hear about her on campus? Where was the space for them to process this with fellow community members and to receive support? Is a single counselor sitting on the other side of a desk enough? It was not until a week after the death that a communal event was held; it was one single community vigil, which still left me feeling just as grieved. In the following weeks, I had many conversations with colleagues and American friends to gain further insight about American views of death and grief.

I started reflecting on why this particular event had left me feeling so grieved, especially since I had not known the student well since she was still in her first semester at our institution. I realized that, first of all, because of my upbringing in a communal society where responsibility for others was strongly valued and stressed, I tend to automatically have a higher sense of responsibility, community, and connection over others in my circle than would be expected in the more individualistic society in which I currently live. This student, as an advisee, was close psychologically to me as she was part of that emotional community I automatically create as a result of my communal upbringing. In addition, human life is greatly respected, and when lost, that becomes a big deal, and the lack of communal mourning rituals and ceremonies immediately following the death felt very unnatural and absurd to me; I could not believe how casually this loss was being treated. In addition, the fact that we had to seek permission to acknowledge, mourn, and grieve this young lady from the family and university administration seemed ridiculous from my cultural lens.

In comparison, when recently a child whose parents are Kenyan immigrants passed away, word was spread within the Kenyan and African communities on social media, in conversations, as well as phone calls. No permission is needed to share this news or attend any events; everyone tells everybody they know, allowing community members to show up even when they did not previously know the parents or child to provide social, emotional, and financial support. Many of us went to the home every day for weeks, ate together, talked about this and many other losses we've had previously, and attended the funeral services and interment because, just as there's nothing like a private death, there's no internment private service where community members are not allowed to attend. People still continue to gather at this couple's home often and I expect that this will continue for many months.

Concluding Words

As discussed, death in the Kenyan setting is expected but treated with utmost respect. Death is considered an important rite of passage into the next world of the ancestors. As such, it is followed by important rituals to escort the departed to the next world, even though he or she is believed to straddle both the visible and invisible parts of our worlds. Even the announcement of a death is ritualized, as death is not described with the finality Americans apply to it. In the event that an American clinician has to inform a Kenyan family of a death, he or she should be aware that referring to a person as being dead or having died is viewed as somewhat disrespectful of the departed individual and their kin. As explained, people attempt to live good lives so they can live on; the term is only utilized for an individual who was viewed as a bad or evil person. In my community of the Gikuyu people, the spirits of the ancestors are referred to as *Ngoma*, a derivative of the word *Gukoma*, which means to sleep. People who have passed on are viewed as being asleep rather than "dead." In fact, I cannot think of a Gikuyu word that would directly translate to the term *dead* or *died*. As such, when death is announced, Gikuyu people, as it is with many other African communities, do not speak of a person as being "dead/having died"; we use terms like *departed, having left us, being called* (as in by God), or *rested* if the individual had been ill prior to death. The spirit and person are viewed as immortal, especially if he or she had lived a life as a good person.

In instances where Kenyans may be troubled by grief, rituals can be performed to help calm their spirits. Many of these rituals will involve some kind of church minister or traditional healer or elder performing a series of prayers. During these prayers, the individual will call upon the spirit of the departed person and his or her other ancestors (by name) and ask that they come and comfort their grieving relative. They will often pour libations of food and drink (alcoholic and non-alcoholic) on the ground and say many prayers and invite ancestral spirits to commune with their living relative and bring them closure. Many of these ritual ceremonies will involve prayers to the spirits of nature and God in addition to ancestral spirits (water, earth, fire). The minister would be accompanied by other community members who will often respond to every stanza of the prayers with "Let it be as you have said" or "Praise Ngai/God; peace be with us." There is a lot of singing and dancing (movement is considered important in restoring well-being, especially when one's spirit is troubled) and eating, as well as words of comfort to the individuals involved. Not too long ago, I was consulted about an African woman who was in a local hospital, admitted with a medical issue but now requiring transfer to an inpatient psychiatric hospital due to "delusions and hallucinations." Upon speaking with her, I realized she had survivors' guilt, having made it to the United States after a difficult journey where many of her relatives, friends, and community members were killed. In this instance, I was able to convince the medical team to allow her to go home, where I arranged for community members and an African pastor to perform rituals to "cleanse" her home, had additional ceremonies with the larger community, and facilitated a small fundraiser that allowed her to send a small amount of money to relatives she had left behind to perform similar ceremonies. I also encouraged and connected her to a Western-trained therapist (even though that did not work out due to a variety of reasons). Upon completion of these three ceremonies, this woman improved greatly and is thriving. In conclusion, it's extremely important for a clinician to be open and find out exactly what may be bothering the individual. Many immigrants are bothered by inability to attend and participate in the funeral and burial rituals, and facilitating travel for the individual where possible may be the only thing that helps resolve the issue.

FIGURE 4.13. Nyame Nnwu Na Mawu

MEANING: "God never dies, therefore I cannot die" (Represents God's omnipresence and the perpetual exist ence of human spirit and soul. It signifies the immortality of the human soul, believed to be a part of God. Because the soul rests with God after death, it cannot die).

References

Alembi, E. (2002). *The construction of the Abanyole perceptions on death through oral funeral poetry.* Retrieved from http://ethesis.helsinki.fi/julkaisut/hum/kultt/vk/alembi/theconst.pdf

Asatsa, S., & Gichuho, M. C. (2014). An investigation in to the Batsotso mourning rituals in Kakamega County, Kenya. *International Journal of Science and Research (IJSR), 3*(9), 794–796.

Baloyi, L., & Makobe-Rabothata, M. (2014). The African conception of death: A cultural implication. In L. T. B. Jackson, D. Meiring, F. J. R. Van de Vijver, E. S. Idemoudia, & W. K. Gabrenya Jr. (Eds.), *Toward sustainable development through nurturing diversity: Proceedings from the 21st International Congress of the International Association for Cross-Cultural Psychology.* Retrieved from https://scholarworks.gvsu.edu/iaccp_papers/119/

Baloyi, M. E. (2014). Distance no impediment for funerals: Death as a uniting ritual for African people—A pastoral study. *Verbum et Ecclesia 35*(1), a1248. doi:10.4102/ve.v35i1.1248

Ekanem, F. E. (2012). On the ontology of African philosophy. *International Journal of Humanities and Social Science Invention, 1*(1), 54–58.

Ekore, R. I., & Lanre-Abass, B. (2016). African cultural concept of death and the idea of advance care directives. *Indian Journal of Palliative Care, 22*(4), 369–372.

Hoy, G. W. (2012). Life and death among the Luo of Nyakach Plateau, Western Kenya. *Grief Perspectives, 3*(3), 19–23.

Iteyo, C. (2009). Belief in the spirits of the dead in Africa: A philosophical interpretation. *Thought and Practice: A Journal of the Philosophical Association of Kenya (PAK),* 1(1), 147–159.

Kenyatta, J. (1938). *Facing Mt. Kenya.* London, UK: Secker & Warburg.

Kinoti, H. W. (2010). *African ethics: Gikuyu traditional morality.* G. Wakuraya Wanjohi & G. J. Wanjohi (Eds). Amsterdam, Netherlands: Rodopi.

Maboea, S. I. (2002). *The influence of life-giving power in the African traditional religion and the Zionist churches in Soweto-A comparative study.* Unisa, Pretoria: CB Powell Bible Center.

Mbiti, J. S. (1969). *African religions and philosophy.* New York, NY: Praeger.

Mbiti, J. S. (1990). *African religions and philosophies.* Oxford, UK: Heinemann.

Musana, P. (2018). The African concept of personhood and its relevance to respect for human life and dignity in Africa and the global context. *African Study Monographs, 56*, 21–32. Retrieved from https://repository.kulib.kyoto-u.ac.jp/dspace/bitstream/2433/230172/1/ASM_S_56_21.pdf

The Impact of Taiwanese Culture Religions on Grief and Loss

Hsiu-Fen Lin, MA, MSW, LSW, PhD Candidate,
Rutgers University, New Brunswick, NJ.

As an international graduate Taiwanese student at Rutgers, enrolled in the School of Social Work PhD program, I am currently working on my dissertation. I received my MSW from Rutgers in 2018 with an "Aging and Health" specialization that required completing the course "Grief and Loss." This topic epitomizes my life-long learning, working experiences, and research. I was a social worker in the field of domestic violence in Taiwan from 2003 to 2013. I served high-risk clients to face their grief and loss along with domestic violence issues. When I pursued my first Master's degree from the National Taiwan University in 2002, my thesis was entitled "The surviving single parent widows: The social support process following the 921 Earthquake, 1999." My prolonged participation in the disaster area provided me a better understanding about how Taiwanese culture and gender roles deeply impact the grieving process of disaster survivors.

FIGURE 4.14. Hsiu-Fen Lin

In the summer of 1999, the weather in Taiwan was stifling and sultry. The pronounced humidity after the large-scale earthquake affected the corpses, and their smell permeated the town. The town became a public mortuary where the trucks were busy transporting bags and bags of dead bodies from the rescue sites. The massive deaths led to a shortage of freezers; the deceased bodies were temporarily stored on the ground covered with white cloths. The humid weather spread the corpses' smell all over. The outside environment was mirrored in the municipal funeral home, where there was an air of extreme somberness. There were hundreds of earthquake survivors in the room, but all that was heard was the sound of religious prayers along with the ringing of bells by ritual specialists. Survivors were still in shock, restless, and grieving their lost loved ones in silence. The gloom was overwhelming and dampened everyone's spirits.

As a social work graduate student, I volunteered to help earthquake survivors in the funeral homes. On the way there, I had confidence in my ability to build rapport, listen attentively, and engage in dialogue with clients. However, my social work skills failed immediately as soon as I was on the scene. I had no answers for questions raised by those survivors who were focused on checking the deceased list, identifying their loved ones, claiming their bodies, finding them in storage, or arranging the cremation procedures. Because of the devastation caused by the earthquake, it was very challenging to recover a complete deceased body. In the Taiwanese culture, people believe that the spirit can only remain in the whole body. The earthquake survivors were therefore further distraught because they could not help their diseased to reach the afterlife.

Inside the funeral home, I was full of empathy for the grieving but failed to initiate a dialogue with distressed survivors. Taiwanese people do not cry or express their grieving in front of others, particularly strangers. I did not realize at the time that I was actually a stranger. Even though I was Taiwanese and introduced myself as a social work student with grieving training, the survivors' faces looked confused because the concept of expressing grieving was so foreign to them. I started to explain who I was more than to engage them to let out their emotions; I was nervous, uncertain, and felt that my presence was an interference.

In contrast, I observed many Buddhist Tzu Chi Foundation[2] volunteers, known throughout Taiwan and easily identified by their clothing, who were able to help. They offered prayers, and the survivors were willing to accept their touch on their shoulders. This touching is not a usual occurrence because Taiwanese are not used to physical touch. As a young girl from the city with good intentions, I found myself so distant from those survivors in rural areas. I was so close to earthquake survivors, but I could not offer any help on the frontline for them to face the death of their loved ones. Without cultural understanding of death and loss, my profession skills were considered of no use.

Disasters: An Overlooked Grief and Loss

After the earthquake in Taiwan, a young mother waited for 3 days to get news about whether her husband survived. Eventually, she learned the grim truth and had to tell her 5-year-old daughter that her father was buried by their collapsed house. The daughter tried to comfort her mother and said, "Mommy, don't cry. Dad is just sleeping." This short poem concisely expresses the deep sorrow of a mother and the innocence of her child following the disastrous earthquake.

The devastation of unanticipated natural disasters makes the grieving and loss process more difficult, particularly for people within Taiwanese culture. The 1999 Jiji earthquake in Taiwan caused unanticipated death of over 2,000 victims and afflicted hundreds of thousands more grieving family members. The Jiji earthquake was a well-known natural disaster, but the widespread global expressions of sympathy did not make the grieving and loss process easier. Even though survivors focused on rebuilding their environment and their life, they were not ready to undergo the grieving process (Lin & Ma, 2004). Survivors of earthquake have a higher risk of complicated grief, PTSD, suicide, or prolonged grief disorder symptoms (Chou et al., 2003; Chou et al., 2007; Li, Chow, Shi, & Chan, 2015; Tsutsui, Hasegawa, Hiraga, Ishiki, & Asukai, 2014). Individuals who are part of a collective grieving society have difficulty in accepting the massive death and loss caused by disaster. In fact, it is the culture of individuals that shapes the grieving and loss in daily life as well as the reaction to death caused by a disaster (Lin, 2005). For Taiwanese, like the mother in the poem, it is typical to face loss silently without emotional expression.

---

2 Short name for Buddhist Compassion Relief Tzu Chi Foundation (http://www.tzuchi.org/), the largest Taiwanese humanitarian and nonprofit organization (NGO), with 10 million members worldwide. Tzu Chi is most well known for its disaster relief from short-term rescue to the long-term rebuilding projects.

Taiwanese Culture: Meaning of Death, Grief, and Loss

Taiwan is a multifaceted society blending traditional Confucian beliefs, ancestral Taiwanese culture, Chinese culture, Japanese colonial heritage, and now Western values. Confucian philosophy, the foundation of Chinese culture, predominately impacts the lifestyle of the Taiwanese people and also constrains their perceptions and behaviors (Tsai, 2006). The political democracy and economic development in Taiwan have fostered a new Asian culture embracing Western values, such as individualism and self-efficacy, to an extent (Weller, 1999). Because Taiwan has a unique cultural perspective with diverse traditions, understanding the way these values are followed is beneficial to interact properly with Taiwanese or Chinese people, for example with regard to superstitions. In Taiwanese culture, superstitions are not legends or stories, but facts of life.

The basic Confucian values have had a profound influence on modern Taiwanese culture, including the idea of the group over the individual, preservation of harmony and propriety, and respect for family and hierarchy (Liu, 2009). The concept of self is defined by one's relationships with others, not by the individual "I." Feedback and recognition from others determine the image of self; in a sense, individuals are not allowed to express their opinions or ideas openly. Taiwanese view harmony as an acceptance of one's social role. As a result, they play roles well in a group and avoid conflicts, so each individual prefers indirect communication. Propriety 禮 (Li), the Chinese code of ethics, dictates proper etiquette in social relationship behaviors; for example, the Western style of greeting with hugs and kisses in public is considered inappropriate as opposed to bowing. In social relations, the family is the fundamental responsible unit for caregiving. Respect for parents, older members, and authoritative figures is viewed as the greatest virtue for Taiwanese. The principle of filial piety 孝 (Xiao) dictates that young children should obey their parents and that the oldest son and his wife are obligated to take care of the son's parents when they grow old. Taiwanese women are expected to subordinate their needs to their father's and husband's families to take care of the home and children; they are not encouraged to prioritize their desires (World Trade Press, 2010).

Death remains a taboo topic in contemporary Taiwanese society, similar to the situation in the United States. Mandarin and its traditional writing/character system, used in Taiwan, has a euphemistic way of referring to death, much as in English. While Americans use "pass away" to avoid direct use of the word "die," most Taiwanese adopt Buddhist wording "往生" (wǎng shēng, which means moving to live) or "走了" (zǒu le, which means departed). Tetraphobia is highly popular because Mandarin pronunciation of the number 4 四 (sì) sounds close to the word of die 死 (sǐ). The language to express condolences to someone is different across cultures. In American culture, "I am sorry for your loss" or "My condolences" are used to validate individuals' emotions of loss. In contrast, Chinese or Taiwanese people use the sentence "節哀順變 (jiē āi shùn biàn)," which means "Repress your grief and obey the irreversible change." The Chinese language itself, in other words, sets the norm that grief must be suppressed. Letting out the deep sorrow in public is considered inappropriate; in turn, the norm may delay the grieving process and set up an obstacle for counselors to build rapport.

In Taiwan, religion cannot be separated from culture. Confucianism, Taoism, and Buddhism significantly impact most Taiwanese people to manage death and bereavement through death practices (Shih, 2010). Confucianism emphasizes the responsibilities of family members to obey ritual propriety that aims to maintain social order. The descendants follow rituals and treat the deceased person as if he or she was alive so that he or she continues to fulfill filial duties during bereavement and afterlife

(Fraser, 2013). It is believed that ancestors have the ability to promote the quality of life for descendants who provide good afterlife care (Yang & Chen, 2009). Since the death of a loved one evokes intense emotions, the funeral rituals regulate the expression of survivors' grief in a specified manner. The Confucian philosophy on death not only denies the fact of death but also fails to validate the sorrow of loss (Fraser, 2013). Buddhist and Taoist beliefs about death, in contrast, assume that human beings exist in nirvana or hell based on their merits before death, and they will be reincarnated in human beings or animals after a period of becoming spirits or ghosts, a belief that may reinforce fear about death (Hui, Chan, & Chan, 1989). Notably, due to the increase of self-harming incidents and suicides at Taiwanese campuses, mental health professionals have advocated for psychological education that may challenge traditional assumptions. The Taiwan Ministry of Education began to implement the life and death education in school curriculum in 2001; accordingly, young generations may be more open to interventions in the grieving process (Yang & Chen, 2009).

Rituals, Customs, and Burial

Taoist priests and Buddhist monks guide the family members to perform death practices that are conducted to transform the deceased into an ancestor in a family line (Shih, 2010). The extensive schedule of religious funeral procedures aims to maintain the social order; therefore, grieving and mourning freely is considered an obstacle. Disclosure of mourning emotions in front of non-family members is considered inappropriate, but grieving silently is acceptable (Tsai, 2005). Ironically, loud crying, weeping, and wailing is integrated into some rituals to symbolize that the descendants perform their filial duties to honor the deceased (Liu, Chen, & Chen, 2003). Non-Asians can watch a Taiwanese noir movie, entitled *7 Days in Heaven*, to understand complicated Taiwanese funeral ritual traditions and prolonged grieving and loss (Wang & Liu, 2010).

Taiwanese people believe that the spirit of the deceased realizes the fact of death on the seventh day after the death and that he or she returns to his or her house at 11:00 p.m. and mourns for him- or herself (Liu et al., 2003). Before that moment, all the family members gather in the living room to mourn for the deceased before their return. They do the ritual mourning every 7 days after death, so-called "doing sevens," which lasts for 7 weeks. In modern Taiwanese society, people shorten 7 weeks into a total of 24 days, but the traditional 7-day ritual must be followed (Liu et al., 2003). Some traditional families continue mourning ceremonies on the 100th day, the first anniversary, until the third anniversary. In addition, Taiwan has the National Tomb Sweeping Day on April 5th for family members to memorize their lost loved ones.

From the moment of death until the funeral, family members begin wearing black or dark colors with armbands to show sorrow for the lost loved one. Males do not shave or cut hair and females do not wear any accessories until the deceased is buried (Liu et al., 2003). At a traditional funeral ceremony, Taiwanese family members wear special filial mourning clothes that are coded by the color and texture according to the degree of kinship between the deceased and the mourners. Married relatives wear long sleeves, and unmarried ones wear short sleeves. The same generation wears the same type of filial mourning clothes. Married daughters are considered family members of the husband's family and wear those designated mourning clothes (Liu et al., 2003).

Application for Clinical Students

This section presents an overview of death, grief, and loss in modern Taiwanese society. Given that bereavement is socially constructed, different factors impact how individuals react to their grieving process, such as age, gender, and relationships between the deceased and their family members (Lin, 2005). The complexity of suffering loss from disasters or other events acquires a deeper understanding of Taiwanese culture and religion on death (Tsai, 2012). Looking back, I was not prepared to face such a graphic scene and to appraise cultural understanding of grieving and loss. Even though I am a native Taiwanese and I know about death, I did not know how to handle different mourning scenarios. My experience with the Jiji earthquake can help clinicians deal with the bereavement after unexpected or expected deaths. For clinical workers who have not had much experience with Taiwanese or Asian death, grief, and loss, my recommendations include the following:

- Encourage your clients to share their religious beliefs and rituals because these play an important role during the grieving process for the Taiwanese.
- Create a safe and supportive environment physically and psychologically for individual grieving counseling. Normalize the grieving process and identify emotional vocabulary.
- Provide alternative ways for mourners to express their grief and loss, such as writing, art, or music therapy, as Taiwanese and Asians in general are not used to verbal expression.
- Provide family counseling if some family members are willing to participate, because loss is the common experience for the entire family.
- Motivate bereaved family members to participate in memorial ceremonies and family activities, particularly on certain meaningful days, such as Tomb Sweeping Day, Lunar New Year, or dates marking the anniversary of the death.

Acknowledgments

My sincere gratitude goes to Eva-Maria Morin, Erin Kelly, and Christopher Hadfield for providing expertise and insight that greatly polished this chapter.

References

Chou, Y. J., Huang, N., Lee, C. H., Tsai, S. L., Tsay, J. H., Chen, L. S., & Chou, P. (2003). Suicides after the 1999 Taiwan earthquake. *International Journal of Epidemiology, 32*(6), 1007–1014.

Chou, F. H. C., Wu, H. C., Chou, P., Su, C. Y., Tsai, K. Y., Chao, S. S., ... & Ou-Yang, W. C. (2007). Epidemiologic psychiatric studies on post-disaster impact among Chi-Chi earthquake survivors in Yu-Chi, Taiwan. *Psychiatry and Clinical Neurosciences, 61*(4), 370–378.

Fraser, C. (2013). Xunzi versus Zhuangzi: Two approaches to death in classical Chinese thought. *Frontiers of Philosophy in China, 8*(3), 410–427.

Hui, C. H., Chan, I. S., & Chan, J. (1989). Death cognition among Chinese teenagers: Beliefs about consequences of death. *Journal of Research in Personality, 23*(1), 99–117.

Li, J., Chow, A. Y., Shi, Z., & Chan, C. L. (2015). Prevalence and risk factors of complicated grief among Sichuan earthquake survivors. *Journal of Affective Disorders, 175*, 218–223.

Lin, C. Y. (2005). 社會文化與悲傷反應 [Social culture and bereaved reaction.] *Journal of Life-and- Death Studies, 2*, 107–127.

Lin, H. F., & Ma, S. P. (2004). The impact of social support on widowed mothers surviving in the 921 Earthquake in Taiwan. *National Taiwan University Social Work Review, 9*, 39–84.

Liu, H. Y., Chen, A. C., & Chen, J. F. (2003). 台灣島民的生命禮俗 [Life Rituals in Taiwan] (1st ed.). Taipei, China: Chang min wen hua.

Liu, A. C. (2009) *Taiwan A to Z: The essential cultural guide*. Taipei: Farm-Mei Printing Company.

Shih, F. L. (2010). Chinese "bad death" practices in Taiwan: Maidens and modernity. *Mortality, 15*(2), 122–137.

Tsai, C. T. L. (2006). The influence of Confucianism on women's leisure in Taiwan. *Leisure Studies, 25*(4), 469–476.

Tsai, P. J. (2012). 華人家庭關係脈絡中悲傷表達模式之探討：以台灣為例 [Exploring grieving expressions in the context of Asian family relationship: A case study of Taiwan.] *Taiwan Counseling Quarterly, 4*(1), 16–38.

Tsutsui, T., Hasegawa, Y., Hiraga, M., Ishiki, M., & Asukai, N. (2014). Distinctiveness of prolonged grief disorder symptoms among survivors of the Great East Japan Earthquake and Tsunami. *Psychiatry research, 217*(1–2), 67–71.

Wang, Y. (Producer), & Liu, E. (Director). (2010). *Seven days in heaven*. [Video file]. Retrieved from https://www.youtube.com/watch?v=GAj_AbC_kpU

Weller, R. (1999). *Alternate civilities: Democracy and culture in China and Taiwan*. New York, NY: Routledge. doi:10.4324/9780429502378

World Trade Press. (2010). *Taiwan women in culture, business and travel: A profile of Taiwanese women in the fabric of society*. Retrieved from https://ebookcentral.proquest.com

Yang, S. C., & Chen, S. F. (2009). The study of personal constructs of death and fear of death among Taiwanese adolescents. *Death Studies, 33*(10), 913–940.

中華文化對悲傷及失落之影響

近年來大規模災害造成重大傷亡，例如台灣九二一地震以及四川汶川大地震，數以萬計的災民無家可歸。無論天然災害或人為災難，造成了生命喪失及建築物損害外，災害存活者內心的悲傷及失落往往讓人疏忽，心靈重建工作更需要長期的關注。即使災害是特殊事件，但人們如何回應災害所造成的失落，並非突如其來，而是深植於先前社會文化如看待死亡及失落。因此，我們必須先瞭解中華文化如何影響悲傷及失落，方能進行後續悲傷輔導。

本章從個人參與台灣九二一地震的親身體驗出發，反思當時身處南投殯儀館，但卻無能協助受災家屬抒發悲傷，反觀慈濟功德會志工透過誦經、摺蓮花陪伴家屬渡過最困難的時刻，進而探究中華文化對死亡及哀悼的詮釋，最後提出個人對悲傷輔導之建議。死亡在現代社會仍是一個禁忌話題，即使台灣從2001年開始在各大專院校及中小學推廣生命教育，再加上喪葬禮儀公司企業化，我們仍然欠缺對於死亡的準備與討論。台灣文化具有其獨特性，融合了傳統儒教、中國文化、台灣先民文化、日本殖民遺跡，以及西方強調個人主義之思想，尤其是儒家思想奠定禮教儀式之基礎，作為待人接物之準則。家庭是社會最重要的基本單位，掌管家族成員的生老病死，家庭成員必須恪守社會規範，視亡者身後事如同生前，一般人相信若能將亡者身後事及祭祀辦理合宜，祖先將能庇蔭後世子孫。喪葬禮儀其實是一套將亡者轉換為祖宗先列的繁複程序，現代人多半商請宗教禮儀師來主持各項喪葬儀式，台灣人大多壓抑面對死亡的失落情緒，先依序完成守喪及後續事宜，因此悲傷的情緒反應往往延後出現。

因此，若為台灣人或深受中華文化的亞洲人進行悲傷輔導，本章提出下列建議：

- 在台灣社會，死亡及喪葬與文化密不可分，可多鼓勵案主分享其宗教信仰及其儀式，了解他們在期間的情緒反應及感受。
- 為個人悲傷諮商創造一個在空間上及心理上的安全環境，並且將悲傷反應過程予以正常化，提供情緒詞彙，幫助個人指認及表達因悲傷所產生的情緒感受。
- 由於台灣人/亞洲人不擅長用口語表達悲傷，可提供其他形式方式協助其宣洩悲傷情緒，例如寫作、藝術創作、或音樂治療等等。
- 提供家族治療。因為死亡是家庭的共同經驗，只要部分家庭成員願意，就可嘗試先進行部份成員的家族治療。
- 鼓勵家庭成員參加喪葬儀式及家庭活動，特別是在重要節日，例如清明節、過年或忌日週年等。

Spirituality Heals: The Maya-Grief and Loss

Linda E. Benavides, PhD, MSW, Widener University

Linda E. Benavides is an Assistant Professor in the Center for Social Work Education at Widener University. Dr. Benavides teaches across both the undergraduate and graduate (land-based and on-line) programs. In addition to teaching practice/field courses, Dr. Benavides also teaches Human Behavior in the Social Environment, Grief & Loss, Spirituality & Social Work, and Interpersonal Processes. Dr. Benavides's research and scholarship focus on spirituality-specifically spirituality as a protective factor, spiritual development, spirituality in the Latino community, and indigenous spiritual healing practices.

FIGURE 4.15. Linda E. Benavides

The Maya are a diverse indigenous people of Latin America. Prior to the Spanish conquest in the 16th century, the Maya civilization was a thriving "complex intellectual and spiritual culture" (Grandin, Levenson, & Oglesby, 2011, p. 11) that encompassed a large region comprising of Guatemala, Belize, Honduras, El Salvador, and southern Mexico—including the Yucatan and Chiapas. The Spanish conquest resulted in mass genocide and displacement of the Maya from ancestral lands, as well as spiritual, political, economic, land, health, and cultural oppression that continues through today (Ceron et al., 2016; Giralt, 2012; Lopez, 2004; Vogt, 2015). Despite such systemic oppression, the Maya continue to be a spiritually rich people with spiritual healing practices that have led to their individual and collective resilience and perseverance.

This is especially true for the Maya of Guatemala, who have endured continual systematic oppression and violence since the Spanish conquest, including a 36-year civil war that ended in 1996 and resulted in the deaths and/or disappearance of almost 200,000 Mayan women, men, and children (Ceron et al., 2016; Grandin, Levenson, & Oglesby, 2011). Today, the Maya of Guatemala make up 45 to 70% of the population of Guatemala (Ceron et al., 2016; Consoli, Tzaquitzal, & Gonzalez, 2013; Marin-Beristain, Paez, & Gonzalez, 2000). There are 23 Mayan ethnic groups in the country, each with their own language, customs, traditional and ceremonial clothing, and traditional authorities (Ceron et al., 2016; Consoli, Hernandez-Tzaquitzal, & Gonzalez, 2013; Lopez, 2004).

In this section, we will begin with an exploration of Mayan spirituality, which will guide an understanding of loss and grief in the Mayan community. Discussion on grief and loss will focus on (a) the historical trauma experienced by the Maya of Guatemala; (b) death and dying in the Mayan community (i.e., views on death, burial traditions, etc.); and (c) expression of grief, bereavement, and mourning in the Mayan community. Finally, implications for spiritually and culturally sensitive social work practice with the Mayan community will be addressed.

**Throughout this chapter, I will be referring to indigenous terms and knowledge gained through my experiences learning about Mayan culture and spirituality in my travels to Guatemala, Mexico, El Salvador, and Honduras.

**I am not of Mayan descent. I am a first-generation Mexican-American, born and raised in Texas.

Sandra: Case Study on Mayan Grief and Loss

Sandra is a 63-year-old Maya from Guatemala. Sandra was born and raised in a small village right outside of Santa Cruz del Quiche. While Sandra's primary language is Quiche, she speaks some Spanish. Sandra is widowed. Her husband Alejandro was killed in 1981 at the height of the Guatemalan civil war. Alejandro was 29 years old when he was executed by the Guatemalan military as he was suspected of being part of the counter-insurgency. Sandra was 25 years old and mother to 1-year-old Micaela when Alejandro was murdered. Sandra has fled the violence and poverty in her home country with her daughter Micaela and Micaela's husband and teenage son. The four of them are currently staying in a make-shift shelter outside the port of entry to El Paso, Texas, waiting for an asylum interview. Sandra is extremely depressed. She did not wish to leave her home country as she did not wish to be separated from her remaining siblings. She also wanted to stay close to Alejandro's grave. She felt his presence there and worried she would lose contact with Alejandro and her parents (also deceased) if she no longer lived close to their graves. Sandra was conflicted about accompanying Micaela and her daughter's family to the United States, but in the end decided she could not bear to be separated from her only daughter and grandchild. Sandra is in extreme pain and malnourished from their journey. Sandra has also been experiencing nightmares and flashbacks of the multiple times she was raped during the *conflicto armado* (civil war) by members of the Guatemalan military. She feels enraged that they never served a day in jail for their violence toward her. Sandra is extremely anxious about what the future holds for her and her family.

Mayan Spirituality

Mayan spirituality is holistic and collectivist. The Maya place great importance on the interrelationship between land, nature, and humankind and believe it to be tied to their very survival. For the Maya, land is life (Martin-Beristain, Paez, Gonzalez, 2000). Through the planting and consuming of maize (corn), "a thread is woven, which connects Mayan people with their ancestors, sacred spirits and with their future through their children" (Kaupisch, 2017, p. 242). As such, the Maya have traditionally looked to the Calendario Ab' (also known as the solar/agricultural calendar), which consists of 365 days, for guidance on the agricultural cycle, the seasons, solstices, and equinoxes (Lopez, 2004; Hart, 2008).

The Maya also look to the Calendario Cholq'ij (also known as the lunar/sacred calendar) to promote balance between nature and human beings. The Calendario Cholq'ij, which consists of approximately 260 days, centers on human beings and guides Mayan conduct, purpose, health, beliefs, and so on (Lopez, 2004; Hart, 2008). Hart (2008) elaborates, stating that the Calendario Cholq'ij is "a zodiac, marking the destiny of every newborn according to his or her date of birth" and "when used in divinations, the calendar indicates where the problems and dangers lie" (p. 40).

Mayan spirituality centers on spiritual ceremonies. According to Hart (2008), there are two types of Kotz'i'j (spiritual ceremonies). The first are ceremonies dictated by the Calendario Cholq'ij, such as New Years. The second type of ceremonies are divinations facilitated by spiritual guides requested by individuals and/or families (Consoli, et. al., 2013; Hart, 2008). Spiritual guides provide insights into the nature and cause of problems and often recommend further ceremonies on days determined by the Calendario Cholq'ij (Hart, 2008).

For the Maya, everything is living and has energy and is therefore spiritual. The earth, sun, moon, mountains, trees/plants, rocks, and animals hold important symbolic familial positions and as such "command love and respect and are personifications of good and of ancestors' souls" (Marin-Beristain, Paez, & Gonzalez, 2000, p. 118). As such, the Maya believe that the souls of ancestors dwell with the living on Earth and are part of the everyday lives of their descendants. Hart (2008) elaborates, stating,

> The Maya say that the dead are always with us. They are in the air; they can give us warnings or advice in dreams; they can clear our path of obstacles or traps. If the dead can help us, we can also help them; the ancestors are offered food and drink in the form of candles, incense, and ceremony. Their names are remembered in prayers, and by their names they are called to be at our side. But there may be a price to pay for those who don't honor their ancestors; sometimes punishments inflicted by the dead upon the living come in the form of illness, or even death. (p. 205)

Mayan traditions and rituals when an individual dies date back to pre-colonization. We will explore these later. For now, it is important to note that for the Maya a burial must be done properly if the soul of the deceased is to have a good afterlife. A proper burial is also necessary for continued good relationship between the ancestors and their descendants (Garrard-Burnett, 2015; Hart, 2008; Kaupisch, 2017). The loss of relationships between ancestors and the living can be detrimental to the well-being of the Mayan community.

It is also important to note that colonization by the Spanish resulted in forced Christianity. For their own survival, Mayans were forced to convert publicly to Christianity and take their Indigenous spiritual beliefs and practices underground. Today, Mayan spirituality is a fusion of pre-colonial Mayan spiritual beliefs and practices with Christian beliefs, practices, and religious figures. While this mixture of Christianity and Indigenous spiritual beliefs is practiced by a large percentage of the Maya, a new spiritual movement rejecting Christianity in Indigenous spirituality has emerged. According to MacKenzie (1999), a pan-Mayan movement, which calls for a "purity" (p. 42) of Mayan spirituality, has gained momentum since the end of the *conflicto armado* (civil war). The pan-Mayan movement rejects Christian/Catholic beliefs and practices and the use of Spanish in all spiritual ceremonies, rather calling for a return to Mayan native languages. We will now explore the historical trauma endured by the Maya of Guatemala.

Historical Trauma

Beginning with the genocide, land displacement, and oppression brought about by the Spanish conquest, to a 36-year civil war that ended in 1996, the Maya of Guatemala have continuously had to fight for their very survival. Led by Pedro de Alvarado, the Spanish invaded what is now known as Guatemala in 1524 and waged war on the various Mayan groups (Grandin, Levenson & Oglesby,

2011). The invasion resulted in mass genocide of the Maya through widespread massacre and carnage carried out by the Spanish. In addition, the introduction of diseases not known by the Maya, such as measles and small pox, contributed significantly to the depopulation of the Mayan people (Lovell, 2011). Displacement of ancestral lands, rape of women and children, *servicio ordinario* (forced labor) to build the Spanish empire, and *reparto* (forced tribute) of cocoa, textiles, and other goods were also the result of the Spanish invasion. The Spanish forced Christianity on the Maya and those not willing to convert were often tortured and/or killed. The Spanish conquest also resulted in the destruction of Mayan cities, sacred sites, and written histories and prophesies. As a result, much knowledge of the Maya before the Spanish invasion was lost (Grandin, Levenson & Oglesby, 2011). While recent archeological advances in deciphering Mayan pre-conquest writing has shed some light on Mayan spirituality before the Spanish conquest (Coe, 2011), many pre-colonization Mayan spiritual beliefs and practices were lost. Forced Christianity also led to a loss of spiritual beliefs and practices and the integration of Christianity with Mayan indigenous spiritual beliefs and practices (Lopez, 2004, Grandin, Levenson, & Oglesby, 2011).

The oppression of the Maya did not end after Guatemala obtained independence from Spain in 1821. Rather, oppression of the Maya continued by the new ruling class, Ladinos/as, who are descendants of both the Maya and Spanish. It is important to note, however, that there exists social classes among the Ladinos and that many Ladinos also face poverty, violence, and oppression (Grandin, Levenson, & Oglesby, 2011). Indigenous individuals in Guatemala, however, have had historically higher poverty rates than Ladinos and suffer from disproportionate health inequalities, including higher rates of child mortality and lower life expectancy than non-Indigenous Guatemalans (Ceron et al., 2016; Consoli et al., 2013).

Already a severely oppressed people, the Maya of Guatemala suffered another genocide during a 36-year *conflicto armado* (civil war), which began in 1960 and ended in 1996. During this time, thousands of Mayans were once again displaced from their ancestral lands and were raped, tortured, killed, or disappeared (Ceron et al., 2016; Grandin et al., 2011; Lykes, Beristain, Cabrera Perez-Arminan, 2007). According to the Comision para el Esclarecimiento Historico (CEH) (Commission for Historical Clarification), 83% of the 200,000 individuals who were killed or disappeared during the *conflicto armado* were of Maya descent (Comision para el Esclarecimiento Historico, 2011). The civil war became a genocide, which according to Grandin, Levenson, and Oglesby (2011), was "executed with a racist frenzy, which included the murder of children—often by beating them against a wall or crushing them with the bodies of dead adults—as well as amputations, impalings, eviscerations, abortions by bayonets, and burning victims alive" (p. 363). The destruction of entire villages resulted in families and communities being torn apart, causing significant breaks in established social structures (Consoli et al., 2013; Lykes et al., 2007). Consoli and colleagues (2013) elaborate on the irreparable damage done to the Maya:

> The numerous massacres that took place in many rural, mostly Mayan communities during the civil war caused extensive social structure difficulties and engendered much distrust among Mayan people. Many Mayan groups lost their places of worship, their holidays and rituals, and some entire communities went into exile in neighboring countries, most frequently Southern Mexico. Many Mayan communities were even forbidden to wear the traje tipico (traditional clothing), a hallmark of ethnic identity and pride. (p.144)

Such trauma as experienced by the Maya is known in as historical trauma. Historical trauma is defined by Brave Heart, Chase, Elkins, and Altschul (2011) as "cumulative emotional and psychological wounding across generations, including the lifespan, which emanates from massive group trauma" (p. 283). For the Maya of Guatemala, their shared historical trauma has resulted in physical and mental health problems, substance use/abuse, and post-traumatic stress disorder (Consoli et al., 2013; Kaupisch, 2017), which has been compounded by systematic barriers in accessing health care that continue through today (Cerron et al., 2016; Consoli et al., 2013). In addition, the Maya were left feeling isolated, fearful, and distrustful toward the Guatemalan government and non-Indigenous Guatemalans (Lykes et al., 2007; Consoli et al., 2013). The historical trauma experienced by the Maya has also resulted in a disruption of burial and mourning rituals, which we will now explore.

Burial Rituals

For the Maya, death does not separate an individual from his or her community. Rather, ancestors are an active part of the lives of their descendants and their community. Mayan burial rituals ensure proper disposition of the body for the overall well-being of the deceased's soul. It is important to note that burial rituals and expressions of grief by the bereaved may vary among the distinct Maya ethnic groups. Some burial rituals include the washing of the body, the offering of food and drinks and other material goods (such as clothes) to the deceased, wrapping of the body in shroud, weeping, and other outward expressions of grief (Beristain et al., 2000; Hart, 2008; Kaupisch, 2017). According to Woodrick (1995), the deceased must also go through the process of exhumation and reburial 3 years after death. The relatives of the deceased are responsible for the exhumation and reburial and accompanying rituals. Per Woodrick, (1995), this is important as "the reburial of bones marks the soul's entrance into a spiritual existence" (p. 416) where they continue their relationship with their family and community.

Expressions of Grief, Bereavement, and Mourning

As we have seen, burial rituals are very important to the Maya, ensuring a continuation between the living and the dead. Lack of proper burial rituals, however, can impede the deceased's journey to the afterlife and can disrupt their relationship with the living. During the *conflicto armado* (civil war), thousands of Mayas were killed and/or disappeared. Their bodies were never found. Without the bodies of their loved ones, the Maya were unable to properly bury their loved ones, inhibiting mourning rituals and leaving loved ones in doubt as to the souls of the deceased. For those who were able to recover the bodies of their loved ones, the violence around them did not allow for proper burials. According to Kaupisch (2017), burial rites of the deceased were condensed out of necessity. As such, loved ones were unable "to establish the postlife relations with them (the deceased) that are essential to the maintenance of family and community coherence and equilibrium" (Garrard-Burnett, 2015, p. 186).

After the *conflicto armado* (civil war), the Guatemalan government began a process of exhuming mass graves as part of the Peace Accords of 1996 (Garrard-Burnett, 2015; Grandin et al., 2011). According to Garrard-Burnett (2015), by 2013, the remains of over 55,000 individuals had been exhumed from several mass graves. The return of the remains to their loved ones and communities ensures proper Mayan burial and the deceased's journey to the spiritual realm and rejoining their loved ones and community. Much work still has to be done to reconnect the victims with their loved ones.

Implications for Practice

You may wonder when the knowledge presented in this chapter might ever come in handy. Possibly sooner than you think. The number of individuals from the Northern Triangle of Central America (Guatemala, El Salvador, and Honduras) fleeing violence, poverty, and oppression in their home countries and seeking sanctuary in the United States is steadily increasing; we saw a 58% increase from 2016 to 2017 (U.N. Refugee Agency, n.d.). As 45–60% of the Guatemalan population is Indigenous and 10% of the population of Honduras is Indigenous (Ceron et al, 2016), it is quite likely that social workers in the United States will be working with Mayans who have immigrated to the there. It is important to note that by leaving their home countries, these individuals and families are separating from their social and cultural supports. It is imperative that social workers be sensitive to these losses when developing spiritually sensitive interventions to work with this population.

The research literature has underscored the risk of post-traumatic stress disorder, depression, anxiety, grief disorders (including prolonged/and or unresolved grief) and other MH disorders in those affected by war and mass violence in general (Brave Heart, Chase, Elkins, & Altschul, 2011; Keller, Joscelyne, Granski, & Rosenfeld, 2017; Morina, Malek, Nickerson, & Bryant, 2017; Schaal, Dusingizemungu, Jacob, Neuner, & Elbert, 2012), and with the Maya in particular (Consoli et al., 2013; Kaupisch, 2017). According to Morina, Malek, Nickerson, and Bryant (2017), MH disorders are exacerbated by the "subsequent social upheaval, poverty, marginalization, lack of infrastructure, and overcrowding" (p. 688) experienced by survivors of war and mass violence. In addition, displacement from one's community and/or country can further exacerbate MH disorders (McPherson, 2012). The Maya of Guatemala are extremely vulnerable, then, to MH disorders. As such, social work interventions grounded in spiritual beliefs and practices and that provide opportunities for mutual social/cultural support are imperative when working with the Maya.

Spiritually sensitive social work interventions can focus on bringing the Maya community together for the purpose of communal coping through commemorations, memorials, rituals, and so on. Communal coping can help individuals who are struggling with unresolved/prolonged grief. As we learned earlier in the chapter, for the Maya, death does not end the relationship between an individual and his or her community. Proper burial rituals ensure continued connection. As a result of the *conflicto armado* (civil war), proper burials were not always possible, leading to a disruption in the relationship between the dead and the living (Garrard-Burnett, 2015; Hart, 2008; Kaupisch, 2017). The *conflicto armado* (civil war) also did not allow time and space for families to mourn their loved ones. In addition, justice for the victims and punishment for the guilty are almost nonexistent in Guatemala. As such, interventions focused on social/cultural support and communal coping are necessary and can have positive outcomes on participants (Gasparre et. al., 2010; Rosenbloom, 1995). In their study of 59 victims of the *conflicto armado* (civil war), 93% who identified as Maya, Gasparre and colleagues (2010) found that "commemoration rites about past traumatic events, funerary rituals, and participation in transitional justice rites … elicit social cohesion and solidarity" (p. 43). In addition, Gasparre and colleagues (2010) found that 95% of the study participants who partook in some type of communal coping reported "some level of post-traumatic change: a higher level of spiritual growth and appreciation of life, and to a lower extent discovering personal strength, improving interpersonal relations, and least frequently new possibilities in life" (p. 44).

Narrative interventions have also been found to be beneficial with survivors of war and mass violence (Kaminar, 2006; Peleg, Lev-Wiesel, Yaniv, 2014; Woodcock, 2001). As the "trauma of genocide produces extensive fragmentation in its survivors—fragmentation of perception, fragmentation of a sense of coherence in their life stories, and fragmentation of their relationships to their families and to the wider human community" (Peleg et al., 2014, p. 411)—narrative interventions allow the survivors to tell their story and make sense of lived experiences.

Kaminar (2006) elaborates, stating,

> The trauma experience can be re-storied, or re-plotted, in order to highlight the skills and knowledge that enabled the person to survive the trauma—awareness of these skills and knowledge can enable the survivor to develop a sense of purpose for the future. (p. 492)

Social workers using narrative interventions are cautioned to broach the subject of the *conflicto armado* (civil war) and subsequent violence, poverty, and immigration with utmost care and respect for the lived experiences of their Mayan clients. It is imperative that social workers create a safe and accepting environment. In addition, social workers must be empathic, nonjudgmental, trustworthy, and encouraging (Kaminar, 2006; Peleg et al., 2014). If facilitated effectively, narrative interventions allow us to "enter the imaginative space of a survivor's experience and work collaboratively to neutralize the horror" (Woodcock, 2001, p. 151).

Navigating U.S. immigration and asylum processes, language barriers, and financial difficulties are additional areas social work interventions are called for when working with the Maya who have fled to the United States. Individuals and families seeking asylum in the United States run the risk of being held for extended periods of time in one of numerous detention facilities, while awaiting disposition of their asylum application (Keller et al., 2017). This is concerning as research has highlighted the risks of detention for asylum seekers and refugees in general, including PTSD (post-traumatic stress disorder), depression, anxiety, and other mental health diagnoses (Keller et al., 2017). It is important to note that not all asylum seekers are held in detention centers; some are released to a sponsor (often times a relative) living in the United States. These asylum seekers are also at risk for mental health disorders. As such, when developing treatment plans, social workers must not only take into consideration the lived experiences of their Mayan client(s) before leaving their homeland, but of potential mental health issues that clients developed as a result of immigration.

Language barriers and lack of financial stability can exacerbate the challenges the Maya face. Social workers can aid in finding needed resources, such as an interpreter who speaks either Spanish or one of the Mayan languages; remember there are over 20 Mayan languages in Guatemala. Social workers can also refer their clients to local social service agencies, food pantries, churches, and so on that can provide resources such as food and clothing.

Conclusion

Despite continued oppression, violence, poverty, and all they have had to endure, the Maya of Guatemala are holding on strong. While a visit to Guatemala will provide you with the opportunity to experience this beautiful people and culture, as social workers we also have the opportunity to do so firsthand here in the United States as more Mayans migrate to our country. I believe that the key to the individual and collective resilience of the Maya is their deep spirituality. It is important to understand that for the Maya, their spirituality is part of their everyday life, from how they cook their food, run their household, harvest their maiz (corn), to how they view the afterlife. As such, interventions with this population must incorporate the deep spiritual beliefs and practices of the Maya (with consent of client). Interventions must be strength/resilience based, acknowledging the numerous internal (spirituality) and external (community) strengths of the Maya. In order to be effective we must practice cultural humility and allow our Mayan clients to guide our work together.

Reflection Questions

1. Are you spiritual? How is your spirituality similar to that of the Maya? How is it different?
2. What knowledge have you gained in this chapter that can help you provide spiritually sensitive practice to any Mayan clients you may have?
3. The Maya have many internal and external strengths. How have these strengths helped the Maya with the loss and grief they have experienced? How can you incorporate these strengths in social work interventions with the Maya?
4. If you were working with Sandra, what might you focus on first? Second? Third? What theories/interventions would guide your work with Sandra?
5. What are Sandra's internal and external strengths?
6. How do your cultural and spiritual background influence your responses to death and loss (any type of loss)?
7. What consequences of colonization still exist today for the Indigenous peoples in your country? How might you be viewed as someone who contributed to or benefitted from colonization?
8. Imagine a foreign country invades your country, killing a large number of your family and friends. You are not allowed to speak your own language but are forced to learn the invader's language. You are not allowed to practice your own spiritual/religious beliefs and practices, but rather are forced to convert to the invaders' religion under the threat of death. What impact, physical, mental, emotional, spiritual, might this have on you? On your loved ones?

References

Brave Heart, M. Y. H., Chase, J., Elkins, J., & Altschul, D. B. (2011). Historical trauma among Indigenous peoples of the Americas: Concepts, research, and clinical considerations. *Journal of Psychoactive Drugs, 43*(4), 282–290. doi:10.1080/02791072.2011.628913

Ceron, A., Ruano, A. L., Sanchez, S., Chew, A. S., Diaz, D., & Hernandez, A. (2016). Abuse and discrimination towards Indigenous people in public health care facilities: Experiences from rural Guatemala. *International Journal for Equity in Health, 15*(1), 1–7. doi:10.1186/s12939-016-0367-z

Coe, M. D. (2011). Breaking the Maya code. In G. Grandin, D. T. Levenson, & E. Oglesby (Eds.), *The Guatemalan reader: History, culture, politics* (pp. 19–23). Durham, NC: Duke University Press.

Commission for Historical Clarification. (2011). Acts of genocide. In G. Grandin, D. T. Levenson, & E. Oglesby (Eds.), *The Guatemalan reader: History, culture, politics* (pp. 386–394). Durham, NC: Duke University Press.

Consoli, A. J., Hernández Tzaquitzal, M. A., & González, A. (2013). Mayan cosmovision and integrative counseling: A case study from Guatemala. In S. Poyrazli and C. E. Thompson (Eds), *International Case Studies in Mental Health* (pp. 141–153). Thousand Oaks, CA: SAGE.

Garrard-Burnett, V. (2015). Living with ghosts: Death, exhumation, and reburial among the Maya in Guatemala. *Latin American Perspectives, 42*(3), 180–192. doi:10.1177/0094582X15570881

Gasparre, A., Bosco, S., & Bellelli, G. (2010). Cognitive and social consequences of participation in social rites: Collective coping, social support, and post-traumatic growth in the victims of Guatemala genocide. *Revista de Psicologia Social, 25*(1), 35–46. doi:10.1174/021347410790193513

Giralt, A. (2012). A decade after Guatemala's agreement on identity and rights of indigenous peoples: Mayan-Tz'utujil women's view on health, healing, and disease. *Heath Care for Women International, 33,* 440–456. doi:10.1080/07399332.2011.610538

Grandin, G., Levenson, D. T., & Oglesby, E. (2011). *The Guatemalan reader: History, culture, politics.* Durham, NC: Duke University Press.

Hart, T. (2008). *The ancient spirituality of the modern Maya.* Albuquerque, NM: University of New Mexico Press.

Kaminar, D. (2006). Healing processes in trauma narratives: A review. *South African Journal of Psychology, 36*(3), 481–499.

Kaupisch, P. (2017). Facing loss: Coping mechanisms of Mayan widows in Guatemala. *Deusto Journal of Human Rights, 2*(2005), 239–256. doi: doi:10.18543/djhr

Keller, A., Joscelyne, A., Granski, M., & Rosenfeld, B. (2017). Pre-migration trauma exposure and mental health functioning among Central American migrants arriving at US border. *PLoS One 12*(1), 1–11. doi:10.1371/journal.pone.0168692

Lopez, R. T. (2004). Mayan spirituality and lands in Guatemala. *Arizona Journal of International & Comparative Law, 21*(1), 223–268.

Lovell, G. W. (2011). Great was the stench of the dead. In G. Grandin, D. T. Levenson, & E. Oglesby (Eds.), *The Guatemalan reader: History, culture, politics* (pp. 62–64). Durham, NC: Duke University Press.

Lykes, M. B., Beristain, C. M., & Cabrera Perez-Arminan, M. L. (2007). Political violence, impunity, and emotional climate in Maya communities. *Journal of Social Issues, 63*(2), 369–385. doi:10.1111/j.1540-4560.2007.00514.x

MacKenzie, C. J. (1999). The priest, the shaman, and "Grandfather Judas": Syncretism and anti-syncretism in Guatemala. *Religious Studies and Theology, 18*(2), 33–65.

Marin-Beristain, M., Paez, C., & Gonzalez, J. L. (2000). Rituals, social sharing, silence, emotions and collective memory claims in the case of the Guatemalan genocide. *Psicothema, 12*(1), 117–130.

McPherson, J. (2012). Does narrative exposure therapy reduce PTSD in survivors of mass violence? *Research on Social Work Practice, 22*(1) 29–42. doi:10.1177/1049731511414147

Morina, N., Malek, M., Nickerson, A., & Bryant, R.A. (2017). Meta-analysis of interventions for posttraumatic stress disorder and depression in adult survivors of mass violence in low-and-middle income countries. *Depression & Anxiety, 34,* 679–691. doi:10.1002/da.22618

Peleg, M., Lev-Wiesel, R., & Yaniv, D. (2014). Reconstruction of self-identity of Holocaust child survivors who participated in "Testimony Theatre." *Psychological Trauma: Theory, Research, Practice, and Policy, 6*(4), 411–419. doi:10.1037/a0033834

Rosenbloom, M. (1995). Implications of the Holocaust for social work. *Families in Society, 76(9),* 567–576.

Schaal, S., Dusingizemungu, J. P., Jacob, N., Neuner, F., & Elbert, T. (2012). Associations between prolonged grief disorder, depression, posttraumatic stress disorder, and anxiety in Rwandan genocide survivors. *Death Studies, 36(2),* 97–117.

Vogt, M. (2015). The disarticulated movement: Barriers to Maya mobilization in post-conflict Guatemala. *Latin American Politics & Society, 57*(1), 29–50. doi:10.1111/j.1548-2456.2015.00260.x

Woodcock, J. (2001). Threads form the labyrinth: Therapy with survivors of war and political oppression. *Journal of Family Therapy, 23*(2), 136–154.

Woodrick, A. C. (1995). A lifetime of grief work among Yucatec Maya women. *Ethos, 23*(4), 401–423.

UN Refugee Agency. (n.d.). Retrieved from https://www.unhcr.org/

American Indian and Alaskan Native Death Culture: Culturally Appropriate Practices for Working With Bereaved Families

Rebecca A. Cobb, PhD, LMFT, Seattle University

Rebecca Cobb, PhD, LMFT, is Assistant Clinical Professor and Clinical Coordinator in Seattle University's Master of Arts in Couples and Family Therapy, a multifaith spiritually-integrated program, where she provides clinical supervision and training to students working with clients from diverse backgrounds and faith traditions, including a course specifically on the systemic treatment of trauma, grief, and loss. She received her MS in Child Development and Family Studies, with specialization in Marriage and Family Therapy from Purdue University, and her PhD in Marriage and Family Therapy from Florida State University. There, she trained at a grief and loss counseling center, working with clients from diverse cultural, religious, and spiritual backgrounds, including those with indigenous cultural and spiritual backgrounds. Dr. Cobb has published and presented on the ethical integration of spirituality and religion in clinical practice, trauma, grief, and loss. She is past president of the Washington Association for Marriage and Family Therapy (WAMFT), a prior recipient of the WAMFT Educator of the Year Award, the WAMFT Volunteer of the Year Award, the American Association for Marriage and Family Therapy (AAMFT) Dissertation Award, and the AAMFT Certificate in Leadership. Additionally, Dr. Cobb is an AAMFT Approved Supervisor, a mentor in the AAMFT Minority Fellowship Program, and maintains a private practice in Seattle, WA, focusing on clinical supervision, grief, loss, and trauma. She has provided supervision to American Indian family therapy interns providing therapeutic services on American Indian reservations.

Elizabeth Theriault, MA, LMFTA, Kitsap Family Wellness

Elizabeth L. Theriault, MA, LMFTA, lives in Washington State on the Kitsap Peninsula. She received her MA in Couples and Family Therapy from Seattle University. As an experiential family therapist, Elizabeth strives to utilize practices and interventions which uphold cultural and spiritual components as paramount factors in every therapy room. Elizabeth is mindful of her own Native American heritage and is a passionate advocate for Native American people of all tribes. Her scope of research includes differences and similarities of tribal tradition and ritual as well as the complexities of grief and bereavement in individuals and families. Through independent study and application of cultural assessment and inclusion in her own therapy practice, she continues to collect data as a service to provide more information where it is currently lacking.

Introduction

There are over four million American Indian (AI) and Alaska Native (AN) people in the United States (U.S. Census Bureau, 2012). In comparison with all other racial and ethnic groups, AI and AN people experience disproportionately higher rates of mental illness (Centers for Disease Control and Prevention, 2017). Yet, many barriers, including lack of culturally appropriate services, prevent AI and AN people from receiving necessary mental health services (American Psychiatric Association, 2014). Therapists working with AI and AN clients must be aware of heterogeneity and differences amongst AI/ANs to provide competent and ethical care. More specifically, therapists supporting clients through grief and traumatic loss must practice cultural humility and be aware of cultural understandings and rituals surrounding the bereavement process to best serve client needs.

This chapter provides a brief overview of AI/AN understanding of death and rituals related to the bereavement process. Examples of specific beliefs and practices from Lakota, Navajo, Mandan, Hidatsa, Arikara, Athabascan, Hopi, and Seminole tribes are provided. Following this, implications for clinical practice are discussed.

American Indian and Alaskan Natives: An Overview

AI and ANs are the Indigenous people of the United States. They comprise 2% of the United States population. Over 560 federally recognized tribes represent rich diversity in location, language, culture, spiritual beliefs, and traditional practices among this population (Brave Heart, Chase, Elkins, & Altschul, 2011; Harper, 2011; McGoldrick, Giordano, & Garcia-Preto, 2005). Additionally, there are over 100 state-recognized tribes and many that are neither federally nor state recognized. While some (22%) live on reservations and other trust lands, most (78%) live in urban, suburban, or rural non-reservation areas.

Health and educational assistance are provided to AI/ANs through the Indian Health Service, a federally funded government agency. However, urban AI/ANs have less accessibility to services provided by Indian Health Services, contributing to more limited health care options.

Historical Trauma

AI/AN people were greatly affected by the European colonization of the Americas. During this time, AI/ANs faced warfare, genocide, territorial confiscation, and slavery and were introduced to diseases that significantly reduced their population. They suffered from discriminatory government policies, racism, forced assimilation, and loss of land through broken treaties. The compounding effects of grief and trauma have been transcribed from generation to generation (BigFoot & Funderburk, 2011; McGoldrick et al., 2005; Olsen, 2003; Spiwak et al., 2012; Walker, 2009) and have forever changed the economic, physical, and social lives of AI/AN people.

Since then, federally recognized tribes are provided some protection of land and access to traditional ceremonial resources (e.g., hunting and fishing rights). Yet, land rights and ceremonial resources continue to remain at risk (e.g., Alaska Department of Fish and Game, 2010) and AI/AN people face many other contemporary issues. There is a high occurrence of poverty, domestic violence, suicide, depression, attachment disorders, post-traumatic stress disorder, alcohol abuse, and other substance abuse disorders (BigFoot & Schmidt, 2010; Gray & Rose, 2012). Many of these concerns are directly linked to intergenerational historical trauma, such as forced removal from home land and separation of children from parents, culture, and spiritual practices (Evans-Campbell, Walters, Pearson, & Campbell, 2012).

Acculturation

AI/ANs that adhere to a traditional foundation may speak their native language, practice only tribal customs, worship, and uphold traditional values and beliefs (Cacciatore, 2009). AI/ANs who have chosen, been forced, or have grown apart from a traditional foundation may ascribe to dominant culture and be viewed as assimilated. Those who have assimilated may have lost touch with their culture and may want to reconnect. Those who adhere to strict traditional baselines may have difficulties dealing with dominant society (Sue & Sue, 2013). Most AI/ANs have varied levels of acculturation and may adhere to a combination of traditional practice and dominant culture.

Spirituality

There are many different spiritual practices and denominations represented in AI and AN populations. Spiritual rituals and ceremonies often differ between and within tribes (Walker & Balk, 2007). Many AI/ANs may practice a combination of Christianity and traditional AI/AN spirituality. Ultimately, the expression of spirituality is largely dependent on the degree of acculturation (Clements et al., 2003). Yet, there are many commonalities amongst spiritual beliefs within AI/AN culture.

AI/ANs traditionally view all aspects of life as interconnected and having a spiritual nature (Limb & Hodge, 2011; Lowe, 2002). These elements are bound together by a universal force (Hunter & Sawyer, 2006; Lowe, 2002; Lettenberger-Klein, Fish, & Hecker, 2013). Mental wellness is not typically separated from spiritual nature (Grandbois, 2005). Health is considered harmony of mental, physical, emotional, and spiritual elements in balance in communal context (Cacciatore, 2009; Lowe, 2002; McGoldrick et al., 2005). Illness or other problematic concerns may be attributed to an imbalance in or between these structures (Choney, Berryhill-Paapke, & Robbins, 1995; Rogers, 2001).

The earth and its processes are revered as powerful and worthy of great care and recognition for giving life (Lowe, 2002). The primary element of worship is the force, which binds all that exists, often referred to as Creator or Great Spirit. Traditionally, the natural world (e.g., animals, plants, rocks, elements) is honored and integrated into ritual and spiritual practices (Hunter & Sawyer, 2006; Lowe, 2002; McGoldrick et al, 2005). Often non-human beings and things are personified and named with familial identifiers (e.g., Mother Earth, Father Sky, Brother Bear) (Hunter & Sawyer, 2006; Lowe, 2002; McGoldrick et al., 2005). This spiritual view is systemic and accurately reflects the significance of family and systemic holistic thought as interwoven into this culture (Limb & Hodge, 2011).

Prayer, song, music, and other ceremonial rituals may be integrated into daily practices (Clements et al., 2003). Ceremonies, rituals, and celebrations often involve the entire extended family. These spiritual beliefs and practices largely influence beliefs and traditional practices related to death.

Beliefs About Death in American Indian and Alaskan Native Culture

Generally within AI/AN culture, death is interpreted as a natural occurrence of the ongoing life cycle, sometimes referred to as the circle of life (BigFoot & Funderbunk, 2011). To the majority of AI/ANs, death is not considered an end to life. Rather, death is recognized as a transformative experience in which the deceased changes form into spirit (Van Winkle, 2000; Walker & Balk, 2007) and continues their journey in the afterlife. The Lakota, for example, believe in an afterlife that exists in a spirit world (i.e., Wakan Tanka) that is free of pain and suffering. According to the Lakota and the Hopi, the deceased's spirit travels to the spirit world 4 days after death. Additionally, the Lakota believe that spirits can watch over and affect the thoughts, feeling, dreams, and visions of the living.

Yet, meanings associated with death may vary between tribes, families, and individuals with differing levels of acculturation (Cacciatore, 2009; Gire, 2011; Walker, 2009; Walker & Balk, 2007; Weaver, 1998). While most do not fear death (e.g., Lakota) (Stone, 1998), others do (e.g., Hopi). Members of the Hopi tribe, for example, attribute untimely death and illness to spiritual imbalance and supernatural experiences. Tribal ceremonies or rituals can redress these misfortunes (Hanson, 1978). In general, different beliefs influence rituals such as burial and mourning (Clements et al., 2003).

Practices Related to Death

Rituals and ceremonies practiced by each tribe are generally meant to encourage the spirit into the afterlife and are an important part of the grieving process (Steele, 1977). Some believe that failure to practice traditional rituals and ceremonies may have negative consequences for the individual, family, or deceased. Elders from the Lakota tribe, for example, believe that if the traditional mourning period is ignored, the deceased's spirit might experience difficulty transitioning to the spirit world and that bereaved family members might experience bad luck (Stone, 1998).

Lakota

Traditional grieving ceremonies among the Lakota include a 4-day formal mourning period and 1 to 2 years of formal mourning (Stone, 1998). All Lakota ceremonies must be led by a trained medicine man or woman within the community. These spiritual leaders provide guidance about the proper ways to channel grief and assist the journey of the spirit.

During the 4-day mourning period, the bereaved typically cry and wail until they are so exhausted that they sleep. Other community members who were not as close to the deceased may join in weeping to support the deceased's family. A wake is conducted on the night before the funeral and burial. During the wake, relatives, friends, and community leaders stay awake all night talking about the deceased. It is appropriate for shared stories to elicit laughter or tears. After 4 days of mourning, excessive mourning could cause the spirit to linger and impede their journey to the spirit world.

One to two years following the death, formal modified mourning continues. Historically, mourners cut their hair or parts of their flesh as a sign of mourning and sacrifice to help the deceased's spirit in their transition. More recently, mourners wear black clothing and avoid favored social activities such as dancing.

Navajo

Navajo death rites also involve 4 days of traditional ceremonies. During this time, families engage in rituals such as cleansing the body, disposing of personal belongings, tying an eagle feather to the hair of the deceased, and active mourning (Cacciatore, 2009; Clements et al., 2003; Walker & Balk, 2007).

Mandan, Hidatsa, and Arikara Nation

On the Fort Berthold Indian Reservation in North Dakota, home of the Mandan, Hidatsa, and Arikara Nation, also known as the Three Affiliated Tribes, weeping is encouraged only until burial. Weeping after burial of the deceased is believed to prevent the spirit from moving into the spirit world (Mazur-Bullis, 1984).

Athabascan

Many AN death rituals may involve "potlatch" ceremonies, which typically involve hunting during the funerary or mortuary cycle (Alaska Department of Fish and Game, 2010). AN communities may participate in funeral potlatches, 20-day feasts, 40-day feasts, and memorial potlatches. The Athabascan potlatch is a religious and social ceremony requiring wild food such as moose and caribou. A funeral potlach is held immediately after a funeral and a memorial potlatch is held within a year of the funeral. The potlatch is hosted by the deceased's family. Over 3 days, hundreds of people typically attend to console the relatives. Speeches, eulogies, dancing, and singing usually occur on the first and second nights. Gifts are then given by the deceased's family to guests. During the feast, the spirit of the deceased may be fed by throwing bits of food into the fire.

Hopi

Among the Hopi, the dead are customarily buried as quickly as possible. Delayed burial could interfere with the soul's ability to reach the underworld. In traditional preparation for the burial, a paternal aunt washes the hair of the deceased with yucca shampoo. The hair is then decorated with prayer feathers, the face is covered with raw cotton, and the body is wrapped in deerskin for men and a wedding robe for women. Preferably on the day or night of the death, the oldest son buries the body of the deceased in a seated position with food and water. A stick may be placed in the soil to allow exit of the soul.

Speaking about death and saying the name of the deceased is traditionally avoided amongst Hopis. Mentioning the name could negatively affect the bereaved and interfere with the journey of the deceased (Clements et al., 2003; McCabe, 1994; Walker & Balk, 2007). Hopis give the deceased a new name for their continuing journey into the afterlife (Cacciatore, 2009; Leming & Dickenson, 2011).

Seminoles

The Seminoles have many "medicine" traditions regarding death and also many interpretations of those traditions (Seminole Tribe of Florida, 2019). Typically, the entire family mourns for 4 days. On the morning of the fourth day, they drink or wash with herbs made by the medicine man. During more traditional burials, the deceased's body may be left on an open platform exposed to the wilderness and surrounded by favorite possessions. The wife of a deceased man wears black and mourns for "four moons." Some believe she must wait 4 years before she remarries.

According to many Seminoles, application of "medicine" and ritual practice may influence success, failure, danger, safety, and luck. However, most details concerning medicine culture are not discussed outside the tribe (Seminole Tribe of Florida, 2019).

Implications for Therapeutic Practice

Understanding general similarities and differences amongst AI/AN people provides a starting point for working with bereaved AI/AN clients. General values and cultural basics attend to a foundation by which to investigate and explore idiosyncrasies, acquire competency, and avoid ethical and culturally insensitive dilemmas (Lettenberger-Klein et al., 2013; Sue & Sue, 2013). Implications for therapeutic practice include remaining curious, inquiring about levels of acculturation, considering client communication style, utilizing a trauma-informed approach, remaining mindful of strengths and resilience of AI/AN people, considering a systemic approach to therapeutic treatment, and attending to self of the therapist when working with AI/AN clients.

Curiosity

There are many similarities and many differences between and within different AI/AN populations. Therapists must apply cultural sensitivity and curiosity in their work, specifically with regards to death beliefs and practices. To prevent assumptions and errors, therapists may acknowledge the unique cultural constitutions of their clients and ask about personal preferences (Brady, 2015). For example, when working with Hopi clients, therapists might gather information directly from the client(s) about their beliefs and practices, and specifically ask whether they prefer to name the deceased. McGoldrick, Almedia, and Hines (1991) suggests that therapists also ask about what the family considers appropriate emotional expression of loss, gender rules for handling death, and whether certain types of death are particularly traumatic or carry a stigma in their culture.

Acculturation

Clinical assessment of the bereaved AI/AN client's level of acculturation should be a prerequisite to treatment planning (Stone, 1998). It may also be helpful to ask questions about the acculturation of the client's family and others from their community. An indication of proximity to native culture may be useful in planning effective treatment and interventions (Kurilla, 1998; Sue & Sue, 2013). Therapists may inquire about tribal affiliation, preferred language, personal identity, or proximity and strength of relationship with their affiliated tribe, band, clan, or other community to gain knowledge of acculturation level (Sue & Sue, 2013). Stone (1998) suggests that intervention with grieving Lakota clients, for example, should include attention to both Western and traditional Lakota bereavement practices. Additionally, it may be helpful to ask if the client's beliefs about death and death practices align with those of their friends, family, and the deceased. Therapists may also ask if alignment or misalignment of beliefs causes personal distress or conflict within the client's system.

Communication Style

AI and AN families may have a communication style that is counter to that of dominant culture. For instance, in traditional talk therapy, lack of eye contact and reluctance to respond verbally and consistently could be labeled as resistance or avoidance or indicate an area of clinical concern such as depression or dissociation (Brucker & Perry, 1998; Cacciatore, 2009; Lettenberger-Klein et al., 2013; McGoldrick et al., 2005). Within AI/AN culture, listening is traditionally valued over speaking and lack of eye contact may indicate honor for the person speaking (Brucker & Perry, 1998; Lettenberger-Klein et al., 2013, McGoldrick et al., 2005; Paniagua, 2005). When this is the case, therapists should not attempt to make eye contact. Instead, therapists should respectfully adapt to the communication style of their clients.

Additionally, AI/AN clients may prefer for therapists to assume an expert role (McGoldrick et al., 2005). This role should not be assumed but should be considered as the therapist learns more about his or her clients and their preferences.

Trauma-Informed approach

Taking into consideration the significant impact of historical trauma on AI/AN populations, it is imperative that therapists utilize a trauma-informed approach to working with AI/AN clients. A culturally competent therapist must maintain a commitment to trauma awareness and understanding of the impact of historical trauma and oppression. Specifically within AI/AN culture, therapists should be aware of historical events such as the European colonization of the Americas, territorial confiscation, slavery, genocide, discriminatory government policies, racism, and forced assimilation. Trauma-informed therapists must also remain aware of lasting consequences of transgenerational trauma and its systemic impact, including economic disadvantage and increased risk of suicidal ideation amongst AI/AN populations (BigFoot & Schmidt, 2010; McGoldrick et al., 2005; Spiwak et al., 2012; Sue & Sue, 2013).

Therapists can create a safe context for therapy by remaining transparent about the therapeutic process, maintaining clear and consistent boundaries, being curious and nonjudgmental, and by demonstrating acceptance, compassion, respect, and willingness for collaboration. Common elements of programs specifically addressing trauma in AI/AN youth include reconnecting youth to traditional tribal culture (Lechner, Cavanaugh, & Blyler, 2016). Additionally, therapists may help to restore power to their clients by promoting choice and empowerment throughout therapy and focusing on client strengths.

Strengths and Resilience

There is tremendous opportunity for accessing strengths and resilience of clients from rich and diverse AI/AN cultures. Accessing the cultural history and philosophies that suggest strength may be important for understanding and processing grief and traumatic loss with this population. Additionally, it may be helpful to inquire about strengths and resources provided by the larger AI/AN community.

One way of assessing strengths and resilience that may be particularly fitting with AI/AN clients is the use narrative (i.e., storytelling), metaphors, and folklore (Alexander & Sussman, 1995; Lettenberger et al., 2013). Cacciatore (2009) suggests giving clients voice by enabling them to "tell and retell their story within their own cultural understanding" (p. 48). Spiritual ecograms and spiritual genograms may also be helpful tools for exploration and providing insight into systemic strengths and resilience (Hodge, 2000; Limb & Hodge, 2011).

Systemic Approach

In general, holistic and systemic approaches are complimentary to AI/AN understanding of the systemic nature of all things (Lowe, 2002; McGoldrick, et al., 2005; Sue & Sue, 2013). Family systems theory complements this holistic world view in its basic tenets, which establish that all things exist in relationship, relationships are reciprocal in nature, and people exist in relationship to the natural world, others, and their surroundings (Lowe, 2002; McGoldrick et al., 2005; Walsh & McGoldrick, 2004). In addition, a life cycle orientation blends well with the life cycle approach of family therapy (McGoldrick et al., 2005).

Collectivism is a standing principle of AI/AN culture, in which the well-being of the family and community come before individual needs (Brave Heart et al., 2011; Lettenberger-Klein et al., 2013; McGoldrick et al., 2005; Sue & Sue, 2013). Families and community hold special importance within AI/AN culture. AI and AN families typically integrate extended family and non-blood-related others from the community into a family unit (McGoldrick, et al., 2005; Sue & Sue, 2013) and may involve them as active participants in child-rearing (BigFoot & Funderburk, 2011; Lettenberger-Klein et al., 2013). Frequently, primary relationships with children are with grandparents, aunts, uncles, cousins, and older elders from the community (BigFoot & Funderbunk, 2011; Lettenberger-Klein et al., 2013;

McGoldrick, et al., 2005; Sue & Sue, 2013). "Brothers" and "sisters" are not always siblings by blood but may be cousins or others from the community (BigFoot & Funderbunk, 2011; McGoldrick et al., 2005). This understanding is paramount in conceptualizing cultural rituals surrounding the bereavement process and a client's experience of loss.

Systemic practices, for example, may help to continue tribal unity and wholeness through bereavement practices. Therapists should consider the possibility of inviting extended family or other members of the community to participate in therapy (Brady, 2015). By making space for family, tribal community, and ceremonial activities in the therapeutic process, the therapist may assist the bereaved in "filling the hole in the circle" left by the deceased (Stone, 1998, p. iv).

Self of the Therapist

Therapists from different cultural backgrounds may need to spend considerable time reflecting on the intersection of client and therapist culture and spirituality or religious beliefs (Limb & Hodge, 2011). Therapists may gain knowledge on how to do this from extant literature, mentors, and experiences (Cobb, Priest, & Strachan, 2016).

One way that therapists may get to know AI/AN culture is by becoming active in communities and groups within these populations. Being active in this manner allows people within these populations to recognize the commitment, support, and ability to work with families that affiliate (Weaver, 1998). Some AI/AN clients may require therapists to connect to the community to gain trust before participating in therapy (Walker & Balk, 2007). Collaborative practices that involve alliances with the community leaders, elders, and healers may encourage trust between therapist and clients.

Therapists may need to reexamine their understanding of therapeutic boundaries in order to support and be present in ways that are expected by a particular tribe. If conducting therapy on a reservation, for example, therapists may be asked and expected to attend bereavement rituals. Therapists should consult with supervisors or other therapists to discuss what clear boundaries should look like within this setting and how they may differ from traditional boundaries within other settings. Furthermore, clinicians under the supervision of supervisors from different cultural backgrounds may need to educate colleagues and supervisors of differing cultural expectations and boundary norms when seeking consultation. Additionally, therapists may tap into the strengths and resilience of AI/AN clients by identifying their own pre- and post-therapy rituals to care for one's self while simultaneously honoring client stories and traditions.

Conclusion

There is a deficit in research examining death, dying, grief, and loss in AI/AN populations. Existing literature describes general beliefs and practices that suggest inclusion of cultural, spiritual, and systemic values within trauma-informed therapeutic care of bereaved AI/AN clients.

References

Alaska Department of Fish and Game. (2010). *Alaska Native funerary ceremonies and hunting regulations*. Alaska Department of Fish and Game Division of Subsistence Special Publication No. BOG 2010-01, Anchorage, AK.

Alexander, C. M., & Sussman, L. (1995). Creative approaches to multicultural counseling. In J. G. Ponterotto, J. M. Casas, L. A. Suzuki, & C. M. Alexander (Eds.), *Handbook of multicultural counseling* (pp. 375–384). Thousand Oaks, CA, US: Sage.

American Psychiatric Association. (2017). *Mental health disparities: American Indians and Alaska Natives.* Retrieved from https://www.psychiatry.org/File%20Library/Psychiatrists/Cultural-Competency/Mental-Health-Disparities/Mental-Health-Facts-for-American-Indian-Alaska-Natives.pdf

Bigfoot, D. S., & Funderburk, B.W. (2011). Honoring children, making relatives: The cultural translation of parent-child interaction therapy for American Indian and Alaska Native families. *Journal of Psychoactive Drugs, 43*(4), 309–318. doi:10.1080/02791072.2011.628924

Bigfoot, D. S., & Schmidt, S. R. (2010). Honoring children, mending the circle: Cultural adaptations of trauma-focused cognitive-behavioral therapy for American Indian and Alaska Native children. *Journal of Clinical Psychology, 66*(8), 847–856. doi:10.1002/jclp.20707

Boyraz, G., Waits, J. B., & Horne, S. G. (2015). Accepting death as part of life: Meaning in life as a means for dealing with loss among bereaved individuals. *Death Studies, 39*(1), 1–11. doi:10.1080/07481187.2013.878767

Brady, M. (2015). Cultural considerations in play therapy with Aboriginal children in Canada. *First Nations Child and Family Caring Society, 10*(2), 95–105.

Brave Heart, M., Chase, J., Elkins, J., & Altschul, D. (2011). Historical trauma among indigenous peoples of the Americas: Concepts, research, and clinical considerations. *Journal of Psychoactive Drugs, 43*(4), 283–290.

Brennen, M. (2010). International conference on death, grief, and bereavement. *Illness, Crisis & Loss, 18*(1), 65–68.

Brucker, P. S., & Perry, B. J. (1998). American Indians: Presenting concerns and considerations for family therapists. *American Journal of Family Therapy, 26*, 307–319.

Cacciatore, J. (2009). Appropriate bereavement practice after the death of a Native American child. *Journal of Contemporary Social Services, 90*(1), 46–50. doi:10.1606/1044-3894.3844

Centers for Disease Control and Prevention. (2017). *Summary health statistics: National Health Interview Survey 2017.* Retrieved from https://www.cdc.gov/nchs/nhis/shs/tables.htm

Choney, S. K., Berryhill-Paapke, E., & Robbins, R. R. (1995). The acculturation of American Indians: Developing frameworks for research and practice. In J. G. Ponterotto. J. M. Casas, L. A. Suzuki, & C. M. Alexander (Eds.). *Handbook of multicultural counseling* (pp. 34–39). Thousand Oaks, CA: SAGE.

Clements, P. T., Vigil, G. J., Manno, M. S., Henry, G. C., Wilks, J., Das, S., & Foster, W. (2003). Cultural perspectives of death, grief, and bereavement. *Journal of Psychosocial Nursing and Mental Health Services, 41*(7), 18–26.

Cobb, R. A., Priest, J. B., & Strachan, T. B. (2016). Spirituality and religion. In M. J. Murphy & L. Hecker (Eds.), *Ethics and professional issues in couple and family therapy* (2nd ed.) (pp. 163–182). New York, NY: Routledge.

Corr, C.A. (1991–1992). A task-based approach to coping with dying. *Omega: Journal of Death and Dying, 24*(2), 81–94.

Devoe, J. E., Darling-Churchill, K. E., & Snyder, T. D. (2008). *Status and trends in the education of American Indians and Alaska Natives: 2008 (NCES 2008–084).* Washington, DC: National Center for Education Statistics, Institute of Education Sciences, U. S. Department of Education.

Doka, K. J. (Ed.). (2002). *Disenfranchised grief: New directions, challenges, and strategies for practice.* Champaign, IL: Research Press.

Evans-Campbell, T., Walters, K. L., Pearson, C. R., & Campbell, C. D. (2012). Indian boarding school experience, substance use, and mental health among urban Two-Spirit American Indian/Alaska Natives. *American Journal of Drug and Alcohol Abuse, 38*(5), 421–427.

Gire, J. T. (2011). Cultural variations in perceptions of aging. In K. D. Keith (Ed.), *Cross-cultural psychology* (pp. 216–240). Hoboken, NJ: John Wiley & Sons.

Grandbois, D. (2005). Stigma of mental illness among American Indian and Alaska Native nations: Historical and contemporary perspectives. *Issues in Mental Health Nursing, 26*(10), 1000–1024.

Gray, J. S., & Rose, W. J. (2012). Cultural adaptation for therapy with American Indians and Alaska Natives. *Journal of Multicultural Counseling and Development, 40*(2), 82–92.

Harper, F. G. (2011). With all my relations: Counseling American Indians and Alaska Natives within a familial context. *The Family Journal, 19,* 434–442.

Hunter, D., & Sawyer, C. (2006). Blending Native American spirituality with individual psychology in work with children. *Journal of Individual Psychology, 62*(3), 234–250.

Keltner, B. R. (1993). Native American children and adolescents: Cultural distinctiveness and mental health needs. *Journal of Child and Adolescent Psychiatric and Mental Health Nursing, 6*(4), 18–23.

Kurilla, V. (1998). Multicultural counseling perspectives: Culture specificity and implications in family therapy. *The Family Journal: Counseling and Therapy for Couples and Families, 6*(3), 207–211.

Lechner, A., Cavanaugh, M., & Blyler, C. (2016). *Addressing trauma in American Indian and Alaska Native youth.* Washington, DC: Mathematica Policy Research.

Leming, M. R., & Dickinson, G. E. (2011). *Death, dying, and bereavement* (7th ed.) Belmont, CA: Cengage.

Lettenberger-Klein, C. G., Fish, J. A., & Hecker, L. L. (2013). Cultural competence when working with American Indian populations: A couple and family therapist perspective. *American Journal of Family Therapy, 41*(2), 148–159.

Limb, G. E., & Hodge, D. R. (2011). Utilizing spiritual ecograms with Native American families and children to promote cultural competence in family therapy. *Journal of Marital and Family Therapy, 37*(1), 81–94. doi:10.111/j.1752-0606.2009.00163.x

Lowe, J. (2002). Cherokee self-reliance. *Journal of Transcultural Nursing, 13,* 287–295.

Mandelbaum, D. G. (1959). Social uses of funeral rites. In H. Feifel (Ed.), *The meaning of death* (pp. 186–218). New York, NY: McGraw-Hill.

Mazur-Bullis R. B. (1984). Pastoral care in Native American context. *Journal of Pastoral Care, 38,* 306–309.

McCabe, M. (1994). Patient Self-Determination Act: A Native American (Navajo) perspective. *Cambridge Quarterly of Healthcare Ethics, 3*(3), 419–421.

McGoldrick, M., Almedia, R., & Hines, P. M. (1991). Mourning in different cultures. In F. Walsh & M. McGoldrick (Eds.), *Living beyond loss: Death in the family* (pp. 176–206). New York, NY: Norton.

McGoldrick, M., Carter, B., & Garcia-Preto, N. (2011). *The expanded family life cycle* (4th ed.). Boston, MA: Pearson Education.

McGoldrick, M., Giordano, J., & Garcia-Preto, N. (Eds.). (2005). *Ethnicity and family therapy* (3rd ed.). New York, NY: Guilford.

Neimeyer, R. A. (Ed.) (2012). *Techniques in grief therapy: Creative practices for counseling the bereaved.* New York, NY: Routledge.

Neimeyer, R. A., Harris, D., Winokeur, H., & Thorton, G. (Eds.). (2011). *Grief and bereavement in contemporary society: Bridging research and practice.* New York, NY: Routledge.

Olsen, M. J. (2003). Counselor understanding of Native American spiritual loss. *Counseling and Values, 47*(2), 109–117.

Paniagua, F. A. (2005). *Assessing and treating culturally diverse clients: A practical guide.* Thousand Oaks, CA: Sage.

Rogers, B. (2001). A path of healing and wellness for native families. *American Behavioral Scientist, 44*(9), 1512–1514.

Seminole Tribe of Florida. (2018). *Medicine.* Retrieved from https://www.semtribe.com/STOF/culture/medicine

Spiwak, R., Sareen, J., Elias, B., Martens, R., Munro, G., & Bolton, J. (2012). Complicated grief in aboriginal populations. *Dialogues in Clinical Neuroscience, 14*(2), 204–209.

Steele, R. S. (1977). Dying, death, and bereavement among the Maya Indians of Mesoamerica: A study in anthropological psychology. *American Psychologist, 32*(12), 1060–1086.

Stone, J. B. (1998). Traditional and contemporary Lakota death, dying, grief, and bereavement beliefs and practices: A qualitative study (Dissertation). *All Graduate Theses and Dissertations.* 4055

Stroebe, M., Schut, H., & Stroebe, W. (2007). Health outcomes of bereavement. *The Lancet, 370*(9603), 1960–1973.

Sue, D. W., & Sue, D. (2013). *Counseling the culturally diverse: Theory and practice* (6th ed.). Hoboken, NJ: Wiley.

U.S. Census Bureau. (2012). American Indians and Alaska Native population: 2010. Retrieved from: http://www.census.gov/prod/cen2010/briefs/c2010br-10.pdf

Valeriote, S., & Fine, M. (1987). Bereavement following the death of a child: Implications for family therapy. *Contemporary Family Therapy, 9*(3), 202–217.

Van Winkle, N. W. (2000). End-of-life decision making in American Indian and Alaska Native cultures. In K. L. Braun, J. H. Pietsch, & P. L. Blanchette (Eds.), *Cultural issues in end-of-life decision making* (pp. 127–144). Thousand Oaks, CA: Sage.

Walker, A. C. (2009). Building bridges in American Indian bereavement research. *Omega, 59*(4), 351–367.

Walker, C., & Balk, D. E. (2007). Bereavement rituals in the Muscogee Creek tribe. *Death Studies, 31*(7), 633–652.

Walsh, F. (Ed.). (2009). *Spiritual resources in family therapy* (2nd ed.). New York, NY: Guilford.

Walsh, F., & McGoldrick, M. (2004). *Living beyond loss: Death in the family* (2nd ed.). New York, NY: Norton.

Walsh-Burke, K. (2006). Cultural and spiritual influences. In *Grief and loss: Theories and skills for helping professionals* (pp. 77–89). Boston, MA: Allyn & Bacon.

Weaver, J. (Ed.). (1998). *Native American religious identity: Unforgotten gods.* Maryknoll, NY: Orbis Books.

Caribbean Blacks

Camille Huggins, PhD, LCSW, University of the West Indies at St. Augustine, Trinidad & Tobago

Dr. Camille Huggins was born and spent most of her life in New York City in the United States. She moved to Trinidad, West Indies five years ago to be a caregiver for her mother and became a lecturer at the University of the West Indies with the Faculty of Social Science since 2015. Dr. Huggins obtained a Ph.D. in clinical social work from New York University; Master's degree in Social Work from Columbia University in New York and a Bachelors' degree in Sociology from the State University of New York at Buffalo. Prior to moving into academia, she worked in administration at various acute and long term healthcare facilities for over 15 years. Her area of research in death rituals and reactions to trauma and grief as she is currently conducting research on grieving mothers of murdered children.

Introduction

With the rise in popularity of Ancestry.com and 23andMe genetic testing, understanding genetic and family history has become important to one's identity. Our genetics allows us to understand what health conditions we may be predisposed to, and our family lineage tells us a story of whence we came (e.g., descendants of Russian monarchs or Holocaust survivors), which may help us determine what we might be evolving toward. It is often assumed all African Americans are the same and the heterogeneity within this population is a neglected dimension (William, Neighbors, & Jackson, 2003). There are 13 sovereign states in the Caribbean Sea with a combined population of approximately 46 million people. Blacks from the Caribbean have been migrating to the United States from multiple Spanish, English, and French speaking Caribbean islands since 1860 (James, 2002). Currently, Caribbean Blacks account for 49% of the Black immigrants (e.g., African-born, Caribbean) living in the United States (Thomas, 2012). Caribbean Blacks tend to settle in the Eastern part of the United States such as Boston, New York City, Miami, Maryland, and Washington, DC, and often live together in ethnic clusters alongside African American and White communities (Denton & Massey, 1989).

Personal Experience

As a first-generation Caribbean Black living in the United States, I find myself always straddling two spheres: born and raised in the United States with a firsthand knowledge of American culture and norms; and the other sphere, born of Caribbean parents who impose the culture and norms of "back home." Although my religion is of Christianity (e.g., Catholic) faith, as most Caribbean Blacks from English-speaking Caribbean islands are of Christian faith (e.g., Catholic, Anglican, Baptist, Methodist), how death and grief is treated among Christian Caribbean Blacks is diametrically different from what I have grown to understand in Christian American (e.g., White or Black) culture. Growing up in a predominately Caribbean community in New York City, what I realized is many Caribbean Blacks from different Caribbean islands had similar experiences with regards to death and grief. When a loved one passes, their Caribbean families utilized both back home bereavement traditions as well as the Christian burial rituals practiced in the United States.

I first understood grief and Caribbean bereavement practices from my mother, an immigrant from Trinidad and Tobago, who was recruited as a nurse during the nursing workforce shortage in the United States during the 1960s. I remember her being visibly upset when she read the bereavement policy of her employment, which stated she had 3 days' leave for a death in the family. She found it ridiculous that you were only allowed 3 days and 1 additional day with a death certificate. Her mother, my grandmother, had passed, and my mother was her caregiver, and although both were living in New York, it was understood my grandmother was to be buried in Trinidad. I was a teenager, in my senior year of high school. I could not attend the funeral, but my mother along, with my grandmother, flew to Trinidad and my mother did not return for 1 month.

Bereavement Rituals

What occurred during her time away were a series of bereavement rituals that were conducted during the practice of burying. Bereavement rituals are used to facilitate relinquishing the dead and helping those who are left to transition to a new role. Family members participate in a combination of rituals that are *intrapsychic,* which is the transformation of the person's sense of self resulting from loss; the *psychosocial* dimension, which is the transition between the individual's pre-death and post-death social status; and the *communal* aspect, where the mourner can see the impact of the deceased from the community perspective (Romanoff, 1998). The experience of the family member is to psychologically let go with the support of the community (Romanoff, 1998). Bereavement rituals continue after the funeral, which provide a structure to the grieving and full incorporation into the new status of the surviving family members (Goldberg, 1981). Part of the bereavement rituals are the burial rituals, which are symbolic enactments that provide meaningful and affirming experiences for the bereaved (Romanoff, 1998). These rituals help facilitate resolution of grief and help people maintain an appropriate connection with the deceased (Silverman & Klass, 1996). Burial rituals also mediate the transition of the deceased from life to death and mediate the transition of the bereaved from one social status to another (Pine, 1989). These rituals provide opportunities for the public display of grief and an opportunity to affirm the relationship of the deceased to the community.

Colonialism in the Caribbean

In the Caribbean, the treatment of a deceased loved one is a prolonged activity that involves immediate family, colleagues, neighbors, and the larger community. These practices are closely tied to its history of colonialism, Christianity, and the African lineage of Blacks living in the Caribbean. The Caribbean has a long history of slavery; slaves of African descent underwent treatment that systematically tried to erase their cultural heritage (Adamson, 1972; Patterson, 1973). Colonizers and Christian missionaries introduced religion, particularly Christian religion, in tandem with enslavement to justify and condone the importance of slavery to the captured. As a result, colonizers criticized and earnestly tried to erode African practices so they could be replaced with Christian practices among slaves. This was true with burial rituals where Africans tried to preserve their burial practices and often rejected the practices of the colonizers (Beasley, 2009). It was a potent statement about African autonomy at a critical personal moment during slavery. Slaves ultimately interwove Christian religious practices along with West African traditions to develop present-day burial rituals (Marshall & Sutherland, 2008).

During slavery, colonizers constantly observed and noted burial practices of Africans, their expression of grief, and their commitment to mourning their dead by using their African rites (Beasley, 2009). Colonizers often discussed the sound of the mourners which is not observed in Christian practices, for example in Barbados, mourning Africans often clapped and wringed their hands, making a doleful sound with their voices (Beasley, 2009). The colonizers felt the practices were demonic and non-Christian in practice but took note of the power of the African burial practices and its regulation of community life. Therefore, colonizers often ban the slaves from meeting and at times stopped them from acknowledging the dead in hopes of stopping any mutinies that might occur. Although a burial was not allowed it did not stop slaves from acknowledging the dead and setting up makeshift services in the dead of the night. In fact, slaves preferred to bury their dead in the night, so they were free to dance, sing and drink without interruption (Beasley, 2009). For colonizers who felt there were circumstances where a burial service was allowed, it would be convened by a Christian minister and infused with Christian practices.

Caribbean Blacks experience stressors associated with immigration, acculturation and compounded with grief due to the passing of a loved one, who may have been living in another country, so they are unable to attend the burial. This can give rise to severe psychological problems that, in many cases, maybe presented as somatic symptoms (e.g., high blood pressure). The distinction between the Caribbean Black immigrant and the U.S. born African American when working with persons dealing with grief should be understood and recognized because its significance as it pertains to each person's culture.

The Caribbean Islands of Barbados, Trinidad and Haiti, while independent countries all experienced some form of colonization by Great Britain, France, and Spain. Barbados was colonized by Great Britain, Haiti was colonized by France and, Trinidad at one time has been colonized by France, Spain and Great Britain. All three islands are in the Caribbean Sea and have similar histories of slavery however their burial rituals are vastly diverse, distinct and equally sacred to its people. In the three Caribbean islands (i.e., Barbados, Haiti and Trinidad) there is a great variety of burial practices and rituals within the Christian religion and of people from African descent.

Burial Rituals by Country

Barbados

Barbados was colonized by the British in 1627 until the abolition of slavery in 1807 with a couple of unsuccessful slave rebellions which helped to ease the hardships of the slaves. In 1966, Barbados became an independent state and Commonwealth realm with the British Monarch (presently Queen Elizabeth II) as hereditary head of state. Most Barbadians are Christians (95%) from various denominations especially, Anglicans and Catholics. The smallest of the Caribbean isles is Barbados with a population of 277,821 people in total, its ethnic composition is 90% of African descent, while 4% are of European descent and the rest are a mixture of immigrants from Guyana, China and Syria (Byfield, Denzer, & Morrison, 2010).

In Barbados, from the 1600s to the 1780s, colonizers ensured that dead bodies of whites even poor ones were treated with a level of care that marked their superior status on the plantation. Whites were buried in order of importance to the community and wealth in a local church, or church yard and based on their importance they were also given a ceremonial plague to commemorate their existence.

For free blacks or mulattos[3] their bodies were placed on a private property separate from whites. Slaves were usually responsible for burying their own dead, in their own areas where they can find space (Handler & Lange, 1978). Even if colonizers may have beheaded and placed the slave's head on a pike to stand outside a public area (e.g., church) as a warning to other slaves. It was the responsibility of the slaves to ultimately bury them. As a result, burials took place in the dead of night with a brief acknowledgement and no marker on the grave (Beasley 2009).

Today, family and community are very important. They not only plan but lead out in the funeral services—from grandchildren, to first and second cousins, and beyond. Basically, any connection to the deceased is recognized to show the connection and love in the family. In large families, there is a funeral planning hierarchy. While the spouse will have an integral role, unless there is some level of dysfunction in the family, the eldest sibling, or child, may also have a similar important role in the final decisions of funeral planning. Traditionally, the family or close loved ones and relative wear mourning colors (white, black, shades of purple) for a period of about 6 months to a year, signifying their grieving, nonverbally yet outwardly and publicly. This highlights their grief so they can still receive support. Even one's activities can be limited to diminish the perception of any type of enjoyment.

One cultural death practice that is unlike other Caribbean islands, prior to the funeral, is that there is little to no gathering at the deceased's families' home. There may be the usual sharing of food and phone calls as people are notified and sympathies are extended, but visiting for any length of time is mainly done immediately after the funeral. Thus, the usual understanding of wakes in other Caribbean islands is not a Barbadian norm. There is also an interesting grieving pattern of not visiting the grave after a loved one has died. Some individuals may visit at certain times, but it is not a common place or a recurring event for most Barbadians. This does not signify the level of attachment or connection to the deceased, but possibly a belief in not wishing to relive the memory of the loss or a recollection of stories from childhood about "duppies" (In Caribbean folklore, a duppy can be either the manifestation (in human or animal form) of the soul of a dead person, or a malevolent supernatural being ghost or spirit. They are believed to come out and haunt people at night, and people from around the islands claim to have seen them. In other islands, duppies are known as *jumbies*, while Barbados and Jamaica use the term. But the word *duppy* more likely originates from African folklore and the Ashanti people) in the cemetery, plus the poor conditions (overgrown grass and trees) of the older cemeteries, which may reinforce the old fears.

Haiti

The country of Haiti is unique in that it shares the same land with another Caribbean island named the Dominican Republic. The western portion of the island was led by France, and this part of the island was originally called St. Dominic and later changed to Haiti. During this time thousands of Africans were brought to work the sugarcane plantations, which led to the colony being among the most lucrative in the world (Colmáin, 2010). When France was experiencing the French Revolution from 1789 to1799, slaves and free people of color revolted in Haiti from 1791 to 1804. This led Haiti to become a sovereign nation in 1804 and successfully abolish slavery. Although Haiti experienced sovereignty in

3 The historic term mulatto meant a biracial person with black and white heritage. This term may be offensive to the reader but it is being used in its historic context in this text.

1804, it experienced several government rebellions and unstable government administrations. It was never able to stabilize its economy.

Although 98% of Haitians are Catholic, many also believe in Vodou, which originated in the Caribbean under the French in the 18th century, among West African slaves when African religious practices were actively suppressed and enslaved Africans were forced to convert to Christianity (Fandrich, 2007). Vodou is a mixture of West African and Catholic practices. Most Haitians, at least in the lower class, are buried with both Catholic and Vodou rites. Haitians believe relationships with the dead last forever and a living Haitian inherit the spirits his or her ancestors worshipped, and these spirits visit him or her in dreams and provide guidance. Many believe if these spirits and ancestors are not respected the dead can return to trouble the living as zombies. Zombies, according to Haitian folklore, are undead beings created through the reanimation of human corpses (Fandrich, 2007). Zombies can be a carriers of mental diseases and viruses and precipitate a serious accident; therefore, burying the dead in a respectful manner is of utmost importance for Haitians.

Worshipping the dead is so important to Haitians that in many villages the cemeteries are more elaborate, with stone crypts and mausoleums, than the home in which they live. When traveling throughout Haiti you will see a small funeral plot with maybe 10 to 15 mausoleums painted in bright pink and blue colors (Grossman, 2010). They can be 10 to 15 feet in height and 10 feet in width. Some of the mausoleums are intact while others have been broken into to put a body of a recently deceased family member, fixed and repainted, while others remain with gaping holes. Some say in times of deep financial strife people break into the mausoleums for various reasons (e.g., clothes from the dead, jewelry (Grossman, 2010). In the remote villages of Haiti, daylong funeral celebrations are convened, with villagers wearing their Sunday best and men playing drums in a processional form. The worshippers can be seen clapping and singing for hours. The average cost for a funeral in Haiti is $600; additional costs may be the celebration itself, with cows, goats, and pigs being slaughtered for the meal after the funeral celebration (Rey & Stepnick, 2013). Villagers celebrate along with the family, preparing for 9 nights of visits and preparing foods. The 9-night celebration is an intermingling of Catholic and West African burial practices. The West African tradition is a belief that on the ninth night after death, the soul of the deceased leaves for its final resting place so the family members of the deceased will pray from the day after the pronouncement of death to the ninth day. For women this time is for prayer and preparation of the homegoing celebration; for men the rhum (rum alcohol) flows freely to the accompaniment of drums. The celebration culminates the night before the funeral and the night after the funeral, with lots of eating and singing for hours.

The Vodou rituals are intermingled with the Catholic celebrations. While most Haitians attend church regularly, they believe God or Jesus Christ is too busy and tending to other needs in the world; therefore, it is important to enlist the help of the ancestor's spirits. A Vodou priest(ess), Hougan, is hired to complete the rituals. The Vodou priest(ess) is usually dedicated to serve the Loa or Lwa or gods and spirits. The funeral participants donate some type of items for the Lwa such as money, rum, Florida water, flowers, or cigars out of a sign of respect. The ceremony for the public involves a lot of drumming, singing, and dancing, and this is considered a spiritual or Vodou party. This event is often encapsulated in the repass after the church service. The purpose of this ceremony is to help the Lwa prophesize, heal people, cleanse people or bless them, and assist them in resolving their issues. Private ceremonies happen only in the presence of immediate family members with special needs and requests

(Fandrich, 2007). There are two such ceremonies, namely the divination/readings, which is a reading with cards, a candle, and water, or getting the Houngan to call a specific Lwa for a special request or a spiritual bath, which is specially composed for a client to achieve goals. Spiritual baths are done to remove negativity, bring up luck, and open doors of opportunity. This is a general understanding of the rituals associated with death and Vodou in Haiti. In all the time, money, and resources involved, just one funeral is massive and exemplifies how important these rituals are to this country.

Trinidad

Trinidad was colonized by the Spanish until 1797, then settled by French colonists and finally the British, who incorporated the two islands of Trinidad and Tobago in 1889. Independence was obtained from the British Empire in 1962 and became a republic in 1976 (Williams, 1965). Trinidad is unique from other Caribbean islands because ownership of the country was transferred three times from Spain, French, and the British and it was only a plantation economy for a short period, the 1780s to the 1830s; therefore, plantation slavery as a labor and social institution only occurred for about 50 years as opposed to 200 years in other countries such as Barbados (Brereton, 2007). Although Trinidad had slavery and experienced the same issues of slavery like the other islands, it was for an abbreviated amount of time. The population of Trinidad and Tobago is approximately 1.4 million of diverse ethnic, religious and cultural groups. As of the 2011 Trinidad and Tobago Census, the population was, 35.43% African, 34.22% East Indian, 7.66% mixed African and East Indian, and 15.16% mixed (various ethnicities). Most Trinidadians are Christians (over 50%) from various denominations.

One of the most significant burial rituals that can be observed in Trinidad is the 9-night celebration, which is an intermingling of Catholic and West African burial practices. The West African tradition is a belief that on the ninth night after death, the soul of the deceased leaves for its final resting place so the family members of the deceased will pray from the day after the pronouncement of death to the ninth day. A wake is held every night until the ninth day, starting at 6:00 p.m. The day of the funeral is a big day of celebration; the 9 days are also celebration on a smaller scale. If it is financially possible, the home of the deceased, along with family and friends, provide food and alcohol for each of the 9 nights. The most important part of the ceremony occurs in the room where the person died, so at approximately 7:00 p.m. the family members retreat to the bedroom of the deceased and begin to recite the rosary and reading passages from the Bible. They are also praying to the prophets of the Old Testament and the saints of the New Testament to ensure the deceased body is committed to the Lord and will ascend into heaven. The person is appointed by relatives of the deceased to lead in the hymns to be sung and passages to be read. A small altar is erected in the room with lit candles and a pan with frankincense and myrrh. The ceremony in the room lasts for 45 minutes and the group joins the other visitors.

In some lower-class households, candles or flambeaus are lit and line the street floor near the deceased house to indicate a recent death. It is also meant to help the spirits find their way. After the ceremony, everyone who visits stays for food and drink and to extol condolences to the immediate family. This event will continue until 11:00 p.m. when the last guest leaves. Sometimes this may continue into the morning hours with the playing of cards and playing of loud music. The day of the funeral is often a whole-day affair with an early service, the ride to the gravesite, and male family members breaking ground for the first time to unearth 6 feet of dirt. Biblical songs are song by the female members until the casket is ready to be lowered. Once the casket is lowered, prayers are said again, and songs begin while dirt is being tossed on the casket. The time at the burial site is about 2–3 hours. After the event the family returns to the repass and a celebration of food, song, and good company continues.

Implications for Grieving and Mental Health

What is clear about these three distinct Caribbean islands are how serious bereavement rituals are taken and how involved the family (nuclear and extended) and the community are in the festivities. Death and the acknowledgement of death is critical to the psychological well-being of the Caribbean Black. The lack of acknowledgement of death for the Caribbean Black is tied to mental illness. For example, in 2010, Haiti experienced the worst earthquake in its history. There were estimates of 200,000 lives lost and the Haitian government buried more than 150,000 people, few of them with any identification (Kolbe, et al., 2010). They were buried in mass graves with no ceremonial burial rituals or identification for families to identify later. For Haitians who place significant emphasis on dying with dignity and holding a funeral, mass graves are unconscionable. Many Haitians believe this treatment of the deceased will have long-lasting effects on the citizens of Haiti as the zombies will haunt them for years to come, which will bring mental illness and disease. Many Haitians who believe in Voodoo acknowledge both natural and supernatural causes of mental illness, so depression and psychosis may be perceived as the consequences of a spell or a curse.

Caribbean Blacks, overall, believe that the causes of mental illness, particularly depression, are due to excessive worry, an impure environment, and bad family genes (Edgerton, 1971; Lawrence et al., 2006). Caribbean Blacks believe that doctors are not sensitive to their cultural perspectives regarding mental health and are overzealous when it comes to prescribing pharmaceutical interventions. Caribbean Blacks prefer to deal with mental health problems without medical interventions (Strothers et al., 2005).

Caribbean Blacks exhibit depressive symptoms that are classified as subthreshold or subsyndromal depression (SSD) (Grabovich, Lu, Tang, Tu, & Lyness, 2010; Vahia et al. 2010), which do not meet the criteria for a diagnosis of depressive disorder but are just as harmful (Cohen et.al, 2005). SSD entails the presence of two or more symptoms of depression for shorter periods of time (e.g., throughout the course of each day or week instead of occurring for a 2-week period typical of major depression) (Grabovich et al., 2010). Subsyndromal depression is associated with declines in overall physical functioning, increase rates of hospitalization, poorer health outcomes, and quality of life, and it is also a strong predictor for the reoccurrence of major depression. Caribbean Blacks also experience symptoms of subsyndromal anxiety (SSA), which do not meet the criteria of generalized anxiety disorder, including pathological worry, sleep disturbance, restlessness, fatigue, and difficulty concentrating but do exhibit some of the symptoms (Cohen, Maggai, Yaffee, & Walcott-Brown, 2006). Subsyndromal anxiety can also have serious negative consequences and affect the course of depressive, cognitive, and medical disorders (Beaudreau & O'Hara, 2008).

Implications for Mental Health Practitioners

As practitioners, there are many aspects of the Caribbean Black bereavement rituals that are unique to American grief and bereavement practices. I am sure when one hears of spirits and images of the walking dead, it is assumed the person is hallucinating but, in some cultures, the spiritual world exists alongside the living. It is important to ask the context (e.g., environmental, familial) in which a person may define a spirit that is present in his or her life. The bereaved person may have rituals he or she may want to share to help alleviate grief.

Grief and the differences in the prevalence of syndromal and subsyndromal depression and anxiety among Caribbean Blacks highlight the importance for mental health providers to understand if the person is experiencing grief or has been participating in bereavement rituals specific to his or her countries' norms as this may alleviate some of the grief. There should also be an accurate and timely detection, identification, and management of mental health issues. This population is under-researched and misunderstood and may at times experience high rates of severe mental health issues as well as physical health issues.

Questions Mental Health Practitioners May Ask

1. Tell me, is there a way you may want to honor your loved one? If you were back home, what practices would you participate in to bury and honor your loved one?
2. Acknowledge what bereavement rituals they can and cannot participate in away from home and provide empathy for the rituals they cannot do.

References

Adamson, A. H. (1972). *Sugar without slaves.* New Haven, CT: Yale University Press.

Beaudreau, S., & O'Hara, R., (2008). Late life anxiety and cognitive impairment: A review. *American Journal of Geriatric Psychiatry, 16*(10), 790–803.

Beasley, N. M. (2009). *Christian ritual and the creation of British plantation colonies.* Athens, GA: University of Georgia Press.

Brereton, B. (2007). *Emancipation in Trinidad. Trinidad and Tobago.* Trinidad: University of the West Indies Press.

Byfield, J. A. M; Denzer, L & Morrison, A. (2010). *Gendering the African diaspora: women, culture, and historical change in the Caribbean and Nigerian hinterland.* Bloomington: Indiana University Press. ISBN 978-0-253-22153-7.

Cohen, C., Maggai, C., Yaffee, R., & Walcott-Brown, L. (2005). Comparison of users and nonusers of mental health services among older urban African-Americans. *American Journal of Psychiatry, 161,* 864–871.

Cohen, C., Maggai, C., Yaffee, R., & Walcott-Brown, L. (2006). The prevalence of anxiety and associated factors: A multiracial sample of older adults. *Psychiatric Services, 57*(12), 1719–1725.

Colmáin, G. O. (2010). France and the History of Haiti. *Global Research*: Center for Research on Globalization (2005–2019) countries index. Global Research.ca https://www.globalresearch.ca/page/428?p=0onOvaj

Denton, N. & Massey, D. (1989). Racial identity among Caribbean Hispanics: The effects of double minority status on residential segregation. *American Sociological Review, 54,* 190–208.

Edgerton, R. (1971). A traditional African psychiatrist. *Southwestern Journal of Anthropology, 27,* 259–287.

Fandrich, I. J. (2007). Yoru` ba′ influences on Haitian Vodou and New Orleans Voodoo. *Journal of Black Studies, 37*(5), 775–791.

Goldberg, H. S. (1981). Funeral and bereavement rituals of Kota Indians and Orthodox Jews. *Omega: Journal of Death and Dying, 12*(2), 117–128.

Grabovich, A., Lu, N., Tang, W., Tu, X., & Lyness, J. (2010). Outcomes of sybsyndromal depression in older primary care patients. *American Journal of Geriatric Psychiatry, 18*, 227–235.

Grossman, C. L. January, 18, 2010. Prayer and praise to God rise from Haiti's ruins. *USA Today.* http://content.usatoday.com/communities/Religion/post/2010/01/faith-prayer-haiti-earthquake-god-/1#.XTSoOZNKiCg

Handler, J. S., & Lange, F. W. (1978). *Plantation slavery in Barbados: An archaeological and historical investigation.* Cambridge, MA: Harvard University Press.

James, W. (2002). Explaining Afro-Caribbean social mobility in the United States Beyond the Sowell (Thesis). *Comparative Studies in Society and History, 44*(2), 218–262.

Kolbe, et al., (2010). "Mortality, crime and access to basic needs before and after the Haiti earthquake: a random survey of Port-au-Prince households". *Medicine, Conflict and Survival.* 26 (4): 281–297. doi:10.1080/13623699.2010.535279. PMID 21314081.

Lawrence, V., Murray, J., Banjeree, S., Turner, S., Sangha, K., Byng, R., ... Macdonald, J. (2006). Concepts and causation of depression: A cross-cultural study of the beliefs of older adults. *The Gerontologist, 46*, 23–32.

Marshall, R., & Sutherland, P. (2008). The social relations of bereavement in the Caribbean. *OMEGA: Journal of Death and Dying, 57*(1), 21–34.

Patterson, O. (1973). *The sociology of slavery. An analysis of the origins, development and structure of Negro slave society in Jamaica.* London, UK: Grenada.

Pine, V. (1989). Death, loss, and disenfranchised grief. In K. J. Doka (Ed.), *Disenfranchised grief: Recognizing hidden sorrow* (pp. 13–24). Lexington, MA: Lexington.

Rey, T. & Stepick, A. (2013). *Crossing the Water and keeping the faith: Haitian religion in Miami.* https://nyupress.org/books/9780814777091. ISBN: 9780814777091

Romanoff, B. D. (1998). Rituals and the grieving process. *Death Studies, 22*(8), 697–711.

Silverman, P. R., & Klass, D. (1996). Introduction: What's the problem? In D. Klass, P. R. Silverman & S. L. Nickman (Eds.), *Continuing bonds: New understandings of grief* (pp. 3–27). Washington, DC: Taylor & Francis.

Strothers, H., Rust, G., Minor, P., Fresh, E., Druss, B; & Satcher, D., (2005). Disparities in antidepressant treatment in Medicaid elderly diagnosed with depression. *Journal of American Geriatric Society, 53*, 456–466.

Thomas, K. (2012). A demographic profile of black Caribbean immigrants in the United States. Washington D.C. Migration Policy Institute.

Thornton, M., Taylor, R., & Chatters, L. (2012). African American, Black Caribbean, and Non-Hispanic White Feelings of Closeness Toward Other Racial and Ethnic Groups. *Journal of Black Studies 43*(7) 749 –772.

Vahia, I., Meeks, T., Thompson, W., Depp, C., Zisook, S., Allison, M., Judd, L., & Jesie, D. (2010). Subthreshold depression and successful aging in older women. *American Journal of Geriatric Psychiatry, 18*(3), 212–220.

Williams, D. R., Neighbors, H. W., & Jackson, J. S. (2003). Racial/ethnic discrimination and health findings come community studies. *American Journal of Public Health, 93*, 2000–2008.

Williams, E. (1965). History of the People of Trinidad and Tobago. International Affairs, 41,2, 389 https://doi.org/10.2307/2610709

LGBT Loss and Grief

M. Aaron Guest, PhD, MPH, MSW, CPH, CSW, Arizona State University, Phoenix, AZ

M. Aaron Guest, an Assistant Professor of Aging within the College of Nursing and Health Innovation at Arizona State University, is a socio-environmental gerontologist whose research interests lie at the nexus of health, identity, and the social & built environments. He holds a PhD in Gerontology from the University of Kentucky, a Master of Public Health, and a Master of Social Work from the University of South Carolina. The emphasis throughout his academic career been on translational community-engaged participatory health equity research. His research specializes in aging among rural marginalized populations, health equity, environmental gerontology, and social network/placed based community-engaged mixed method research. Specifically, his research centers on how marginalized, particularly LGBTQ, rural older adults social networks affect their health and quality of life. He focuses on the interrelationship between identity, place, networks, and health. He applies his interdisciplinary background as a community-based scholar to address health inequities, improve health equity, and improve health outcomes through decreasing disparities among rural older adults.

FIGURE 4.16. M. Aaron Guest

Introduction

Perhaps one of the greatest strengths of social work practice is the reliance on the person-in-environment model. The person-in-environment model recognizes that people are continuously impacted by organizations, policies, people, cultural beliefs, and societal practices that surround them. In practice, as clinicians, we use this model to recognize the inherent intersectionality of our clients. No two clients are the same. We must approach each client, and especially clients experiencing grief and loss, with a fresh perspective. Even so, and despite our best efforts, at times we may find ourselves relying too much on our attitudes and what is viewed as the societal "norms." In doing so, we may not only alienate our clients but cause additional emotional stress when they are most vulnerable.

This section seeks to provide an overview of working with lesbian, gay, bisexual, or transgender (LGBT) people who are experiencing grief and loss. The chapter is not meant to imply that the LGBT population is homogenous with the same belief systems, experiences, and support networks. Indeed, there are major differences even among LGBT populations. Instead, it is my hope you will see how identities intersect for those experiencing loss and the need to remain vigilant in your assumptions.

About the LGBT Community

The lesbian, gay, bisexual, transgender community across the world is growing as individuals have more freedom to express their sexual orientation and sexual identity. In the United States it is estimated that between 3% to 4% of the total population is LGBT (Choi & Meyer, 2016).

Lesbian, gay, and bisexual refer to sexual identities that individuals may adopt that are non-heteronormative, or straight. These sexual identities are often referred to as sexual orientations, which refers to the general pattern of sexual/romantic attraction one feels. Gay is most often used to describe men who are attracted to men while lesbian refers to women attracted to other women. Individuals who identify as bisexual are attracted to those of the same gender or other genders. On the other hand, transgender refers to a gender identity that people may adopt if they do not identify with their assigned sex at birth or their body characteristic or identify as some gender beyond the binary male/female system (GLAAD, n.d.)

LGBT individuals face stigmatization and marginalization that lead to poorer health outcomes and increased amounts of stress (Cochran & Mays, 2017). LGBT individuals may be afraid to disclose their identity for fear of persecution or denial of service. They also may suffer the loss of friends, family, or community due to their identity (Erosheva, Kim, Emlet, & Fredriksen-Goldsen, 2016; Orel, 2017). Although there have been major strides in LGBTQ equality over the last decade, homophobia (the fear of individuals who identify as homosexual) and homomesia (the hatred of individuals who identify as homosexual) remain prevalent across societies. As clinicians, it is vital we recognize these prejudices and are aware of how to work best with our LGBT clients, especially as they face grief and loss.

LGBT Perspectives on Experiencing Loss and Grief

LGBT individuals face unique challenges in experiencing and processing loss and grief. In working with this client population is it critical to take into considerations these realities, especially as they may be unfamiliar to you. In this section, we will address four of these challenges: limited biological family, limited community support, assumptions of heteronormativity, and the unique experiences of LGBT older adults.

Limited Biological Family

LGBT individuals may face additional challenges in locating individual social support. Unfortunately, it is still common for LGBT individuals to be disowned by family and friends as they come to accept their identity (Alencar Albuquerque et al., 2016). The loss of biological family members results in holes within the support networks, and as such LGBT individuals may have smaller support networks to turn to or no network at all (Erosheva et al., 2016). The loss of family, friends, and community networks can be a significant experience of loss and grief in and of itself for LGBT individuals. As coming out is not a one-time process, but rather a constant experience of identity management, this loss and grief can occur throughout the individual's life (Kaufman & Raphael, 1996).

One way that LGBT individuals have navigated the loss of biological family and friend networks is through the development of chosen families. Chosen families refer to the selected individuals people have surrounded themselves with and who can take on specific roles such as a cousin, aunt, uncle, mother, father, and so on. The form of fictive kin exchange allows for the replication of previously existing social support networks (Allen, Blieszner, & Roberto, 2011).

Limited Community Support

In addition to the challenges posed by limited individual social support networks, members of the LGBT community who are experiencing grief and loss may also find themselves limited by the availability of community supports and services (McGovern, Brown, & Gasparro, 2016). It can be terrifying for an LGBT person seeking out counseling, medical, or social services. Individuals may feel the need to hide their sexual orientation for fear of being turned away. Individuals may be afraid of identifying as a deceased individual's spouse or partner and may opt to refer to themselves as friend. While the LGBT community, as with many marginalized groups, has often turned inward for the development of community resources, not all communities can offer every service or be easily identified as being welcoming or accepting. Smaller communities and rural areas can exacerbate these challenges due to the limited number of providers or services available.

The development of Pink Pages is one ways the LGBT community has worked to overcome these barriers. Pink Pages can be found in many communities and list LGBT-friendly or LGBT-owned businesses across a variety of sectors. One other way has been the identification of areas as "safe zones"—areas that preemptively identify as being welcoming to LGBT individuals. You can learn more about the Safe Zone Project at thesafezoneproject.com.

Assumptions of Heteronormativity

One of the most uncomfortable factors that affects grieving LGBT individuals is society's pervasive assumptions regarding heteronormativity (Hoy-Ellis & Fredriksen-Goldsen, 2017). Much of society is organized around a heterosexual male/female system. Think about the last time you went out to eat or to go shopping; what type of bathrooms did they have available? Which one would an individual transgender use? What about the last time you filled out a form; did it have a space for spouse(s) or for husband and wife?

Individuals experiencing loss and grief may face the additional challenge of correcting medical professionals' assumptions regarding who is the spouse (Shiu, Kim, & Fredriksen-Goldsen, 2017). Recommendations such as "call in the family" may be exceptionally hurtful if the family is not in the picture. As previously mentioned, medical forms may only have a space for husband and wife or only provide two gender options to select from. In working with funeral homes, LGBT individuals may be forced to explain why the deceased do not want to list their biological family members but put others in their place. Transgender individuals may have to explain the use of a chosen names versus legal names and why it matters. Assumptions of gender identity can make grieving individuals take part in uncomfortable conversations while seeking comfort.

Providers should work to ensure all intake, medical, legal, or other forms provide for the expression of all sexual orientations and gender identities. Forms should be as inclusive as possible. In addition, as professionals working with the community, we must actively work not to assume heterosexuality and to avoid heterosexist language in our work proactively.

LGBT Older Adults

Grief and loss can be experienced across the life span. Within the LGBT community, one particular age group that should be of note to clinicians moving forward are aging LGBT individuals. The aging population of the United States continues to diversify (Ortman, Velkoff, & Hogan, 2014). This includes the number of self-identifying LGBT older individuals (Choi & Meyer, 2016). Aging LGBT individuals may face unique challenges in the grief process due to the combination of smaller social support networks than their heterosexual peers and loss of social support network members due to death. At the same time, these individuals may not want to burden other LGBT persons they know under the assumption they have similar challenges.

Furthermore, it is not uncommon for LGBT individuals in long-term care to go back into the closet in order to avoid revealing their sexual orientation out of fear of neglect or maltreatment for health professionals and fellow residents (Shiu, Muraco, & Fredriksen-Goldsen, 2016). As individuals attempt to avoid outing themselves—revealing their sexual orientation—they may deny themselves the opportunity to grieve the loss of friends and loved ones. Likewise, as individuals die their friends and family may not have the opportunity to appropriately grieve them or visit in the final days due to individuals returning to the closet.

One method of addressing these challenges has been the development of competencies for health professionals in working with LGBT older adults (Portz et al., 2014). Additionally, many organizations now offer specific training for working with LGBT clients in order to create more affirming environments for aging LGBT individuals.

In Practice

LGBT individuals may fear accessing counseling or grief services due to the need to disclose their identity and a fear of judgment. They may also lack the social support structures to navigate loss and grief events. As clinicians, there are a few things we can do to improve the experience of the LGBT clients we see.

1. Review documentation to ensure it does not assume heteronormativity. For example, do intake forms only list male and female? Are there spaces for husband and wife or spouse and spouse? You can find many best-practice forms and tools online, including from the William Institute at UCLA Law.
2. Reach out to the local LGBT organization. Familiarize yourself with the resources they offer. Pink Pages are a great resource if your community has one. Many cities have local LGBT groups, and every state has a statewide equality association.
3. Think about your office environment. What message are you conveying? You do not have to hide your own beliefs, but would a nonreligious or LGBT client feel comfortable in your space?
4. Do not be afraid to ask questions. Clients are infinitely diverse. If you are unfamiliar with a particular community or tradition, seek clarification.
5. Seek out training opportunities that will make you better informed about working with the LGBT population. Training on loss and grief are essential, but also consider training that informs you more about the community.

References

Alencar Albuquerque, G., de Lima Garcia, C., da Silva Quirino, G., Alves, M. J., Belem, J. M., dos Santos Figueiredo, F. W., … & Adami, F. (2016). Access to health services by lesbian, gay, bisexual, and transgender persons: Systematic literature review. *BMC International Health and Human Rights, 16*, 2. doi:10.1186/s12914-015-0072-9

Allen, K. R., Blieszner, R., & Roberto, K. A. (2011). Perspectives on extended family and fictive kin in the later years: Strategies and meanings of kin reinterpretation. *Journal of Family Issues, 32*(9), 1156–1177. doi:10.1177/0192513x11404335

Choi, S. K., & Meyer, I. H. (2016). *LGBT aging: A review of research findings, needs, and policy implications.* Los Angeles: The Williams Institute.

Cochran, S. D., & Mays, V. M. (2017). Advancing the LGBT health research agenda: Differential health trends within the lesbian, gay, and bisexual populations. *American Journal of Public Health, 107*(4), 497–498. doi:10.2105/AJPH.2017.303677

Erosheva, E. A., Kim, H. J., Emlet, C., & Fredriksen-Goldsen, K. I. (2016). Social networks of lesbian, gay, bisexual, and transgender older adults. *Research on Aging, 38*(1), 98–123. doi:10.1177/0164027515581859

GLAAD. (n.d.). GLAAD media reference guide. Retrieved from: https://www.glaad.org/reference/lgbtq

Hoy-Ellis, C. P., & Fredriksen-Goldsen, K. I. (2017). Depression among transgender older adults: General and minority stress. *American Journal of Community Psychology, 59*(3–4), *295–305* . doi:10.1002/ajcp.12138

Kaufman, G., & Raphael, L. (1996). *Coming out of gay shame: Transforming gay and lesbian lives.* New York, NY: Main Street Books.

McGovern, J., Brown, D., & Gasparro, V. (2016). Lessons learned from an LGBTQ senior center: A Bronx tale. *Journal of Gerontological Social Work, 59*(7–8), 496–511. doi:10.1080/01634372.2016.1255692

Orel, N. A. (2017). Families and support systems of LGBT elders. *Annual Review of Gerontology & Geriatrics, 37*(1), 89–109.

Ortman, J., Velkoff, V., & Hogan, H. (2014). *An aging nation: The older population in the United States.* Washington, DC: U.S. Census Bureau

Portz, J. D., Retrum, J. H., Wright, L. A., Boggs, J. M., Wilkins, S., Grimm, C., … & Gozansky, W. S. (2014). Assessing capacity for providing culturally competent services to LGBT older adults. *Journal of Gerontological Social Work, 57*(2–4), 305–321. doi:10.1080/01634372.2013.857378

Shiu, C., Kim, H. J., & Fredriksen-Goldsen, K. (2017). Health care engagement among LGBT older adults: The role of depression diagnosis and symptomatology. *Gerontologist, 57*(1), S105–S114. doi:10.1093/geront/gnw186

Shiu, C., Muraco, A., & Fredriksen-Goldsen, K. (2016). Invisible care: Friend and partner care among older lesbian, gay, bisexual, and transgender (LGBT) adults. *Journal of the Society for Social Work Research, 7*(3), 527–546. doi:10.1086/687325

Inside Hospice

Lisa Quinn-Lee, PhD, MSSW, LICSW, University of Wisconsin, Eau Claire

Dr. Lisa Quinn-Lee is an associate professor in the social work department at the University of Wisconsin-Eau Claire. She received her bachelor's in social work from the University of Wisconsin-Eau Claire, her master's of science in social work from the University of Wisconsin-Madison, and her doctorate in philosophy from the University of Minnesota. Before teaching full time, she spent many years as a clinical social worker in the areas of grief, loss, and end-of-life care, especially related to children's grief. She has worked as a hospice social worker, grief therapist, and hospital social worker. Now she teaches courses and presents nationally about grief, loss, and end-of-life care, along with conducting research on these topics. Her expertise and connection to this topic come from both professional experience, going back to college, and personal experience, going all the way back to her childhood.

> *You matter because you are you, and you matter to the end of your life. We will do all we can not only to help you die peacefully, but also to live until you die.*
>
> – Dame Cicely Saunders (Clark, 1999, p. 498)

> "*We live in a very peculiar, death-denying society. We isolate both the dying and the old, and it serves a purpose I guess. They are reminders of our own mortality.*" (Death with Dignity: An Inquiry into Related Public Issues, 1972, p. 12). "*We should not institutionalize people. We can give families more help with home care and visiting nurses, giving the families and the patients the spiritual, emotional, and financial help in order to facilitate the final care at home.*" (Death with Dignity: An Inquiry into Related Public Issues, 1972, p. 14).
>
> -Dr. Elisabeth Kübler-Ross

Personal Reflection

I have spent my life around death and dying. I have run straight to it, when most people run away from it. Since there will always be people who have to go through the death and dying process, I would rather them go through it with me (and hospice) than without it. Most people think that I am a little "weird" or "crazy" to dedicate my life to death and dying, grief and loss—and even be enthusiastic and passionate about the work. However, when I talk to or meet other people who work in hospice, they just "get it."

A few of the most emotionally challenging times for me in hospice were when my own family members, friends, and colleagues were patients in the same hospice program in which I worked. Seeing their paper and then electronic charts right in front of my face every day, hearing them talked about in team rounds, hearing their names when colleagues used the phone to arrange or discuss services or visits was extremely difficult. My colleagues were supportive, but it was still difficult. However, it was comforting to me to know that my loved ones were in the best hands of my beloved colleagues. And, it was actually my colleagues who informed me of the deaths, and I was able to share my grief with them.

The other difficult times for me were when I was reminded of my own experiences of death and loss: when a young parent was dying and the children were the same age I was when I experienced parental loss; when young parents were grappling with how to say goodbye to their children and/or their partner/spouse; when a young woman my age was diagnosed with a terminal illness.

The most important thing for me to cope with working in hospice was to do consistent, daily, constant self-reflection before, during, and after my work in hospice. I also made sure that I processed my emotions with my supervisor, my colleagues, my family, my friends, and a therapist. The second most important thing for me to cope was to have rituals in order to say goodbye and remember each patient who died. Some of these rituals were already embedded at my hospice team meetings and memorial services, and some of the rituals I completed on my own. Some of these include singing, saying the name of the person who died, sharing memories, saying goodbye verbally and/or via letter/note, picking out a special rock for each person who died, lighting a candle, taking moments of silence, using a Tibetan singing bowl, being by the water, doing meditation, and breathing.

Every patient and family that I worked with holds a special place in my heart. I cannot drive around my city without being reminded of all of the hospice patients and families I've worked with. I am surrounded by memories. Although I am now a college professor and do not work as a hospice social worker anymore, I teach courses in death and dying and also do research in these areas. When I retire many years from now, I plan to be a hospice volunteer because I miss it.

Brief Introduction to Hospice

When most people hear the word *hospice*, they think death. However, the term *hospice* is from a Latin word meaning "host" or "guest" and dates back to medieval times when it referred to a place of rest and shelter for tired or ill people on a long journey. The name hospice was first applied to the care for dying patients by Dame Cicely Saunders (social worker, physician, nurse, writer) who created the first modern hospice, St. Christopher's Hospice, in London in 1967. Later, she brought her ideas of specialized care for the dying to the United States. In 1974, the first U.S. hospice opened in Connecticut.

Hospice is a philosophy, not a place. This philosophy of caring at the end of life includes quality, compassionate care that involves a team-oriented approach of expert medical care, pain management, and emotional and spiritual support personalized to the patient's wishes and needs. The goal is the relief of symptoms to promote comfort and to improve quality of life. Hospice is not just for the patient; emotional and spiritual support is also extended to the family and loved ones during a patient's illness and 13 months or longer after the patient dies. Although most hospice services are provided in a patient's home, they can be provided wherever patients live, including assisted-living facilities, group homes, and nursing homes. There are also some free-standing hospice facilities.

Hospice is characterized by care provided by an interdisciplinary team, expertise in pain relief and symptom management, treating the family and resident as the unit of care, and focusing on both medical and nonmedical needs such as psychosocial and spiritual well-being (Munn, 2012). Hospice emphasizes quality of life instead of quantity; however, it neither hastens nor postpones death. Hospice focuses on caring instead of curing. The philosophy/hope changes from hope for a cure to hope for living life fully until one dies.

Many hospice programs have added palliative care to their names to reflect the range of care and services they provide, since hospice and palliative care both reflect the same core values and philosophies. Palliative care extends the principles of hospice care to a broader population that can benefit from receiving this type of care earlier in their illness/disease process; patients do not have to have a prognosis of 6 months or less to live. Palliative care is sometimes seen as a transitional step between chronic care and hospice care.

Chronic Care Versus Palliative Care Versus Hospice Care

Chronic diseases are defined broadly as conditions that last 1 year or more and require ongoing medical attention or limit activities of daily living or both; six in 10 adults in the United States have a chronic disease and four in 10 adults have two or more (Centers for Disease Control and Prevention [CDC], 2018). Chronic diseases such as heart disease, cancer, chronic lung disease, stroke, Alzheimer's disease, diabetes, and chronic kidney disease are the leading causes of death and disability in the United States, along with being leading drivers of the nation's annual health care costs (CDC, 2018).

Palliative care is applicable early in the course of illness, in conjunction with other therapies that are intended to prolong life, such as chemotherapy or radiation therapy, and includes those investigations needed to better understand and manage distressing clinical complications (World Health Organization [WHO], 2019).

Palliative care is an approach that improves the quality of life of patients and their families facing the problems associated with life-threatening illness, through the prevention and relief of suffering by means of early identification and impeccable assessment and treatment of pain and other problems, physical, psychosocial and spiritual (WHO, 2019). Palliative care is defined as care, services, or programs with the primary intent of relieving suffering and improving health-related quality of life, including dimensions of physical, psychological/emotional, social, and spiritual well-being (Ahluwalia et al., 2018). Palliative care provides relief from pain and other distressing symptoms, affirms life and regards dying as a normal process, intends neither to hasten or postpone death, integrates the psychological and spiritual aspects of patient care, offers a support system to help patients live as actively as possible until death, offers a support system to help the family cope during the patient's illness and in his or her own bereavement, uses a team approach to address the needs of patients and their families (including bereavement counseling if indicated), will enhance quality of life, and may also positively influence the course of illness (WHO, 2019).

Palliative care extends the principles of hospice care to a broader population that could benefit from receiving this type of care earlier in their illness or disease process (National Hospice and Palliative Care Organization [NHPCO], 2019). To better serve individuals who have advanced illnesses or are terminally ill and their families, many hospice programs encourage access to care earlier in the illness or disease process (NHPCO, 2019). Health care professionals who specialize in hospice and palliative care work closely with staff and volunteers to address all the symptoms of illness, with the aim of promoting comfort and dignity (NHPCO, 2019).

Transitions in disease states occur, from acute to chronic and sometimes chronic to terminal. Palliative care can be thought of as the step or stage before hospice care. Palliative care is provided to someone who has a life-limiting illness but still has more than 6 months to live; hospice care is provide for people who have a prognosis of 6 months or less to live. During palliative care, patients are often still opting to receive curative treatments, whereas in hospice care, patients are no longer seeking curative options. Hospice care focuses only on the final stages of a terminal disease.

Role and Purpose of Hospice

Hospice is specialized and holistic care for patients who are dying and their family members. It focuses on the physical, spiritual, and psychosocial needs of the patient and family. The hospice team places the patient in the middle and develops a plan of care with the patient, family, and team members that meets each patient's individualized needs and wishes. The interdisciplinary team includes the patient's primary physician, the hospice physician/medical director, nurses, social workers, clinicians, home health aides, chaplains, and volunteers. If needed, some other team members may include speech therapists, physical therapists, occupational therapists, music therapists, art therapists, massage therapists, registered dietitians, pharmacists, advanced practice nurses, the patient's personal spiritual/religious care support, and even animal-assisted therapy.

Hospice provides a circle of support for the person who is terminally ill and his or her loved ones. The goal is to help patients to live every day to the fullest by managing their symptoms so that their last months, weeks, days, and hours may be lived with dignity and on their own terms. For each patient and family, the interdisciplinary team writes an individualized care plan that is regularly reviewed and updated as needed to make sure any changes and new goals are in the plan. The patient and family are involved in this care plan so that they receive the care they need and want.

Members of the hospice team/staff make regular visits to assess the patient's and family's needs and to provide regular care and services; the visits are based on the patient and family needs and condition during the course of the illness. The staff is also on call 24 hours per day, 7 days a week. However, the staff does not provide 24-hour care, so there usually needs to be a family member or other person who serves as the primary caregiver for the patient. If a patient or family member need/want 24-hour care, then they have the option of paying for either.

One of the many factors that makes hospice unique in the world of health care is its volunteers. The role of volunteers is so important that it is written into the hospice reimbursement policy and requires that volunteer hours equal at least 5% of the hospice agency's total patient care hours. Volunteering can be a good way to find out if hospice work is for you.

Hospice Services

Services usually include assistance with the emotional and psychosocial aspects of dying, assistance with the spiritual aspects of dying, education about the dying process, education about caring for the patient, managing the patient's pain and symptoms, providing the necessary medications, providing the necessary medical supplies and equipment, assistance with ADLs, medication management and delivery, resources, providing other therapies a needed, arranging short-term inpatient care if pain or other symptoms become too difficult to manage at home, arranging respite if needed, and providing bereavement services to surviving loved ones for 13 months after a patient's death.

The types and frequency of all hospice services varies based on patients' and families' particular choices, needs, and wishes throughout their hospice period. However, the use of hospice services also varies according to multiple other factors, including the patients' and families' cultural attitudes toward death, pain relief, suffering, trust, and so on.

Qualifying for Hospice Services

A patient is eligible for hospice care if he or she has a terminal illness (which is defined as having a prognosis of 6 months or less to live if the disease or illness runs its normal course) and is seeking comfort instead of cure. Patients no longer seek aggressive treatment, but instead choose comfort care. Although many patients have a diagnosis of cancer, hospice services are not limited to people with a cancer diagnosis; people qualify for hospice with any terminal illness, including heart disease, AIDS, ALS, stroke, liver disease, pulmonary disease, dementia, Parkinson's, and so on. Patients must be reassessed for eligibility at regular intervals, but there is no limit on the amount of time a patient can spend under hospice care as long as they continue to be eligible. At any time, patients can change their mind and discharge from hospice.

Hospice Care at Home Versus in a Facility

The use of hospice in long-term care has been growing (Munn, 2012). Hospice services provided at home versus in a facility are similar. When patients live at home, they need to have a main caregiver who takes care of them most of the time. When patients live in a facility, the paid staff at the facility provide most of the care to the patient. Facilities have a signed agreement to collaborate with hospice agencies and staff, and together they write a care plan that includes the roles and responsibilities of each. Although hospice services (wherever they are provided) are covered by the Medicare hospice benefit, the facility costs are not, unless the hospice team deems that respite or inpatient care is needed, as discussed more later.

Some of the documented benefits of hospice for residents and families of residents who die in long-term care settings include the following: There are lower rates of hospitalization and, in part consequently, lower costs of care at the EOL for hospice residents when compared with nonhospice residents; hospice recipients are shown to have better pain management, including use of alternative models of pain relief; and there are higher levels of family satisfaction with care (Munn, 2012).

Funding for Hospice Services

Hospice care is typically paid for by Medicare or Medicaid and most health insurance plans. The hospice benefit payment generally covers visits from the hospice team, medical care and medications related to the life-limiting/terminal illness, medical supplies (bandages, catheters, etc.) and equipment (wheelchairs, commodes, walkers, hospital beds, etc.), and inpatient acute hospice care to manage symptoms (if needed) (Centers for Medicare and Medicaid Services [CMS], 2018). Many hospice programs, through donations and other funding sources, still provide care for people without insurance.

While people are receiving hospice care, they do not give up their existing health insurance/Medicare/Medicaid. These policies continue to cover other health services, treatment, and medical care that are medically necessary but not related to the terminal illness (CMS, 2018). The hospice benefit does not cover room and board in a facility; however, if the hospice team determines that a patient needs short-term inpatient services (for pain or symptom management) or respite care services (up to 5 days) that they arrange, Medicare will cover the stay in the facility (CMS, 2018).

Patients and their families are more satisfied with care when hospice services are provided. Hospice services are highly valued by patients and their families, reduce general health service use and costs, and increase the likelihood of effective pain management and of death not occurring in hospital (Candy, Holman, Leurent, Davis, & Jones, 2011).

Function/Roles of Hospice Clinical Staff

Hospice staff have myriad responsibilities and roles, and here are just a few of the duties of the core team. Hospice physicians and nurses manage the patient's medical care. Home health aides provide assistance with ADLs (activities of daily living like bathing, dressing, feeding, grooming, toileting, ambulating/transferring). Chaplains provide spiritual support. Social workers provide counseling, assist with advance directives, lead family care conferences, facilitate communication, and coordinate resources. All hospice staff advocate for patients' wishes and needs, provide emotional support and crisis intervention, provide education, and help patients and families say goodbye. Social workers and chaplains are often involved with providing bereavement support to families after patients die. Hospice staff should be observant, self-aware, non-judgmental; have empathy, good listening skills, and strong communication skills; be comfortable with silence; and have the courage to be with someone's suffering.

Physical Signs That a Person Is Near Death

Educating patients and family about the dying process is one of the roles of hospice staff. Understanding the process can help them prepare and can help take some of the fear away. The dying process often begins months before the death actually occurs. Although dying is a personal journey that may be unique to each individual, there are changes that take place physically, behaviorally, and psychologically in the journey toward death that are signs that the end of life may be nearing.

Within 1–3 months of death, patients usually start to withdraw and detach and separate from people and the world, eat less, and sleep more. Within 1–2 weeks of death, patients may withdraw more and decrease or stop speaking, become confused, restless, disoriented, sleep most of the time, eat very little or nothing, and have congestion; there may be changes in vital signs (temperature, respiration, blood pressure, pulse), incontinence, increased perspiration, breathing changes (more rapid and labored); skin color may become more pale and blue; and they may see visions (these are usually experiences patients have of seeing and hearing and talking to people who are deceased). Within days or hours of death, patients may be unresponsive and have decreased blood pressure, irregular breathing (including periods of no breathing at all and also sometimes a loud, rattle), a weak pulse, decreased urine output, increased restlessness, cool and "mottled" skin (cold, purple, and blotchy), half-opened/glassy/teary eyes, and a sudden surge of energy. The surge of energy is usually short; family members are often surprised to know that this is a sign that a person is moving toward death, rather than away from death. It is important to note that it is widely believed that hearing is the last sense to go, so dying patients can probably still hear.

Personal Joys and Challenges for a Hospice Worker

The joys of being a hospice worker are that you know you make a difference simply by being there. Dying and grief can be a lonely process for some patients and families, especially since we live in a death-denying culture; friends, family members, neighbors, community members, and so on avoid the dying person and/or his or her family because they are uncomfortable with death. The hospice team helps the patient and family to not feel alone. Hospice workers help make patients comfortable;

talk to them about their memories, fears, and wishes; and build relationships with them and their families that are meaningful for both parties. You support the dying person and their family. You listen. Presence and listening are some of the best gifts we can give each other.

Another joy is helping patients know they still have control over some aspects of their living and their dying. Encouraging patients to have a voice and advocating for choices and needs is rewarding. Helping them to fulfill last wishes is incredibly rewarding and gratifying. Helping provide quality of life and a peaceful, dignified, and loving end to their life's journey is fulfilling.

One of the challenges is saying goodbye. It is often difficult to not get attached to your patients and their families. Since you deal with death daily, there will be a lot of goodbyes. Sometimes the sadness and grief of losing a person while remaining professional can be challenging. However, hospice staff usually find comfort in participating in and attending memorial services, visitations, and funerals. The interdisciplinary teams often have their own rituals of honoring a hospice patient who died, which may include reflecting on the memories they share of the patient and family, allowing for silence, saying the name, lighting a candle, singing, putting a rock in a special place, and so on.

Working With People at the End of Life

Being with hospice patients is like being with other patients—talking to them and treating them like people first and not their terminal illness first. Talk to them with warmth, compassion, caring. Of course, it is important to model to patients and families that talking about death is not only acceptable, but important. But, the entire visit does not have to focus on death. It can focus on life. Most people do not work in hospice until they have some other experience working in health care; therefore, seeing people very ill is usually not a shock or surprise to hospice workers.

Seeing people at the end of their life can be sad and difficult and can sometimes remind you of your own losses. Seeing older people at the end of life is sad, yet it is often easier to accept than younger people, people with young children, and children and teenagers who are dying. It is sometimes more difficult for hospice workers to see people who remind them of themselves or who are at a similar stage in life. However, it is important to accept that death is part of life. If you are not okay with that, then hospice work is not for you.

Many hospice workers will say they feel honored and privileged to serve patients and families during their most vulnerable time and that they often personally gain a lot from the experiences.

Hope

Hospice does not mean that "nothing more can be done" or to "give up hope" when a cure is no longer an option; there is still a great deal that can be done to control symptoms and provide care, comfort, and support. The hope changes from hope of a cure to other areas of hope. Hospice focuses on life and living!

Believe it or not, most hospice workers do not find it depressing to work with terminally ill patients every day. It is sad sometimes, but the job is full of hope, connectedness, joy, laughter, meaning, and every member of the interdisciplinary team gets to know and understand the patients and families because in hospice there is time to do so. It is usually a quieter, slower pace than other types of health care where things may seem frenetic. The staff-to-patient ratio in hospice allows staff and patients to spend time together. Although the days can be busy, it is a different attitude. Hospice staff work fairly independently, so they are able to arrange the hospice visits in a way that they can focus on the needs and wishes of the patient and family.

Self-Care Strategies

Hospice social workers are exposed to multiple stressors, both in their work with dying patients and their families and in functioning as professionals within rapidly changing health care organizations; ongoing exposure to such stressors prompts concern about the emotional and psychological effect working with people who are dying may have on those who do it (Pelon, 2017). Barnett, Martin, and Garza (2018) found that workplace social support and hospice nurses' satisfaction with the balance between their work and family lives play a role in supporting their mental health. Make sure to seek out workplace support and rituals; if these mechanisms are not already in place, then advocate to change this and create them.

Understanding and contemplating how one makes meaning of life events like death, dying, loss of hope, suffering, and healing is essential. Service professions like social work and nursing have always been about working with and for others, and these origins remind us of the importance of the individuals' attention to their own journey as they work with and for others (Jacobs, 2015). Sometimes, a physical space can be helpful in order to assist in contemplation. This may be a place that already exists inside or outside of the workplace space, or it may be something that you need to create or find.

The more important self-care strategy is to be emotionally healthy, which may mean making sure that you take care of your own mental health needs. If you have unfinished business of grief, or you experience your own personal loss during working in hospice, make sure that you are emotionally and psychologically ready to work in hospice or come back to work. The other self-care strategies for working in hospice are similar to those in non-hospice fields: Take all of your vacation time; talk to your fellow team members; seek spiritual support, meditation, exercise, yoga, journaling, reading; find a way to honor your patients; say goodbye; pause; be aware of your body; focus on your breath, get enough sleep, laughter, art, music; have a ritual to separate the end of your work day from the beginning of your personal time, and so on. It is imperative to do self-reflection, especially when you notice that certain patients/situations affect you more, and take action to help yourself.

When all (or almost all) of your patients die, and there are new ones on your caseload to take their place, there may not feel like there is time to grieve. However, taking a moment, a pause, to honor and remember a patient who died is healthy and important in order to move on to serve and care for the new patients.

One former social work student learned several things as an intern working with children who were seriously ill and dying. The first and most important lesson was how to deal with her own emotions and not feel guilty for having good health herself and having healthy children at home. Second, it was crucial for her to be able to have supervision and be able to discuss her feelings about the cases with her supervisor and field instructor. Third, it was also important for her to be able to understand that it was appropriate for me to be sad and also grieve some of the losses of her patients/clients, especially when she had spent so much time with them (Vargas & Ostrander, 2012).

Ways to Improve Hospice Care Delivery

There are ways we need to improve hospice care. We need to continue to provide education to the public about hospice and advocate for earlier admission to hospice, because patients and families benefit more from hospice services when patients are admitted earlier.

We need to learn more about and provide more sensitive and appropriate care and options to multi-cultural populations and populations that have not utilized hospice as high as White, middle-class populations. Learning more about the needs and histories and backgrounds of all cultural and ethnic groups, along with all populations, could greatly enhance the care that is provided as could being culturally sensitive to all needs, including providing services and information in languages other than English, providing care to the underserved and vulnerable populations, meeting the multi-cultural needs and information provision to all populations, recruiting culturally diverse providers, making efforts to educate community spokespeople/leaders in underserved cultural populations, and bringing the message of hospice to their communities. We need to increase services to rural and otherwise less accessible hospice patients and their families, perhaps by considering telecommunications and/or other options.

Recommendations for Clinicians

End-of-life and hospice care challenges the emotional strength of all workers who provide care to dying individuals and their family members; however, these challenges may be amplified for interns who are not only new to the field, but also new to the field of hospice and palliative care. Many of these students are enrolled in programs that lack adequate course offerings in the subject of death and dying (Huff, Weisenfluh, Murphy, & Black, 2006). This lack of formalized instruction leaves students feeling unprepared or underprepared and may require additional support and supervision from field instructors and individual faculty members (Vargas & Ostrander, 2012). If you are not receiving adequate support, education, and supervision, it is your responsibility to advocate for this.

The most important recommendation for new clinicians is to "do your own work," meaning, make sure that you work through your own emotional and mental health needs. If you are not healthy, you cannot help others; in fact, you might even do harm. The second recommendation is to find a way to transition from work to home. With all clients/patients, it is easy to bring work home, but this is especially true for dying patients. Creating some transition between work and home is crucial, and this transition will look different for each person—journaling, exercising, meditating, talking, listening to music, observing silence, various breathing techniques, and so on. A third recommendation is to seek and utilize supervision frequently. Fourth, maintain consistent boundaries. When working with people who are dying (and their family members), especially in the home setting, sometimes the boundaries and expectations can get blurred. Fifth, practice good self-care, which is different for each person. Make sure that you remember to live your life, as you will be reminded every day that death is a part of life and that life is ephemeral.

Reflection Questions

1. What unresolved grief do you have that may interfere with clinical work?
2. What will you do and how will you cope with working with a patient who reminds you of yourself or someone close to you?

3. What will you say to a patient who says, "Why is this happening to me?"
4. What are your greatest fears about dying? Why? Most hospice workers are not anxious about death. Why do you think this is?
5. Medical marijuana for the dying is becoming legalized in more states, and the majority of Americans think it should be legalized. What are your own personal beliefs about this? If it is legal in your state, how will you respond to a patient if he or she asks you about this option? If it is not legal in your state, how will you respond to a patient who asks about this option?

References

Ahluwalia, S. C., Chen, C., Raaen, L., Motala, A., Walling, A. M., Chamberlin, C., ... & Hempel, S. (2018). A systematic review in support of the National Consensus Project Clinical practice guidelines for quality palliative care fourth edition. *Journal of Pain and Symptom Management, 56*(6), 831–870. doi:10.1016/j.jpainsymman.2018.09.008

Barnett, M., Martin, K., & Garza, C. (2018). Satisfaction with work-family balance mediates the relationship between workplace social support and depression among hospice nurses. *Journal of Nursing Scholarship, 51*(2), 187–194. doi:10.1111/jnu.12451

Candy, B., Holman, A., Leurent, B., Davis, A., & Jones, S. (2011). Hospice care delivered at home, in nursing homes and in dedicated hospice facilities: A systematic review of quantitative and qualitative evidence. *International Journal of Nursing Studies, 48*(1), 121–133. doi:10.1016/j.ijnurstu.2010.08.003

Centers for Disease Control and Prevention (CDC). (2018, November 19). About chronic diseases. Retrieved from https://www.cdc.gov/chronicdisease/about/index.htm

Centers for Medicare and Medicaid Services (CMS). (2018, March). *Medicare hospice benefits*. Retrieved from https://www.medicare.gov/pubs/pdf/02154-medicare-hospice-benefits.pdf

Clark, D. (1999). An annotated bibliography of the publications of Cicely Saunders – 2: 1968–77. *Palliative Medicine, 13*(6), 485–501. https://doi.org/10.1191/026921699677249209

Death with Dignity: An Inquiry into Related Public Issues: Hearings before the Special Committee on Aging, United States Senate, 92nd Cong. 10–22 (1972) (Testimony of Dr. Elisabeth Kübler-Ross). Retrieved from https://www.aging.senate.gov/imo/media/doc/publications/871972.pdf

Huff, M., Weisenfluh, S., Murphy, M., & Black, P. (2006). End-of-life care and social work education: What do students need to know? *Journal of Gerontological Social Work, 48*(1–2), 219–231.

Jacobs, C. (2015). Contemplative spaces in social work practice. *Journal of Pain and Symptom Management, 49*(1), 151–155. doi:10.1016/j.jpainsymman.2014.10.004

Katz, R. S., & Johnson, T.A. (Eds.) (2016). *When professionals weep: Emotional and countertransference responses in end-of-life care* (2nd ed.). New York, NY: Routledge.

Munn, J. (2012). Telling the story: Perceptions of hospice in long-term care. *American Journal of Hospice & Palliative Care, 29*(3), 201–209. doi:10.1177/1049909111421340

National Hospice and Palliative Care Organization (NHPCO). (2019). Retrieved from https://www.nhpco.org/nhpco-0

Pelon, S. (2017). Compassion fatigue and compassion satisfaction in hospice social work. *Journal of Social Work in End-of-Life & Palliative Care, 13*(2–3), 134–150. doi:10.1080/15524256.2017.1314232

Scheffey, C., Kestenbaum, G., Wachterman, M.W., Connor, S. R., Fine, P. G., Davis, M. S., & Muir, J. C. (2014). Clinic-based outpatient palliative care before hospice is associated with longer hospice length of service. *Journal of Pain and Symptom Management, 48*(4), 532–539. doi:10.1016/j.jpainsymman.2013.10.017

Vargas, M., & Ostrander, N. (2012). Learning to be: Reflections of a social work student on a pediatric hospice internship. *Journal of Social Work in End-Of-Life & Palliative Care, 8*(4), 281–285. doi:10.1080/15524256.2012.732443

World Health Organization (WHO). (2019). *WHO definition of palliative care.* Retrieved from https://www.who.int/cancer/palliative/definition/en/

Credits

CHAPTER FIVE

Discussion and Experiential Exercises for the Classroom

In this chapter, experienced clinicians and educators share best-practice techniques, case studies for analysis, and experiential exercises for the classroom. Some authors have also chosen to share how their personal grief impacted their development of these exercises. These may be adapted for individual or group educational instruction.

Tools #1–4

Kalpana Parekh, LCSW, Wellness Around the World, LLC, Westfield, New Jersey

FIGURE 5.1 Kalpana Parekh

Kalpana is a psychotherapist, personal and executive coach, speaker, author, and singer whose life purpose is bringing light and inspiration into the world. She is the Founder of Wellness Around the World, LLC, an international practice whose mission is to inspire people and empower them with the tools they need to live flourishing lives. Author of "Light The Way!," a chapter in *Spiritual Leaders* (2017) and "Hold On To The Paperclip," a chapter in *The Empowerment Manual* (2015), Kalpana earned her MSW from Columbia University in New York City, holds certificates in applied positive psychology, music therapy, yoga instruction, and is a licensed Heal Your Life® teacher. Kalpana can be reached at www.wellnessaroundworld.com or e-mail: wellness1027@gmail.com

Personal Introduction

FIGURE 5.2. My beloved grandmother, Jayalaxmi R. Daftary (1953)

When I was 11 years old, my grandmother taught me that sooner or later, life would bring difficulties, and when it did, I should not fall apart, but find a way to stand up and forge a path ahead. I write this chapter in memory of my grandmother, on the anniversary of the auspicious day when she transitioned from this life to the next. She was my spiritual and life mentor, and, along with my uncle and my music teacher, a second father, made me who I am today. The tools they passed on to me allowed me to face life's challenges with resilience. After losing numerous family members starting in my adolescence through the next 2 decades, it was my mentors' wisdom that provided me with the foundation to overcome the shock and pain of each loss and eventually grow and find new meaning. They exposed me to yoga and other philosophical traditions of the world that provided meaning, comfort, and perspective and served as a foundation and catalyst for my becoming a psychotherapist.

After providing trauma counseling to hundreds of 9/11 survivors in New York City and hearing countless accounts of what people witnessed on that day, this solid foundation not only protected me from vicarious trauma, but also allowed me to grow personally and professionally. Shortly after completing my study of positive psychology, I went through personal tragedy that shook me to my core, and my own resilience was tested. I received news, just 3 hours apart on the same day, that both my grandmother and my music teacher had been diagnosed with end-stage cancer. This was one of the most devastating days of my life, learning that two people fundamental to my development would no longer be physically present within a few months. Shortly after this news, my third mentor, my uncle, suffered a massive stroke and fell into a coma, with little to no chance of survival. Whereas I was not affected by vicarious trauma during 9/11, I *was* impacted by the anticipatory grief of losing all my mentors at the same time.

Anticipatory grief is a range of intensified emotional responses that can be experienced prior to a loss of function, identity, or impending death (Shore, Gelber, Koch, & Sower, 2016). It is not only experienced by the terminally ill person, but also by friends, family, and caregivers. After an initial period of shock, disbelief, denial, deep sadness and anger, I knew that *I had to make a choice to cope.* Otherwise, my clinical work would have been impacted. I actively used many tools of resilience that helped me to cope during this period of anticipatory grieving, gradually moving from a place of deep despair and questioning of the world as I knew it to healing, growth, and a renewed sense of meaning.

I encourage all my clients to (a) practice self-care that includes physical movement, medical attentiveness, balanced eating, and rest; and (b) carve out a daily grieving period—a time in their day dedicated to thinking about their loved one, processing what is going on, and engaging in contemplation, meditation, releasing, self-expression, and/or reaching out to a support system. Clinical instructors in grief and loss can share the following *tools for coping with anticipatory grief* with beginning clinical students.

Tool #1: Control/No Control

This is a tool I created in 2001, when working with newly diagnosed HIV-positive patients, as they faced a grim diagnosis and prognosis.

Have the client draw a circle in the middle of an 8.5" × 11" sheet of paper (a paper of any size may be used, including a flipchart or white board), and then draw a line through the middle of the circle, dividing it into two equal halves. Label one half of the circle "Control" and the other half "No Control." Encourage your clients to consider what aspects of the circumstance they are facing that are within their control. They can draw a line from inside the control zone to the blank space outside the circle and write down each individual factor. Clients can continue to draw as many lines as they would like, from the "Control" zone to the outside of the circle, in order to note down other factors under their control. Repeat the same for the "No Control" zone.

The following is an example of a diagram that a hypothetical client might create, whose family member was recently diagnosed with advanced stage cancer and given 3 to 6 months to live.

"Control" zone: Finding a good doctor for treatment, researching holistic health remedies for palliative care, focusing thoughts on enjoying the present with them, etc.

"No Control" zone: The diagnosis, feelings of sadness that overcomes me, other negative feelings that I experience, how other people in my family react to the diagnosis, etc.

Explain to the client that the "Control" zone and "No Control" zone may not be 50–50. It may look more like 80% ("No Control") and 20% ("Control"), or any other percentage division. The key point is that no matter how small the control zone may be, it is imperative that clients maintain their mental and physical focus in this empowering zone.

Encourage clients to redirect their attention and focus on those things over which they have control, and actively work on them. This shift in attention from what cannot be helped to what can be helped can provide a newfound sense of purpose and energy. We have a natural tendency to focus on those things over which we have no control, but doing this is like trying to punch a wall of rock with our fist and expecting to make a dent. What is uncontrollable is immovable. A survivor of the Holocaust, Dr. Viktor Frankl (1984) once said that "[e]verything can be taken from a man but one thing: the last of the human freedoms—to choose one›s attitude in any given set of circumstances, to choose one's own way" (p. 86). I often share Dr. Frankl's experience and ideas with my clients to illustrate the point that even if everything has been taken from us, one thing that cannot be taken is our right to choose how we respond to a situation. Taking control of what we choose to focus on is empowering and life-enhancing. Some ideas in the control zone might be the following:

1. Saying what needs to be said to a loved one, or saying what one wants to say
2. Educating oneself about what to expect regarding the illness and its progression
3. Discussing end-of-life wishes, legal and financial matters
4. Joining a support group
5. Creating enjoyable moments with a loved one
6. Continuing to live one's life and staying engaged in activities/interests

Clients may ask how to handle their no control zone. Explain that any time they catch their thoughts focusing on, or lingering in, the no control zone, they can practice *redirecting their focus* from what they cannot control to what they can, from accepting what they cannot change to focusing on what they can. We become aware that we are focusing on the no control zone when we are predominantly feeling more helpless, hopeless, depressed, overwhelmed, and other disempowering emotions. The client can learn to recognize these as friendly signs that it is time to redirect focus. Once clients are aware that those feelings are arising, they might try one of the following tips for redirecting focus:

1. Observe the feelings that are arising as a result of feeling no control. Name the feeling and identify in which part of the body you feel it. Simply observe the feelings and the effect they are having on you, as a witness, without judging the feelings. This application of mindfulness to your emotions can help you to identify less with them, remembering you are the witness of these emotions. (e.g., "The feeling of helplessness is passing through my body and mind" versus "I am helpless" or "I feel helpless").
2. Visualize the control/no control pie in your mind's eye. Visualize yourself smack in the middle of the no control zone. Visualize this zone as an area that is a dead-end or a bottomless pit. After remembering this is the zone you are currently in, visualize yourself voluntarily bringing yourself out of this zone, and back into your zone of control, a place where there are possibilities and an opportunity for empowerment.
3. Visualize placing all the contents of the no control zone into a box that you now surrender to something or someone you believe in. This could be a higher power, the universe, a personal deity, a wise elder, or an angel, for example. Mentally surrender the box of the no control zone to that power, asking for that power to do its job (one that is beyond your job description), while you do your job. Remind yourself that the no control zone is a zone of no entry for you.

Meditation exercises that guide clients in becoming a witness to physical and emotional pain can be helpful in working through the multi-dimensional impact that no control factors can have on clients.

Classroom instruction: Present two case studies in anticipatory grief (following are two example case studies) and have students practice the control/no control tool for each case study. The instructor can divide the students into pairs (with one person as therapist and other as client). Alternatively, break the class into groups of three or more students to brainstorm together. For the pair or group's case study, the following are some possible discussion questions:

1. What ideas did you come up with for the control and no control zones?
2. Are there any overlaps between pairs or groups? Any differences? What accounts for the differences? Do some people see what is within their control differently?
3. How did clients in the exercise respond? Was it challenging for them to come up with what they could control?
4. What could you, as the therapist, be prepared to discuss if the client cannot come up with ideas for what is under his or her control?
5. What are potential challenges you foresee with this exercise and how might you mitigate them?

Sample Case Study 1: Samina

Samina is a 42-year-old mother of three who was recently diagnosed with stage 4 metastatic lung cancer and given a maximum of 6 months to live. Samina has a large, extended family by her side, who take turns in helping with her medical care. Samina has been a stay-at-home mother for the past 15 years and has become more and more isolated with time. She has friends but has not kept in regular touch with any of them, focusing more time on taking care of her family. She was generally quite healthy, but medical tests started a few months after she told her doctor that she had been having frequent migraine headaches. In the prime of her life, the diagnosis devastated her and her family.

You are a social worker part of a collaborative treatment team for patients in a large cancer hospital, and have been assigned Samina as a new patient. You met with her once for an intake session, during which you discovered Samina's feelings of helplessness and hopelessness. You will now be meeting with her again for the second session. You were recently exposed to the control/no control tool. Discuss with your group how you might utilize this tool in your work with Samina.

Sample Case Study 2: Nelson

Nelson is a self-referred client in your private practice. He is a 35-year-old married man whose father was diagnosed with ALS a year ago and told at the time that he would likely have 2 years to live. Nelson has been holding on to hope that his father will beat the odds, but over the past year, he has watched his father's condition deteriorate rapidly and decided to seek counseling when his wife suggested that he needs it. He reports feeling depressed, hopeless, and overwhelmed with watching his father "disappear before [his] eyes." He accompanies his father to medical appointments and tries to spend as much time with him as possible, but finds it difficult to balance his high-powered marketing career with his life with his wife and two young children and his father. Nelson's mother divorced his father when Nelson was just a teenager, and she has not been involved in his life ever since. Nelson feels a sense of guilt for not being able to be with his father 24/7 and for not being able to "do anything for him." You were recently exposed to the control/no control tool. Discuss with your group how you might utilize this tool in your work with Nelson.

Tool #2: End-of-Life Visualization Exercise

This can be a useful tool for clients whose loved ones are actively dying and who are feeling confused, overwhelmed, and unclear about what to do or how to spend the remaining time with their loved one. It can help clients to gain clarity about how they want to spend their time, help to minimize regret, and help with overcoming obstacles that mixed emotions can present. Ask your client if he or she would be comfortable with you guiding him or her through the exercise during your session. *After practicing this visualization exercise on myself, I was clear about how I wanted to spend my time with my loved ones, bringing about a sense of peace within me and also them.*

End-of-Life Visualization Script

*Please note that this visualization exercise could potentially trigger emotional responses that may be difficult for some people to handle, depending on their personal history. It is advisable for the student or client to be made aware ahead of time of the content of the exercise, so that they can choose whether they want to participate, or participate with a robust support system in place.

> Select a time of day and environment in which you can experience some peace and calm. If it helps to put on some soft, soothing music, you may do that. Then, lie down, or sit in a comfortable position, with your eyes closed. Take a deep, cleansing breath. Continue to do this for the next few moments. Slowly scan your entire body from your toes to the crown of your head and notice any areas of tension. With each exhalation, imagine that the tension is slowly leaving your body and allowing you to settle deeper and deeper into your comfortable position. When you are ready to start visualizing, take a journey into the future, through your life, toward the very end of your life. Imagine that you are in your last days and looking back on your life in a very contented way. Your life has had both ups and downs. In some places, there have been dark moments, in other places, bright moments, and every kind of experience in between. Imagine yourself at the end of your life having navigated all of your life's ups and downs successfully, in a way that brings you contentment. Think back to your loved one (who is currently not well). Imagine that you spent time with him or her before he or she transitioned to the next realm, in a way that brought you peace of mind. What did it look like? (Pause) What did you do with them? (Pause) How did you spend your time with them? (Pause) What did you say to them? (Pause) Was there anything to be forgiven or let go of? (Pause) Were there any questions you asked? (Pause) If he or she was unable to communicate or speak, in which ways did you choose to communicate? (Pause) How did you show up when with him or her? (Pause) What attitude, spirit, and body language did you choose to bring to him or her? (Pause) What gift did you give to him or her in the form of your time, words, body language, actions, or your spirit? (Pause) Now, imagine that all of the things you did for and with your loved one are now traveling back in time with you to the present. Your mission now is to spend time with your loved one in the way that you have imagined would be best.

After the exercise is complete, you can ask the following questions:

1. What was it like to do this exercise?
2. Were you able to think about how you want to spend time with your loved one? Can you articulate this? Or, did you have difficulty coming up with these ideas?
3. If you had difficulty visualizing this, are you okay with the way you are spending time with them now? Would you like to do anything differently? Or, are you at peace with it? *Educate the client that this is a process and that clarity may come with time and not necessarily in one session. The exercise can be repeated as often as desired or needed.*

Classroom instruction: Have students pair up. One can be client and the other can serve as the therapist. Have the therapist practice introducing the exercise, guiding the client through it and discussing it after the exercise. Students can switch roles, time permitting. Please see previous warning and discuss the exercise with students prior to using it in the classroom.

Tool #3: Savoring

Savoring can be actively practiced in the present moment and applied to the present, past, and even the future. *I took a long video interview of my grandmother, asking her questions about her life, views on wisdom and happiness, and life philosophy. Not only is this video a treasured memory of her, but it fully engaged her, giving her a sense of fulfillment in being able to share her life with the three generations below her.*

Encourage your client to think of ways he or she would like to savor his or her time with his or her loved one in the present moment. The previous visualization exercise may help with clarifying this. Some ideas for savoring are (a) having a meaningful conversation with questions and topics that clients want to discuss with their loved ones, (b) reminiscing, (c) looking at photographs or watching videos of happy memories, (d) taking an interview of the loved one, (e) playing a game, (f) watching movies or shows together, (g) playing music for them, (h) if possible, going to a park or serene place in nature together, or a favorite place of the loved one, (i) giving a meaningful gift to the loved one, and (j) working on creating something together. There are countless other ways, and ideas can be brainstormed with the client, with the goal of helping the client create happy memories with his or her loved one. Clients can be encouraged to really tune into their five senses and be in the moment when with their loved one, paying attention to what they see, smell, touch, hear, and even taste. They can be encouraged to take mental snapshots of these moments so that they can go back to them in their mind at a later time and continue to savor these moments.

Some clients may not have a good relationship with the person who is dying. A strained relationship with someone who is dying may bring up many complex emotions, including anger, guilt, confusion, and numbness, along with sadness, disbelief, and shock. The social worker can work with clients to explore how they would like to look back on this time with their relative or friend. Even if their relationship is currently or historically strained, they can give thought to what they may have liked to have done with them or things they wished they had been able to say in the past if their relationship had been different. In thinking about this, they can take action steps to realize this vision. The social worker can also work with the client to explore other possibilities about the person: Are there things they would like to know about the person? Memories they would like to share? Are there lessons they feel they could learn from the person, setting aside their personal differences? The control/no control tool can help here as well. Clients can try to separate out the past with the person (no control), and focus on the present as their control zone. If they are able to shift their attention to the present moment and create a more open mind about the possibilities with the person who is dying, they may be able to engage in a few or many of the suggestions listed.

Tool #4: Therapeutic Writing Exercises

The following are seven therapeutic writing exercises that may help clients release emotion, gain perspective, experience gratitude, and/or find meaning. Clients who indicate they are not "writers" are the best candidates for stream of consciousness exercises. These exercises encourage them to write whatever is on their mind without editing or judgment.

> **Stream of consciousness:** Set a timer for 5 minutes and have clients write whatever is on their mind in the moment. There is no editing, proofreading, or need for "perfect" grammar or content. This is simply a place for them to release what is on their mind and in their heart onto paper, or the computer screen, in a confidential place. This exercise can be repeated as needed.

Guiding prompt: Write whatever is on your mind right now for the next 5 minutes. An example of the first few sentences might be "I am supposed to write what is on my mind right now … I have no idea what is on my mind. How do I write about that? Well, I'll do the best I can … I guess what's on my mind right now is that I feel awful about what has happened to my aunt."

Lessons learned: Write a list of things they have learned from their loved one. This can also be done in prose style. If this is a conflicted relationship, think of what knowing this person has taught them about life or about how not to live.

Guiding questions: What are some of the most important lessons (big or small) that I have learned from my loved one? What has their life taught me? What have I learned about how to live, or even, how not to live?

Gratitude: Write a letter of gratitude to their loved one for how they have touched their life, or what an example they have been. The client may hand deliver or mail it to their loved one, read it to him or her, or choose not to send it.

Guiding prompt: "Dear XYZ relative/friend, I am grateful to you for …"

General letter: This exercise is a variation on #3. The client may want to write a letter to his or her loved one about any topic, not focused on gratitude only.

Guiding prompt: "Dear XYZ, I can't believe that a year from now, you may not be physically here anymore … just the other day I was remembering the time when we enjoyed that summer picnic in Provence …"

Write about the pain: Write a stream of consciousness about their pain or write a letter to their pain. They can set a timer for this exercise for up to 20 minutes, so as to contain the amount of time they are writing about something painful, and this can be repeated daily for 4 consecutive days (Pennebaker & Chung, 267).

Guiding prompt: "Dear Unbearable Pain, You are a force to reckon with … I cannot get a handle on you right now. You are taking over my life."

Write a story or article about loved one: Invite the client to write a story about his or her loved one in any way he or she chooses, to be shared with his or her loved one, others in his or her life, or not to be shared. Some may choose to write an article that is published in a magazine or newspaper, or self-published.

Finding new meaning: Create a mind map of words and phrases that they associated with their loved one. These could be personal qualities or traits, interests or hobbies, work they do in the world, causes they work on, or habits. Ask clients if there is something from this list that they would like to carry forward into the future to keep their loved one's work alive. Or, there may be a personality trait of theirs that they would like to work on developing. Let clients write about how they would like to keep their loved one's memory alive.

Sample Mind Map

These tools may provide clients who are experiencing anticipatory grief with the opportunity to release their emotions, gain clarity about how they would like to spend their remaining time on Earth or with their loved one, minimize regret, gain perspective and meaning, and ultimately grow through the experience of facing impending loss.

References

Frankl, V. E. (1984). *Man's search for meaning: An introduction to logotherapy.* New York, NY: Simon & Schuster.

Pennebaker, J., & Chung, C. (2007). Expressive writing, emotional upheavals, and health. In H. S. Friedman & R. C. Silver (Eds.), *Foundations of health psychology* (pp. 263–284). New York, NY: Oxford University Press.

Shore, J. C., Gelber, M. W., Koch, L. M. & Sower, E. (2016). Anticipatory grief: An evidence-based approach. *Journal of Hospice and Palliative Nursing, 18*(1), 15–19.

Tool #5: Life-Mapping: An Adaptation for Self-Reflection on Mortality Awareness

Abigail Nathanson, MSW, LCSW, APHHSW-C, ACS, New York University and Meredith Ruden, DSW, LCSW, APHSW-C, ACS, Feather Foundation & New York University, New York

FIGURE 5.3. Abigail Nathanson

Abigail Nathanson is a clinical social worker and doctoral candidate at New York University, specializing in palliative care and bereavement. She teaches grief, loss and bereavement and developed the curriculum for and teaches the Clinical Practice with Chronic and Life-Limiting Illness class in the Master of Social Work program at New York University. She has extensive experience in healthcare social work, including leadership and program development positions in hospice and other nonprofit social service agencies. She received her MSW from New York University and her bachelor of arts in psychology from the University of North Carolina at Chapel Hill. She has lectured and presented at conferences on the national level and been published in the *Journal of Social Work in Palliative and End-of-Life Care*. She has received post-graduate certificates in palliative and end-of-life care, as well as in clinical supervision, and has national designations as an approved clinical supervisor (ACS) and advanced hospice palliative social worker, certified (AHPSW-C).

FIGURE 5.4. Meredith Ruden

Dr. Meredith Ruden specializes in oncology social work, palliative car,e and end-of-life counseling. She received her master's and doctorate of social work at New York University (NYU), and bachelor's of art at Brown University. She has received advanced training in end-of-life studies, spiritually integrated psychotherapy, and psychodynamic psychotherapy. She currently acts as an adjunct at NYU and Columbia University, teaching grief, loss, and bereavement and research courses. She also serves as executive director at the Feather Foundation, a nonprofit she founded that supports parents who have cancer. Previously, she counseled patients at Mt. Sinai Hospital and supervised social workers and students in that capacity. Dr. Ruden has presented in national hospice and palliative conferences on hope at end of life and therapeutic writing for physically ill people.

Introduction

Preparing students to work in bereavement means helping them navigate the intersection of their own death anxiety with a death-avoidant society (McClatchey & King, 2015). Death anxiety can be understood as more than just a fear of death; it also encompasses the degree to which a person is aware of, or anticipating, the reality of dying (Lehto & Stein, 2009). It can be understood as having both conscious and unconscious elements, and has a substantial impact on clinical grief work.

Life-mapping is a technique that helps people construct a meaningful narrative of major events in their lives and is used in many non-clinical contexts for self-reflective practice. In professional death education, life-mapping can be an important tool in encouraging reflection of otherwise unconscious clinician death anxiety. It can help "students examine significant events in their lives in terms of grief, loss, and transitions" (Doughty, Horn, Crews & Harrowood, 2013, p. 77). The adaptation presented combines several commonly used approaches to grief-related life-mapping and proposes a useful clinical guide and a suggested script appropriate for an academic setting. It was developed by Abigail Nathanson in her work teaching grief, loss, and bereavement in an MSW program.

This exercise combines *individual* and *group* process. It involves a substantial preparation phase, followed by intervention and reflective group discussion. The preparatory phase aims to induce a mindful and motivated approach toward the exercise to follow. It also establishes group rules and expectations so that the students can better observe and explore their own reactions. The intervention and group process phases build awareness of students' own death anxiety and comfort in discussion of death, and engenders greater empathy toward both dying patients and grieving friends and relatives. *This exercise takes approximately 30 minutes.*

Preparation

A. *Rationale*: A major aim at this stage is to promote buy in, conveying the importance of self-reflection on thoughts and feelings related to mortality. A rationale for the exercise is provided through introduction to the listed concepts. First, a brief summary of Becker's (1973) generative death anxiety theory and its consequences are shared. It is also explained that when individuals defend against such painful material, it can result in psychic numbing, which leaves them both preoccupied with that material and struggling to connect emotionally overall (Leichty, 2000). Repressed death anxiety and lack of appropriate education about it can result in clinicians being unfamiliar with, and therefore ill-equipped to face, death and dying in their clients (McClatchey & King, 2015). On a professional level, the impact of unprocessed death anxiety on clinicians is outlined as (a) seeing patients as a sick "other": "They're sick, not me"; (b) approaching dying patients with false assurances as part of a "messianic reaction" to avoid own feelings of powerlessness: "I can save them!" (Liechty, 2000); and (c) burnout or lack of empathic attunement (Cacciatore, Thieleman, Killian & Tavasolli, 2015). The benefits of death anxiety awareness on professional development, such as greater empathic attunement, maintaining emotional engagement in work, and personal reflection on one's own life meaning, are explicitly stated.

B. *Group expectations*: The aim of this exercise is to help students be present to their own thoughts, feelings, and reactions. Students are told that this exercise is intended to help them to increase their awareness of their own mortality and they are asked to be sensitive to maintaining an environment that is conducive to this kind of work for other students. The instructor notes that it may elicit unexpected or strong emotions such as sadness, anger, or fear; a lack of strong response is also normalized. They are encouraged to participate in the written portion of the exercise and are informed that the decision to share their work and reaction to it is optional. Students are told that noticing when they feel discomfort and choosing not to participate is an important reflective exercise, too.
C. *Mindfulness*: Students are asked to remove all objects from their desk and take out a piece of paper and pen. They are asked not to leave their desk throughout the exercise and to notice their body (posture, changes, levels of tension, etc.) and awareness of the environment as indicators to their own reactions. Do they find the urge to fidget, look out the window, reach for phones, drink water? Do they feel any tension or changes in their body? How does it feel to sit with these feelings? The instructor encourages students to stay present with their experience and avoid distracting behaviors or chatting with classmates.

Intervention

After each question, the instructor pauses to allow for students to become more attuned to their internal dialogue about the exercise, their decisions, and their reactions. Some students may share their experiences without prompting. For others, open-ended questions should be posed by the instructor to invite "noticing" of student thoughts about own mortality and death.

Part one: Students are asked to turn a piece of paper sideways and draw a straight line across the middle, marked by two vertical tick marks at either end. The instructor says, "The line to the left is the date of your birth. The line on the right is the date of your death," notes that their entire life happens along this line, and encourages them to reflect on the finiteness of their life and how it feels to see it on paper.

Part two: Then, the instructor continues: "Put an X on the line for where you think you are now." The instructor asks them to reflect on how it felt to be asked to do this, how it felt to choose and write it down, how they chose, and what it feels like looking at it afterward. Were there struggles, a sense of superstitious power? Did they decide intellectually based on normative statistics, emotionally based on what they wanted to see, or based on family legacy? How does it feel to look at the life lived, and the rest of their lives? The instructor notes that not everyone has a strong reaction to the first two parts of the exercise and asks students to check in on feelings, bodily sensations, thoughts, and the general energy of the room, and begins the third part.

Part three: The instructor states, "Now, look at your X for where you are now and the space between now and the date of your death. You will likely experience many losses between now and the date of your death. Put three more marks down between now and your death, representing three losses you anticipate experiencing, and write down what they are." Processing questions after this part can include "How did it feel to be asked to do this? How did you decide what losses to include, and where? Were there losses that you felt unable to put on paper? Were all losses deaths? How does it feel to look at them now? What was it like to contemplate your own mortality versus the loss of others? What do they notice differently in their bodies and in the energy of the room?"

Discussion

The intervention proceeds with a guided discussion to reflect on awareness of the defense against one's own mortality and death anxiety. The instructor can say, "Think about how aware you were of these feelings 20 minutes ago, when the idea of your own death was just intellectual. Now, without any specific knowledge of your own health or physical vulnerabilities, many of you are feeling it more acutely, and you can see how hidden we keep these feelings on a daily basis. Note what it feels like over the next several hours as this feeling becomes less salient and we begin to defend against it again, and notice your energy levels and desires for proximity and connections. Take a few moments to write how you're feeling now, and when you go back later and re-read it, notice if it still resonates in the same way."

Then, the discussion is intentionally directed toward theory and practice and away from the self: What happens when our clients' health status (i.e., a new diagnosis or life-threatening prognosis) causes them to quickly and unexpectedly be faced with their own mortality? How can you use this knowledge of defensive functioning around death anxiety to manage your own feelings of empathic attunement and the needs of your clients?

Wrap-Up and Reintegration

At the close of this exercise, a review of major learning points and objectives is provided. Students are encouraged to get out of their seats and physically move and stretch their bodies, in order to shift the energy before moving to didactic instruction, which is explained. It is not recommended to do this at the end of class when students would be leaving with heavily charged material.

References

Becker, E. (1973). *The denial of death*. New York, NY: Free Press.

Cacciatore, J., Thieleman, K., Killian, M., & Tavasolli, K. (2015). Braving human suffering: Death education and its relationship to empathy and mindfulness. *Social Work Education, 34*(1), 91–109. doi:10.1080/02615479.2014.940890

Doughty Horn, E. A., Crews, J. A., & Harrawood, L. K. (2013). Grief and loss education: Recommendations for curricular inclusion. *Counselor Education & Supervision, 52*(1), 70–80. doi:10.1002/j.1556-6978.2013.00029.x

Lehto, R. H., & Stein, K. F. (2009). Death anxiety: An analysis of an evolving concept. *Research and Theory for Nursing Practice: An International Journal, 23*(1), 23–41.

Liechty, D. (2000). Touching mortality, touching strength: Clinical work with dying patients. *Journal of Religion and Health, 39*(3), 247–258.

McClatchey, I. S., & King, S. (2015). The impact of death education on fear of death and death anxiety among human services students. *OMEGA: Journal of Death and Dying, 71*(4), 343–361. doi:10.1177/0030222815572606

Tool #6: Speaking Your Truth: Using Creative Writing to Process Grief and Negotiate Self-Disclosure in Trauma-Informed Care

Lizzie McAdam, MA, RDT, LCAT, Hetrick-Martin Institute, New York City, New York

FIGURE 5.5. Lizzie McAdam

Lizzie McAdam, MA, RDT, LCAT is a drama therapist, educational consultant, and adjunct faculty member at New York University. She is also currently the assistant director of counseling at the Hetrick-Martin Institute supporting LGBTQ+ youth. Prior to that she was the associate director of the ALIVE Program at the Post Traumatic Stress Center in New Haven, Conneticut, providing trauma-centered drama therapy services in both clinical and public school settings. As a former educator turned drama therapist, she works with students to connect their lived experience to their learning process. Lizzie can be reached at em1726@nyu.edu

Personal Case Study

Last year, I lost my mother suddenly, primarily due to hypoglycemia caused by her diabetes, but also influenced by alcohol addiction. At the time of the loss, I was running a group for adolescents focused around telling their stories of loss, toxic stress, and trauma. As a drama therapist doing trauma-informed work in schools, this group in particular was focused not only on trauma-informed embodied work, but also on activism and creating spaces of community and connection (Boal, 1993; Sajnani, 2009; Sajnani, Jewers-Dailley, Brillante, Puglisi, J., & Johnson, 2014). Loss was a common theme in the group, and one of the norms of the group was that the co-facilitators shared from their own lives with boundaries as a way to model strength and overcoming struggle. This is where I got stuck. When my mother passed, I did not know how to reenter the group, much less support my students as a therapist.

My mom and I always had a very close, loving but complicated relationship. I grew up going to work with my mom, a dance and movement therapist who worked primarily with adults with multiple disabilities. Times when I helped my mom run groups were my favorite; we could communicate seamlessly, and I was skilled at anticipating her needs before she spoke them out loud. We were close. We made a good team.

The loss of my mother was both sudden and gradual at the same time. At 63 years old, no one expected her to die, much less from the diabetes she had been managing well for many years. Hers was a spirit that worked hard to be joyful, loving, and kind. Her passing occurred, however, during a time of intense hardship. Due to significant multiple losses in our family, my mom struggled with taking care of herself, using alcohol to cope, which made things worse. The mother I knew faded from view. Her passing felt like a shock wave in our family, and my assumptive world shattered (Gerrish, Dyck, & Marsh, 2009). I experienced waves of anxiety often correlated with grief and strong attachment (Xu, Fu, He, Schoebi, & Wang, 2015). I craved spaces where I still felt attached to her, where I could feel close to her even when it caused me pain, a common part of early grief (Kosminsky & Jordan, 2016).

Eventually, as I prepared to return to work, I turned to *creative writing and poetry* as a way to begin processing this loss. As a therapist, a parentified child, and an adult child of an alcoholic, I can support others with ease, but learning to support myself has been a journey. This was especially true when facing sudden loss. This struggle is understandable, but dangerous if not addressed proactively. Creative writing became the conduit that allowed me to begin to heal myself and create a space for communication in the work.

Returning to Work

In the immediate aftermath of my loss, I struggled with how I would return to my students, and how I could support them when I myself felt so anchorless without my own mom.

"Yasmine," a 17-year-old Latinx student I was working with, had lost her mother several years previous. She was part of an after-school group I co-led focusing on the impact of trauma and toxic stress and students' lives and how to cultivate strength. It was a creative group, where students spoke their truth, located these experiences within their communities and cultures, and worked to build a project of their own that would help transform the school (Sajnani, 2012). It was important that every member of the group, including the coleaders, locate themselves, because the personal is political (hooks, 1994), and intersections matter (Crenshaw, 1993).

It was the case that every student in the group had experienced the loss of at least one family member or close friend due to illness or gun violence. Yasmine, in particular, had decided to focus her project on the loss of her mother and was working on creating a monologue that gave voice to the conflicting thoughts in her head. There was no question that in returning to the group, I would need to find a way to talk about my loss in a way that supported Yasmine's work. I struggled with two big questions:

- How would I share this news with the group in a way that was contained enough?
- Would I be able to maintain my role as facilitator and hold space for the group without burdening my students?

Many of my students were more experienced in dealing with grief as a result of the high rates of death in their communities due to violence and illness, and they were impacted by racism, poverty, and police brutality. As a White clinician for whom loss was never associated with violence or White supremacy, I worried about the space I would take up in the group. For Yasmine, who was so close with her mother and often flooded in group, would it be helpful or problematic for me to share my own loss? The literature shows that parentally bereaved adolescents report higher post-traumatic growth and grief reactions than adolescents who have lost another family member (Hirooka, Fukahori, Ozawa, & Akita, 2017), and that female adolescents report higher levels of internalized grief responses than males (Shulla & Toomey, 2018).

It is also the case that adolescents are more likely to experience greater intensity of grief and distress without proper supports (Palmer, Saviet, & Tourish, 2016). In my return I was careful to plan each step and ensure there were always multiple supports in place. My co-facilitator was ready to hold the group in case I needed to step out. I decided to let Yasmine know individually before I told the group, as I knew she would react strongly to the news and I wanted to give her space to have her own reaction. When I did tell the group, I started by reading the Waheed (2013) poem that begins with "i wake" (p. 43). I told them it captured the sense of disbelief I felt at her being gone and asked if anyone could relate. The group became energized, sharing their own stories of loss. While the group opened up, I struggled with staying present, flooded with memories of my mom. The poem helped ground me. My co-facilitator was a big support, prompting the group with questions and holding the therapeutic space.

What surprised me was that Yasmine shared it was helpful to know the truth about what had happened to me. She told a story about a time in the hospital when her mom told her the dreams she had for Yasmine, that she would break patterns in the family and go on to higher education and a career she loved. This is perhaps connected to the conclusions that Palmer, Saviet, and Tourish (2016) draw: Adolescents need others who can help normalize their feelings, understand that grief experiences are unique, and listen with genuine interest while connecting them with supports that normalize individualized styles of grieving. While this does not necessitate that therapists share their own experiences, it opens the possibility that there are ways for clinicians to share their stories of grief in a way that is helpful in therapeutic spaces.

The Role of Creative Writing in Processing Grief

My loss necessitated that I increase the amount of work I was doing to process my grief; that was the only way to make myself available for holding therapeutic spaces again. There were days where I could hear stories of loss and days I couldn't. I worked to develop a practice of checking in with myself about what I could handle that day. I worked to lighten my workload outside of the group. I found a therapist who could support me. I spent time in my own supervision processing this group work. This, in turn, became a larger plan for self-care and healing. Radical self-care is not effortless; it is brave work where I hold myself accountable and cultivate practices that allow me to stay grounded, attuned, present, regulated, and open to feedback.

Creative writing and finding poems that spoke to my experience became another outlet for healing, one that offered grounding while also evoking an emotional understanding of loss I was struggling to find words for. There are many questions that I am left with, but two in particular resonate deeply:

1. Who am I in the world, and how do I hold/locate myself?
2. How can I work toward continued meaning making and growth through storytelling and encourage my clients to do the same?

These central challenges are echoed in the work of therapists who have written about loss in the context of healing work (Kouriatis & Brown, 2013; McPherson & Mazza, 2014). There is no one answer, but rather these questions stand as a call to action in grief work.

Discussion Questions

1. Do you agree with the therapist's approach to self-disclosure? What would you have done differently?

2. What are the risks associated with talking about personal loss with clients/students? What are the benefits? How would you navigate this boundary in a way that was beneficial for clients?
3. How is utilizing creative writing or poetry an effective technique for clinicians experiencing loss?

Group Experiential Activity

1. Take 5 minutes to journal about an experience in your life that you struggled with (pick something that you feel comfortable sharing with the group). Find or write a poem that connects with that experience and bring it to your group.
2. In small groups, do the following:
    - Read your poem to the group. After reading, ask the group members to share themes, images, or words that stuck out to them during the reading.
    - Share a little bit about why the poem speaks to you. You may choose to speak directly about the event from your life it connects to if you feel comfortable doing so.
    - Once each person has shared, reflect on how this experience is different from verbally telling the group what happened. How can using creative writing be helpful or healing in therapeutic work? How does this inform the process of navigating self-disclosure with clients?

References

Boal, A. (1993). *Theatre of the oppressed.* New York, NY: Theatre Communications Group.

Brabant, S., & Martof, M. (1993). Childhood experiences and complicated grief: A study of adult children of alcoholics. *International Journal of Addictions, 28*(11), 1111–1125.

Crenshaw, K. (1993). Mapping the margins: Intersectionality, identity politics, and violence against women of color, *Stanford Law Review, 43*(6), 1241–1299.

Gerrish, N., Dyck, M., & Marsh, A. (2009). Post-traumatic growth and bereavement. *Mortality: Promoting the Interdisciplinary Study of Death and Dying, 14*(3), 226–244.

Hirooka, K., Fukahori, H., Ozawa, M., & Akita, Y. (2017). Differences in posttraumatic growth among adolescents by relationship with the deceased. *Journal of Advanced Nursing, 73*(4), 955–965.

hooks, b. (1994). *Teaching to transgress.* New York, NY: Routledge.

Kosminsky, P. S., & Jordan, J. J. (2016). *Attachment-informed grief therapy: The clinician's guide to foundations and applications.* New York, NY: Routledge.

Kouriatis, K., & Brown, D. (2013). Therapists' experience of loss: An interpretative phenomenological analysis. *OMEGA: Journal of Death and Dying, 68*(2), 89–109.

McPherson, J., & Mazza, N. (2014). Using arts activism and poetry to catalyze human rights engagement and reflection. *Social Work Education, 33*(7), 944–958.

Sajnani, N. (2009). Theatre of the oppressed: Drama therapy as cultural dialogue. In D. R. Johnson & R. Emunah's (Eds.), *Current approaches in drama therapy* (pp. 461–482). Springfield, IL: Charles C. Thomas.

Sajnani, N. (2012). Response/ability: Imagining a critical race feminist paradigm for the creative arts therapies. *The Arts in Psychotherapy, 39*(3), 186–191.

Sajnani, N., Jewers-Dailley, K., Brillante, A., Puglisi, J., & Johnson, D. R. (2014). Animating learning by integrating and validating experience. In N. Sajnani & D. R. Johnson's (Eds.), *Trauma-informed drama therapy: Transforming clinics, classrooms, and communities* (pp. 206–240). Springfield, IL: Charles C. Thomas.

Shulla, R. M., & Toomey, R. B. (2018). Sex differences in behavioral and psychological expression of grief during adolescence: A meta-analysis. *Journal of Adolescence, 65*, 219–227.

Palmer, M., Saviet, M., & Tourish, J. (2016). Understanding and supporting grieving adolescents and young adults. *Pediatric Nursing, 42*(6), 275–281.

Xu, W., Fu, Z., He, L., Schoebi, D., & Wang, J. (2015). Growing in times of grief: Attachment modulates bereaved adults' posttraumatic growth after losing a family member to cancer. *Psychiatry Research, 230*(1), 108–115.

Waheed, N. (2013). *Salt*. Lexington, KY: CreateSpace.

Tool #7: Case Study–Conducting a Suicide Assessment

Elizabeth Murdoch, LCSW

A Case Study in Suicide Assessment: Sam

The first acutely suicidal client I saw for therapy was a 20-year-old young man, Sam. He came to his intake session with me accompanied by his parents who were tearful and terrified. He was a student at a local university, hated it, and had recently been dumped by his girlfriend. He had a near-genius IQ, was not challenged by his physics curriculum, had no interest in socializing, and reported that he felt that he had no options in his life. I had been told by the referral source that he was depressed, but had little other information, other than that he had been hospitalized for a week a few months prior. When he was asked to clarify the reasons for his hospitalization, he stated it was for suicidality with a plan. The inpatient stay was followed by a stint in an intensive outpatient program; he reported that he hated both and would never return to either.

As the first step in a suicide assessment, I asked him if he was currently feeling suicidal; he responded that he was, and, anticipating my next question, he said he did not have an immediate plan. I asked him how he would do it, if he did kill himself. Often clinicians will say that this is a very difficult question to ask, and indeed it is, but talking about suicide does not cause it. He reported that he would shoot himself. I determined that he did not have immediate access to a gun. I asked him what he needed from his family, or anyone else, to stay safe and he then asked his mother to make sure he had no access to money so he could not buy a gun. His mother complied and kept him by her side for a number of days, which he allowed.

By any criteria, he was depressed. He had been seeing a psychiatrist and was on antidepressants, which he hated and did not believe to be effective. He did not see a future for himself. He came to see me without fail on Sunday mornings, despite his belief that there was no point to therapy. He was able to tolerate my weekly questioning about his degree of suicidal thinking. I consistently asked him if there changes in passive versus active suicidal thinking, changes in his choice of method, changes in his degree of hopelessness. He agreed that talking about his suicidal thoughts made them less powerful. He grudgingly admitted that it was good to have somebody to talk to, although he told me later that the only useful thing I ever said to him was that if he was going to stop his medication, which he did, then he had to start doing a lot of aerobic exercise. He began running, working out, and has now completed two marathons.

Working with suicidal clients is, minimally, challenging. Friends and family are apt to say such things as "You have so much to live for!" or "Things will get better!" which the clients I have had contemplating suicide find at best annoying, at worst enraging. Finding alternative, clinical ways to say the same thing takes a great deal of thought and an understanding of your patient. Treatment with Sam consisted of building a human connection, known of course as the therapeutic relationship, and working to instill hope in specific ways. I attempted to utilize some CBT techniques with him, but he rejected them. He just wanted to talk, so talk we did, and sometimes we just looked across the room at each other. We explored what he could do to keep busy, what kind of adult he wants to be, what kind of woman he wants to be with. He remained suicidal for a few months, but in typical analytical

Sam style, he thought that he should wait and see how things went. He did a risk-reward analysis of suicide. Talking openly with him about suicide, the effect it would have on his family and friends, the concept that he might be wrong that his life was hopeless, appeared to help him reach a decision that he would stay alive. He gradually stopped coming to therapy, but he texts me from time to time when he's done well in a race.

Performing a suicide assessment with a patient is not simply going through a checklist. Think of it as an ongoing conversation, an ongoing assessment of your patient's state of mind. Many people think very abstractly about suicide, but that does not necessarily mean they are suicidal. It is undeniable that these conversations about suicide are difficult for patients, family, and clinicians. Family members often say that they are afraid to talk to their loved ones about their suicidal thoughts for fear that somehow it will make things worse. It is our job to thoughtfully, carefully, and collaboratively explore what is going on for the client.

When working with a new client or one who may be suicidal, familiarize yourself with the following:

Risk Factors Specific to Clients

- Historical suicidal behavior, including past attempts or self-injurious behavior
- Psychiatric disorders, including psychotic and/or mood disorders, alcohol or drug abuse, personality disorders
- Symptoms such as lack of enjoyment or interest in anything, impulsivity, hopelessness, command hallucinations, anxiety, depression, poor distress tolerance
- Family history of suicide, suicide attempts, or serious psychiatric disorders
- Recent discharge from psychiatric hospital or provider(s)
- Access to firearms, pills

Protective Factors

- Ability to cope with stress, ability to tolerate negative emotions and frustration, religious/spiritual beliefs
- Awareness of responsibility to and the effect of suicide on family/friends
- Strong support network, including family, friends, community

Assessment for Risk of Suicide

- Is the suicidal thinking passive (I wish I wouldn't wake up tomorrow) or active (I am going to make sure I don't wake up tomorrow)?
- If there is active suicidality, is the plan imminent? When and how?
- Does the person have the means to do it?
- Does the client believe the attempt will be fatal?
- If there is a plan, an assessment at a hospital is a necessity. If you work in an agency, be sure you are familiar with the agency's protocols on how to handle a client at imminent risk. If you are in private practice, do not hesitate to call 911. Don't let actively suicidal patients walk out of your office. If they do, have the police attempt to find them and transport them to the hospital.

Questions for Discussion

- As a practitioner, what are your own thoughts about people who commit suicide?
- What do you think the role of a family might play with a client of yours who is suicidal? How might you utilize family members—or not?
- To what degree, if any, is it the clinician's responsibility to keep a client from dying by suicide?
- What interventions might you use with a client who has consistent suicidal thoughts but does not have a plan to die?
- Where would you find support if you did have a client who died by suicide?

Classroom Exercise

1. Take 15-20 minutes to write down, individually, your personal and your spiritual beliefs about suicide.
2. Next, write down your fears as a behavioral health student around discussing suicide with your clients. Is it something you feel prepared to do or not prepared to do? What advice or training have you been given as part of your educational experience?
3. As a small group, discuss Sam's case:
    a. Create a checklist of his risk and protective factors.
    b. What questions would you have asked him about his suicidal ideation?
    c. What level of risk would you have determined Sam was at during that intake session?
4. Sam's therapist tried to engage in CBT as part of his treatment plan and ended up using a psychodynamic approach. Discuss other modalities such as psychoanalysis, DBT, strengths-based, task-centered, or creative expressive models and how you might integrate them into your work with Sam.

Columbia-Suicide Severity Rating Scale (C-SSRS)

Posner, Brent, Lucas, Gould, Stanley, Brown, Fisher, Zelazny, Burke, Oquendo, & Mann

RISK ASSESSMENT

Instructions: Check all risk and protective factors that apply. To be completed following the patient interview, review of medical record(s), and/or consultation with family members and/or other professionals.

Past 3 months	Suicidal and self-injurious behavior	Lifetime	Clinical status (recent)	
☐	Actual suicide attempt ☐ Lifetime	☐	☐	Hopelessness
☐	Interrupted attempt ☐ Lifetime	☐	☐	Major depressive episode
☐	Aborted or self-interrupted attempt ☐ Lifetime	☐	☐	Mixed affective episode (e.g., bipolar)

☐	Other preparatory acts to kill self ☐ Lifetime	☐	☐	Command hallucinations to hurt self
☐	Self-injurious behavior *without* suicidal intent	☐	☐	Highly impulsive behavior
Suicidal ideation **Check most severe in past month**			☐	Substance abuse or dependence
☐	Wish to be dead		☐	Agitation or severe anxiety
☐	Suicidal thoughts		☐	Perceived burden on family or others
☐	Suicidal thoughts with method (but without specific plan or intent to act)		☐	Chronic physical pain or other acute medical problem (HIV/AIDS, COPD, cancer, etc.)
☐	Suicidal intent (without specific plan)		☐	Homicidal ideation
☐	Suicidal intent with specific plan		☐	Aggressive behavior toward others
Activating events (recent)			☐	Method for suicide available (gun, pills, etc.)
☐	Recent loss(es) or other significant negative event(s) (legal, financial, relationship, etc.)		☐	Refuses or feels unable to agree to safety plan
Describe:			☐	Sexual abuse (lifetime)
			☐	Family history of suicide (lifetime)
☐	Pending incarceration or homelessness		**Protective factors (Recent)**	
☐	Current or pending isolation or feeling alone		☐	Identifies reasons for living
Treatment history			☐	Responsibility to family or others; living with family
☐	Previous psychiatric diagnoses and treatments		☐	Supportive social network or family
☐	Hopeless or dissatisfied with treatment		☐	Fear of death or dying due to pain and suffering
☐	Noncompliant with treatment		☐	Belief that suicide is immoral; high spirituality
☐	Not receiving treatment		☐	Engaged in work or school
Other risk factors			**Other protective factors**	
☐			☐	
☐			☐	
☐			☐	
Describe any suicidal, self-injurious, or aggressive behavior (include dates)				

Tool #8: Timeline of Loss

Kelly Zinn, LCSW

Objective

Students will gain a greater understanding of how grief and loss can impact individuals in various ways across the lifespan.

*Please keep in mind that thinking about loss can be triggering and it is important to take care of yourself during this process. As you work through this activity, take a break if you need one.

**Instructor note: It may help to end the class with a meditation or some other grounding activity.

Directions

1. *Brainstorm:* Think of the losses you have encountered throughout your own life. Do not limit these losses to deaths; include losses such as important friendships, loss of community (e.g., moving or changing schools), normative losses such as those that come about as a result of maturing, etc.
2. *Activity:* As you consider these losses, create a timeline of your life. Include as many losses as you can think of and plot them on your timeline as they relate to your age/developmental stage at the time of the loss. Annotate the timeline with information about how you coped (or did not cope) with these losses. Think about the following:
    a. What supports were available to you?
    b. Did you deal with the loss alone or did you have help?
    c. Who helped you and how did this support come about?
3. *Pair and share:* Talk with a classmate about your timeline. Be empathetic during this process, keeping in mind that there is no measure for loss. Listen to learn from your classmates about their experience.

Discussion Questions

1. How can reflecting on our own losses help us to understand the losses of others?
2. How can developmental stage impact the experience of loss?
3. How does support or lack of support play a role?
4. Were any of the losses you endured transformative for you? How so?

Tool #9: The Bliss List

Beth Counselman Carpenter, Co-editor, PhD, LCSW

Objectives

To enhance student awareness about self-care techniques and to deepen students' tools to practice self-care when working with grief and loss.

Directions

1. Take a piece of lined or blank paper. Do not prompt students by sharing the purpose or the title of the exercise. Students will have 5 minutes to make a list of all the things that inspire "bliss" for them. Encourage them to fill the page with as many items, behaviors, or experiences that they can think of and to write for the entire time, if possible. It is preferable to complete this activity by handwriting it, but adaptive technology can be used, particularly if there is use of a drawing tool.
2. Once the time is up, ask students to spend 2–5 minutes reflecting on their list. After this period of reflection, ask them to take another piece of paper and organize the list into groups:
   a. Things that are easy to implement
   b. Things that require some sort of investment (time, energy, supplies)
   c. One time or large-scale events
   d. Practices in which they can engage on a daily, weekly, or monthly basis
3. Alternative: Students may decorate their list with stickers, colored pencils, or collage materials.
4. Ask students to break up in groups of three to five and share their lists with one another. Use this time to look for common or differing themes and to discuss challenges and ease with which they completed the activity. Have students compare the groupings they completed after the initial brainstorm.

Discussion Questions

1. How is bliss defined?
2. What community supports need to be in place to create a feeling of or experience of bliss?
3. What was it like to share your list in the small group? In the large group? Was there any comparing of the "value" of one's list?
4. What barriers are in place that prevent someone from engaging in the activities in this list?

Instructor note: For students who may be startled or triggered by the difficulty of completing the exercise, the dearth of things that are blissful for them or a list of behaviors that are unhealthy, encourage students to process this with a supervisor or personal therapist. Be sure to frame that learning how to take care of oneself is a skill that is learned in school and throughout one's clinical career.

Tool #10: Invoking Rituals

Beth Counselman Carpenter, Co-editor, PhD, LCSW

Objective

For students to deepen their understanding of the connection between rituals and loss and to deepen their self-awareness about the role of ritual in their own history. This activity is best done in the last weeks of a class as part of termination.

Directions

This portion of the class should be done the week before ritual is shared as a class experience. Have students break up into small groups, or, alternately, this can be done as a reflective writing assignment for homework or in class.

Reflective Discussion/Writing Assignment

Write or share about the rituals that framed important events in your life growing up. What rituals were observed? What food was served? Are there certain terms or phrases that are shared to convey meaning and respect to the situation? Now, write or share about the rituals in your family, community, and spiritual identity around death, grieving and loss. How may loss be recognized and observed? Be as detailed and specific as you can, and supplement the words with images if possible.

Class Activity

Following the writing assignment/class discussion about rituals, plan your own ritual feast for the class. Ask students to bring in food that has meaning (in some way to them). Make sure that you are prepared to accommodate all food needs including allergies, vegan, kosher, gluten-free, and other dietary observances. For students who may experience food insecurity, also offer opportunities to sign up and serve as an organizational point person, to serve as lead story teller, or to share music or choose media to share during the class.

While feasting, discuss how different communities and spiritual traditions come together around food. Ask students to share what they wrote or discussed last week in terms of their own communities of origin.

Credits

CHAPTER SIX
Self-Care

Self-Care for the Grieving Therapist: An Essay Written in Real Time

Beth Counselman Carpenter, Co-editor, PhD, LCSW

FIGURE 6.1. Beth Counselman-Carpenter

My coeditor and I conceptualized this book after meeting at the Council on Social Work Education (CSWE) Conference's annual program meeting. Both passionate clinicians, researchers, and educators in the fields of trauma, grief, and loss and their related symptomology, Alex's mother died in 2013 after battling a prolonged illness and I had lost my father at the age of 7 to a sudden heart attack. We felt there was a gap in the literature about how grief and loss inform and impact our work as behavioral health providers and were thrilled to work with a publisher to create this textbook. The essays we planned to write focused on more recent loss (Alex's) and historical loss (mine).

About 2 months before the full draft of this textbook was due, my mother was admitted to the hospital with what appeared to be mild pneumonia and died 7 days later of an aggressive and rare form of mantel cell non-Hodgkin's lymphoma. Suddenly, I had a front row seat on what it means to instituting self-care for grief and loss while in practice. The irony of the timing has certainly not been lost on me, and I want to directly thank my coeditor for pushing me to sit in my grief and my sadness to write this piece.

My Story

It was the last week of classes on a Wednesday when my mom went to the ER with some difficulty breathing. Reporting unusual pain, doctors treated her breathing issues, but within 48 hours as I drove home from work, the attending physician called to say my mother had become unresponsive and I needed to override her DNR (Do Not Resituate) order if I wanted her to keep breathing. Within 2 hours, she was in the Critical Care Unit, intubated on a respirator and I was never able to talk with her again. The next 4 days brought worse news with each following test: higher white blood cell counts, the need for a central line, the potential of cancer, and rapidly swelling internal organs. On Thursday night, they said her cancer was too far advanced, and she would die in 2 weeks at most. There was no treatment available and things would happen quickly. By Sunday morning, despite her lack of consciousness, I could tell she was in pain. I asked the doctors on Monday to switch her to morphine and to extubate her. My children and extended family came to say goodbye, final rites were conducted, and 6 hours after extubation she died in my arms.

It all happened so fast and I can hardly believe, even as I write this some months later, that I lived through and survived it all. I was completely exhausted and completely numb. I was grateful to give her a dignified death. I was relieved she never knew how sick she was. I was heartbroken that the sun in my solar system was gone. To this day, the to-do list is never ending. December is a difficult time in my chosen profession: four classes and 100 students' worth of work to grade and clients who struggle around the triggers of the holidays, and it was a week before Christmas, a very significant family holiday. My loss was exponentially complicated by my other roles as professor, clinician, mother, only child, and now orphan.

FIGURE 6.2. Terry Dankel Counselman, summer 2018

There are not too many resources that explain the sheer amount of phone calls, paperwork, meetings, and death-related minutiae that you will have to manage. Nor do people warn you that the people you professionally encounter during this time may not be the most compassionate and empathic. My stressors were enormous; I handed off my practice to be covered for 3 weeks and luckily had finished grading while waiting for her admission that Monday. I contacted my program coordinator and said I would be unavailable for the next 3 weeks as well and promptly turned off my instructor brain.

My stressors felt endless. The first stressor was that she was gone. It was Christmas and how were we going to plan a funeral and burial? Our family cemetery refused to bury her on the weekend and would only honor our request if it was on Christmas Eve. I refused back and had to find a new cemetery and new headstone carvers and pay extra for the grave to be opened on a Saturday at lunch time. There were also bright spots. Celebrating her life was actually and unexpectedly joyous; it was a relief to be surrounded by friends, but choosing memorial picture boards, Bible readings, hymns, church availability and her cemetery view (yes seriously!) were all things I had not anticipated contemplating. Navigating the holidays of wrapping presents for the kids, making it festive even though they had lost one of their primary caregivers, and getting through a New Year celebration that was the opposite of festive came next.

Through all of this was the paperwork and the phone calls. It is amazing how thoroughly you need to prove the death of someone in order to turn off his or her Internet and cancel the paper, let alone the legal and business aspects of frozen credit cards, electrical bills, and bank accounts. And then came packing up her house, what to keep, to sell, to donate, to give to family, to recycle. She had my entire childhood in her basement, so it became a time to revisit four generations' worth of family memories, ghosts, and history—all things so emotionally laden that it is hard to describe.

Six days after she died, I closed on my own new house. I had been through a difficult break-up just 3 months before and then had to deal with owning my new house (in reality a 160-year-old house with lots of historical quirks), and her house, managing my pets and her pets, in addition to meetings with accountants, realtors, lawyers, bankers, painters, tag sale brokers, contractors, and moving companies, to name just a few of the calls, meetings, e-mails and texts that filled my weeks.

Suddenly, my holiday break was over and I need to tackle a return to my new normal in which I balanced these stressors along with the regular demands of my life. I was not sure I would be able to work, and how I would be able to do so effectively. I have rarely doubted my ability to execute my role as an effective and competent clinician, until this point. Self-care became a necessity in order for me to live my new life in a way that did not compromise any of my responsibilities. It has been imperfect, messy, and emotional and altered my worldview in the most unexpected of ways.

Note: I want to name that the positionality of my voice and that my privileges as a cisgender female White educator and clinician impact the lens through which I see my world, my loss, and how I have coped.

Why Self-Care Is Key in Behavioral Health Professions

It is an ethical responsibility to provide the best possible service to clients). This is referred to as the "oxygen mask" metaphor often shared when flying; in the event of an emergency, you need to put on your own rescue oxygen mask before you assist someone else with their mask so that you both do not end up incapacitated. In other words, we cannot help others if we have not yet helped ourselves. We know that taking care of ourselves lets us be more available to our clients, students, and supervisees, yet we struggle to institute it. It is widely understood that self-care directly correlates to burnout (Dalphon, 2019). Even the World Health Organization (2014) recognizes self-care as a process of both promoting and maintaining health and as a form of disease prevention. Yet although it is our ethical responsibility to care for ourselves; professional self-care is not yet a requirement in social work curriculum or professional standards (CSWE, 2008; Moore, Perry, Beldsoe & Robinson, 2019 NASW 2009; Newell & Nelson-Gardell 2014).

Definitions

There are a variety of different definitions that attempt to capture the experience and practice of **self-care**:

> *Self-care* is purposeful, intentional and is intended to enhance well-being. It is meant to be continuous and involves all dimensions of self, in order to keep the individual appropriately fit to help others. (Moore et al., 2019)).
>
> The concept of *professional self-care* involves the utilization of both strategies and skills for social workers to maintain their own needs (personal, emotional, familial, and spiritual) while simultaneously attending to the needs of their clients (Newell & Nelson-Gardell, 2014).
>
> A *self-care plan* involves the development of a collection of practices from which a social worker can draw to help regular both workplace and interpersonal stress (Dalphon, 2019).

What Is Compassion Fatigue?

Compassion fatigue is an occupational hazard associated with the work-related effects of providing empathically oriented care to others over any length of time and includes both physical and emotional responses that came at the expense of using one's own energy to provide this care (Worley, 2005; Adimando, 2017). Newell and Nelson-Gardell (2014) see compassion fatigue as a particular combination of secondary traumatic stress and professional burnout. This "Bermuda Triangle" of exhaustion is a blend of *bearing witness and holding the pain* of others while providing trauma-informed care (Durall, 2011; Figley, 1995). It can affect behavioral health care workers, child welfare workers, animal rescue veterinarians and rescue support staff, nurses, and physicians.

What Is Burnout?

While there is no one generally accepted definition of burnout, it is considered a prolonged response to chronic professional stressors. Burnout includes physical, emotional, psychological, and spiritual exhaustion when working in human services fields and is typically conceptualized as a process (Maslach, Schaeufelit & Leiter, 2001; Newell & Nelson-Gardell, 2014; Pines & Aronson, 1988). This process involves emotional exhaustion; depersonalization, which can look like cynicism; detachment from the job; and impaired/reduced personal accomplishment connected to a sense of professional ineffectiveness, such as feeling inadequate.

What Is Secondary Traumatic Stress (STS)?

STS develops when a clinician who is supporting trauma survivors becomes traumatized him- or herself from the work (Glennon, Pruitt, & Rouland Polmanteer, 2019). It is defined as the emotional duress that results from exposure to hearing about the first-hand trauma experiences of another and has multiple symptoms that mimic those of PTSD. Particular to STS is the presence of distortions around alterations in sense of self-efficacy, changes in memory and perception, and increased arousal and avoidance reactions. These intrusive clusters of symptoms and level of re-experiencing differ slightly from vicarious trauma.

Symptoms include hypervigilance, hopelessness, and inability to listen thoroughly and to embrace complexity. Feelings include fear, anger, hopelessness, and cynicism and behaviors include avoidance of clients. Somatic symptoms can include sleeplessness and chronic exhaustion. Left untreated, the presence of secondary traumatic stress highly predicts that helping professionals will leave the field for a completely different line of work.

What Is Vicarious Trauma (VT)?

VT refers to internal changes in the experience of the therapist in the session and at work due to this indirect exposure to traumatic events. Engagement at work is often impacted. Unlike STS, which focuses more on experiencing trauma symptoms, VT focuses on covert subtle changes that occurs following cumulative exposure to someone else's trauma. Primary symptoms can include a disturbed cognitive frame related to trust, safety, and control over one's environment and intimacy.

Self-Care Practice Models

Dalphon (2019) offers the Holmes-Rahe Life Stress Inventory (LSI) as a way of evaluating one's stress level, which can help strengthen understanding about possible stress-induced health issues that are correlated with high levels of constant stress. By identifying what demands make life stressful in a clear and operationalized way, one can understand exactly what it is about the position that makes it stressful. In the case of grief and loss, it is easy to determine what has caused one's stress but does not make the development and adaptation of a self-care plan quite so clear.

Dalphon (2019) makes the following suggestions, and I have added reflection questions:

1. *Taking a personal inventory of stressors.*
    a. It is extremely important to actually quantify what is stressful, rather than just saying "work is stressful"; the key is to figure out exactly what aspects of work are stressful.
    b. Dalphon encourages the use of valid scales, such as the LSI, to measure levels of stress.
    c. By naming the stressors, one can then develop a targeted plan to address them.
    d. In grief and loss, there are just some stressors you cannot avoid! So, how can you lessen other professional stressors in the mean time until the tasks related to death and grief are less present?
2. *Seeing one's identity beyond social work/counseling.*
    a. Who are you outside of your role as a clinician? We often refer to behavioral health professions as a calling, which can also mean that it is challenging to turn off who we are professionally.
    b. What other roles do you hold? How do you elevate these roles to help hold boundaries between your personal and professional lives?
    c. Where do you see the intersection between griever and clinician? Can you hold these roles together, or can you compartmentalize between the two roles effectively?
3. *Personal relationships.*
    a. Who are the people in your life who are *not* clinicians? How can you more regularly engage with these folks or strengthen these bonds? What lens do they see the world through and how does it differ from your behavioral health approach?
    b. Who do you let take care of you in your time of loss? Why or why not?
    c. How can you ask for more help? Although you may the primary executor/executrix, or the person tasked with making all the calls or cleaning out a family home, how can you let people help you during this time?
4. *Saying no.*
    a. I picked up the phrase "No is a complete sentence" from some online meme, and while I cannot give credit to the original author, this is a statement that I try to practice more, not less, personally and professionally.
    b. When you are going through the Herculean tasks of early grief, particularly the logistical ones, or supporting other family members through their navigation of these challenges, what becomes optional? It is helpful to do a cost-benefit analysis of what is no longer charging your emotional batteries.
5. *Mindfulness.*
    a. Mindfulness exercises
    b. Mindful seeing (taking in visual stimuli without judgments about what is being seen)
    c. Body-conscious exercise
    d. Safe place guided imagery
    e. Guided imagery script

In grief, it can be hard to sit still, and sit silent, but finding pockets to let yourself be sad, be angry, or to feel whatever it is you want to feel can help process and integrate the powerful feelings that come from a loss. Mindfulness can also include art about the person who you've lost, guided meditation through readings, classes or yogic practice. As one's attention span can be limited, particularly in early grief, it is important to set yourself up for success by choosing short and manageable practices.

1. *Physical care.*
    a. Activity
    b. Sleep
    c. Accountability partners to help one follow through on a regular basis

Grief is physically and emotionally exhausting. It is completely normal for your entire body to feel tired, and it is okay if you do not jump right into to a regular exercise routine immediately after loss. For me, I found the physicality of moving furniture and packing up a lifetime's worth of house items was exactly the outlet that I needed to process how I was feeling. Sleep can be very challenging when you are grieving, particularly if you are simultaneously providing trauma-informed care, so talk to your medical professionals if your sleep challenges continue past the early months of loss.

One of the most powerful tools of healing for me has been having both a non-social work and social work accountability partner to remind me to take care of myself these days as I work to take care of others. They typically check in with me every other week or so via text. It can be a funny meme, a shared moment about their loss, or a pointed question about how many glasses or water I have had that day.

Other strategies for self-care in behavioral health work include personal strategies of humor, spiritual practice and faith, and seeking balance between work and your personal life. Other professional strategies to help manage loss include creating an atmosphere of respect within your institution of practice, diversifying one's workload, and creating meaningful context for your work (Rashotte, Fothergill-Bourbonnais, & Chamberlain, 1997).

Self-Care Lessons

1. Take the Time That You Can

There is no time table when it comes to the scheduling of loss. As an only child, family caregiving has always fallen to me since a young age, which has been a handy skill for my chosen profession. As my mom's health unexpectedly and rapidly deteriorated over a 48-hour period, the timing was fortuitous only in that the semester was ending and that I would not have to worry about teaching four classes a week. Being a university professor, work life during the semester often includes 16-hour days, 7 days a week, so I would normally have little to no time to grieve, being overwhelmed by student and faculty expectations. This allowed me to focus on her final days and the significant decisions ahead of us without sacrificing time dedicated to my students and academic responsibilities. However, in nearly 15 years, I have never taken 3 unplanned weeks off from work or my practice and, initially, before I knew the gravity of the situation, I would have never imagined being unplugged from my clients or my office for so long. Even in the whirlwind of early grief, it seemed a bit terrifying to be away from my work for so long because I had simply never taken than much unplanned time off before. However, I learned that my practice could survive and even thrive without me, which gave me the time to heal enough to return to my clients ready to hold the space. Clinical work requires a mindful, intentional, nuanced lens in which we as clinicians must offer to bear witness to, acknowledge, and help integrate our clients' pain.

What I Learned

Your work, your practice, your supervisees, and your students will be okay. For clinicians, know that your clients will learn how to cope, or to learn to work with a trusted colleague in your absence, and it gives them an opportunity to lean on others to support them until you are able to return. Give yourself the gift of time to *not* care for your clients and others in your life while you attend to your own needs.

Concrete Strategies

1. Have a colleague pick up your voicemails for you and check your e-mails. Have them put up an "Away" message that states you have had a family emergency and will be out of the office from THIS DATE until THAT DATE. Have your colleague triage what information you need to know until you are ready to return to your practice. Preferably have a short list in your mind of colleagues who would be a good fit for the population of clients you see and have conversations with those colleagues prior to any difficult personal situations about the potential of covering your practice in an emergency.
2. If you work for an agency or other institution consider using the Family Medical Leave Act (FMLA) of 1993, if possible, for some extra time. Typical employers may only offer 1 to 3 days of bereavement leave. FMLA is a federally guaranteed right for some employees to take unpaid time off work for up to 12 weeks each year with no threat of losing your job. FMLA can be taken for you, an immediate family member, or an adopted or foster child. If you have sick days, you can use those hours to continue to receive your paycheck. Consider FMLA because you will be exhausted. You are more likely to get sick. And while I have worked through pregnancies, post-partum, the stomach flu and strep throat, grief brought a different level of exhaustion that was unexpected. My whole body felt flattened by fatigue; at times, my heart seemed to physically hurt, and the level of emotion could be physically dizzying.
3. If you have access to FMLA, perhaps it means taking just Fridays off for a few weeks, and during that time, you can meet with banks, lawyers, tally the bills, clean out your loved ones' things, or simply lay on the couch and cry. Carving out blocks of time to manage the tasks of grieving and the logistics of a family death is key. I teach full time, have a family, and a private practice. I have learned to have any e-mails related to post-death logistics such as turning off phones/cable, estate matters, and medical bills sent to a specific, newly created e-mail address so I could have control over when I checked in and when I did not. It prevented, for a majority of the time, the blindsides that come weeks and months after your loss via medical billing and life details that are unexpected. I learned to only pick up my mom's mail and voicemail after work, not before because it would have derailed my ability to focus at work. I tried to reserve more flexible work days, such as Thursday late afternoons and Monday mornings on my way into the office, for phone calls and estate-related appointments.
4. Consider not taking on any new clients for a period of time. Grief changes you at a cellular level, and you will be a different therapist than you were before your loss. Allow yourself to work with the familiar as you find your sea legs in grief before introducing new clients to the mix.
5. Take a hiatus from optional/voluntary or more flexible work responsibilities even if you have a leadership role. As a junior faculty member, there is an expectation to sit on a certain number of committees to show that you are invested in the institution. However, the amount of meetings combined with the number of personal appointments I had was simply not possible for nearly the entire semester after my mom's death. I came up with a plan to stagger which

meeting responsibilities were critical, and which could wait for me for a semester and was able to negotiate a staggered time to return to all of my responsibilities.

2. Self-Care in Grieving is UNIQUE

What I Learned

Writing this chapter has been a bit challenging, simply because what has worked for me may not work for you. I have received so many suggestions of what to do and what not to do that sometimes even that "help" is overwhelming. Your process of grieving while doing grief work is unique. Embrace that concept. Borrow what works and discard what does not. This journey is truly one of a kind.

For example, everyone recommended meditation and breathing exercises to help calm the mind and focus. I found that focusing on my breathing made me more anxious! And for those who know me, sitting still is not one of my strengths. However, a lot of the literature recommends adding exercise and movement for kinesthetic healing, and as a former long-distance athlete, I couldn't agree more. But I found after holding the space for clients, during this grief journey, anything physical was just too much for my body. I also was moving and packing furniture, which is a fully kinesthetic experience and the only outlet that my particular body was able to tolerate. Grief is an all-encompassing, overwhelming physical experience, and sometimes we just need to rest.

Concrete Suggestions

1. Try different things. Many people suggested bibliotherapy; in fact, this book has a whole chapter dedicated to it! For me, reading did not keep my attention, and I found many grief and loss books trite. I also struggled to write in a journal to express my thoughts and feelings. For me, I wrote bullet point lists on paper and in my phone about how I was feeling, what I needed to do, and lists of what aspects of my identity had changed and that was a better fit for me.
2. I appreciated all the advice that was given to me and tried to be very mindful about saying thank you. You will receive many suggestions about what to try or not try. I remained open to trying what was suggested, even if it was something I would never have considered prior to my loss. I have found myself surprised by what has brought some relief and what has not.

3. Manage Your Expectations of Others

What I Learned

Just because we are mental and behavioral health providers does not necessarily breed empathy from others for our grief. Grief, as shared by so many authors in the personal grief chapter, tends to make people uncomfortable. I had a number of colleagues simply not ask about my loss, or neglect to bring it up in any way. Conversely, if I referenced it, they ignored my statements, and that was hurtful. However, as the personal grief chapter and grief theory chapter repetitively state, Western culture often shies away from the discomfort and pain that come with grief. It takes some practice, but I have learned not to take it personally—and I have also learned to gently share with coworkers when a colleague may need a reminder as to why I am having a difficult or distracted day.

4. Change Your Routine

What I Learned

My long commute was a time that I often talked with my mom and it became extremely painful to be in the car and not be able to talk to her. Grief is distracting, and suddenly the podcasts and music I loved could not keep the tears away. One of the first and biggest changes I needed to make in order to cope was turning my routine into something totally different!

Concrete Strategies

1. Phone calls were no longer an option and speaking out loud to my mom felt strange and inauthentic. Humorous memoir audiobooks have now become my car companion. Because of what we do as behavioral health providers, long phone calls in the car can actually make me more tired before I even step into the office. Listening to books fills the time, massages my brain, and signals me that it's time to get my "game face" on for work. Find what works for you to keep you safe on the road and also, perhaps, a little less lonely. My world is different now, and changing my routine has helped me adjust to this difference.

5. Keep Your Loved Ones Close

What I Learned

Grief has a deceiving time-space warp quality to it. Some days, it seems as if my loss was yesterday, and other days it feels as if this has been my way of life forever. My office has often been a place of neutrality for me; I do not keep personal pictures of my family nor do I display anything particularly revealing. I already do a remarkable amount of grief and loss work in practice, so that did not feel like a change. However, it has felt important to find a way to carry my mom with me throughout the work day.

Concrete Strategies

1. For me, wearing a piece of my mom's jewelry—and I mix it up depending on the day—has allowed me to feel connected to her even though life keeps moving ahead. I carry so many life lessons, positive, complex, and everything in between, from my experiences with her that looking down and seeing her ring on my finger or a simple beaded bracelet that she loved helps ground me in my day-to-day professional life. I have colleagues who keep fresh flowers in their office, add a small photo in a frame to a hidden corner of their office, or chose office artwork with an image that represents their loved one.
2. Using technology: Although this is a strategy that sometimes can provoke strong reactions in me, it can be helpful to listen to old voicemails, to revisit screenshots of texts/e-mails, to write to them through social media (continuing to post on the FB page, for example) or scrolling through saved pictures. Smartphones and other technology allow us to access people who are no longer with us and keep them close in a way that does not involve heavy and irreplaceable photographs. I am mindful to save these touchstones for when I am done with my academic/clinical work for the day. Touchstones are anything "concrete" in a sensory manner—an image, an item, a song, for example, that helps you feel connected to Other, person or an experience.

6. Self-Disclosure

What I Learned

Prepare for the Unexpected

I had been significantly mindful to not disclose the nature of my loss to certain clients for therapeutic reasons. I did not want to make the session about my loss or encourage the client to comfort me. We always need to remember not to burden our clients with our own stuff. They come into our clinical space with a need for us to accompany them on their journey of integration and healing. Our own healing should never happen at the expense of a client's time. Be very intentional about deciding to share about your loss with clients (and see chapter 3 for how different clinicians have mindfully walked through this choice).

I had a well-intended colleague inadvertently ask a mutual client if she had heard what had happened to my mom. Out of the blue, on bereavement leave, I received a text from this client expressing her condolences, and in our second session after I had returned, she said that she was experiencing a lot of guilt in talking about her own parents who were both surviving and thriving. About an hour later, I received an apology text from the colleague that it had "just slipped out" as they were wrapping up their session (work that was less clinical in nature). I accepted my colleague's apology and prepared myself to unpack it in session with my client. I made sure that I mentioned it early in our first session back together.

While on leave, I had thought about my caseload and possible scenarios of my bereavement leave and knowledge about my loss being triggering with certain clients, but this was not something I had expected. We were able to process it in the moment, and use it as a way that informed our work, but it was a helpful reminder that no matter how thorough we are, our personal information may creep into our work and we need to prepared to address it.

Be Mindful of Boundaries Versus Transparency

We need to be very careful about sharing aspects of our losses in practice. Please see chapter 3 for examples of how colleagues chose to judiciously share information about their losses and how it informs their work. However, due to the physicality of grief, clients will notice! I have had clients comment on circles under my eyes or that I looked tired that day. Rather than brushing it off, I typically thank them for their concern, validate that it has been a tough day/week, and say (authentically) that I'm grateful to be in the office today and that I'm ready to jump into our work together. I am occasionally asked, by clients who know of my loss(es), if I can recommend an estate lawyer, sale firm, accountant. I provide a list of references that may or may not include whom I have worked with personally. Whenever my boundaries begin to feel a little diffuse, particularly related to loss or the impulse to overshare, I check in with my peer supervision team.

7. Get Supervision From Someone Specifically in the Field of Grief and Loss

I cannot say this enough! Even if you are an expert at what you do, find a professional mentor who can guide you through the pitfalls and speedbumps of transference and counter-transference during this time. It is okay to ask for help and to have a trusted colleague help you navigate for vulnerabilities such as having clients try and take care of you, over-disclosing your loss, or helping you manage the days it seems you cannot be at work. Make sure, however, it is a supervisor who understands the experience of grief and loss specifically. A note about confidentiality: Within the supervisory contract (and it is vitally important to have one), disclosing about clients and professional processing is ethically responsible and not a violation of confidentiality.

HOW DO I KNOW WHEN I NEED TO SEEK SUPERVISION?

by Kelly Zinn

After suffering a loss, it is important to become aware of your triggers, and equally important to respond to these triggers by seeking supervision. Clinical work demands a high level of self-reflection because we are helping professionals. As such, we must take into consideration the nuanced ways in which grief may impact our work. The saying "you can't pour from an empty cup" comes to mind. Clinicians deal with the emotional concerns and challenges of clients, and when we are grieving these may be triggering to us. So how can you tell when you need to seek supervision?

Here are a few tips:

Engage in reflective practice: Journaling about your work can be very helpful. Take some time each day to reflect on the challenges you faced. Were there any times when you felt emotionally triggered or struggled to get through a session? These instances represent topics for discussion in supervision.

Note any visceral reactions: Once a child said something to me and the statement left me feeling as though I had been punched in the stomach. After the session, I called one of the counselors at my school and told her about it. She helped me to see that the strength of my reaction required further discussion, and I spoke with my supervisor later that day to determine next steps. It is important to be in tune with yourself, to be aware of these visceral reactions, and to be willing to examine them in supervision.

Identify an accountability partner at work: Peer supervision can be just as important and impactful as formal supervision. Having a peer with whom you can process sessions can lead to improved practice at any time, but for a person who is grieving this support is essential. Choose a peer with whom you have a strong relationship, a person who will provide support without judgement. Process sessions with this person often and utilize his or her support to help plan for upcoming sessions.

Resist the fear of reaching out: Being a clinician does not mean you need to have all the answers or be unaffected by grief; the reality is quite the opposite. Do not hesitate to reach out for supervision when your grief is triggered or activated in your work.

Give yourself some of the grace you are most likely offering others: As clinicians, we often excel at listening without judgement and providing unconditional support to our clients. Yet we do not treat ourselves nearly so well, focusing on our weaknesses and missteps. At all times, but especially when we are grieving, we need to be kind to ourselves. Keep in mind that even though you are a clinician, you are also human and asking for help is advised. Supervision can assist with this process, as we often need others to point out when we are being too hard on ourselves.

Also, a note about therapy in addition to supervision. As a clinician, of course I am biased in believing we can always go back to our own treatment to address any issues that have come up in the difficult work that we do. Supervision for professional challenges, to enhance boundary maintenance and to address work-related triggers, is incredibly important. However, the week of Mom's death journey was emotionally and visually traumatic. Early grief brought with it intrusive memories and thoughts about all I had seen and the decisions I had had to make, and going to see a clinician to process this experience and get therapeutic support was incredibly helpful to the self-care and integration process. I am profoundly grateful that I carved out 50 minutes a week in those early months to be able to say out loud and have some else bear witness to my own pain.

8. Find Your Village

What I Learned

People do not know what to say. Find the people who do. I found that posting aspects of my mourning on social media drew out people's other experiences, and I received messages of blog posts to read and poems with meaning, and I have ended up with a community that understands how some days you can be filled with laughter about something silly that reminds you of your loved on, and how on other days it can cripple you with tears. I will also warn the reader that public displays of grief can make people uncomfortable on social media and they may be silent, tell you to get over it, or say something trite and hurtful. It is important to be careful about who you let in to observe your grief on social media so that you can feel safe to grieve authentically.

My village was not other social workers in this case, but people who also identified as only children, who had lost both parents, or any of my friends and acquaintances who had lost their mothers unexpectedly. Having a tribe who understands your mourning and holds the space for you has provided tremendous support through this process.

Concrete Strategies

As stated, having accountability partners to talk me through their grief experiences as they compare to mine has been one of the most profoundly important parts of my healing and integration experience. Losing someone close to you/surviving trauma is like becoming a member of a club that no one particularly wants to be a part of. Yet, once you're a member, finding more "senior" survivors has been life changing. These women know what it means to have a "death bag" (a bag in which you carry every single paper that you may need for any appointment with any bureaucrat ever), why you hold on to things that may seem odd to others outside the club (a hairbrush with your mother's hair), know what it is like to feel like you've lost all sense of normalcy and show you that eventually, you will adapt to your new life of normal, and eventually feel a different kind of okay.

9. Take a Break From Social Media When You Need to

What I Learned

I am still at the point where seeing happy pictures of intact families hurts a lot of the time, particularly as we head toward some big holidays. Sure, we can intellectualize how we should not compare oneself to others, and we have all read the research on how people filter the perfect life into their social media feed, but seeing happy grandmothers with their grandkids on Christmas was emotionally crippling in the days after my mom's death. Whereas social media had been a fun escape for me after a long day with clients, and a great way to keep in touch with friends all over the world, it suddenly became a place where I felt like an outsider.

Timing is everything! Choose wisely about when you access your social media because of the triggers it can bring. Grief sneaks up on you in unexpected ways, and if you need to have your professional persona active with all the responsibilities it brings, it may make sense to wait and access your social media at a time when you have the luxury to fall apart. Social media should be a way for you to find support and community and connect to your tribe and maybe even your lost loved one. Pay attention to the timing and choice you make to open the door to your virtual world.

Concrete Strategies

1. I took Facebook off my phone completely for a while. Most days in early grief, I did not begrudge friends who got to spend time with their moms (it is actually something that has gotten harder with time), but there were moments where I would become profoundly sad or jealous. Other times, Timehop (a feature that pulls up your posts from a year to many years ago about what you were doing) was too hard to see (and some days, it brought me great joy). I have learned to listen to my mood before I log in and scroll, particularly before trying to sleep.
2. I found Instagram to be a little easier to control in terms of what came up in my feed. Quickly, I followed grief bloggers, recipes, and nature hiker/yogis so that my feed was a distraction, and an inspiration, as opposed to a reminder of my loss. It has balanced out now that I can hold my friends' joys with these other sources, but in the early days, it was a coping necessity.
3. Texts and direct messages are so helpful! On the days that it was too exhausting or too late to talk after work, a quick text to one of my tribe mates or a family member would help me feel connected when I was lonely. Also, if I was feeling overwhelmed, texts stayed in my phone so I could track who I needed to get back to and control how and when I connected with them.

10. Create Things

What I Learned

In the early days, creating things for me was very specifically related to the rituals of death and loss. In my religious and cultural traditions, the immediate tasks surrounding all of my losses have been designing the funeral service, planning a memorial feast, creating memory boards of pictures of my loved ones, and designing headstones. The next stage of "creating" was actually destroying my mom's house in order to create a new reality in which my things were merged with hers. This was the purging of things—deciding what could be sold, what should be kept, and what should be donated. This was a very painful and exhausting process overall, and, as is common with downsizing, the process still continues today as I write. The painful emotions that came up for me included seeing someone's life reduced to objects they will no longer use, feeling that throwing something out was a betrayal, and the emotional exhaustion of making decision after decision about thousands of items big and small. But the creation of this merged home helped me also feel connected to my mom, how I carry her forward, and had a profoundly cathartic quality to it. My home reflects the stages of integrating her loss: displaying things that remind me of the joy she had in her home, a little beaded flamingo that made her laugh, and boxes of things in the basement that I am not quite ready to go through.

By nature, since childhood, and particularly since graduate school, I have been a crafty person (although I might argue I enjoy collecting craft supplies even more than I do making the crafts). The body fatigue and limited attention span that come with grief initially inhibited my ability to knit, draw, sew, which was frustrating. I could not craft anything for a while, although I occasionally colored or did a craft known as diamond painting (small beads affixed to a canvas in a color-by-numbers fashion).

Concrete Strategies

1. Reframe your view of creating. My mom died right before Christmas, a holiday in which she took great pleasure in planning and decorating. Her home looked absolutely magnificent every year. Although it was hard, I chose to spend some time being in her home in the weeks after death, and hosting a few friends to celebrate her life and her hard work, and then mindfully pack up her lovely things to merge with my own. It was breathtakingly hard work, but I tried to envision how I would recreate her looks in my home and recreate the stories and history that she carried forward from other generations.
2. Pick manageable creations! For now, I've stopped sewing. It was a new craft I had learned and it still requires a lot of attention for me to be successful. I've gone back to knitting, and I try to find bright, easy-to-work-with yarn, and simple patterns for dishcloths and placemats so that my hands can work and my mind can wander. While I love to cook, I've gone back to simpler recipes so that the automaticity of cooking kicks in on those longer, more tired days. Creating allows me to feel a sense of permanence in things that had been shaken.

11. Surround Yourself With Living Things

What I Learned

Private practice can be very isolating—long hours, nights, and weekends, and being on call are all part of the job. I'm lucky to share my suite with some fantastic colleagues, but it is still not a traditional office or agency environment. Likewise, working in the university academy is also unexpectedly distancing; other faculty are often as busy and overwhelmed as you may be, you may be teaching at off hours alone, and most of your time is spent with students as a mentor-role model more than a colleague or friend. These are some connections to the greater, living world that have helped me feel a continued sense of connection to others.

Concrete Strategies

1. Plants/nature/flowers
   Anyone who knows me will say that I have the opposite of a green thumb. I am the worst at keeping plants alive! So, every few weeks, I try and pick up a bunch of freshly cut flowers from the local market to add some color to my table (particularly during the gray Northeast/New England winter). Some people find cut flowers dying as particularly sad, so it depends on what

floral arrangements bring up for you. For me, a brightly colored sunflower that I do not have to regularly water just reminds me about the cycle of life and the need to include beautiful things in your every day.

2. Pets/animals
   I am an animal person! However, walking my dogs is not something that has brought me tremendous joy in my grief and for reasons unbeknownst to me, seems like one of the Herculean tasks on my every day list. Cuddling my sleeping dog though, brings tremendous joy and forces me to simply just sit and be. I also foster and rescue kittens; taking care of them in their early stages and preparing them to find their fur-ever home gives me the balance between pet care and also something from which I can take a break whenever I need it.
3. Other humans
   Working in a people-centric environment while grieving can be overwhelming. But grief can also trap you in your own head in the early days and weeks. So, putting on a pair of noise-cancelling headphones and simply sitting and observing people going about their daily lives can remind you that a new sense of normalcy is out there, and one day, you too will be part of it. Taking hikes and simply nodding and smiling down at others you pass on the trail can be another way of finding a brief, non-attached moment of connection. Other days, it can be a kind word and thank you to someone who holds open the door for you, or a cashier who makes your change. Connecting to others in a way that feels manageable reminds you that there is a life that one day you will get back to, and although it will be different, it is there waiting for you when you are ready.

Self-Care Is a Journey

Where am I now? It is still early on my road of grief and many days bring a lot of challenges and strong feelings. However, whether I wanted to learn it, this process has taught me that I can only take things one day at a time. I have learned so much more about myself in the past few months: what my needs are and that no is a complete sentence, and I have a visceral understanding about the necessity of self-care to sustain oneself in this line of work. I have worked in the field of grief and loss since 1999 and I learn more, not less, with each passing year and through my own relationship with grief. Being grateful sounds trite, but with every difficult moment, beauty has also never been far behind. Even after a series of very hard days, something will inevitably happen that will make me say, "Yes, thank you, I had taken that for granted until now and I am so grateful for this moment to remind me to have hope and positivity (or to at least acknowledge that it's not all miserable!).

I am learning to cultivate and to restore. To cultivate new relationships that sustain me professionally and personally now that my support system looks different. I am learning to cultivate an environment that charges and not depletes my batteries, that this environment may be fluid and that my needs will evolve over time. My loss has taught me that this is not optional, but necessary. I am learning to listen to myself, my body, and my heart more in this raw emotional state to protect myself so that I can show up for others. I am learning to restore my sense of faith in the world and in the universe and to restore my energy and patience. A wise member of my tribe said to me, "You will be okay. It will be different than it was before. You will feel things differently than you did before. And some days may hurt more than others. But the pain will lessen, and time will pass and you will keep going. And the going won't always look like just surviving, you will get back to thriving." My self-care practices are an investment and my goal for my practice is one of sustainability and future-oriented thinking so that I can keep showing up and holding the space for my clients, my students, my supervisees, and especially myself.

References

Adimando, A. (2018). Preventing and alleviating compassion fatigue through self-care: An educational workshop for nurses. *Journal of Holistic Nursing, 36*(4), 304–317. doi:10.1177/0898010117721581

Council on Social Work Education. (2008). *Educational policy and accreditation standards.* Retrieved from: https://www.cswe.org/Accreditation/Standards-and-Policies/2008-EPAS.

Dalphon, H. (2019). Self-care techniques for social workers: Achieving an ethical harmony between work and well-being. *Journal of Human Behaviors in the Social Environment, 29*(1), 85–95. doi:10.1080/10911359.2018.1481802

Durall, A. (2011). Care of the caretaking: Managing the grief process of health care professionals. *Pediatric Annals, 40*(5), 266–273.

Figley, C. R. (1995). Compassion fatigue: Coping with secondary traumatic stress disorder in those who treat the traumatized. Levittown, PA: Brunner/Mazel.

Glennon, A., Pruitt, D., & Rouland Polmanteer, R. (2019). Integrating self-care into clinical practice with trauma clients. *Journal of Human Behavior in the Social Environment, 29*(1), 48–56. doi:10.1080/10911359.2018.1473189.

Moore, S. E., Bledsoe, L. K., Perry, A., & Robinson, M. A. (2011). Social work students and self-care: A model assignment for teaching. *Journal of Social Work Education, 47,* 545–553.

National Association of Social Workers. (2009). *Social work speaks: National Association of Social Workers policy statements, 2009–2012.* Washington, DC: Author

Newell, J. M. & Nelson-Gardell, D. (2014) A competency-based approach to teaching professional self-care: an ethical consideration for social work educators, *Journal of Social Work Education, 50,* 427–439, doi: 10.1080/10437797.2014.917928

Rashotte, J., Fothergill-Bourbonnais, F., & Chamberlain, M. (1997). Pediatric intensive care nurses and their grief experiences: A phenomenological study. *Heart Lung, 26*(5), 343–353.

Shoji, K., Lesnierowska, M., Smoktunowicz, E., Bock, J., Luszczynska, A., Benight, C., & Cieslak, R. (2015). What comes first, job burnout or secondary traumatic stress? *PLoS One, 10,* e0136730.

World Health Organization (2014). Self care for health: a handbook for community health workers & volunteers. WHO Regional Office for South-East Asia. Retrieved from: https://apps.who.int/iris/bitstream/handle/10665/205887/B5084.pdf?sequence=1&isAllowed=y

Worley, C. (2005). The art of caring: compassion fatigue. *Dermatology Nursing, 17,* 4–16.

Annotated Bibliography

This chapter includes journals, books, and articles recommended by the contributors and editors of this text. Some of these are appropriate for scholarly use while others are informative and instructive for working with clients. It is by no means exhaustive in terms of the depth and breadth of resources available, but cultivated carefully to reflect the earlier entries in this anthology.

Death, Bereavement, and Grief Journals

Death Studies, Taylor & Francis
Publishes significant research, scholarship, and practical approaches in bereavement and loss, grief therapy, death attitudes, suicide, and death education. https://www.tandfonline.com/action/journalInformation?show=aimsScope&journalCode=udst20

Journal of Hospice and Palliative Medicine, SAGE Journals
Interdisciplinary team approach to hospice and palliative medicine related to the care of the patient and family. https://journals.sagepub.com/home/ajh

Journal of Hospice and Palliative Nursing, Hospice and Palliative Nurses Association
The official journal for the Hospice and Palliative Nurses Association and is focused on the clinical, educational, and research aspects of end of life nursing care. https://journals.lww.com/jhpn/Pages/aboutthejournal.aspx

Journal of Palliative Care, SAGE Journals
Original research, opinion papers/commentaries, narrative and humanities works, case reports/case series and reports on international activities and comparative palliative care. https://journals.sagepub.com/home/pal

Journal of Palliative Medicine, Liebert Publishing
Medical, psychosocial, policy, and legal issues in end-of-life care and relief of suffering for patients with intractable pain. https://home.liebertpub.com/publications/journal-of-palliative-medicine/41/overview

Journal of Religion and Health, Springer Publishing
Physical and mental health in relation to religion and spirituality of all kinds. https://link.springer.com/journal/10943

Journal of Social Work in End-of-Life & Palliative Care, Taylor & Francis
Publishes articles related to serious, life-threatening, and life-limiting illness for individuals and their families across the lifespan. End-of-life communication, decision making, pain management,

palliative care, grief and bereavement, ethical issues, sudden traumatic death, secondary trauma, and compassion fatigue. https://www.tandfonline.com/toc/wswe20/current

Omega: Journal of Death and Dying, SAGE Journals

A reliable guide for clinicians, social workers, and health professionals who deal with death and dying, terminal illness, fatal accidents, catastrophe, suicide and bereavement. https://journals.sagepub.com/home/ome

Palliative Medicine, SAGE Journals

Multidisciplinary approach to effective palliative care. https://journals.sagepub.com/home/pmj

Books or Religious Texts

Amer, M. M., & Ahmed, S. (2013). Islam, Muslims, and mental health. In S. Ahmed, S., & M.M. (Eds.), *Counseling Muslims* (pp. 23–34). New York, NY: Routledge.

This book provides a comprehensive overview to counseling Muslims and includes topics such as sex therapy, substance abuse counseling, university counseling, and community-based prevention. The guide takes into account the significant cultural stigma and shame that can accompany the access of mental health services in Muslim communities. This book reviews interventions ranging from the individual to community levels. The volume includes chapters that discuss Muslims born and raised in the West, converts to Islam, and those from ethnic minority communities. It is a thorough guide for practitioners on effective service delivery for counseling Muslims.

Ashry, Z. H. (2018). *Death crossing the bridge to the hereafter.* Kuwait: IPC Islam Presentation Committee. Retrieved from https://www.muslim-library.com/dl/books/English_Death_Crossing_the_Bridge_to_the_Hereafter.pdf

This text provides several quotes from the Quran and accompanying interpretations regarding the nature of death, the process of mourning, and expectations for the hereafter.

Cable, D. G. (1998). Grief in the American culture. In K. J. Doka & J. D. Davidson (Eds.), *Living with grief. Who we are, how we grieve* (pp. 61–70). New York, NY: Routledge.

Doka and Davidson have put together this comprehensive work for the Hospice Foundation of American. It is a good resource text for people in grief, students of social work or psychology, or any other person who wants to understand the phenomenon of grief. The content, from contributing authors, offers experiences and perspectives on multiple issues such as spirituality, loss and grief, ethnicity and culture, and the myriad influences and responses to grief. Specifically, Cable frames a Western perspective of dying, death, and grief and the changing paradigm and social attitudes and behaviors over the centuries. The author provides a social context in which, even now, years later into the 21st century, death and grief are considered taboo and are often pathologized. It is important to understand that this is the culture, for those who have experienced the death of someone or another loss or life transition, into which people are catapulted. It is useful information for teaching the griever and helping personnel to provide support that others are unable to.

Carmack, B. J. (2002). *Grieving the death of a pet.* Augsburg Books, Minneapolis, MN

In this book, Carmack establishes a "virtual pet-loss support group." Pet loss continues to be known as a type of disenfranchised loss but Carmack normalizes the experience of readers through personal narratives from people experiencing the loss of a beloved pet. She discussed the range of emotions that a pet guardian may experience, as well as the difficult decisions regarding euthanasia and ways to memorialize a pet after death. This book is a must-read for any person seeking to more fully understand the complex and deep nature of the human-animal bond.

Chan Master Sheng Yen, & Gildow, D. (2007). *Orthodox Chinese Buddhism: A contemporary Chan Master's answers to common questions* Berkeley, California: North Atlantic Books.

This book was written by Chan Master Sheng Yen, one of the foremost contemporary teachers of Buddhism, in a solitary retreat in early 1960s. It explores a wide range of common questions regarding Buddhism, including clarifying fundamental doctrines and differentiating authentic Buddhist teachings from folk norms. It is one of the most influential Buddhist books in Chinese Buddhism. This translated edition includes annotations, appendixes on bodhisattva stages and Buddhist cosmology, and a glossary of Buddhist terminology for readers new to Buddhist literature.

Chan Master Sheng Yen. (2011). *The four steps for handling a problem. Living in the 21st century: A Buddhist view.* Taiwan, China: Sheng Yen Education Foundation.

This book delineates the four steps for handling a problem or encountering adversity. The teaching is essentially a contemporary distillation of the crux of meditation practices, to be applied in daily living. It encourages one to face a problem squarely instead of hiding in denial. Only by facing the problem and accepting the existing situations can we do our best to deal with it and then let go, regardless of the outcomes.

Chan Master Sheng Yen. (2017). *Common questions in the practice of Buddhism.* New York, NY: Sheng Yen Education Foundation.

As a sequel to Orthodox Chinese Buddhism, this book explores additional topics of practical relevance such as funeral services, rituals for the deceased, chanting or reciting the Buddha's name to redeem sins, and the state between death and rebirth. In exploring these topics, it distinguishes Buddhist doctrines from outdated cultural norms. This book is of particular interest for those who would like to gain a better understanding of commonly seen Buddhist practices and their significance, especially those pertaining to Chinese Buddhism.

Devine, M. (2017). *It's okay that you're not okay: Meeting grief and loss in a culture that doesn't understand.* Boulder, CO: Sounds True

After losing her boyfriend/life partner to a tragic accident, this former psychotherapist closed her practice and has dedicated nearly the past decade to confronting the challenges embedded in how Western culture views and addresses grief. Devine challenges the normed belief that one can heal from grief and encourages the reader to sit in his or her grief and build his or her life incorporating it. The book includes how well-meaning friends and family can actually be very harmful in their well-intended words, practical tips to manage the symptoms that come along with grief, and tools to educate friends and family of those who are grieving.

Diamant, A. (1998). *Saying Kaddish.* New York, NY: Schoken.

This book is an excellent resource for anyone who wants to know more about the ritual practices of Jewish mourning. While it is an exhaustive account of these Jewish traditions, it is also very illuminating in its discussion on how these ancient rituals are practiced today by Jews living in a secularized world.

Dickenson, D., Johnson, M., & Katz, J. S. (Eds.). (2000). *Death, dying and bereavement.* Thousand Oaks, CA: SAGE.

This book combines academic research with professional and personal reflections on practical and metaphysical aspects of death.

Doughty, C., (2017) *Traveling the world to find the good death: From Here to eternity.* New York, NY: Norton.

This book is an exploration of how non-American cultures care for death, which includes compelling, powerful rituals unknown in America.

Durkheim, E. (1965). *The elementary forms of the religious life.* J. W. Swain (Trans.). New York, NY: Free Press.

French sociologist Émile Durkheim first published this volume in 1912 as an analysis of religion as a social phenomenon. Durkheim attributes the development of religion to the emotional security attained through communal living. He finds the essence of religion to be the concept of the sacred, a unified system of beliefs and practices that sets somethings apart as holy and others as forbidden. Durkheim argues that these beliefs and practices unite into a morally defined community that becomes known as religion.

Farquhar, M. (2016). *Circuits of faith: Migration, education, and the Wahhabi mission.* Palo Alto, CA: Stanford University Press.

Farquhar analyzes a contingent within Sunni Islam known as Salafism, which has gained increasing attention from scholars and journalists. Critics of Salafism have described this phenomenon as rigid, intolerant, exclusivist, misogynist, and anti-modern. It has also been described as an "export version of Wahhabism" (p. 1), the dominant form of Islam in Saudi Arabia. Farquhar explores the connection between Salafism and Wahhabism through a history of the Islamic University of Madinah. Farquhar argues that petrodollars alone cannot explain the advent of Salafism, but that Saudi material investments still play an important role in the proliferation of both the Salafi tradition and its Wahhabi sub-tradition.

Geertz, C. (1973). *The interpretation of cultures.* New York, NY: Basic Books.
In this seminal work, Geertz described culture as "a system of inherited conceptions expressed in symbolic forms by means of which men communicate, perpetuate, and develop their knowledge about and attitudes toward life" (p. 89). Geertz believed that the role of anthropologists was to try to interpret the guiding symbols of culture.

Gilanshah, F. (1993). Islamic customs regarding death. In *Ethnic variations in dying, death, and grief: Diversity in universality* (pp. 137–145). In D. P. Irish, K. F. Lundquist, & V. J. Nelsen (Eds.), Ethnic variations in dying, death, and grief: Diversity in universality (137–145). Philadelphia, PA: Taylor and Francis.
This article begins with a brief overview of Islam, then delves deeper into Islamic views on life and death. The article covers customs and traditions that typically occur surrounding death and funerals in Muslim traditions.

Goel, M. (2008). *Devotional Hinduism: Creating impressions for God.* iUniverse.
This book touches on the core of Hindu spirituality through the surrender of everyday actions or a love affair with the Divine.

Hasan, I. Y., & Salaam, Y. (2007). Faith and Islamic issues at the end of life. In C. M. Puchalski (Ed.), *A time for listening and caring: Spirituality and the care of the chronically ill and dying* (pp. 183–192). New York, NY: Oxford University Press.
Co-written by an imam, a Muslim religious leader, this manuscript begins with a preliminary overview of the principles of Islamic religion, then focuses on faith in times of distress and methods toward healing. End-of-life considerations are reviewed, including resuscitation orders, Islam and medical technology, care for the dying, funeral rituals, and family needs.

Heschel, A. J. (2005). *The sabbath.* New York, NY: Farrar, Straus, and Giroux.
A classic work by one of the foremost 20th-century rabbis, this book on the Jewish sabbath makes clear why Judaism is a religion of time that attempts to sanctify the various phases of life, from birth to death, and does so in a way that requires the Jew to perform intricate ritual practices.

Hickman, M. W. (1994) *Healing after loss: Daily meditations for working through grief.* New York, NY: William Morrow Paperbacks.
Martha Hickman wrote nearly two dozen texts, many that focus on transitions in life and loss. This palm-sized text is designed to be read on a daily basis and provides a quote followed by a paragraph-long reflection. These meditations tend to be spiritually connected.

Inagaki, H., & Stewart, H. (1995). *The three pure land sutras: A study and translation from Chinese.* Kyoto, Japan: Nagata Bunshado.
This is a translation of the three primary scriptures of pure land Buddhism, namely Amitabha sutra, sutra on the Buddha of infinite life, and Sutra on the contemplation of Amitabha Buddha. Together,

they describe the Western pure land, its origin, the salvific vows of Amitabha Buddha, and specific practices to access the salvific power of Amitabha Buddha. These texts are indispensable for those who would like to gain an in-depth understanding of pure land practices.

Jones, L. G. (2012). "He cried and made others cry": Crying as a sign of pietistic authenticity or deception in medieval Islamic preaching. In E. Gertsman (Ed.), *Crying in the Middle Ages* (pp. 132–165). New York, NY: Routledge.

This text investigates the phenomenon of crying in medieval Islamic preaching and how tears were seen as ways of both remembering and causing suffering to the deceased. Crying could also be seen as acknowledgement of taqwa, or piety/fear of God.

Johns, B. (Ed.). (1999). *Old dogs remembered.* Santa Fe, New Mexico: Synergistic Press.

This book is an amazing collection of stories, memories, and recollections of aging, dying, and already mourned dogs by some of the world's most famous authors, including James Thurber, John Updike, Eugene O'Neill, Elizabeth Barrett Browning, and John Cheever, among others. The stories are heartfelt, deeply personal, and incredibly beautiful. Readers should make sure to have a box of tissues with them as they read, since you are guaranteed to cry. Although not a book on grief counseling, this book helps people of all backgrounds understand that pets are an integral part of our families and their loss can profoundly change us all.

Karma-Lingpa, P. S., & Thurman, R. A. F. (1994). *The Tibetan book of the dead: The great book of natural liberation through understanding in the between.* New York, NY: Bantam Books.

This is the translation of the "Bardo-Thodol"—the quintessential Tibetan Buddhist classic that deals with the issues of death, rebirth, the intermediate states, and how one may attain natural liberation through understanding these intermediate states. In recent times, its descriptions of the processes of death and dying have been recognized to be great psychological insights. This book is especially important for those who would like to have an in-depth understanding of the intermediate states between death and rebirth.

Lamm, M. (2000). *The Jewish way in death and mourning.* Middle Village, NY: Jonathan David.

This book is considered the classic account of Jewish mourning rituals. Lamm's book should be thought of as the go-to book for both Jews and non-Jews alike who want to better understand Jewish mourning.

Levine, S. (2005). *Unattended sorrow: Recovering from loss and reviving the heart.* Rhinebeck, NY: Monkfish.

Steven Levine was a personal friend of Elizabeth Kübler-Ross and worked in end-of-life care for more than 25 years. He also worked with concentration camp survivors, Vietnam veterans, and victims of sexual abuse. Having been a witness to the suffering of people on their deathbed or living with historical loss and exposure to trauma and violence, Levine produced a resource on the grief experience. The notion of unresolved grief is core to this seminal work. This book is informative and broadens the perspective on grief with its limited contemporary perceptions or allowances for it.

Levine normalizes and gives a name to the unresolved pain from any kind of loss that can become cumulative and destructive over time if left unresolved. The book is an invitation for readers to see unresolved grief for what it is and how it impacts the mind, body, and spirit. Readers are encouraged to claim their pain and find healing, beauty, and joy. This is a must-read for students and anyone who may be struggling with spiritual wounds.

Lewis, C. S (1961). *A grief observed.* New York, NY: HarperOne.
A classic in grief literature, this book was written after C. S. Lewis's beloved wife of 4 years died of cancer. Written as a form of coping with his grief, it is an honest account of how even the most faithful can lose their sense of identity and meaning after losing someone they love. In this small text, Lewis explores the meaning of life, death, the role of faith in grief, and how people can find their way again.

McClelland, N. C. (2018). *Encyclopedia of reincarnation and karma.* Jefferson, NC: McFarland.
This encyclopedia contains over 1,200 entries on diverse and detailed topics such as reincarnation and karma.

Meagher, D. K., & Balk, D. E. (Eds.). (2013). *Handbook of thanatology: The essential body of knowledge for the study of death, dying, and bereavement.* New York, NY: Routledge.
This text is required reading in the credentialing processes for students in the American Death Education and Counseling certification program in Thanatology. The work provides context related to death education including dying, decision making at the end of life, grief loss and bereavement, assessment and intervention, and traumatic death. These categories are presented in contexts of cultural, religious, spiritual, and developmental frames; practitioner issues; temporal perspectives, social, institutional, family, and individual perspectives; and related to the legal and ethical aspects of death and dying. In itself a comprehensive resource, one complete chapter is committed to resources and research in the field of death, dying, and bereavement and includes dying and loss-specific, end-of-life decision making, and grief organization names, assessment, and intervention resources.

Neimeyer, R. (Ed.) (2001). *Meaning reconstruction and the experience of loss.* Washington, DC: American Psychological Association.
This volume seeks to debunk the notion that there is a sequential and stage-like process to grief. Instead, Neimeyer posits that highly individual processes of meaning making guide the dynamics of grief. Neimeyer focuses on the role of continued symbolic bonds following loss as a means of appreciation and growth. The author posits that symptoms in the bereaved have significance in meaning making, and that reconstructing this meaning in response to loss is the central process in grieving. For practitioners, there are clinically informed models to tackle issues pertaining to grief and loss.

Ravel, J. F., Ricard, M. (1999). *The monk and the philosopher: A father and son discuss the meaning of life.* New York, NY: Schocken.
This book records the conversations between a father and son, the former a philosopher and the latter a Buddhist monk, about the meaning of life. It explores profound questions on ethics, consciousness,

freewill, scientific and material progress, suffering, rights, and responsibilities, among others. It is an engaging book that will lead one to think more deeply about one's own life, and, ultimately, to self-discovery.

Rosenblatt, P. C. (2001). A social constructionist perspective on cultural differences in grief. In *Handbook of bereavement research: Consequences, coping, and care* (pp. 285–300). Stroebe, Margaret S. (Ed); Hansson, Robert O. (Ed); Stroebe, Wolfgang (Ed) & Schut, Henk (Ed). (2001). Washington, DC, US: American Psychological Association

The article argues that grief is not primarily an internalized process, but rather is social. The bereaved commonly seek meaning in not only personal and familial life, but also broader community and cultural spheres. Under this perspective, mourning is interpretive and cultural. Expressions of grief may be policed to ensure they fit with the prevailing social and political order.

Sandberg, S. & Grant, A. (2017). *Option B: Facing adversity, building resilience and finding joy.* New York, NY: Knopf.

Written from the perspective of grief after the sudden death of her husband, and combined with the psychological lens of resilience theory, this text explores a variety of losses including loss of employment, ability, and natural disasters and how resilience in the face of heartbreaking adversity can occur.

Skovholt, T. M., & Trotter-Mathison, M. (2016). *The resilient practitioner: Burnout and compassion fatigue prevention and self-care strategies for the helping professions* (3rd ed.). New York, NY: Routledge.

This book is grounded in research and is written for practitioners in professional service to others and who are giving of themselves on an emotional or spiritual level. These professions include educators at all levels, mental health and health care workers, law enforcement and criminal justice, and faith-oriented professions. The book is well organized and easy to read and provides practical content on the cycles of caring, compassion fatigue, burnout and resilience, with applications for the practitioner related to self-care and professional sustainability.

In this third edition, the authors added a resiliency chapter and enhanced the self-care content in this important work. They outline the benefits and emotional pitfalls of working in service to other people and offer useful and informative exercises, tools, and approaches to the identification of stress-related impacts of giving of oneself on an ongoing basis. This book could be useful as a required text with writing and discussion exercises or recommended reading for students. It can be a tool for clinical practitioners or in supervision groups as a way to keep self-care and resiliency at the forefront of any practice.

Vecchio, K. D., & Saxton-Lopez, N. (2013). *The pet loss companion: Healing advice from family therapists who lead pet loss groups.* North Charleston, SC: CreateSpace.

This book is the definitive guide on grief counseling for pet loss. It includes a complete description of the bereavement process as specific to pet loss. It normalizes the feelings, thoughts, and experiences of those who are grieving and discusses the different types of loss that they may encounter. This is a book that I always send to any family member or friend who has just suffered the loss of a pet. Countless people have told me that this book brought them significant relief and I as well found some solace in this book after the loss of my own pet. I highly recommend this book, not only for the bereaved, but also for clinicians seeking to understand more about the pet loss experience.

Walter, T. (1999). *On bereavement: The culture of grief.* Buckingham, UK: Open University Press.
Walter analyzes the social position of the bereaved, who may be searching for guidelines or may find their grief pathologized.

Warner, J. (2018) *Grief day-by-day: Simple practices and daily guidance for living with loss.* San Antonio, TX: Althea Press.
This is a very practical guide that offers exercises and mindful reflection that can be completed daily or weekly to accompany the feelings that come with day-to-day living through and with grief. Each week has its own theme, with daily meditations and weekly exercises, mostly written, that help process feelings and strengthen coping skills. It is written with a practical and empathic tone and can be completed chronologically or in a random order, depending on preference.

Wolfelt, A. (2002) *Healing your grieving heart series: 100 practical ideas.* Fort Collins, CO: Companion Press.
This series includes books tailored to particular types of loss including the adult child, the parent, the spouse, and teens. The book is broken down into an easy-to-read format where one topic, exercise, or activity is suggested per page. It is meant to be read in small, digestible portions and includes practical tips.

Zimmerman, L. J. (2011). *The sacred wisdom of the Native Americans.* New York, NY: Watkins.
This book captures an expansive reflection of Native American history, culture, artistry, sacrament, wisdom, and myths of various tribes. It identifies and explores the main concepts of belief, sacred rituals, traditions, symbolism, and resilience of Native American and Alaska Native peoples. Its pages are enhanced by vivid pictures, illustrations, selected poetry excerpts, stories, and quotes from tribal leaders and advocates. This book is a diversely rich tribute and celebration of Native American people and the gifts they have bestowed in legacy to this world. Zimmerman's knowledge of anthropology and his passion intended for his readers is apparent throughout the book. It is not only diverse in its subject matter, but is captivating. Each page seems a work of art, which comes alive with color. It is not only a good read, it is a memorable experience of life, beauty, wisdom, and depths between and within tribes.

Articles Suggested by Authors

Abu-Rabia, A., & Khalil, N. (2012). Mourning Palestine: Death and grief rituals. *Anthropology of the Middle East, 7*(2), 1–18.
This article presents mourning rituals and death rites as practiced in Palestine. The authors focus on differences in the mourning experience among fellahin and Bedouin Arabs, but also shows parallels in their mourning and grieving customs with other Arab communities. The article highlights the set

of rituals that Palestinians perform, beginning with how the body is treated and the way that it is prepared for burial. Mourning practices that differ between women and men are also highlighted, namely women lamenting loudly and scratching their faces, while tears were not encouraged among men.

Abu-Lughod, L. (1993). Islam and the gendered discourses of death. *International Journal of Middle East Studies, 25*(2), 187–205.

This article provides a personal reflection on an experience that the author had in January 1987 when visiting the Awlad 'Ali bedouin community. Experiences of bereavement and the gendered discourse of death are reviewed in this manuscript.

Beaty, D. D. (2015). Approaches to death and dying: A cultural comparison of Turkey and the United States. *OMEGA: Journal of Death and Dying, 70*(3), 301–316.

In this text, the author theorizes three principles that guide the bioethics movement in the United States and other Western societies that apply to death and dying in both the United States and Turkey. These three principles are autonomy, beneficence, and justice. Beatty argues that autonomy is of greater concern to those in the United States, whereas in Turkey, medical decisions are made entirely with family and physician involvement. Beatty also highlights similarities and differences with end-of-life experiences between Islam and Christianity. Differences in approaches to death, such as how to handle advance directives, are examined in light of the spiritual, cultural, legal, and political factors that inform the experience of dying for people in Turkey and in the United States.

Firth, S. (2005). End-of-life: A Hindu view. *The Lancet, 366*(9486), 682–686.

This article explores the beliefs that Hindus have in common that influence their beliefs about death, end of life, transitions to another life, reincarnation, and life in heaven with God or absorption into Brahman (the ultimate reality).

Goss, R. E., & Klass D. (1997). Tibetan Buddhism and the resolution of grief: The Bardo-Thodol for the dying and the grieving. *Death Studies, 21*(4), 377–395.

This article is an introduction to "Bardo-Thodol"—the quintessential Tibetan Buddhist classic that deals with the issues of death, rebirth, and the intermediate states. In particular, it explores the issue of grief and how it is resolved in Tibetan Buddhist practices, connecting the classic to the Western concept of grieving.

Gupta, R. (2011). Death beliefs and practices from an Asian Indian American Hindu perspective. *Death Studies, 35*(3), 244–266.

This article explores cultural views of death and dying for Asian Indian American Hindu populations through three focus groups of all ages.

Hedayat, K. (2006). When the spirit leaves: Childhood death, grieving, and bereavement in Islam. *Journal of Palliative Medicine, 9*(6), 1282–1291.

This manuscript explores the death of a child and the long-lasting impact this loss has on families. Focusing on Muslims, this text seeks to explore the parents' relationship and their ability to bond with and take care of surviving children. Hedayat seeks to explain how Islamic beliefs contextualize the meaning of life and death and how Muslims are expected to grieve upon a child's death. The paper seeks to aid those who care for Muslim families to better attend to the social and emotional needs of Muslim parents and siblings after the death of a child.

Hoffner, E. (2015). As we lay dying. Stephen Jenkinson on how we deny our mortality. *The Sun,* 476. Retrieved from https://thesunmagazine.org/issues/476/as-we-lay-dying

This 2015 article in *Sun Magazine* is a narrative written in the context of an interview with Jenkinson, a theologian and a social worker. From his view at the death bed of the dying, for many years as a grief program coordinator, the goal is seemingly to inspire conversation about dying and death in our culture and its relationship to life. Jenkinson stated, in conversation with Hoffner, "We have no language for the experience of dying, we live in a grief illiterate culture." He shared that life and wellness include conversations about illness and dying. As a narrative from someone with years of clinical experience with death, dying, grief, and the practicalities and contemporary barriers to these conversations, this is an informative piece from a spiritual rather than academic perspective. Jenkinson also created a documentary, *Griefwalker,* in 2008 that captures more of his experiences and wisdom in the work of grief counselor.

Hunter, J. (2007). Bereavement: An incomplete rite of passage. *Omega: Journal of Death & Dying, 56*(2), 153–173.

This text is the result of anthropological fieldwork in Peru, from observations of a bereavement ritual. Bereavement is posed as an incomplete rite of passage. The article reviews the role of rituals and rites of passage and how these practices are incongruent with the long-term emotional needs and reconstruction of meaning within grief. Hunter recommends that bereavement counselors offer to help the bereaved construct a "ritual of remembrance and new meaning" after time has passed to allow for the reconstruction processes of making sense of the death, finding benefits from the experience, and changing identities as a result of the loss.

Hussein, H., & Oyebode, J. R. (2009). Influences of religion and culture on continuing bonds in a sample of British Muslims of Pakistani origin. *Death Studies, 33*(10), 890–912.

This study considered the nature of continuing bonds with deceased relatives in a sample of Pakistani Muslims living in the United Kingdom (U.K.). Ten participants were interviewed following a cultural psychology approach. Participants reported experiencing tension when expressing emotion or communality through their assimilation into a new cultural framework in the UK. The study sought to highlight how understanding different cultural and religious influences may enrich the concept of continuing bonds.

Iqbal, Z. (2011). McDonaldization, Islamic teachings, and funerary practices in Kuwait. *OMEGA: Journal of Death and Dying, 63*(1), 95–112.

Based on personal observations and random interviews, Iqbal explores the transformation of burial practices in Kuwait. He argues that traditional, religious, and private ways of dealing with death have been modernized using the fast-food model of McDonald's. Iqbal examines Islamic teachings on burial and how that model has been applied to traditional Muslim funerary services, including cemetery management, grave excavation, funeral prayers, burial, and condolences. Iqbal finds that the state bureaucracy in Kuwait has made burial rituals more efficient, standardized, calculable, and controlled.

Johnson, M. C. (2009). Death and the left hand: Islam, gender, and "proper" Mandinga funerary custom in Guinea-Bissau and Portugal. *African Studies Review, 52*(2), 93–117.

This article explores Islam, gender, and Mandinga funerary rituals in Guinea-Bissau and Portugal. Some of these rituals include shaking hands with the left hand, public wailing at funerals, and having healers investigate the nature of particular deaths. Johnson argues that these contradictions and debates are central to how Mandinga imagine themselves in a changing world.

Karmali, A. S. (2008). *Role of religious community support among bereaved South Asian Muslim children living in America* (Doctoral dissertation). Retrieved from *ProQuest*. 2008-99240-219

This dissertation focuses on how South Asian Muslim children living in America handle bereavement through systems of religious community support, including increased frequency of visiting and praying at the mosque and engaging in other faith-based activities.

Klass, D., & Goss, R. (2003). The politics of grief and continuing bonds with the dead: The cases of Maoist China and Wahhabi Islam. *Death Studies, 27*(9), 787–811.

This article examines the relationship between individual/family continuing bonds with the dead and cultural narratives that legitimize political power. Klass and Goss posit the political question, "Which collective—family, community, church, party, nation—owns the dead and controls the rituals by which bonds with the dead are maintained or relinquished?" The authors discuss periods of rapid change in power arrangements and how bonds with the dead have shifted during these historical moments. Focusing on China under Chairman Mao and the Wahhabi movement in Islam, Klass and Goss argue that ancestor rituals that support identity as a family or tribal member have been replaced by allegiance to collective representations of the new political order.

Kleinman, A. (2012). Culture, bereavement, and psychiatry. *The Lancet, 379*(9816), 608–609.

This article follows the author's personal experience of death, following his own wife's passing. Kleinman highlights that there is no conclusive scientific evidence to indicate a normal length of bereavement. Cultures vary widely in their appreciation for a "normal" grieving period. He notes that some societies regard a year as the standard length of mourning whereas others use the death anniversary as a marker for memorial. Still others sanction even longer periods for grieving, perhaps even a lifetime

Kristiansen, M., Younis, T., Hassani, A., & Sheikh, A. (2016). Experiencing loss: A Muslim widow's bereavement narrative. *Journal of Religion and Health, 55*(1), 226–240.

This article explores how Islam, minority status, and refugee experiences intersect in shaping meaning-making processes in bereavement. The authors utilize a phenomenological analysis of a biographical account of personal loss told by a Muslim Palestinian refugee living in Denmark, who narrates her experience of losing her husband to lung cancer.

Madan, T. N. (1992). Dying with dignity. *Social Science & Medicine, 35*(4), 425–432.

This is a historic description of paradigm shift in how cultures understood death and dying while examining the modern medical culture.

Neimeyer, R. A. (2004). Research on grief and bereavement: Evolution and revolution. *Death Studies, 28*(6), 489–575.

This editorial discusses how research on bereavement has entered a period where new theories, research methods, clinical practices, and empirical research have been introduced.

Sarhill, N., LeGrand, S., Islambouli, R., Davis, M. P., & Walsh, D. (2001). The terminally ill Muslim: Death and dying from the Muslim perspective. *American Journal of Hospice and Palliative Medicine, 18*(4), 251–255.

This article reviews Islamic notions of holding life as sacred coupled with the belief that that all creatures belong to God and will one day die. The article reviews the Islamic notion that death is only a transition between two different lives. It also reviews how "Do Not Resuscitate" (DNR) orders are acceptable, but suicide is forbidden. Finally, death rituals for the washing and burial of the corpse are also provided.

Suhail, K., Jamil, N., Oyebode, J., & Ajmal, M. A. (2011). Continuing bonds in bereaved Pakistani Muslims: Effects of culture and religion. *Death Studies, 35*(1), 22–41.

This study explores the bereavement process in Pakistani Muslims, focusing on how culture and religion influence these processes. For this study, 10 participants were interviewed and their transcribed interviews were analyzed using a grounded theory approach. The analysis showed that Pakistani Muslims maintain their link with the deceased through cultural and religious rituals, such as performing prayers, reciting holy verses, talking and dreaming about the deceased, doing charity, visiting graves, and arranging communal gatherings. The main purpose of these practices is to receive the forgiveness of the deceased.

Thrane, S. (2010). Hindu end of life: Death, dying, suffering, and karma. *Journal of Hospice & Palliative Nursing, 12*(6), 337–342.

This article educates the practitioner on how to provide culturally sensitive care by understanding Hindus' belief of community interconnectedness, karma, and reincarnation as major beliefs of Hinduism.

Venhorst, C. (2012). Islamic death rituals in a small town context in the Netherlands: Explorations of a common praxis for professionals. *Omega-Journal of Death and Dying, 65*(1), 1–10.

This manuscript focuses on the context of Muslim communities in the Netherlands, which are largely from Indonesian, Turkey, Moroccan, and Tunisian backgrounds. Noting the diversity within Islamic traditions, the author covers the ritual purification of the deceased in Muslim funerals.

Hallaq, W., (2005). *The origins and evolution of Islamic law.* Cambridge, UK: Cambridge University Press

Hallaq provides an introduction to the origins and evolution of Islamic law. Beginning with Muhammad's prophecy, Hallaq provides a historical context in which Muhammad began his prophecy, and in which the Quran became the foundation for the religion, paying special attention to the development of the Muslim judge or qadi. Judges became responsible for overseeing litigation, evaluating witness testimony, and ruling on disputes. Both the qadi and the ulama, or the juristic class, were mutually involved in the development of Islamic law and the formation of the various madhab or Islamic schools of thought.

Yasien-Esmail, H., & Rubin, S.S. (2005). The meaning structures of Muslim bereavements in Israel: Religious traditions, mourning practices, and human experience. *Death Studies, 29*(6), 495–518.

In this manuscript, Yasien-Email and Rubin discuss grief and mourning processes for Muslim citizens in Israel, covering main perspectives: the requirements of the Islamic Sunni tradition and the manner in which Islamic mourning rituals are practiced. The author also provides a synopsis of the personal experiences of two adult children who have lost their elderly father.

Index

D

E

F

G

H

S

T

U

V

W

Y

Z

www.ingramcontent.com/pod-product-compliance
Lightning Source LLC
LaVergne TN
LVHW062113200926
848484LV00007B/1660
* 9 7 8 1 5 1 6 5 7 7 9 6 5 *